STRATEGIC ASIA 2020

STRATEGIC ASIA 2020

U.S.-CHINA COMPETITION
for Global Influence

Edited by

Ashley J. Tellis, Alison Szalwinski, and Michael Wills

With contributions from

Frédéric Grare, Ji-Young Lee, Syaru Shirley Lin,
Joseph Chinyong Liow, Chris Miller, Liselotte Odgaard,
Sheila A. Smith, Ashley J. Tellis, Michael Wesley, and Carol Wise

 THE NATIONAL BUREAU *of* ASIAN RESEARCH
Seattle and Washington, D.C.

THE NATIONAL BUREAU *of* ASIAN RESEARCH

Published in the United States of America by
The National Bureau of Asian Research, Seattle, WA, and Washington, D.C.
www.nbr.org

ISBN (print): 978-1-939131-59-1
ISBN (electronic): 978-1-939131-60-7

Cover images

Front: Crack in grey concrete surface © rtyree1/iStock

Back (left to right): Bridge construction © Zhangguifu/iStock; Roundtable meeting of leaders at the Belt and Road international forum ©① The Russian Presidential Press and Information Office; HY-6 and two J-10Bs at PRC70 parade ©① Jing ju Jing duan; Businessman using futuristic VR © Wonry/iStock

Design and publishing services by The National Bureau of Asian Research.

Cover design by Stefanie Choi.

Publisher's Cataloging-In-Publication Data
(Prepared by The Donohue Group, Inc.)

Names: Tellis, Ashley J., editor. | Szalwinski, Alison, editor. | Wills, Michael, 1970- editor. | Grare, Frédéric, contributor. | National Bureau of Asian Research (U.S.), publisher, sponsoring body.

Title: U.S.-China competition for global influence / edited by Ashley J. Tellis, Alison Szalwinski, and Michael Wills ; with contributions from Frédéric Grare [and 9 others].

Other Titles: United States-China competition for global influence | Strategic Asia ; 2020.

Description: Seattle ; Washington, D.C. : The National Bureau of Asian Research, [2020] | Includes bibliographical references and index.

Identifiers: ISBN 9781939131591 (print) | ISBN 9781939131607 (electronic)

Subjects: LCSH: China--Strategic aspects. | United States--Strategic aspects. | Competition--China. | Competition--United States. | China--Foreign relations--United States. | United States--Foreign relations--China.

Classification: LCC JZ1313.3 .U55 2020 (print) | LCC JZ1313.3 (ebook) | DDC 327.1140973--dc23

Printed in the United States.

The paper used in this publication meets the minimum requirement of the American National Standard for Information Sciences—Permanence of Paper for Printed Library Materials, ANSI Z39.48-1992.

Contents

Preface

Alison Szalwinski and Michael Wills

There is no longer any question that the United States is in a long-term strategic competition with China. Over the past few years, bilateral suspicion and tension have grown over issues ranging from the ongoing trade war to contested interpretations of the Belt and Road Initiative and other Chinese activities that suggest a desire to change the international order. This shift from putative strategic partners to strategic competitors should be no surprise. The widespread recognition of China as a strategic competitor across the U.S. policy community is the culmination of a decade-long intensification in bilateral relations, as China's international presence and military and economic power continued to expand. The real surprise is perhaps that it has taken so long for broader public recognition of the challenge to take hold.[1]

U.S. history offers two examples of a similar lag between the emergence of a strategic competitor, widespread public awareness of the challenge, and the formation of a unified national response, both intellectually and then in policy terms. The first occurred as Franklin D. Roosevelt watched the rise of fascism in Europe and imperial militarism in Japan during the 1930s with growing concern but against a backdrop of isolationism and the pressure of the powerful America First Committee at home. A significant part of the American public thought that the United States should focus inward to recover from the Great Depression instead of expending resources on costly international interventions. Even after the outbreak of World War II in Europe in 1939, it took a shock to the system—the surprise Japanese attack on Pearl Harbor in 1941—before American sentiment shifted away from isolationism and Roosevelt was able to lead the United States into the global struggle.

---

[1] Niall Ferguson, "The New Cold War? It's With China, and It Has Already Begun," *New York Times*, December 2, 2019, https://www.nytimes.com/2019/12/02/opinion/china-cold-war.html.

Similarly, George Kennan published his famous "X article" on the sources of Soviet conduct in *Foreign Affairs* in 1947. But it took another decade, one that featured the deep partisan divisions of the McCarthy hearings and divergent opinions on the nature of the challenge from the Soviet Union, before the Sputnik moment in 1957 brought the U.S. government and electorate into alignment. The coherent strategy of containment that emerged afterward, with strong bipartisan support, lasted for another three decades until the end of the Cold War in 1989–91.

In this context, it is perhaps less surprising that public discussions about the nature of, and appropriate response to, the challenges posed by the People's Republic of China (PRC) are now being widely aired. And in fact, there are important signs of a bipartisan recognition of the need for a coherent response. Threads of recognition that the United States would need to engage with China as a strategic competitor were evident in the Bush and Obama administrations, although both continued to pursue policies based on the belief that positive engagement with Beijing could lead to a more democratic and open China. As Ashley Tellis illuminates in his introductory chapter, those initial threads have since become a largely bipartisan consensus across both the public and private sectors that acknowledges China as a strategic competitor, while the arguments in favor of continued engagement have waned. A more comprehensive understanding of the nature of the U.S. relationship with China will be crucial for Washington to craft an effective national strategy.

The emergence of a bipartisan consensus on China that openly acknowledges the competitive relationship and proposes tougher responses has perhaps inevitably prompted some pushback and even more soul-searching within the policy community. Some have argued for a return to the *status quo ante* and a deliberate search for bilateral cooperation where possible, given the risks that a prolonged period of strategic competition or, even worse, a military confrontation would pose. Unfortunately, the strategic drivers of the competition, as demonstrated in recent volumes in the *Strategic Asia* series, are too deeply rooted for cooperation to be anything more than limited to specific issues where U.S. and Chinese interests genuinely align, such as antipiracy missions in the Persian Gulf and Gulf of Aden.

From China's perspective, the achievement of, or return to, great-power status is the inevitable outcome of fundamental historical processes that naturally lead to China playing the dominant strategic role in East Asia and beyond. The Chinese Communist Party (CCP) uses a particular interpretation of China's long history as evidence for its peaceful rise. It claims that China has historically been a benevolent civilization whose greatness its own people and neighbors naturally accept. However, as Christopher Ford argued in the 2016–17 edition of *Strategic Asia*, Chinese strategic culture is influenced by both this deep-rooted historical ideology and realpolitik. This combination results in a defensive realist culture that does not shy away from the use of force.[2] And as Ashley Tellis outlined in last year's volume, China's path to great-power status and increasing assertiveness in recent decades can be clearly defined in three distinct periods: (1) creating domestic stability and establishing legitimacy, (2) integrating with the global system and preparing for the challenges ahead, and (3) asserting global leadership. During the first phase, under Deng Xiaoping's tenure, China followed the "hide and bide" (*taoguang yanghui*) policy, in which it veiled its capabilities and focused on securing internal stability. Following the collapse of the Soviet Union and the emergence of a unipolar world order in which no serious challenger faced the United States, the CCP became increasingly concerned about its continued security and legitimacy. As a result, the party both stoked nationalist fervor and opened up its markets to promote economic growth and development. In the third stage of China's ascension, Xi Jinping has promoted the "four strengths" aimed at increasing China's global leadership, improving its global image, becoming a moral leader, and enhancing economic influence.[3]

Given this combination of a strategic culture that places China naturally among the pantheon of great powers, the ideological framework espoused by the CCP, and a belief that the United States, along with its democratic allies and partners across the region, represents a significant existential threat to China's national interests, it is no surprise that China today is seeking to push back against the United States across the Indo-Pacific. From the perspective of Beijing, all of China's recent actions—island-building in the South China Sea, the Belt and Road Initiative, deepening strategic cooperation with Russia, pressure on U.S. allies and partners, and other attempts to assume global leadership and reshape the international order—make complete strategic sense.

From the United States' perspective, an equally deep-rooted set of drivers influence U.S. grand strategy in the Indo-Pacific and shape the hardening U.S. response. Since the middle of the nineteenth century, if not earlier, the United States has looked west across the Pacific and engaged in

---

[2] Christopher A. Ford, "Realpolitik with Chinese Characteristics: Chinese Strategic Culture and the Modern Communist Party-State" in *Strategic Asia 2016–17: Understanding Strategic Cultures in the Asia-Pacific*, ed. Ashley J. Tellis, Alison Szalwinski, and Michael Wills (Seattle: National Bureau of Asian Research [NBR], 2016), 29–60.

[3] Ashley J. Tellis, "Pursuing Global Reach: China's Not So Long March toward Preeminence," in *Strategic Asia 2019: China's Expanding Strategic Ambitions*, ed. Ashley J. Tellis, Alison Szalwinski, and Michael Wills (Seattle: NBR, 2019), 3–46.

the "effective application of military, diplomatic, economic, and ideational tools of national power" to ensure open access to Asia, unchallenged by any other hegemonic power.[4] This understanding drove the United States' first forays across the Pacific to counter the threat from imperial Britain and other European colonial powers. It later drove the United States' entrance into World War II to push back against Japanese expansionism. And it underpinned U.S. engagement throughout the Cold War—from the Korean and Vietnam Wars through the opening to China under Richard Nixon to take advantage of the Sino-Soviet split. For decades, and over multiple administrations, U.S. policy toward the Indo-Pacific has emphasized the importance of alliances and a forward military posture for securing the region.

Given the strength and deep roots of these strategic drivers, the hope for a return to a period of Sino-U.S. cooperation seems highly wishful. The international system in the decades ahead will likely be defined by an escalating strategic competition between the United States and China and the return to an era of bipolar competition, though one in which the protagonists are deeply interconnected. Building on the analysis of previous *Strategic Asia* volumes, the 2020 volume elucidates how states will manage their own interests in this global competition by attempting to align with either China or the United States or by hedging and trying to play both sides to their advantage. Each chapter examines and assesses these dynamics in a key state or region. To frame the issue, we offer some thoughts about four significant elements of success in this strategic competition and what aspects of national power the United States should therefore prioritize in order to craft an effective strategy for competition with China.

The first element is hard power and military capabilities. Despite China's massive military modernization program, the U.S. military remains the dominant force in the Indo-Pacific. Since World War II, the United States has employed forward power projection in order to meet security challenges far from its own territory and secure global primacy. As a result, it has developed strong alliances and advanced military capabilities. Although the United States still has the advantage in power projection, China is investing in its own military and shifting power from the army to develop a stronger navy and air force. In some domains, the People's Liberation Army is catching up with or posing significant challenges to long-standing U.S.

---

[4] Michael J. Green, *By More Than Providence: Grand Strategy and American Power in the Asia Pacific Since 1783* (New York: Columbia University Press, 2017), 4.

military advantages.[5] As Thomas Mahnken argued in the 2015–16 *Strategic Asia* volume, Washington needs to prioritize investments in U.S. military capabilities and critically assess its force posture needs to maintain its current advantage.[6]

Second, in economic terms, the competition is already far more evenly matched. While the United States retains great economic strengths and a culture of technological innovation, since the 2008 financial crisis, China has pursued a series of blunting strategies against the United States by creating parallel economic structures to the ones designed under the Bretton Woods system that help underpin U.S. economic and financial primacy.[7] Through developing alternative systems and structures, China has been able to achieve economic leverage over its neighbors and subsequently gain regional power. The United States is only now beginning to design an effective plan for long-term economic competition with China. Such a plan would limit the costs of the trade war for American consumers while maintaining restrictions on some Chinese imports.[8] The United States must also invest in innovation, technology, and education. China partly acquires its advanced technology through its own development and investment, but also significantly through illegal means such as intellectual property theft, which damages the U.S. economy and diminishes incentives for innovation.[9] China understands the importance of cutting-edge technology for its rise, and the United States must recognize that protecting U.S. intellectual property and investing in innovation are imperative to effectively compete with China.

Third, as noted above, dating back to the end of World War II, the United States has had a clear sense of national purpose in the Indo-Pacific. Washington has sought to support the advancement of "security, development, and democracy" in the region by promoting a rules-based and value-driven world order.[10] China, in contrast, does not yet appear to have a clear vision for the world it seeks to create. Although Beijing is unequivocal in expressing its discontent with the current U.S.-led order and ultimately

---

[5] Oriana Skylar Mastro, "Ideas, Perceptions, and Power: An Examination of China's Military Strategy," in *Strategic Asia 2017–18: Power, Ideas, and Military Strategy in the Asia-Pacific* (Seattle: NBR, 2017), 19–43.

[6] Thomas G. Mahnken, "U.S. Strategy: Confronting Challenges Abroad and Constraints at Home," in Tellis, Szalwinski, and Wills, *Strategic Asia 2017–18*, 227–29.

[7] Rush Doshi, "China's Role in Reshaping the International Financial Architecture: Blunting U.S. Power and Building Regional Order," in Tellis, Szalwinski, and Wills, *Strategic Asia 2019*, 279–308.

[8] Charles W. Boustany Jr. and Aaron L. Friedberg, "Partial Disengagement: A New U.S. Strategy for Economic Competition with China," NBR, NBR Special Report, no. 82, November 2019, 2.

[9] Commission on the Theft of American Intellectual Property, *The IP Commission Report* (Seattle: NBR, 2013), 1–7.

[10] White House, *National Security Strategy* (Washington, D.C., February 2015), 24.

seeks to become a conventional global power, how it aims to achieve this goal is still shrouded in vague discourse.[11] Nonetheless, this discourse reveals that China envisions a world incompatible with Western liberal values, one where authoritarian regimes are not ostracized. For now, the enduring vision of a free and open world order that the United States offers remains an advantage.

A fourth element of a successful strategy is the sustainment of an effective coalition of allies and partners both to complement the capabilities that a great power alone possesses and to serve as a conduit for the projection of power in the region. In this area, the United States' alliances and partnerships in the Indo-Pacific provide Washington with a distinct comparative advantage. China, despite growing strategic cooperation with Russia and an alliance with North Korea, remains relatively isolated. A critical variable in determining the prospects for continued stability in the region will be the United States' ability to sustain its alliance relationships in ways that work toward common regional objectives. However, with Washington seemingly focused on the dollar amount that allies contribute over the capabilities offered or enabled, with political tensions between treaty allies rising, and with trade disputes between like-minded nations escalating, the United States will need to tread carefully to preserve the goodwill and ready support of its allies and partners in order to maintain this advantage.[12]

Today, the United States faces a stark challenge: to create an effective strategy for competing with China in an age of deep partisan division and political tribalism. U.S. policymakers and the American public must come together, despite the polarization of domestic politics, to create a strategy that addresses the long-term challenge of competing with China without overcorrecting. This challenge is not insurmountable. History illustrates that we have faced similar challenges before, and if the various elements of American power—from the White House, to Capitol Hill, to the business community, to the public at large—can agree on a common path, as they have begun to do, a coherent, competitive strategy can emerge. China's rise will remain a focal point for U.S. foreign policy for years to come. A bipartisan consensus that builds on the commonalities evident in the Bush, Obama, and Trump administrations and then extends to future administrations will be critical for success.

---

[11] Nadège Rolland, "China's Vision for a New World Order," NBR, NBR Special Report (forthcoming in 2020).

[12] See Ashley J. Tellis, Abraham M. Denmark, and Greg Chaffin, eds., *Strategic Asia 2014–15: U.S. Alliances and Partnerships at the Center of Global Power* (Seattle: NBR, 2014).

Acknowledgments

As with all previous books in the *Strategic Asia* series, many talents have gone into making this year's volume possible. Above all, we acknowledge the hard work of our nine contributing authors, who join a group of more than 150 scholars who have written for the Strategic Asia Program over the past nineteen years. We also thank the fifteen anonymous reviewers—both scholars and current U.S. government officials—whose comments on the draft chapters during the summer helped strengthen our collective findings.

Within NBR, we owe thanks to our tireless colleagues Naomi Garcia, Jessica Keough, John Morreale, Ian Smith, and above all Joshua Ziemkowski, who brought this book to life with their first-rate editing and production work. Thanks also to Stefanie Choi for another classic cover design and to Dan Aum, Audrey Mossberger, and Sandra Ward for their work in promoting the book. As always, a team of incredible research assistants helped our authors meet the unreasonable deadlines that we imposed on them, and this year we acknowledge Rachel Bernstein, Joseph Michaels, Eliot Roberts, and Aimee Tat. And all of us owe an enormous debt of gratitude to Richard Ellings, who first conceived of the Strategic Asia Program two decades ago, and who stepped down this summer after 30 years as president of NBR.

Finally, special thanks and deep appreciation are due to our colleague Ashley Tellis, now in his sixteenth year serving as research director of the Strategic Asia Program. The care and attention that he devotes to each book—from crafting the research guidelines, conversing with the authors during and following the planning meeting, reviewing chapters, and writing an outstanding introduction—are unparalleled. It is a privilege to have spent another year collaborating with him and deepening our professional friendship to bring this book to fruition.

Alison Szalwinski
Vice President of Research
NBR

Michael Wills
Executive Vice President
NBR

STRATEGIC ASIA 2020

EXECUTIVE SUMMARY

This chapter analyzes the progression of China into a strategic competitor to the U.S. and the geopolitical implications of this evolving development.

MAIN ARGUMENT

Under the Trump administration, the U.S. has shifted from viewing China as a strategic partner to a strategic competitor. The administration has challenged China in five key areas: control over the Indo-Pacific rimland, trade and the economy, China's quest for alternative technical standards, the pursuit of technological dominance, and Chinese military advancement. However, this contestation is complex due to both the close economic relationship between the U.S. and China and the interconnectedness of global trade networks. Nonetheless, states are attempting to exploit the growing U.S.-China competition for their own benefit, avoid being penalized by it, or use each rival to protect their own national interests.

POLICY IMPLICATIONS

- The U.S. must act like a responsible hegemon by recommitting to uphold the liberal international order built by U.S. power, provide the global public goods that bestow legitimacy upon its primacy, and strengthen its power-projection capabilities to protect its allies and friends.

- The U.S. should use coordinated action with allies to confront China's trade malpractices while simultaneously expanding plurilateral free trade agreements to accelerate U.S. economic growth and deepen the U.S. relationship with its partners.

- The U.S. should pursue targeted decoupling of the U.S. and Chinese economies, mainly in order to protect its defense capabilities, rather than seeking a comprehensive rupture that would fracture global trade networks, impose economic losses on the U.S. and its allies, and strengthen Beijing's determination to establish its own trading bloc.

The Return of U.S.-China Strategic Competition

Ashley J. Tellis

After a little over two decades of simmering geopolitical suspicion between Washington and Beijing, President Donald Trump's administration finally declared China to be a major strategic competitor of the United States. The December 2017 National Security Strategy plainly described China as a "revisionist" power that "seeks to displace the United States in the Indo-Pacific region, expand the reaches of its state-driven economic model, and reorder the region in its favor."[1] The summary of the National Defense Strategy issued subsequently by the U.S. Department of Defense elaborated on this assessment by declaring that "China is a strategic competitor" and further noting:

> China is leveraging military modernization, influence operations, and predatory economics to coerce neighboring countries to reorder the Indo-Pacific region to their advantage. As China continues its economic and military ascendance, asserting power through an all-of-nation long-term strategy, it will continue to pursue a military modernization program that seeks Indo-Pacific regional hegemony in the near-term and displacement of the United States to achieve global preeminence in the future.[2]

This transformation of China from an ambiguous partner to a strategic rival was a long time coming. The Trump administration only articulated

---

Ashley J. Tellis is the Tata Chair for Strategic Affairs and a Senior Fellow at the Carnegie Endowment for International Peace. He is also Research Director of the Strategic Asia Program at the National Bureau of Asian Research. He can be reached at <atellis@ceip.org>.

[1] White House, *National Security Strategy of the United States of America* (Washington, D.C., December 2017), https://www.whitehouse.gov/wp-content/uploads/2017/12/NSS-Final-12-18-2017-0905.pdf.

[2] U.S. Department of Defense, "Summary of the 2018 National Defense Strategy of the United States of America: Sharpening the American Military's Competitive Edge," January 2018, https://dod.defense.gov/Portals/1/Documents/pubs/2018-National-Defense-Strategy-Summary.pdf.

boldly what both the George W. Bush and the Barack Obama administrations feared as a possibility but hoped to avoid through deepened engagement and prudential hedging. Yet this aspiration was unlikely to ever be realized because, irrespective of what the United States tried or did, the steady growth of Chinese power since the reforms began in 1978 would have bestowed on Beijing greater influence and control over the Indo-Pacific space at Washington's expense—this, in turn, enabling China to seek parity with, if not supplant altogether, the United States globally.[3]

This chapter analyzes the progression of China as a strategic competitor of the United States and the geopolitical implications of this evolving development. Toward that end, it is divided into four major sections. The first section assesses why the U.S. quest for a partnership with China was fated to fail once China's growth in economic capabilities was gradually matched by its rising military power. The second section explores why the United States took so long to recognize that China was in fact steadily becoming a strategic competitor, even though that was increasingly evident after the end of the Cold War. The third section describes the contours of the Trump administration's current confrontation with China and elaborates its significance for U.S. interests. The fourth section summarizes the chapters gathered together in this volume—whose theme is the impact of U.S.-China competition on the global system—to underscore the point that most states enjoy significant agency, which enables them to pursue choices that go beyond exclusive solidarity with either the United States or China in the ongoing Sino-U.S. rivalry. The conclusion argues that the Trump administration should consider significant correctives to its current strategy for confronting China if the United States is to secure enduring strategic advantages over the long term.

The Doomed Quest for a U.S.-China Strategic Partnership

Although U.S.-China relations had gradually improved despite numerous hiccups since President Richard Nixon's landmark 1972 visit to China, the quest for a "constructive strategic partnership" received a decisive boost during President Bill Clinton's administration, when "comprehensive engagement" became the watchword for growing ties between the two countries.[4]

---

[3] Ashley J. Tellis, *Balancing Without Containment* (Washington, D.C.: Carnegie Endowment for International Peace, 2014), 1–15.

[4] "Joint U.S.-China Statement," White House, October 29, 1997, https://1997-2001.state.gov/regions/eap/971029_usc_jtstmt.html.

This phrase signaled the United States' desire to sustain a relationship that could survive disagreements about China's human rights practices—an issue that became particularly important after the Tiananmen Square massacre—and led in time to a dramatic deepening of bilateral economic ties and China's systematic integration into the liberal international economic order built and preserved by U.S. hegemony. These developments, in turn, contributed to the acceleration of China's growth in power. Despite the misgivings generated by this development, successive administrations in Washington sought to sustain a productive partnership with Beijing on the presumption that assuaging its fears about any U.S. desire to suppress China's rising power would protect bilateral cooperation and preserve broader stability in the Indo-Pacific region.

Consistent with this expectation, President Bush told the Chinese people in 2002 that "my nation offers you our respect and our friendship," believing that all the changes he perceived within China would "lead to a stronger, more confident China—a China that can astonish and enrich the world."[5] Speaking in a similar vein, President Obama went one step further when he declared that "the United States welcomes the rise of China as a prosperous, peaceful and stable state. I want to repeat that....We welcome the rise of a prosperous, peaceful and stable China." In emphasizing this idea, he noted that "over recent decades the United States has worked to help integrate China into the global economy—not only because it's in China's best interest, but because it's in America's best interest, and the world's best interest. We want China to do well."[6]

These sentiments are fundamentally consistent with the liberal worldview that generally dominates U.S. policymaking. It presumes a harmony of interests in international politics and, accordingly, concludes that the aims of both established and rising powers can be reconciled without unyielding conflict. Weaker versions of this conception hold that conflicting interests can be mitigated if the parties involved make conscious efforts to compromise, thereby defusing what would otherwise degenerate into malignant rivalry.[7]

In the case of U.S.-China relations, liberal optimism played an important role in leading Washington to support Beijing's ascent to power long after it

---

[5] "President Bush Speaks at Tsinghua University," White House, Office of the Press Secretary, February 22, 2002, https://georgewbush-whitehouse.archives.gov/news/releases/2002/02/20020222.html.

[6] "Remarks by President Obama at APEC CEO Summit," White House, Office of the Press Secretary, November 10, 2014, https://obamawhitehouse.archives.gov/the-press-office/2014/11/10/remarks-president-obama-apec-ceo-summit.

[7] For good examples of such an expectation, see Lyle J. Goldstein, *Meeting China Halfway: How to Defuse the Emerging U.S.-China Rivalry* (Washington, D.C.: Georgetown University Press, 2015); and James Steinberg and Michael E. O'Hanlon, *Strategic Reassurance and Resolve: U.S.-China Relations in the Twenty-First Century* (Princeton: Princeton University Press, 2014).

was necessitated by the exigencies of the Cold War.[8] Thus, since the Clinton presidency, the United States has provided China with asymmetric access to the U.S. market, while U.S. firms have used their capital and technology to build a manufacturing base in China. Over time, this would enlarge their markets and profitability even as it simultaneously raised China's living standards, its technological capabilities, and ultimately its national power.

Such mutually productive intercourse, it was assumed, would deepen economic ties between the two countries and thereby diminish the political irritants that might otherwise inflame bilateral relations. Since the expansion of political liberty was also assumed to be a natural byproduct of economic openness, the expectation that China would slowly evolve toward democracy gained strength as well, and this possibility further reinforced the conviction that peaceful relations between the two countries were possible. Economic interdependence and the possibility of democratization in China would, taken together, consequently defuse the prospect of a lethal rivalry—the kind that marked the interactions previously witnessed between all hegemonic powers and their rising challengers.[9]

These expectations, however, progressively came to naught in the case of the United States and China for three reasons. First, despite the widespread expectation that bilateral differences could be managed, if not actually reconciled, the divergences in Chinese and U.S. interests sometimes proved to be acute, especially on key strategic issues. For example, China and the United States have fundamentally different aims regarding Taiwan. China believes that Taiwan is inherently part of China, and accordingly Beijing reserves the right to use force if required to prevent any formal assertion of independence by Taipei. In contrast, the United States is strictly speaking agnostic about the Chinese claim and seeks only to prevent the use of force to change the current status quo.[10] While these mismatched aims could be managed for a while, they are increasingly hard to harmonize. Taiwanese democracy, the demographic dominance of the indigenous Taiwanese population, and the dramatic increases in prosperity have pushed the island toward either seeking to preserve the status quo indefinitely (the preference of the majority) or even contemplating independence (the desire of a significant minority)—at

---

[8] An excellent early review of the dilemmas facing U.S. policymakers about managing China can be found in Richard K. Betts, "Wealth, Power, and Instability: East Asia and the United States after the Cold War," *International Security* 18, no. 3 (1993/1994): 34–77.

[9] Ibid. See also, Kurt M. Campbell and Ely Ratner, "The China Reckoning: How Beijing Defied American Expectations," *Foreign Affairs*, March/April 2018.

[10] The complex issues implicated herein are reviewed masterfully in Alan D. Romberg, *Rein In at the Brink of the Precipice: American Policy toward Taiwan and U.S.-PRC Relations* (Washington, D.C.: Henry L. Stimson Center, 2003).

exactly the time when rising Chinese power has resulted in Beijing seeking to complete its nationalist project of "reunification."[11]

Similarly, China, as the most powerful state in Asia, seeks to preserve its periphery as a sanctuary free from the presence of competitors and other security threats.[12] All great powers in history, including the United States, have sought to maintain such zones of privileged influence along their frontiers, and China is no different. But this ambition strikes directly at the interests of other major states located around China's borders, such as Japan, South Korea, and India, all of which want to limit China's military reach and capacity to threaten their security and autonomy.[13] Because the United States is obligated by its alliance ties to defend Japan, South Korea, and the Philippines, and because it arguably is motivated by its interests to preserve India's well-being, Washington cannot acquiesce to Beijing's desire to maintain a periphery either that is free of U.S. presence or where China's neighbors are neutered in order to satisfy Chinese preferences.

Second, although Washington's hope that the liberal vision of international politics might finally prevail was understandable, it stood little chance of realization given China's troubled history. Spanning nearly four thousand years, the country's recorded past is marked by unrest, violence, intranational conflicts, and foreign invasions.[14] The lessons imbibed by Chinese elites from this experience is that order is rare and must be produced by an accumulation of power that is sufficient both to uphold monadic rule within the state and to provide a measure of predominance vis-à-vis its neighbors. Such an understanding of political necessity would inevitably drive China, as circumstances permitted, toward building up its national power and using it first for authoritarian ends within China itself and thereafter to construct an Asian hierarchy with China at its apex in order to ward off those threats that might otherwise endanger Beijing.[15]

While these remedies suffice to undermine the liberal vision of what constitutes good order both inside and outside China, the more recent memory of the "century of national humiliation" threatens the hope for

---

[11] For a sobering overview, see Richard C. Bush, "Danger Ahead? Taiwan's Politics, China's Ambitions, and U.S. Policy," Brookings Institution, April 15, 2019, https://www.brookings.edu/on-the-record/danger-ahead-taiwans-politics-chinas-ambitions-and-us-policy; and Brendan Taylor, *Dangerous Decade: Taiwan's Security and Crisis Management*, Adelphi Series 470 (New York: Routledge, 2019).

[12] Michael D. Swaine and Ashley J. Tellis, *Interpreting China's Grand Strategy: Past, Present and Future* (Santa Monica: RAND Corporation, 2000), 9–20, 97–150.

[13] Ibid.

[14] Ibid.

[15] See Christopher A. Ford, "Realpolitik with Chinese Characteristics: Chinese Strategic Culture and the Modern Communist Party-State," in *Strategic Asia 2016–17: Understanding Strategic Cultures in the Asia Pacific*, ed. Ashley J. Tellis, Alison Szalwinski, and Michael Wills (Seattle: National Bureau of Asian Research [NBR], 2016), 29–62.

China's peaceful rise conclusively. The birth of the People's Republic of China (PRC) itself was a long-gestating reaction to the colonial penetration of China. Colonialism produced a multitude of ills for China, including humiliating defeats in wars with neighboring countries and various European powers as well as losses of territory that were formalized in what China refers to as "unequal treaties."[16] Inasmuch as the contemporary Chinese state represents a desire to recover the greatness that China once enjoyed in Asia and globally, the revanchist impulse is indelibly etched into its governing regime's psychology: only the full retrieval of its claimed territories would satisfy China's desire for rejuvenation. Yet this ambition, almost by definition, undermines the expectation that China might be able to live in peace with its neighbors because both the character of the Chinese Communist Party (CCP) regime and its aspirations to right historical wrongs conspire against that hope.[17]

Third, the liberal expectation that China (the rising power) and the United States (the established hegemon) would find reasons to cooperate because of shared economic gains also proved fallacious for reasons that were understandable at either end. Given the traditional animosity between the United States and China since the founding of the PRC in 1949—a hostility that abated but never fully evaporated even after their rapprochement during the latter years of the Cold War—it is not surprising that the CCP, with its Leninist ideology, never bought into the idea that the reconciliation between Washington and Beijing was anything other than a tactical adjustment.[18] The CCP viewed this détente as a product of necessity precipitated by the ideological and security threats posed by the Soviet Union. As Chen Jian succinctly summarized, the Chinese perception was that "U.S. imperialism remained China's enemy but no longer the primary one."[19] When this perception was conjoined with China's own abiding desire to restore its national grandeur and the CCP's enduring ideological suspicion of the United States as a liberal hegemon, it was highly unlikely that the U.S.-China rapprochement engendered by their common interests vis-à-vis the Soviet Union could have survived in perpetuity the circumstances that begat it.[20]

[16] Ford, "Realpolitik with Chinese Characteristics."

[17] Ibid. For a more expansive elaboration, see Christopher A. Ford, *The Mind of Empire: China's History and Modern Foreign Relations* (Lexington: University Press of Kentucky, 2010).

[18] See Odd Arne Westad's discussion of Mao Zedong's initial strategy of allying with the United States as a tactical measure similar to the CCP working with the United States to confront Japan. Odd Arne Westad, *Restless Empire: China and the World since 1750* (New York: Basic Books, 2012), 367–75.

[19] Chen Jian, *Mao's China and the Cold War* (Chapel Hill: University of North Carolina Press, 2001), 243.

[20] See the insightful discussion in Gary J. Schmitt, "The China Dream: America's, China's, and the Resulting Competition," American Enterprise Institute, January 18, 2019.

Political realists, and Leninists even more so, would have no difficulty accepting this conclusion given that, as Lenin phrased it, "war is not only a continuation of politics, it is the epitome of politics."[21] As China began to rise, therefore, it was not surprising that many Chinese leaders began to fear the possibility that the United States might seek to contain its ascendency either directly or through euphemistic devices such as "peaceful evolution."[22] Consequently, China labeled every U.S. action, be it diplomatic, economic, or military, that did not advance Chinese interests as "containment," not because Beijing was necessarily being disingenuous, but because it could not conceive of how Washington's strategy could have been any different.

Thus, for example, at exactly the time when the Obama administration was trying to most deeply engage China, the CCP's *Qiushi Journal* published a detailed analysis of the six strategies that the United States was supposedly pursuing to contain China.[23] To defeat that objective, it recommended seven counterstrategies that subsumed everything from economic warfare to attacking near enemies to prosecuting space wars. It should not be surprising that Chinese theorists would suggest such responses. Not only is it consistent with China's "parabellum" political culture,[24] but China would have arguably behaved in exactly the same way that it imagines the United States to have done had the two countries' positions been reversed in the global system—a natural consequence of the conviction that relentless competition is the essence of international politics.

While the United States supported China's international integration and, by implication, its rise even after the end of the Cold War because of the U.S. desire to secure absolute gains from trade (and because China was still viewed as relatively weak and incapable of threatening the United States), that view was increasingly strained by growing Chinese power after the turn of the century. Washington gradually perceived this problem but attempted—again for understandable reasons—to defuse it by half measures. Despite George W. Bush's anxieties about China, his administration, pressed by the challenges of terrorism, softened its early view of the country as a competitor, a position reflected in then secretary of state Colin Powell's disinclination to label Beijing

---

[21] V.I. Lenin, *Collected Works*, vol. 30, ed. George Hanna (Moscow: Progress Press, 1963), 224, https://archive.org/details/collectedworks0030leni/page/224.

[22] Russell Ong, "'Peaceful Evolution,' 'Regime Change' and China's Political Security," *Journal of Contemporary China* 16, no. 53 (2007): 717–27.

[23] "How China Deals with the U.S. Strategy to Contain China," *Qiushi Journal*, December 10, 2010, trans. by Chinascope, http://chinascope.org/archives/6353/92.

[24] Alastair Iain Johnston, *Cultural Realism: Strategic Culture and Grand Strategy in Chinese History* (Princeton: Princeton University Press, 1995).

as either a partner or an enemy on the grounds that "U.S.-China relations are too complicated and comprehensive to simply summarize in one word."[25]

The Obama administration tried a different approach, seeking to reassure China by declaring the "abolition" of great-power competition. As Hillary Clinton put it during her term as Obama's first secretary of state, "our approach to foreign policy must reflect the world as it is, not as it used to be. It does not make sense to adapt a 19th-century concert of powers, or a 20th-century balance of power strategy. We cannot go back to Cold War containment, or to unilateralism."[26] But even as the United States was thus trying to reassure China, it went about—sometimes without conviction, while at other times with more resolution—strengthening its alliances in Asia, developing new partnerships with the nations located on China's periphery, restructuring U.S. military capabilities for more effective power projection, completing new exclusionary trading agreements such as the Trans-Pacific Partnership (TPP), and generally seeking to revitalize U.S. global leadership in exactly the ways that would heighten anxiety in Beijing about Washington's intention to check China's growing power.

Both the Bush and the Obama administrations pursued such realist policies in more or less effective ways—and, obviously, they could not do otherwise. To do so would imply a dereliction of duty, a disavowal of U.S. interests, and a disregard of U.S. allies. But that only proves why the United States and China could never assure each other sufficiently to realize the common gains that otherwise supposedly lay within reach. For such reassurance to have been effective, both countries would have had to make costly sacrifices that increased each one's vulnerability to the other, thereby conclusively proving their benignity.[27] The risks involved in conveying the honesty of good intentions in this way, however, are often prohibitive enough that no self-regarding state—let alone great powers that have major equities or weaker allies to protect—will ordinarily undertake them.[28] Consequently, the hope that major potential competitors like the United States and China will sufficiently lower their guard to eliminate the corrosive suspicions that prevent strategic cooperation also flies out the window, despite the ensuing costs to both.

[25] Cited by Yu Wanli, "Breaking the Cycle? Sino-U.S. Relations under George W. Bush Administration," *China's Shift: Global Strategy of the Rising Power*, ed. Masafumi Iida (Tokyo: National Institute for Defense Studies, 2009), 81–98.

[26] "A Conversation with U.S. Secretary of State Hillary Rodham Clinton," Council on Foreign Relations, July 15, 2009, https://www.cfr.org/event/conversation-us-secretary-state-hillary-rodham-clinton-1.

[27] See the insightful discussion in Andrew H. Kydd, *Trust and Mistrust in International Relations* (Princeton: Princeton University Press, 2005).

[28] Evan Braden Montgomery, "Breaking Out of the Security Dilemma: Realism, Reassurance, and the Problem of Uncertainty," *International Security* 31, no. 2 (2006): 151–85.

For all these reasons, the United States and China could never realize their quest for a strategic partnership. As long as Chinese power continued to grow, as long as it embodied latent threats to U.S. allies in Asia, and as long as it contained the potential to undermine U.S. interests and hegemony in the global system more generally, Beijing would inevitably be viewed not as a collaborator but as a challenger in Washington. And as long as the United States attempted to protect, and even buttress, its extant primacy—both to preserve its prevailing privileges in the international system and to effectively defend its allies in the face of growing Chinese power—any initiatives undertaken by Washington toward this end would be inescapably perceived as threatening by Beijing. The structural contradiction between these two objectives could never be overcome by any strategy of reassurance, no matter how well-intentioned.

Why Did U.S. Pushback Take So Long?

Given this judgment, why did it take so long for the United States to recognize the threat that China posed to the preservation of its primacy in Asia and globally? To be sure, there are still some who deny that China poses any fundamental threats to the United States.[29] But, leaving such views aside, the official mind in Washington clearly has moved toward the view that China is today, and will be for the foreseeable future, the principal challenger to overall U.S. hegemony in the international system.[30] No other countries come close because they lack comparable levels of comprehensive national power, even though several states, such as Russia, North Korea, and Iran, oppose the United States locally or on important specific issues. The question of why the United States failed to appreciate the gravity of the challenge posed by China earlier thus remains. A complete answer will have to await the verdict of history, but for the moment a few explanations rooted in historical circumstances, misjudgments about China's capacity to thrive, the failure to anticipate China's ambitions, the difficulties of pursuing strategic competition under conditions of economic interdependence, and the character of state-society relations in the United States can all be proposed.

The first explanation is rooted in how the U.S.-China relationship evolved during the later stages of the Cold War. The decision by Nixon to seek a rapprochement with China in 1972—a process that his successors brought to full conclusion in 1979—was motivated fundamentally by a desire to tighten

---

[29] See, for example, M. Taylor Fravel et al., "China Is Not an Enemy," *Washington Post*, July 2, 2019, https://www.washingtonpost.com/opinions/making-china-a-us-enemy-is-counterproductive/2019/07/02/647d49d0-9bfa-11e9-b27f-ed2942f73d70_story.html.

[30] Aaron L. Friedberg, "Competing with China," *Survival* 60, no. 3 (2018): 7–64.

the containment of the Soviet Union. Exploiting the earlier Sino-Soviet split, Nixon hoped to entice Beijing into partnering with the United States to oppose the Soviet Union at a time when U.S. power was perceived to be weakening because of overextension in Southeast Asia and economic crises at home.[31] This engagement, which continued until the end of the Cold War despite bumps along the way, made sense at the time because U.S. and Chinese interests in limiting Soviet power happily converged. It also laid the foundations for viewing China as a de facto U.S. partner whose influence in Asia and globally could be exploited to advance the vital objective of defeating the Soviet Union.

This perception of China as a U.S. collaborator, however, survived well after the end of the Cold War because Beijing, as a result of Deng Xiaoping's reforms, renounced its previous Maoist objective of fomenting world revolution. China would remain a revisionist but not a revolutionary state, with its revisionism judged in the early post–Cold War period to be limited insofar as it was focused mainly on integrating Taiwan. To the degree that this goal was pursued peacefully and did not implicate larger military challenges to the United States, China's limited revisionism was viewed as manageable from the perspective of U.S. grand strategy. Some facsimile of this view persists in several quarters of the United States to this day, and this residual perception arguably prevented Washington from treating Beijing as a significant challenger long after it had evolved into one.[32]

The U.S. failure to recognize that China contained the preconditions for rapid growth compounded the problem of anticipating its rise as a major challenger. The fact that China was a relatively poor country at the time when its rapprochement with the United States matured reinforced Washington's complacency. China's development challenges were undoubtedly immense, and U.S. leaders in the 1980s and 1990s simply did not imagine that the country's economic revitalization could be rapid enough to change the global balance of power in their lifetimes.[33] Nor did they appreciate, after several decades of Mao's political and economic disruptions, that China could grow

---

[31] J. Stapleton Roy, "Engagement Works," *Foreign Affairs*, July/August 2018.

[32] For useful overviews of the evolution of U.S. strategic attitudes to China, see Harry Harding, "The U.S. and China from Partners to Competitors," Carter Center, https://www.cartercenter.org/resources/pdfs/peace/china/china-program-2019/harding.pdf; Evan A. Feigenbaum, "China and the World: Dealing with a Reluctant Power," *Foreign Affairs*, January/February 2017; and Evan A. Feigenbaum, "Reluctant Stakeholder: Why China's Highly Strategic Brand of Revisionism Is More Challenging Than Washington Thinks," MacroPolo, April 27, 2018.

[33] As William Safire would record, "Before Nixon died, I asked him—on the record—if perhaps we had gone a bit overboard on selling the American public on the political benefits of increased trade. That old realist, who had played the China card to exploit the split in the Communist world, replied with some sadness that he was not as hopeful as he had once been: 'We may have created a Frankenstein.'" See William Safire, "The Biggest Vote," *New York Times*, May 18, 2000, https://www.nytimes.com/2000/05/18/opinion/essay-the-biggest-vote.html.

effervescently if favorable circumstances were to present themselves. And it is exactly these conditions that obtained once the reform period began in 1978.

Deng Xiaoping's reforms, which involved the gradual replacement of Mao Zedong's socialism with state-directed and -controlled liberalization, finally succeeded for several reasons. For starters, the Communist party-state had penetrated Chinese society completely and was thus able to implement national policy at the farthest reaches of the country without any meaningful local opposition, while simultaneously creating channels of information and feedback for understanding what was happening even in far-flung provinces.[34] This penetration, which was novel in China's history, had a remarkable impact once the reforms began. It allowed Beijing to initiate and control the character and pace of economic liberalization in ways that would have been impossible to sustain without pervasive political control. It also permitted the reformers to countenance local experimentation at different levels, which could be rapidly emulated elsewhere if successful and contained if a failure. In so doing, China enjoyed what can be best described as "embedded liberalization"—that is, the measured introduction and maintenance of limited markets designed to enhance the resources accruing to, and thus the power of, the party-state.[35]

Furthermore, despite other failures in both agriculture and industry, the Maoist regime had made significant investments in the health and education of its people, thus creating a labor force that could become remarkably productive when the overarching circumstances changed.[36] When the reform era finally resulted in foreign capital entering China to manufacture goods destined for external markets, even low-cost Chinese labor was able to create products of extremely high quality that were capable of capturing markets in both developed and developing countries around the world. This skillfulness and efficiency led in time to huge capital and technology inflows as major multinational corporations all sought a foothold in China for a manufacturing base. The resulting expansion of industry in the country fueled the growth of incomes and savings domestically. As Chinese exports grew internationally, Beijing received increased revenues and accumulated huge foreign-exchange reserves that could be used both as a prophylactic in the

---

[34] For details, see Zheng Yongnian, *The Chinese Communist Party as Organizational Emperor* (New York: Routledge, 2010); and Mary E. Gallagher, "China: The Limits of Civil Society in a Late Leninist State," in *Civil Society and Political Change in Asia*, ed. Muthiah Alagappa (Stanford: Stanford University Press, 2004), 419–54.

[35] The concept of embedded liberalism was coined by John Gerard Ruggie in "International Regimes, Transactions, and Change: Embedded Liberalism in the Postwar Economic Order," *International Organization* 36, no. 2 (1982): 379–415. The term used here is borrowed from Wen Xie, "Embedded Liberalization and Paths toward Capitalism in China" (unpublished manuscript).

[36] See, for example, Thomas G. Rawski, "Human Resources and China's Long Economic Boom," *Asia Policy*, no. 12 (2011): 33–78.

event of future crises and for further internal investments and technological innovation—and eventually for outward investments that would produce enormous international influence.[37]

Finally, for all the repressiveness of Mao's tenure, the Communist state was unable to extinguish the remarkable entrepreneurialism of the Chinese populace, which, although then oriented primarily to surviving the cataclysms of Communism, proved remarkably adept at productively exploiting the opportunities offered by Deng's reforms when they finally came.[38] This effusion of Chinese entrepreneurship was initially eclipsed by the spectacle of foreign direct investment in China, but it proved to be just as consequential. Through the dramatic productivity growth in agriculture and the upsurge in rural industry, the new profit-seeking behaviors of state-owned enterprises, and the unprecedented expansion of private economic activities, China began to grow at double-digit rates for a prolonged period of time as new forms of capitalism took root in areas where the state permitted market activity. In time, the quality of China's labor force and vibrant entrepreneurship set the stage for a transition in which Chinese products soon shifted from "made in China" to "innovated in China."[39] This process was aided by the requirement that all international investors could operate in China only through joint ventures with a local partner, the periodic theft of foreign intellectual property, and generous state subsidies. The steady increase in China's technological proficiency that followed, which has now been further stimulated by large state-driven projects such as the Made in China 2025 plan, rapidly transformed China into a sophisticated competitor to even the advanced economies of Japan, Western Europe, and North America.

The three elements—state penetration, human capital investment, and latent entrepreneurism—thus operated synergistically to pave the way for China's rapid growth in power once the reforms began in 1978. Consequently, China would have grown even if external integration with the West had not occurred as a result of the United States' decisions to permit access to its markets first on an annual basis and then permanently in 2000. But this growth arguably would have been slower had the expansion of China's

---

[37] See, for example, Barry Naughton, *The Chinese Economy: Transitions and Growth* (Cambridge: MIT Press, 2006), 375–424; and David Dollar, "China as a Global Investor," in *China's New Sources of Economic Growth: Reform, Resources and Climate Change*, vol. 1, ed. Ligang Song et al. (Acton: ANU Press, 2016), 197–214.

[38] Dwight H. Perkins, "The Transition from Central Planning: East Asia's Experience," in *Social Capability and Long-Term Economic Growth*, ed. Bon Ho Koo and Dwight H. Perkins (New York: St. Martin's Press, 1995), 221–41; and Rawski, "Human Resources and China's Long Economic Boom."

[39] Shang-Jin Wei, Zhuan Xie, and Xiaobo Zhang, "From 'Made in China' to 'Innovated in China': Necessity, Prospect, and Challenges," *Journal of Economic Perspectives* 31, no. 1 (2017): 49–70.

domestic market not been complemented by the outward-looking strategy centered on expanding international trade.[40]

It is in this context that the failure to anticipate China's enduring strategic ambitions would prove costly to the United States. The integration of China with the West clearly accelerated the country's domestic growth dramatically, but as long as this expansion was directed principally toward commercial ends, it would have elicited little strategic anxiety in Washington. After all, Japan, the smaller East Asian states, and Western Europe too trod similar paths to recovery in the aftermath of World War II and became economic powerhouses in the process. Although these developments caused episodic concern in the United States because of their impact on its domestic economy—with the heartburn caused by the Japanese displacement of the U.S. automobile industry in the 1980s being a good example—such fears ultimately abated because the rising economic power of these countries was not used to underwrite the production of military capabilities directed against U.S. power.[41]

In the case of China, however, this is exactly the direction that Beijing pursued. Unlike the other postwar European and Asian states that flourished because of their integration with the global economic system, China had no intention of subsisting as a postmodern "trading state."[42] Although in the beginning of the reform period Deng Xiaoping had relegated military modernization to the last of the "four modernizations," this priority altered dramatically when forced by political necessity. Thus, from the 1991 Gulf War, and even more so from the 1995–96 Taiwan missile crisis onward, China began to develop ever more potent military instruments designed to limit the U.S. military's effectiveness in and around Asia.[43] As China's economic power continued to expand, its military capabilities, which were initially designed to constrain the United States along the Asian rimland, were extended to challenge U.S. dominance of the global commons more resolutely.[44]

These developments took place in an evolutionary way but nonetheless were motivated by China's singular objective of recovering its traditional

---

[40] Zuliu Hu and Mohsin S. Khan, "Why Is China Growing So Fast?" *Economic Issues*, no. 8 (1997), https://www.imf.org/external/pubs/ft/issues8/index.htm.

[41] Ashley J. Tellis, "Power Shift: How the West Can Adapt and Thrive in an Asian Century," German Marshall Fund, Asia Paper Series, January 2010, https://carnegieendowment.org/files/GMF7417_Power_Shift_Asia_Paper_for_web_Final.pdf.

[42] Richard Rosecrance, *The Rise of the Trading State: Commerce and Conquest in the Modern World* (New York: Basic Books, 1986).

[43] See the discussion in David Shambaugh, *Modernizing China's Military: Progress, Problems, and Prospects* (Berkeley: University of California Press, 2002).

[44] For a comprehensive estimate of the Chinese military developments in comparison with the United States, see Eric Heginbotham et al., *The U.S.-China Military Scorecard: Forces, Geography, and the Evolving Balance of Power 1996-2017* (Santa Monica: RAND Corporation, 2015).

primacy in Asia and, when possible, globally. This goal ultimately underlay all of China's grand strategic choices since the founding of the PRC, if not earlier, although the strategies employed toward "the attainment and maintenance of geopolitical influence as a major, and perhaps primary, state" varied depending on its relative capabilities.[45] But both the goal and the instrumentalities it spawned were overlooked by U.S. policymakers, especially after the Cold War, because liberal triumphalism led them to believe that China's interests would be best served by the evolution of the country into a democratic trading state rather than a traditional great power that focused its energies on military competition. The United States, at any rate, ought not to have done anything that pushed China in this direction. As Clinton argued toward the end of his presidency,

> Now we hear that China is a country to be feared. A growing number of people say that it is the next great threat to our security and our well being.... Clearly, if it chooses to do so, China could pursue such a course, pouring much more of its wealth into military might and into traditional great power geopolitics. Of course this would rob it of much of its future prosperity, and it is far from inevitable that China will choose this path. Therefore I would argue that we should not make it more likely that China will choose this path by acting as if that decision has already been made.[46]

With due respect to Clinton, that decision had already been made in 1949. Mao's ambition to recreate "great China" carried within itself the seeds of the eventual reach for global preeminence. Sulmaan Wasif Khan's judgment captures this idea succinctly: "[Mao's] state was just a fragment of what it would later become, but that would change in time. Ambition alters with circumstance; as success followed success, Mao's China would sweep out to encompass ever more."[47] Fearing that China was already en route to realizing the goal of becoming a traditional great power—with the military instruments commensurate to that end—Zalmay Khalilzad and his colleagues at RAND argued as early as 1999 that the prevailing U.S. policy of engagement with China needed to be reconsidered and replaced by an alternative policy of "congagement."[48] Such a policy would, among other things, avoid doing anything that directly helps the growth of Chinese military power, strengthen the Western export-control regime to choke Chinese access to militarily relevant high technology, strengthen U.S. alliances and build new partnerships

---

[45] Swaine and Tellis, *Interpreting China's Grand Strategy*, x.

[46] "Transcript: Clinton Outlines China Policy," CNN, April 7, 1999, http://edition.cnn.com/ALLPOLITICS/stories/1999/04/07/clinton.china/transcript.html.

[47] Sulmaan Wasif Khan, *Haunted by Chaos: China's Grand Strategy from Mao Zedong to Xi Jinping* (Cambridge: Harvard University Press, 2018), 10.

[48] Zalmay M. Khalilzad et al., *The United States and a Rising China: Strategic and Military Implications* (Santa Monica: RAND Corporation, 1999), 72.

in Asia, and preserve U.S. global supremacy—economically, geopolitically, and militarily—indefinitely.[49] Other assessments produced at RAND during this period elaborated on these themes,[50] and one of the earliest studies of China's grand strategy then argued that while Beijing's focus centered for the moment on maximizing its power peacefully,

> growing Chinese power will most likely result, over the very long term, in a more assertive China. As part of this process, China could reasonably be expected to pursue most, if not all, of the core elements of those assertive grand strategies pursued by major powers in the past. These elements include efforts to augment its military capabilities in a manner commensurate with its increased power; develop a sphere of influence by acquiring new allies and underwriting the protection of others; acquire new or reclaim old territory for China's resources or for symbolic reasons by penalizing, if necessary, any opponents or bystanders who resist such claims; prepare to redress past wrongs it believes it may have suffered; attempt to rewrite the prevailing international "rules of the game" to better reflect its own interests; and, in the most extreme policy choice imaginable, even perhaps ready itself to thwart preventive war or to launch predatory attacks on its foes.[51]

While this message fell on the receptive ears of many individuals who would later serve as senior officials in the administration of George W. Bush, the vigorous balancing of China that might have occurred during his term in office was derailed by the September 11 attacks. The Bush administration undertook several critical initiatives, including transforming U.S. relations with India, as part of the effort to prevent an "untethered" China from dominating Asia.[52] However, more comprehensive balancing of China was postponed because of the need to secure Beijing's cooperation in the global war on terrorism.[53] The Obama administration, in turn, was equally unable to confront China's growing power and assertiveness—which began to be unabashedly manifest after the 2008 global financial crisis despite earlier appearances—because its first term was spent recovering from the

---

[49] Khalilzad et al., *The United States and a Rising China*, 72–75; and Zalmay Khalilzad, "Congage China," RAND Corporation, 1999.

[50] Zalmay Khalilzad and Ian O. Lesser, eds., *Sources of Conflict in the 21st Century: Regional Futures and U.S. Strategy* (Santa Monica: RAND Corporation, 1998); Mark Burles, *Chinese Policy Toward Russia and the Central Asian Republics* (Santa Monica: RAND Corporation, 1999); Mark Burles and Abram N. Shulsky, *Patterns in China's Use of Force: Evidence from History and Doctrinal Writings* (Santa Monica: RAND Corporation, 2000); and Zalmay Khalilzad et al., *The United States and Asia: Toward a New U.S. Strategy and Force Posture* (Santa Monica: RAND Corporation, 2001).

[51] Swaine and Tellis, *Interpreting China's Grand Strategy*, xii. China's current trajectory confirms this assessment abundantly, although Beijing shifted toward assertiveness somewhat earlier than was anticipated by this analysis, which was completed before the turn of the century.

[52] Condoleezza Rice (remarks at Sophia University, Tokyo, March 19, 2005), https://2001-2009.state.gov/secretary/rm/2005/43655.htm.

[53] Michael J. Green, *By More Than Providence: Grand Strategy and American Power in the Asia Pacific Since 1783* (New York: Columbia University Press, 2017), 482–517.

destructiveness of the economic meltdown. Although Obama initially attempted to defuse the China challenge by proposing a deepened relationship with China that appeared akin to a "group of two," he eventually came around to the idea that Chinese power needed to be countered, thus giving rise to the concept of the "rebalance" to Asia in his second term.[54]

Unfortunately for the United States, Obama could not muster the resources necessary to make the rebalance a meaningful response to growing Chinese power. He neither found a solution to arresting the increased relative gains accruing to China as a result of its integration with the U.S. economy, nor could he mitigate U.S. deindustrialization to the degree that it was caused by China. The problems associated with Chinese theft of intellectual property, the structural obstacles to U.S. investments in China (such as coerced technology transfer and lack of market access), and the challenges posed by state subsidies to Chinese private and governmental enterprises also eluded meaningful solutions beyond a commitment to seeking remedies through a continued strategic and economic dialogue.[55] Finally, the dangers posed by Chinese counter-intervention military technologies, which threatened to limit the effectiveness of U.S. power projection in Asia, were undoubtedly recognized but could not be conclusively negated by the administration's sensible "third offset strategy," which came too late in Obama's term in office.[56]

When considered in a historical perspective, therefore, the residual sentiment surviving from China's Cold War partnership against the Soviet Union, the U.S. failure to anticipate that China would grow rapidly once its internal reforms and lopsided access to Western markets yielded their fruit, and the distractions imposed by the war on terrorism, the U.S. invasion of Iraq, and later the global economic crisis all combined to prevent the United States from treating China seriously as a strategic competitor, even as Beijing was evolving in that direction. When the normal lags afflicting all translation of perception into policy are also considered, it is not surprising that Washington moved more slowly than was prudent in deliberately balancing China.

Underlying these historical accidents, however, the languid U.S. response to China's rise was deeply shaped by two other factors that served to effectively paralyze the development of a more resolute response. For starters, the United States found it extremely difficult to devise a strategy for competing with China under conditions of economic interdependence. During the Cold War, pursuing a strategy of containment against the Soviet Union was conceptually

---

[54] Green, *By More Than Providence*, 518–40.

[55] Cheng Li, "Assessing U.S.-China Relations under the Obama Administration," China-US Focus, August 30, 2016.

[56] Green, *By More Than Providence*, 518–40.

simple, however challenging it was to implement in practice, because the two competing blocs were not tied by any meaningful economic links. In other words, the prosperity enjoyed by each side—and by extension, each side's capacity to sustain military competition—was not dependent on its ties with the other. The realities of globalization had transformed this situation entirely. With the United States and China now tied by deep bonds of interdependence, any effort by Washington to fundamentally limit China's growth in power would require the United States to suffer losses in its own prosperity and welfare, even if reducing commercial ties weakened a rising China.[57]

Equally important was the fact that thinning U.S. economic ties with China by itself would be insufficient. Washington would also need to interdict China's economic links with other states in order to prevent China from compensating for its reduced trade with the United States by deepening its intercourse with others. In other words, competing with China in ways that would structurally limit its capacity to grow faster than the United States would require Washington to undo the very webs of globalization that the United States has fostered since the beginning of the postwar era. Because limiting China's relative gains would require the United States to suffer losses in its own absolute gains, while demanding similar sacrifices on the part of China's other trading partners, Washington wilted at the prospect of pursuing such a difficult policy because of the fear that it would fail. It was simply unclear whether the United States could compel other states to significantly limit their trade ties with China, even if Washington were to pursue such a course of action unilaterally. If this outcome could not be enforced, the United States would find itself in a position of sacrificing its own absolute gains (and, by implication, its ability to militarily compete with China more effectively) even as China continued to enjoy such benefits thanks to its ongoing—perhaps even rising—trade with other countries.[58]

The difficulties of engaging in strategic competition under conditions of economic interdependence remain unresolved to this day. Because any of the actions described above would be both ruinous to the United States and destructive of the international order it had created, successive administrations before the Trump administration were deterred from attempting to stymie China's rise by engaging in the principal form of nonmilitary competition that could have produced that outcome: comprehensive economic warfare.

This diffidence was only enhanced by the character of state-society relations in the United States—another important element that prevented various presidents from resolutely confronting China. The fact that the United

---

[57] Tellis, *Balancing Without Containment*, 18–32.

[58] The theoretical foundations for this argument were first laid out in Duncan Snidal, "Relative Gains and the Pattern of International Cooperation," *American Political Science Review* 85, no. 3 (1991): 701–26.

States is a pluralist democracy gave societal institutions an outsized voice in shaping national policy, and there was no greater champion of persistent engagement with China than the U.S. business sector.[59] This should not have been surprising because U.S. multinational corporations view their interests primarily through the prism of the fiduciary obligations owed to shareholders rather than patriotic sentiments involving the country in which they are headquartered. Consequently, corporations, which had invested heavily in China since 1979, argued vigorously against any U.S. governmental pressures on Beijing because of their fears that it might retaliate against their commercial operations inside China. Although the U.S. corporate sector had many grievances about China's business environment, their fears about losses arising from either Washington's or Beijing's actions made them extremely reluctant to support U.S. attempts at confronting Chinese strategic challenges. Where these issues were concerned, geopolitical considerations took a back seat to corporate interests.[60]

Because of the intimate relationship between large U.S. businesses and the major political parties in the United States, both Republican and Democratic administrations before Trump also acted as if what is good for U.S. companies is always good for the United States. But even when supporting corporate interests was not at issue, the fears about the impact of pressing China on important domestic matters, such as employment and competitiveness, made policymakers reticent to push Beijing too hard.[61] This hesitation was only reinforced by elements in civil society. Both U.S. academics who studied China and U.S.-China friendship organizations often argued against tougher policies, sometimes for self-serving reasons and at other times because the risks of pugnacious policies were judged to be high in the face of their potential ineffectiveness.[62]

The inability to easily redress the problem of relative gains, combined with the pressures emanating from business and civil society, thus left successive U.S. presidents settling for liberal solutions. They hoped that the deepening interdependence between China and the world would weaken

---

[59] Naná De Graaff and Bastiaan Van Apeldoorn, "U.S.-China Relations and the Liberal World Order: Contending Elites, Colliding Visions?" *International Affairs* 94, no. 1 (2018): 113–31.

[60] Bill Powell, "How America's Biggest Companies Made China Great Again," *Newsweek*, June 24, 2019, https://www.newsweek.com/how-americas-biggest-companies-made-china-great-again-1445325; and James Mann, *The China Fantasy: Why Capitalism Will Not Bring Democracy to China* (New York: Penguin, 2007).

[61] Stewart Paterson, *China, Trade and Power: Why the West's Economic Engagement Has Failed* (London: London Publishing Partnership, 2018).

[62] For a useful examination of the complex relationship between American Sinology and China, see David L. Shambaugh, ed., *American Studies of Contemporary China* (Armonk: M.E. Sharpe, 1993). A more critical assessment of the role of U.S. academics in Washington's China policy can be found in Mann, *The China Fantasy*; and Friedberg, "Competing with China."

Beijing's assertiveness and that continued bilateral dialogue and engagement might help persuade China to correct its most egregious economic behaviors, including by strengthening the hands of those factions that sought to reform the Chinese economy from within.[63] Because none of these approaches offered any guarantees of success, however, policymakers often took solace in the fact that the larger size and the greater dynamism of the U.S. economy would yet take the United States across the finish line, no matter how impressive China's trade-driven growth appeared in the interim.[64]

Just to be sure that China did not employ its steadily improving power to U.S. disadvantage, however, the United States continued to invest in its military capabilities, sustain its partnerships and alliance relations, and deepen its trade ties through various preferential agreements—despite the possibility that these developments would continue to fuel Chinese suspicions of its motives. Standing U.S. policy toward China before Trump, therefore, reflected a constrained liberalism, with Washington desiring that common interests would preserve bilateral stability but preparing for dangerous eventualities in any case. This hybrid posture was viewed as the best alternative to the tyranny of a manic realism that might demand active and thorough decoupling of the U.S. and Chinese economies to weaken China's power, new crusades directed against the authoritarian CCP regime and the ill treatment of its people, and energetic confrontations with China on the major geopolitical disputes between the two countries.

By the last two years of the Obama administration, however, the dangers posed by China's growing power were gradually perceived as outweighing the habitual U.S. interest in avoiding a strategic confrontation with China.[65] The combination of U.S. myopia (and sometimes hubris), the power of U.S. commercial interests, the distractions imposed by the greater Middle East, the intensifying Chinese integration with the U.S. economy, and the differing political priorities of previous Chinese leaders such as Jiang Zemin (in contrast to Hu Jintao and even more emphatically in contrast to Xi Jinping) and their U.S. counterparts all played a critical role in minimizing the dangers posed by China in Washington's national security consciousness. By the time Obama left office, however, the dangers posed by a rising China were simply too pronounced to ignore. But it would take the arrival of Trump as

---

[63] De Graaff and Van Apeldoorn, "U.S.-China Relations and the Liberal World Order."

[64] Former vice president Joe Biden inadvertently gave voice to such sentiments when, while campaigning for the 2020 Democratic presidential nomination, he dismissed claims that China poses a serious economic threat to the United States: "China is going to eat our lunch? Come on, man....They're not competition for us." James M. Lindsay, "Election 2020: Joe Biden, Democratic Presidential Candidate," Council on Foreign Relations, September 17, 2019.

[65] Robert D. Blackwill and Ashley J. Tellis, *Revising U.S. Grand Strategy Toward China* (New York: Council on Foreign Relations, 2015).

president to inaugurate the return of bare-knuckled competition with China in a manner not witnessed since the early years of the Cold War.

Jousting with China Again

Trump arrived in office supported by a coalition of voters who were deeply insecure about their political and economic future. The rise of this group, which consists significantly of evangelicals, non-college-educated whites with low incomes, and those threatened by both the changing social composition of and the changing cultural trends within the United States, propelled Trump to an unexpected victory.[66] Many in this constituency were unduly affected by the deindustrialization of the United States, which had accelerated after China's admission to the World Trade Organization (WTO), as well as by the losses suffered as a result of the financial crisis (not to mention that many attributed their economic misfortunes to the presence of immigrants within the country). Thus, it was not surprising that Trump focused his ire on three specific targets from the beginning of his presidency: hegemonic order, globalization, and China.

Long before Trump became president, he had acquired the view that the liberal international order established by the United States after World War II did not serve U.S. interests because it created opportunities for other nations to become more secure and richer at the United States' expense. He framed this position in his inaugural address as follows:

> For many decades, we've enriched foreign industry at the expense of American industry; subsidized the armies of other countries, while allowing for the very sad depletion of our military. We've defended other nations' borders while refusing to defend our own. And spent trillions and trillions of dollars overseas while America's infrastructure has fallen into disrepair and decay. We've made other countries rich, while the wealth, strength and confidence of our country has dissipated over the horizon.[67]

This worldview expressly rejects one of the key ideas inherent in the notion of hegemonic order—that hegemonic powers both construct international systems that serve their interests disproportionately and make supernormal contributions toward preserving them precisely because these countries have the most to lose in the absence of those systems.[68]

[66] Sean McElwee, "Who Is Trump's Base?" Data for Progress, August 23, 2018, https://www.dataforprogress.org/blog/2018/8/21/data-for-politics-14-who-is-trumps-base.

[67] Donald J. Trump, "Inaugural Address" (Washington, D.C., January 20, 2017).

[68] For an insightful summary of this thesis, see David A. Lake, "Leadership, Hegemony, and the International Economy: Naked Emperor or Tattered Monarch with Potential?" *International Studies Quarterly* 37, no. 4 (1993): 459–89.

Because Trump has been more attuned to the tangible costs accruing to the United States in upholding the liberal order than he has been to both the tangible benefits deriving from threats mitigated and the intangible benefits of legitimacy accruing to U.S. primacy, he has not focused on protecting international institutions or projecting American values abroad, as presidents before him did insistently. Instead, he has concerned himself mainly with limiting their costs to the United States. Even when those structures bear directly on U.S. security, such as alliances, Trump has raised doubts about their value. For example, he has questioned the importance of fulfilling deterrence obligations, concentrating more on getting allies to increase their national contributions in order to minimize what seems like an unnecessary subsidy borne by U.S. taxpayers.[69] Consistent with this emphasis, Trump has harangued the United States' European allies to raise their defense expenditures, even as he declared NATO to be "obsolete," and has demanded a fivefold increase in South Korea's contribution to the U.S.–South Korea alliance, thereby imperiling the partnership at a time when the dangers from both North Korea and China are increasing in intensity.

There has been no greater skepticism demonstrated about hegemonic order than Trump's animus toward globalization. It is easy to recognize that globalization, understood as the ever-deepening webs of international economic interdependence, could never have occurred without the hegemonic stability provided by the United States.[70] If Washington had refused to bear the costs of upholding the global trading system—costs that range from providing military security both in the commons and for key trading partners to developing the rules and institutions that foster trade—international economic intercourse would have been stymied as nations would have ceased to trade beyond a point for fear that the greater relative gains enjoyed by some partners could at some point be weaponized and used against them. Because superior U.S. military power—the highest manifestation of U.S. hegemony—effectively guarantees that trading states will not be permitted to abuse their gains in this way (since such abuse would undermine the United States' own ability to benefit from deepened global trade), the entire international system benefits as a result from the steadily enlarging exchange across national borders.[71]

---

[69] See, for example, John Vandiver, "Trump on NATO Burden Sharing: 'We Are the Schmucks,'" *Stars and Stripes*, July 6, 2018, https://www.stripes.com/news/trump-on-nato-burden-sharing-we-are-the-schmucks-1.536329.

[70] For an excellent analysis of the deep structure underlying globalization, see Christopher Chase-Dunn, Yukio Kawano, and Benjamin D. Brewer, "Trade Globalization since 1795: Waves of Integration in the World-System," *American Sociological Review* 65, no. 1 (2000): 77–95. For a critical treatment of the relationship between U.S. power and globalization, see John A. Agnew, *Hegemony: The New Shape of Global Power* (Philadelphia: Temple University Press, 2005).

[71] The foundational arguments can be found in Robert Gilpin, *Global Political Economy: Understanding the International Economic Order* (Princeton: Princeton University Press, 2001).

Ever since Japan's economic ascendancy became visible from the 1970s onward, Trump appeared to be increasingly skeptical about the value of international trade.[72] He came to view the multilateral trading system as a threat to the United States because underwriting it cost Washington significant resources, and it produced new competitors in Europe and Asia. This focus on relative gains to the neglect of absolute gains—the benefits that the United States as a whole enjoys because of trade—seems to have strengthened Trump's conviction that the multilateral trading system is flawed and must be replaced by purely bilateral arrangements wherein the United States can ensure that it is not taken advantage of by its international partners. Not surprisingly, Trump described the WTO as a "disaster," refused to support the appointment of new members to its appellate body, and chided the body as being "very unfair" to the United States.[73] Consistent with this view, he also pulled the United States out of the TPP and renegotiated the North American Free Trade Agreement, offering as supplements or substitutes new bilateral trade deals with various U.S. partners.

While many of Trump's complaints about the multilateral trading system are justified, these concerns were concatenated in a dramatic way by the rise of China. The Trump administration was particularly peeved by the WTO's treatment of China, which, despite becoming the world's second-largest economy, was still permitted to enjoy the status of a developing country and thus put off opening its markets.[74] That China meanwhile had become the world's largest exporter, had contributed to the displacement of U.S. manufacturing on a large scale, was pursuing a gigantic state-supported strategy aimed at dominating the leading sectors of the global economy of the future, and was now determinedly threatening U.S. military primacy all coalesced toward making the country the primary example of everything that was wrong with globalization. The U.S. effort at upholding a hegemonic order was now producing resolute threats to the United States itself.[75]

The Trump administration, accordingly, lost no time in designating China as a strategic competitor, something its predecessors were reticent to do even when they recognized the more pernicious aspects of China's rise. Given his hostility to multilateral trade and his skepticism about the benefits of the liberal international order to the United States specifically, Trump's

[72] Jennifer M. Miller, "Let's Not Be Laughed at Anymore: Donald Trump and Japan from the 1980s to the Present," *Journal of American–East Asian Relations* 25, no. 2 (2018): 138–68.

[73] Ana Swanson and Jack Ewing, "Trump's National Security Claim for Tariffs Sets Off Crisis at WTO," *New York Times*, August 12, 2018.

[74] Jacob M. Schlesinger and Alex Leary, "Trump Denounces Both China and WTO," *Wall Street Journal*, July 26, 2019.

[75] Donald J. Trump, "Remarks by President Trump to the 74th Session of the United Nations General Assembly" (New York, September 25, 2019).

decision to confront China was not particularly difficult. It was made easier, in any case, by the diverse resentments toward Beijing that had accumulated across the U.S. political system by the time he had arrived in office.

The U.S. corporate sector, once China's strongest ally in the United States, was chagrined by years of Chinese theft of U.S. intellectual property, coerced technology transfers, and the absence of a level playing field within China, even after close to three decades of investment there.[76] Various domestic constituencies that were hurt by Chinese trade practices, such as organized labor, as well as the Office of the U.S. Trade Representative, which is now led by Robert Lighthizer, a confirmed skeptic irate about China's unfair exploitation of the global trading system, sought to strike back at the roots of China's problematic economic expansion.[77] Rising Chinese authoritarianism at home, especially as manifested by the Xi Jinping regime's treatment of Uighurs and Tibetans, left those Americans who were concerned about human rights and political freedoms more dismayed than usual.[78]

The foreign policy establishment, which for years assessed China's behaviors in Asia and elsewhere largely benignly, was now increasingly perturbed by Chinese assertiveness in the South China Sea and toward neighbors such as Japan, South Korea, Taiwan, and India. It also was concerned about the impact of the Belt and Road Initiative (BRI) on the expansion of China's influence globally and appeared startled by the dramatic enlargement of China's foreign presence in areas far from Beijing's traditional interests, such as the Arctic, Latin America, and increasingly outer space and cyberspace.[79] Finally, U.S. military planners, as well as the United States' Asian allies, were alarmed at the pace of China's military transformation and the burdens it was imposing on Washington's ability to credibly underwrite U.S. security commitments in Asia and beyond. They thus pushed for far-reaching solutions that could restore the effectiveness of U.S. power projection and thereby balance China effectively.[80]

---

[76] Michael Martina, "U.S. Firms No Longer 'Positive Anchor' for Beijing Ties: AmCham in China," Reuters, April 17, 2019.

[77] See Matt Peterson "The Making of a Trade Warrior," Atlantic, December 29, 2018.

[78] Olivia Enos, "The Administration Should Be Bold in Condemning Human Rights Abuses in China," Forbes, August 6, 2019.

[79] See, for example, Aaron L. Friedberg, "Hegemony with Chinese Characteristics," National Interest, June 21, 2011; and Aaron L. Friedberg, "The Sources of Chinese Conduct: Explaining Beijing's Assertiveness," Washington Quarterly 37, no. 4 (2014): 133–50.

[80] See, for example, Elbridge Colby, "The Implications of China Developing a World-Class Military: First and Foremost a Regional Challenge," testimony before the U.S.-China Economic and Security Review Commission, Washington, D.C., June 20, 2019, https://www.cnas.org/publications/congressional-testimony/the-implications-of-china-developing-a-world-class-military-first-and-foremost-a-regional-challenge.

With these elements converging for the first time in U.S. politics to support a fundamental restructuring of U.S.-China relations, the stage was set for the Trump administration's transformation of Washington's approach toward Beijing. This new, and still evolving, U.S. policy toward China consists of preparing for multidimensional competition on the premise that China is, and will remain for some time to come, the most important great-power competitor of the United States. Toward that end, the administration has challenged China in five domains.

The first avenue of resistance toward China has focused on resisting its attempts to dominate the Indo-Pacific rimland by controlling the commons and subordinating its neighbors into accepting a new hierarchy in Asia rooted in a legitimization of Chinese centrality. The Trump administration, early in its term in office, accepted Prime Minister Shinzo Abe's concept of a "free and open Indo-Pacific" to mobilize various regional partners to resist potential Chinese coercion.[81] This effort subsumes both the power-political and ideational dimensions. The power-political dimension includes challenging excessive Chinese claims in the South China Sea through conducting freedom of navigation patrols; deepening strategic ties with key Asian states, such as Japan, Australia, Taiwan, Vietnam, and India, that have a vested interest in resisting the rise of Chinese power; reinvigorating ties with Oceania to neutralize Chinese penetration; and re-energizing newer forms of institutional engagement, such as the Quad, to enhance geopolitical cooperation vis-à-vis China.[82]

The ideational element, however abstract, is just as important. It consists of affirming the principle that although states are differentiated by material power, stronger nations (read China) cannot compel deference on the part of their weaker neighbors whose desire for autonomy is supported by the United States.[83] To aid this effort, Trump administration officials have consciously amplified their criticism of China's authoritarian party-state, highlighting its egregious policies toward its own citizenry, especially minorities, though the effectiveness of this critique is often undermined by Trump's peculiar personal affection for Xi. The administration, however, has attempted to give several Asian states pressed by China respite on other grounds. Consistent with Trump's personal predilections, the administration has downplayed the traditional U.S. emphasis on democracy and human rights—which has been

---

[81] Tsuneo Watanabe, "Japan's Strategy in the Trump Era," *Japan Times*, January 16, 2018.

[82] See U.S. Department of Defense, *Indo-Pacific Strategy Report: Preparedness, Partnerships, and Promoting a Networked Region* (Washington, D.C., June 2019).

[83] "Remarks by President Trump at APEC CEO Summit," White House, November 10, 2017, https://www.whitehouse.gov/briefings-statements/remarks-president-trump-apec-ceo-summit-da-nang-vietnam.

welcomed by many regional states, particularly in Southeast Asia—in favor of exhorting good governance and the rule of law.[84]

The second avenue of resistance to China has taken the form of strident opposition to China's economic behavior. On this issue, the administration has targeted China's huge trade surpluses vis-à-vis the United States by using heavy-handed tariffs on a variety of Chinese goods to compel Beijing to both reduce its trade surpluses and restructure its domestic economy so as to eliminate intellectual property theft and coerced technology transfers, increase market access for U.S. products, and eventually limit the role of state-owned enterprises in international trade.[85] The administration has levied increasing tariffs in successive rounds on China (and others), even as it has conducted negotiations with Beijing intended to force concessions. The failure of the tentative agreement reached by both sides in May 2019 highlighted the fact that not even Trump's much ballyhooed personal relationship with Xi was sufficient to motivate China to ultimately agree to tough U.S. demands. These included not merely relief on the substantive issues but also commitments to memorialize Beijing's promises into Chinese law, permit the United States to be the sole judge of whether these obligations were adhered to, and recognize the U.S. right to reimpose *ex parte* penalties on China if it were judged to contravene its promises.[86] The administration has recently announced an interim "phase one" trade agreement with China that will lower some U.S. tariffs in exchange for increased U.S. market access and agreement on a dispute settlement mechanism, with more hazy—and likely vacuous—claims of progress on coerced technology transfers, intellectual property theft, and currency manipulation, thus strengthening the suspicion that Trump may have gained less than he had aimed for in his spat with China.[87]

At any rate, even as the administration has pursued this high-profile trade war with China, it has also opposed BRI, Xi's signature initiative, because of the fear that the expanding Chinese infrastructure network will be used to both strangulate weaker partners in Asia and Africa and secure new logistics nodes that would be used ultimately to support the expansion of Chinese military operations worldwide.[88] As part of this effort, the United

---

[84] "Advancing a Free and Open Indo-Pacific Region," U.S. Department of State, Fact Sheet, November 18, 2018.

[85] For a useful analytical overview of the Trump administration's trade complaints against China, see Steve Charnovitz, "Grading Trump's China Trade Strategy," George Washington University Law School, Research Paper, May 2019, https://ssrn.com/abstract=3393083.

[86] Chris Buckley and Keith Bradsher, "How Xi's Last-Minute Switch on U.S.-China Trade Deal Upended It," *New York Times*, May 16, 2019.

[87] Gina Heeb, "Here's the Full List of Everything Covered by Trump's Phase-One Trade Deal with China," *Markets Insider*, December 16, 2019.

[88] White House, *National Security Strategy of the United States of America*, 51–52.

States has also looked dimly at, if not actually opposed, Chinese efforts to develop alternative financial institutions that might compete with the original Bretton Woods financial infrastructure. And having withdrawn from new regional multilateral trading agreements such as the TPP, the administration has proffered the alternative of bilateral trade arrangements with the United States as a superior substitute to both global multilateral trade institutions and shallow Chinese trade multilateralism in Asia of the sort represented by the Regional Comprehensive Economic Partnership (RCEP).[89]

The third avenue of resistance to China has focused on stymieing Beijing's efforts to create alternative technical standards to those established in the West.[90] As China's domination of global manufacturing and the expansion of its markets continue—both within its huge domestic economy and in its large and growing external outlets—the country will be well-positioned to exploit its growing commercial reach to disadvantage its Western competitors through the development and promulgation of new standards.[91] The ability to burden competitors by threatening their product lines with obsolescence or by imposing adaptation costs on them as they seek to meet the standards established by the largest Chinese suppliers in the market has far-reaching, even if still relatively underexplored, consequences for Western economies.[92]

Some of these new standards could arise as a natural result of emerging innovations, in which case there is less room for concern if well-functioning markets exist. The fear that animates the Trump administration, however, is that Chinese firms, which are often subsidized by the state, might use their national backing to produce new technologies and to penetrate new markets, and by so doing, force their less advantaged competitors to either bear the higher costs of catching up or live with fragmented and smaller markets that operate on different standards.[93] This problem implicates all dimensions of economic activity—from agriculture to electronics to manufacturing.

---

[89] Geoffrey Gertz, "What Will Trump's Embrace of Bilateralism Mean for America's Trade Partners?" Brookings Institution, February 8, 2017; and Chad P. Bown and Douglas A. Irwin, "Trump's Assault on the Global Trading System: And Why Decoupling from China Will Change Everything," *Foreign Affairs*, September/October 2019, https://www.foreignaffairs.com/articles/asia/2019-08-12/trumps-assault-global-trading-system.

[90] Richard P. Suttmeier, Xiankui Yao, and Alex Zixiang Tan, "Standards of Power? Technology, Institutions, and Politics in the Development of China's National Standards Strategy," NBR, NBR Special Report, no. 10, June 2006.

[91] Dan Breznitz and Michael Murphree, "The Rise of China in Technology Standards: New Norms in Old Institutions," U.S.-China Economic and Security Review Commission, January 16, 2013, http://uscc.gov/sites/default/files/Research/RiseofChinainTechnologyStandards.pdf.

[92] Hilary McGeachy, "Tech Standards and China's Rise," United States Studies Centre, May 2, 2019, https://www.ussc.edu.au/analysis/tech-standards-and-chinas-rise.

[93] See the discussion in U.S. Chamber of Commerce, "Made in China 2025: Global Ambitions Built on Local Protections," 2017, https://www.uschamber.com/sites/default/files/final_made_in_china_2025_report_full.pdf.

Many of the issues pertaining to standards will be negotiated within industry organizations, but the weight of the firms operating in the market will have a decisive impact on who the winners and losers might be. The current confrontations over 5G technology and the "digital Silk Road" are only manifestations of the deeper danger that China might use its national champions to build new electronic infrastructure networks that either shut out the West or incorporate deliberate vulnerabilities that the Chinese government can exploit either in peacetime or in crises.[94]

The fourth avenue of resistance, which is related to the third but quite distinct from it, is confronting China's quest for technological dominance in the global system. It has long been recognized that great powers arise as a result of their domination of the leading sectors of the global economy.[95] This domination enables them to reap economic and strategic benefits simultaneously, and hence it is not surprising that China is making concerted efforts to master the critical technologies that are likely to shape the future. The Made in China 2025 plan identifies ten critical technologies in this regard, including agricultural machinery, aerospace and aviation equipment, biomedicine and associated devices, electrical equipment and new energy vehicles, advanced materials, numerical control machinery and robotics, and information and communications technology.[96]

To the degree that China seeks to master these areas by investing in education and domestic research and development, the United States cannot complain. But the fact that the Chinese government is committing vast state resources to compete against predominately Western private companies (while pilfering their technology whenever possible) has earned the ire of the Trump administration. It has, accordingly, responded by attacking the Chinese state's technology development programs through tightened export controls at home, limiting Chinese high-tech firms' ability to procure a variety of U.S. goods and components, tightening the constraints on China's ability to invest in the United States (including the ability to acquire U.S. firms), seeking to limit China's access to intangible knowledge in the United States (including by reviewing the opportunities afforded to Chinese students to study advanced science and technology at the best U.S. institutions of higher learning), and by directly preventing some Chinese technology companies

---

[94] Ned Ryun, "We Cannot Allow China to Set the Standards and Control the Technology for 5G," *Hill*, March 7, 2019; and Kadri Kaska, Henrik Beckvard, and Tomáš Minárik, "Huawei, 5G and China as a Security Threat," NATO Cooperative Cyber Defence Centre of Excellence, 2019, https://ccdcoe.org/uploads/2019/03/CCDCOE-Huawei-2019-03-28-FINAL.pdf.

[95] George Modelski and William R. Thompson, *Leading Sectors and World Powers: The Coevolution of Global Economics and Politics* (Columbia: University of South Carolina Press, 1996).

[96] U.S. Chamber of Commerce, "Made in China 2025."

from doing business in the United States.[97] The administration is aware of the challenges to this strategy. It has concluded, however, that the quest for technological supremacy is too important to be left to markets alone to decide—because it bears fundamentally on the United States' ability to protect its global hegemony. Therefore, the administration has settled for a strategy that reflects, as one scholar phrased it, the "securitization of economic policy and economization of strategic policy."[98]

Finally, the fifth avenue of resistance that characterizes the Trump administration's approach to China is manifested by its initiatives in the military realm. Recognizing that China has made enormous strides in developing technological capabilities to undermine the United States' capacity to operate in support of its Asian allies, the administration's defense investment programs have been focused squarely on neutralizing these Chinese advances.[99] To its credit, the administration has continued many of the critical initiatives inherited from its predecessor, but with an intensification of focus. The clear declaration that China is a strategic competitor and that the Department of Defense must accordingly concentrate on checkmating this evolving threat has created new opportunities for revising U.S. operational plans; increasing investments, especially in long-range and stealth weapons; upgrading the basing infrastructure around the Asian periphery; enlarging the inventory of sophisticated munitions; and developing technologies such as hypersonic systems, unmanned systems, and new advanced missiles to raise the costs of Chinese aggression.[100]

The United States' deepening of military cooperation with Japan, Australia, Taiwan, and India—oriented in some cases toward better meeting the needs of collective defense and in other cases toward better targeting China's expanding military presence in the Indo-Pacific—has resulted in a new willingness to sell sophisticated systems that were previously unavailable. These transfers will allow U.S. allies and partners in Asia to better defend their interests in the face of growing Chinese military capabilities while at the same time holding at risk Chinese military assets that were previously secure.[101] Perhaps most important of all is the administration's decision not to

---

[97] Christopher A. Ford, "Huawei and Its Siblings, the Chinese Tech Giants: National Security and Foreign Policy Implications" (remarks at the U.S. State Department, Washington, D.C., September 11, 2019), https://www.state.gov/huawei-and-its-siblings-the-chinese-tech-giants-national-security-and-foreign-policy-implications.

[98] Michael Wesley, "Australia and the Rise of Geoeconomics," Australian National University, Centre of Gravity Series, November 2016, 4.

[99] U.S. Department of Defense, "Summary of the 2018 National Defense Strategy of the United States of America."

[100] U.S. Department of Defense, Indo-Pacific Strategy Report, 17–20.

[101] Ibid., 21–46.

cede any geographic spaces around China, despite the increase in its military capabilities. Instead, by using both existing and emerging technologies, as well as new concepts of operations, the U.S. military plans to deploy even in highly contested environments close to the Asian rimland, exploiting windows in space and time to bring different capabilities to bear in order to deny the military success that China will seek in a conflict.[102]

The Global Impact of U.S.-China Strategic Competition

Whether the United States succeeds in achieving its aims in this multidimensional competition in whole or in part remains to be seen, but there is no debating the fact that both Washington and Beijing now view each other warily as rivals. Although there are many in each capital who hope that the current confrontation will disappear and the previous equilibrium will be restored once the Trump administration departs from office, it is unlikely that the U.S.-China competition will simply evaporate given the realities of great-power rivalry that have now come to the fore. This tussle for power and influence has already had an impact on almost every geographic region and functional area in international politics.

The studies gathered in this volume of *Strategic Asia* document, analyze, and evaluate this competition and its consequences both for the various nations and regions that are affected and, ultimately, for China and the United States. In order to analyze how a country or region is responding to the re-emergence of acute Sino-U.S. rivalry, each chapter elucidates the aims of the United States and China with respect to the country or region in question to examine the extent of U.S.-China divergence and to assess how U.S. and Chinese objectives interact with elite interests and other domestic factors, as well as with local security competitions and other economic, historical, and ideological factors. Each chapter also analyzes the strategies adopted by various countries in response and the implications both for the country's (or region's) interests and for the relative success of U.S. and Chinese goals.

When the chapters are read synoptically, what becomes amply clear is that although the United States and China are steadily evolving toward a relationship of "asymmetrical bipolarity,"[103] the political order across the world neither exhibits nor suggests an evolution toward tight bipolarity. The realities of globalization have in fact created a dense substructure of

---

[102] U.S. Department of Defense, *Indo-Pacific Strategy Report*, 20.

[103] Evelyn Goh, "U.S. Strategic Relations with a Rising China: Trajectories and Impacts on Asia-Pacific Security," *The Rise of China and International Security: America and Asia Respond*, ed. Kevin J. Cooney and Yoichiro Sato (New York: Routledge, 2009), 81.

intermeshing economic connectivity over which the patterns of U.S.-China power-political competition are being superimposed. While these competitive elements are forcing changes in the underlying substructure of economic relations, the evidence suggests that U.S.-China geopolitical competition is still unable to radically restructure the elemental economic ties that operate across national borders. In part, this is because the costs of restructuring the economic links are immense and the majority of states—including the Asian states most threatened by China—seek to avoid bearing these burdens if possible.[104] Consequently, they seem to have settled on an evolving strategy of "China diversification," but this does not yet imply any fundamental severing of economic ties with China.[105]

Moreover, at a time when China's military power, although growing, is still weaker than that of the United States, unwieldy to deploy, and unable to secure easy successes as long as Washington continues to provide hegemonic security (even if the Trump administration does so only reluctantly), all the states examined in this volume enjoy significant agency, which enables them to pursue choices that go beyond exclusive solidarity with either the United States or China. In fact, the analyses indicate that many countries or regions are attempting to avoid being penalized by the evolving U.S.-China competition, seek to exploit it for their own ends, or hope to enmesh both rivals in order to protect their own interests. Consequently, if the Trump administration's approach is perceived by states caught in the middle or by various bystanders as forcing them to choose between bandwagoning with Washington or Beijing, it is unlikely to enjoy enduring success. Few states desire a world characterized by Chinese primacy, but even in the context of emerging bipolar competition, U.S. strategies marked by support for economic interdependence (with the appropriate corrections both against Chinese trade malpractices and for the protection of U.S. technological superiority), coupled with deepened support for U.S. partners, provide greater assurance that Washington's larger aims will be realized. That conclusion, if no other, stands out in the studies gathered in this volume.

Sheila Smith's chapter on Japan highlights the fact that although growing Chinese power threatens Japanese security in unprecedented ways, Tokyo still seeks to avoid making decisive choices between the United States and China in the context of the ongoing strategic competition. Japan is undoubtedly the staunchest U.S. ally in Asia, partly because it has few other choices to

---

[104] For an early assessment of the impact of the U.S.-China competition on the patterns of trade in Asia, see "U.S. Trade Policy and Reshoring: The Real Impact of America's New Trade Policies," AT Kearney, Report, 2019.

[105] Jennifer Smith, "'Reshoring' Report Finds Factory Work Not Returning to U.S.," *Wall Street Journal*, July 12, 2019.

reliably protect its security in the face of its own rivalry with China—at least for now. But because Japan remains reliant on China for its economic prosperity, even as it depends on the United States for its safety, U.S.-China competition has posed difficult dilemmas for Tokyo. To be sure, Japanese policymakers welcome the fact that the United States now takes China's rise seriously as a strategic challenge. They have responded by beefing up their own military capabilities, more resolutely resisting Chinese claims over the disputed island territories, tightening security cooperation with the United States, strengthening partnerships with other regional powers such as India and Australia, offering various Indo-Pacific nations alternative possibilities to China's BRI investments, and even diversifying economic investments away from China to the degree possible. But Japan cannot pursue any comprehensive economic decoupling from China; instead, it has sought to limit tensions at a time of increased concerns about U.S. reliability and pressures from the Trump administration for greater burden sharing and more trade concessions. Fearful that Trump's idiosyncratic policies might lead to hasty compromises with both China and North Korea that undermine Japanese interests, Tokyo has pursued multiple mutually reinforcing hedging strategies. Although Japan clearly recognizes that the United States will remain its principal external protector and as such will decisively side with Washington in any crisis involving China, it still seeks to avoid such a denouement for as long as possible.

South Korea's response to current U.S.-China competition is arguably even more complex than Japan's. Seoul seeks to defuse the dangers posed by North Korea (a country that still counts on China for ultimate protection), manage South Korea's recently intensifying problems with Japan, and avoid treating China as a conspicuous threat despite its hostile response to the deployment of Terminal High Altitude Area Defense (THAAD) and rising U.S. perceptions of China as a revisionist power. South Korea pursues these objectives while trying to preserve its security alliance with the United States in the face of uncertainties caused by Trump's overtures to North Korea, his demands for greater burden sharing, and the evolution of command arrangements within the alliance. The difficulties of developing a satisfactory strategy in such complicated circumstances are only exacerbated by the deep divides in South Korean domestic politics. Hence, it is not surprising, as Ji-Young Lee's chapter details systematically, that Seoul has settled on "strategic nondecision" precipitated by its inability to reconcile the important but conflicting incentives that mark its dealings with Washington and Beijing. Thus, for example, South Korea under Moon Jae-in has voiced nominal support for the U.S. Indo-Pacific strategy—in part to boost Trump's ambitions to solder a rapprochement with Pyongyang—but out of care for Chinese sensitivities has not done much to advance its aims. Similarly, South Korea has been careful not to join the United States in confronting Chinese technology companies, condemning Chinese initiatives such as the Asian Infrastructure Investment Bank or BRI, or even publicly conveying discomfort with rising Chinese power—even though some Korean companies are beginning to consider shifting a portion of their current investments in China to alternative locations such as Vietnam and India. Lee's broader conclusion that South Korea will continue to be indecisive and vacillate in the face of escalating U.S.-China competition thus has unsettling implications for South Korea's ties with both Japan and the United States. This once again suggests that expectations that U.S. allies and partners might uncritically support the United States in its rivalry with China will turn out to be misplaced in the face of the complex economic and political realities that surround their decision-making.

Frédéric Grare's chapter on India drives home this point. Like Japan, India is directly threatened by Chinese assertiveness, given its outstanding disputes with China over territory, BRI, Chinese support for Pakistan and India's smaller South Asian neighbors, and China's increasing penetration into the Indian Ocean. Accordingly, New Delhi welcomed the Trump administration's policy to confront China's rise because balancing China has long been part of India's own foreign policy. India is not as deeply dependent on trade with China as Japan is, and hence it is easier for New Delhi to support Washington's pushback against Beijing. India has already deepened its military partnership with the United States toward that end. Yet Indian policymakers are still queasy about the Trump administration's approach to confronting China because they have also become targets in Washington's war on globalization. That the Trump administration has not treated allies differently from adversaries is India's biggest concern. Moreover, given India's proximity to China, Indian policymakers emphasize the importance of subtly limiting Chinese gains through targeted policies that deny China technology, limit its political freedom of maneuver, and degrade its military advantages. They fear that Trump's strategy instead undermines the possibility of sustaining a global coalition that will balance China effectively even as it cooperates with Beijing when appropriate. Because of the risk that Washington treats as a zero-sum game what is a mixed-sum rivalry with China, Grare concludes that it will be harder for U.S.-India collaboration to yield actual cooperation, despite the two sides sharing congruent objectives.

In principle, Taiwan may be the greatest beneficiary of renewed U.S.-China competition. Given Taipei's long-standing problems with Beijing over its status and the fact that the current Democratic Progressive Party (DPP) leadership has long sought greater distance from China, the

Trump administration's active balancing of China clearly serves the DPP's, if not Taiwan's, interests. In fact, the administration has proved to be, for well-founded reasons, more strongly supportive of strengthening Taiwan's autonomy than any previous U.S. government in recent memory. Despite the persistence of trade disputes with Taiwan, the Trump administration has encouraged greater leadership interactions with Taipei, authorized major sales of advanced weapons, and deepened defense cooperation aimed at warding off potential Chinese military attacks undertaken in support of forcible reunification. For all these gains, however, Syaru Shirley Lin's chapter on Taiwan describes how Taipei finds itself on the horns of very difficult dilemmas. Apart from the sharp divisions in domestic politics between the DPP, which favors protecting an independent Taiwanese identity, and the Kuomintang, which still holds out the hope of peaceful reunification, the Taiwanese economy is deeply integrated with China's. Taiwanese companies remain critical sources of advanced electronic components for Chinese industry and cannot disengage at will, and many of these firms have been hurt by the U.S. tariffs. Consequently, even if it wants to, Taiwan cannot pursue policies that irreparably alienate China without further increasing the risks to its security. Lin details the domestic considerations that constrain Taiwan on this score and concludes that all the available options—deepening ties with the United States, accommodating China meaningfully, or hedging by deepening ties with other Asian states—bring enormous risks and hence are unlikely to win easy acceptance within Taiwan anytime soon.

The impact of U.S.-China competition on Russia and other countries in the post-Soviet space shares similarities with, but also important differences from, the impact on other regions of the world. Russia is a competitor to the United States, and the Trump administration views it as one of the two most significant revisionist states in the international system, along with China. Continuing the trends witnessed in recent years, Sino-Russian relations are deepening as Washington persists with its efforts to limit Moscow's influence in Eastern Europe and Central Asia. Although growing Chinese interest in both these regions holds the potential to undermine Russia's traditional primacy, Chris Miller's chapter analyzes how both China and Russia, viewing the United States as their most important external threat, have artfully managed their relations to focus on the common objective of degrading U.S. power. Managing this convergence is not easy, but the partnership between Moscow and Beijing has been sufficiently resilient in the face of U.S. power, and the escalating U.S.-China strategic competition in fact provides new opportunities for Russia to exploit its rivalry with the United States. If the Russian posture thus illustrates the proposition that "the enemy of my enemy is my friend," the attitudes of the Eastern European and Central Asian states reflect the dilemmas witnessed elsewhere in Asia. The Eastern European states recognize the benefits of welcoming Chinese investment—and Beijing itself has focused on the region as part of BRI—but they must juggle this interest with their desire for a closer partnership with the United States to protect their security vis-à-vis Russia. The Central Asian republics are trapped in a different dilemma. They too seek increased Chinese investment at a time when there are few alternatives available to them. Increased Chinese resources promise to satisfy these states' desire for greater autonomy from Russia but could come with unwelcome political strings that replace one experience of subordination with another. In these circumstances, U.S. support would provide a welcome escape, but Washington's interest in democratization invariably runs against the aims of the authoritarian governments that populate the region.

Michael Wesley's discussion of Oceania in this volume shows that the intensification of U.S.-China competition has left its imprint on even remote parts of the globe. Australia, New Zealand, and the Pacific Island states are situated in an ordinarily tranquil locale. But lying as they do on the southern flank of the critical line of communication through which the United States brings military power to bear across the Pacific to the Asian rimland, they too have become critical elements in U.S.-China competition. The strategic importance of the area was highlighted during World War II, when the United States and Japan fought intense battles in this region. Given the interest that contemporary Chinese military planning has in obstructing a similar U.S. advance in the future, it is not surprising that Beijing has focused attention on cultivating Oceania's smaller island states through economic and military assistance—an objective that was aided by the migration of ethnic Chinese to the region. This attention in turn provoked U.S., Australian, and New Zealand counter-responses, which have taken the forms of economic assistance and political engagement aimed at limiting the spread of Chinese influence. While the island states obviously benefit from this competitive attention, Wesley notes that their leaders have refused to be "stampeded into making binary choices between China and their traditional partners, Australia and New Zealand." Not only have they rejected the notion of a China threat, but the island states also appear committed to deepening links with China and all other states that enable them to realize their dreams of expanded access to the wider globalized world. If even small states such as those in the South Pacific resist the notion of decoupling, any U.S. effort to compete with China through exclusionary strategies suggests poor chances of success.

Joseph Chinyong Liow's chapter on Southeast Asia deals with a region that is no stranger to U.S.-China competition, having witnessed previous iterations of this rivalry during the Vietnam War. Yet the states that populate this region are now buffeted by U.S.-China rivalry in dangerous ways because the renewal of this competition signals the demise of the equilibrium that they had come to rely on during the last several decades. This equilibrium had allowed them to increase their economic prosperity by deeper integration with the Chinese, Japanese, and U.S. economies, while relying on the United States' military power and presence to protect their security and autonomy vis-à-vis China. Liow points out that, caught between expanding Chinese presence and assertiveness in the region and Trump's unpredictable foreign policy and protectionist instincts, the Southeast Asian nations are struggling to preserve local stability. China has managed to penetrate domestic politics within the regional states, there are renewed questions about the effectiveness of the Association of Southeast Asian Nations (ASEAN) as a security organization, and Washington's new animus toward economic interdependence threatens collective prosperity without any compensating gains in security. All these factors have left the regional states uncertain about how to deal with what they see as the dangerous erosion of the traditional U.S. hegemonic compact whereby Washington used its superior power to protect weaker states and nurture their prosperity because it contributed to a global order that ultimately advanced U.S. interests. Consequently, they have responded by deepening regional cooperation, engaging other extraregional powers such as Japan and India, and looking for ways to avoid getting caught up in the intensifying U.S.-China disputes over trade, technology, and the South China Sea. Although some regional states seek benefits from the U.S. competition with China, Southeast Asia as a whole appears more interested in weathering the rivalry than taking sides.

Liselotte Odgaard's chapter on Europe analyzes the predicament facing strong U.S. allies who are caught in the crossfire despite their distance from the immediate physical locus of rivalry. The European case is also unique because it involves various independent states, with different kinds of national relationships to Washington, that are increasingly unified in an evolving supranational organization, the European Union. Western Europe's own internal desire for unity and the external pressures imposed on it by challenges emerging from Russia, China, and now U.S.-China competition have accelerated this movement toward unified action, especially in the economic realm and increasingly in the security space—despite all the subnational forces that frequently threaten this evolution. Because Europe remains an incredible concentration of economic, industrial, and technological capabilities, it remains a great prize in U.S.-China competition. Its choices have a major impact on outcomes in a variety of areas, ranging from industrial standards to global institutions. While Western Europe's traditional status as a U.S. ally inclines it toward the United States in the first instance, Trump's disdain for the liberal international order has imposed unwelcome stresses on the transatlantic relationship. Odgaard emphasizes that, despite the region's historical affinities with the United States, the renewal of U.S.-China competition will witness Western European powers taking a more independent position. They will cooperate with either Washington or Beijing depending on the issue in question and increasingly with an eye to protecting European interests. This demonstration of agency on the part of even the closest U.S. allies suggests that the United States simply cannot presume European allegiance in its rivalry with China, in part because the threats posed by the latter to Europe are not military as they were in yesteryear with the Soviet Union. Given this fact, Odgaard argues that a more self-regarding European approach to U.S.-China competition may actually temper the competition's intensity by encouraging both sides to consider compromises. Whether or not this expectation is realized, the European attitude toward the continuing U.S. rivalry with China provides startling evidence of the complexities that Washington must confront when thinking about great-power competition under conditions of economic interdependence.

Nothing confirms the importance of U.S.-China competition more than the fact that it has reached the Western Hemisphere, long the backyard of the United States. It is often forgotten, and hence needs repeated emphasizing, that the ability of the United States to sustain global competition with other great powers is immensely advantaged by its capacity to preserve a secure hemispheric base. This geopolitical insight has shaped the United States' relations with its American neighbors since the earliest years of the nation's founding. While the traditional U.S. approach to hemispheric security was preclusive—preventing others from securing any foothold in the region—that strategy, except in the military realm, has become obsolete in the era of globalization. Today, when trading links crisscross the globe and even weaker states have enough agency to make independent choices regarding their trading partners, success for the United States will derive less from its capacity to constrain the productive links offered by its competitors and more from its responsiveness to the economic and political interests of its immediate and extended neighbors. Carol Wise's chapter on China's dramatically growing trade and investment in the Western Hemisphere in recent years drives home this point with clarity. Examining Chinese economic ties with various countries in South and Central America, as well as with Canada and Mexico in North America, Wise notes that these relationships have been enhanced precisely because they provide joint gains to the parties involved. In most instances, China imports primary goods from these countries in exchange for low- to medium-value-added manufacturing goods. The United States, in contrast, exports services and higher-value-added manufacturing goods, a pattern that reflects the complementarities of the parties' strengths and needs all around. Emphasizing that China's relationships in the Americas are fundamentally developmental in nature, Wise's analysis underscores the need for a more sophisticated U.S. approach to the hemisphere. Instead of picking petty trade fights with its neighbors, the United States would do more to protect its interests in the hemisphere by pursuing even deeper economic integration of the kind once envisaged by the idea of the Free Trade Area of the Americas rather than trying to limit China's commercial intercourse with regional states.

Conclusion: Competing for Success

The most important change in U.S.-China relations since the beginning of the Trump administration has been the United States' acknowledgment that China has evolved into a strategic competitor. Prior administrations, also recognizing this reality but fearful of professing it openly, proceeded to surreptitiously hedge against Beijing. The Trump administration has made this competition transparent. In so doing, it has plainly affirmed what has long been appreciated by China itself.[106] Such a public declaration is critical to bringing bureaucratic coherence to how Washington responds to Beijing, but it is equally important to keeping U.S. engagement with China honest despite the difficulties. Without this shift, both nations would remain trapped in a charade of each side professing partnership even as they furtively engage in activities that undermine it.

The Trump administration, however, has gone beyond merely owning up to the reality of Sino-U.S. competition, and has in fact intensified it. Several of the initiatives pursued have undoubtedly been overdue. For example, revitalizing the U.S. capacity to project power in Asia is desirable and necessary for reasons that go beyond competition with China. The efforts to build an Indo-Pacific coalition of partners are similarly valuable because each of the major rimland states has an interest in protecting its autonomy vis-à-vis China. Taking measures to protect against the loss of U.S. technological dominance is likewise imperative, including by tightening export controls and better regulating Chinese business acquisitions in the United States.

For all these actions, other policies of the Trump administration have raised questions about the viability of its larger strategy toward China. Several issues are relevant in this regard. While acknowledging that the competition with China is a reality, the administration's pronouncements

---

[106] Michael Pillsbury, *The Hundred Year Marathon* (New York: St. Martin's Press, 2015); Jonathan D.T. Ward, *China's Vision of Victory* (New York: Atlas, 2019); and Rush Doshi, *The Long Game: China's Grand Strategy and the Displacement of American Power* (forthcoming).

and strategies have not indicated what, if any, the limits of that rivalry may be. The fact that China will continue to grow in power, even if more slowly in the future, only suggests that the future international order will once again return to bipolarity.[107] If bipolarity, however asymmetrical, represents the face of the global system for the next few decades, the United States will need to discern not only what the most advantageous modes of competition might be but also what their inherent limits are. China will remain a peer (or a near-peer) competitor that cannot be defeated conclusively as the Soviet Union was, nor will its regime be changed from without.

In other words, U.S. interests will not be served by treating U.S.-China competition as a zero-sum game if it is in fact something other. Both U.S. allies and bystanders in the international system are anxiously seeking to understand what the long-term objectives of the United States vis-à-vis China might be, what Washington regards as the desirable rules of the game, and what roles others are expected to play as this competition evolves. The Trump administration thus far has focused on correcting the weaknesses of past policies—the inability to admit to strategic competition with China—but it has spent insufficient time framing what the nature of the contestation might be in a world where the United States and China will have to cooperate on many issues despite their persistent rivalry.[108] How the United States proposes to cooperate with its allies in managing the ongoing competition with China is also still unclear.

What complicates these problems further is that there is little evidence that the American public, despite heightened concerns about China, views the administration's offensive against Beijing as the most pressing strategic problem facing the country. Unlike the Soviet Union, which was viewed as an existential threat to the United States, contemporary China is not perceived similarly thanks in part to its economic integration with the global economy. As Richard Fontaine notes, that "could pose a problem for the United States' new competitive strategy. A generation-long great-power competition demands national-level focus and new economic and military approaches, all of which will be difficult to achieve without popular support."[109]

The character of the U.S.-China economic competition itself also requires greater clarity. The Trump administration has used tariffs on various Chinese goods to both correct U.S. trade deficits and force Beijing to rectify the

---

[107] Øystein Tunsjø, *The Return of Bipolarity in World Politics: China, the United States, and Geostructural Realism* (New York: Columbia University Press, 2018).

[108] For a sensible analysis of this challenge, see Kurt M. Campbell and Jake Sullivan, "Competition without Catastrophe: How America Can Both Challenge and Coexist with China," *Foreign Affairs*, September/October 2019.

[109] Richard Fontaine, "Great-Power Competition Is Washington's Top Priority—But Not the Public's," *Foreign Affairs*, September 9, 2019.

structural problems afflicting U.S.-China trade relations. Attempting to reduce the trade deficit through tariffs is a quixotic enterprise because this deficit is caused by many factors that transcend China. Moreover, as economist David Goldman observes, "China's export dependence on the United States is shrinking, not growing."[110] Hence, the effectiveness of the Trump tariffs to force a permanent reduction of China's trade surplus is questionable.

Using tariffs as a negotiating instrument to compel China to address its trade barriers is more defensible, but whether tariff wars are the best means of overcoming these obstacles remains to be seen. Moreover, it is still not obvious whether Trump—as opposed to his administration—cares as much about rectifying China's structural impediments to trade as he does about reducing the U.S. trade deficit and whether his current strategy will suffice to redress the underlying problems that bedevil the U.S.-China economic relationship. Irrespective of whether Trump succeeds in inflicting lasting pain on China, his trade war has already contributed toward slowing global growth, with 90% of the world's economies now experiencing a downturn.[111] The consequences of slowing growth not only for U.S. allies and numerous other friendly nations but also for the United States itself over time are significant in both economic and geopolitical terms. Hence, the administration's decision to simultaneously target many other trading partners, including U.S. allies, is even more dubious because, among other things, China's trade surpluses with the United States are an order of magnitude larger than those enjoyed by all other states. Moreover, many partners targeted by U.S. tariffs also have problems with China's restrictive trade practices, and thus building a coalition to confront China first arguably might have produced better results than concurrently alienating both friends and competitors alike.[112]

In any event, what seems most unclear about the trade confrontation with China—and this remains a source of disquiet across Asia and Europe at large—is whether the Trump administration is seeking merely to level the playing field or whether it is actually pursuing the comprehensive decoupling of the U.S. and Chinese economies.[113] Whether the systematic decoupling of the world's two largest economies can be achieved through state policy alone remains a difficult question. The answer depends greatly on the degree

[110] David P. Goldman, "Open Letter to Larry Kudlow: You Need a Different China Strategy," Townhall, July 19, 2018.

[111] Desmond Lachman, "When China Stumbles, the World Economy Will Shudder," Hill, December 1, 2019, https://thehill.com/opinion/international/472289-when-china-stumbles-the-world-economy-will-shudder.

[112] Wendy Cutler, "Strength in Numbers," Asia Society Policy Institute, April 9, 2019.

[113] Geoffrey Gertz, "Trump Can't Decide What He Wants from China," Foreign Policy, September 11, 2019, https://foreignpolicy.com/2019/09/11/trump-cant-decide-what-he-wants-from-china.

to which private economic activities can be constrained by governmental decisions and whether exogenous factors like technology will subvert state choices.[114] But the prospect of globalization unraveling as a result of deliberate decisions made by the hegemonic power that fostered international economic integration for over 70 years leaves almost every U.S. partner uneasy. Even if such decoupling were ultimately incomplete, the fracturing of global supply chains will impose economic losses not only on the United States but also on its allies, as well as on China, and will only strengthen Beijing's conviction that it must move toward building its own trading bloc so as to limit its vulnerability to Washington's decisions.[115]

Any evolution toward rival trading systems will only impose higher economic costs on all trading states and increase the risks of conflicts between blocs. But more importantly, it will force U.S. partners in Asia and Europe that trade with both the United States and China into having to make unpalatable choices. Most states, however friendly they are to Washington, find this prospect distasteful and will resist U.S. pressures aimed at limiting commercial ties with China. Even the staunchest U.S. partners in Asia, such as Japan and Taiwan, are not exceptions in this regard.[116] Many allied states will accept targeted decoupling by the United States if this is directed at ensuring the security of the U.S. defense supply chain or some other narrow strategic objectives (if such disengagement can actually be effective). Some U.S. partners, such as Japan and Taiwan, are already pursuing limited retrenchment from China to protect their national security. Many European states, too, have become conscious of the need to avoid giving China free access to key strategic industries or technologies. But all U.S. allies would prefer that the global trading system, with its broadly enmeshed supply chains, be protected to the degree possible because of the benefits that each enjoys as a result.[117]

---

[114] For an argument that economic exigencies will trump state choices, see Geoffrey Garrett, "Why U.S.-China Supply Chains Are Stronger Than the Trade War," Wharton School, Knowledge@Wharton, September 5, 2019.

[115] For more on this issue, see David A. Lake, "Economic Openness and Great Power Competition: Lessons for China and the United States," *Chinese Journal of International Politics* 11, no. 3 (2018): 237–70.

[116] Edward Wong, "U.S. versus China: A New Era of Great Power Competition, but Without Boundaries," *New York Times*, June 26, 2019.

[117] For a discussion of how focused decoupling should be managed, see Charles W. Boustany Jr. and Aaron L. Friedberg, "Partial Disengagement: A New U.S. Strategy for Economic Competition with China," NBR, NBR Special Report, no. 82, November 2019. It is worth remembering that China has pursued its own version of decoupling for a long time prior to Trump's trade war. Beijing's effort to restrict the access enjoyed by U.S. technology companies in China, while creating its own national substitutes, is a good example of how China has sought to create an entire information-management regime that shares minimal links with the outside world, especially the United States.

The Trump administration, like its predecessors, has not yet found the right balance between protecting absolute and relative gains. President Trump has exacerbated this problem by suggesting that he cares little about upholding the liberal international order. If U.S. partners come to be convinced that Washington is interested neither in protecting their prosperity, which sometimes derives importantly from trade with China, nor in protecting their security, because burden sharing takes precedence over the common defense, many might be tempted to conclude that collaborating with Washington in confronting Beijing is not worth it. Only the assurance of the United States' continued willingness to protect its partners and treat them differently will forestall these temptations—to the ultimate benefit of the United States itself.

Obviously, Washington cannot bear the burdens of protecting the postwar system if U.S. power seriously hemorrhages in the interim. Consequently, it must consider correctives that enable the United States to compete with China successfully without this rivalry degenerating into violent conflict or fissuring the global economy. Achieving these goals will require diverse and subtle policies that are detailed elsewhere, but the broad strategy that Washington should pursue must focus less on pushing China down than on keeping the United States well ahead.[118]

Toward that end, the United States needs first and foremost to reinvest in itself in order to ensure that it remains the global fountainhead of innovation—from where all power ultimately derives. Washington also must work on protecting and reforming the global trading system in its multilateral form using coordinated actions with allies to confront China's malpractices. At the same time, it should selectively enlarge international trade through high-standard plurilateral free trade agreements that more tightly knit the United States with its partners while also more effectively limiting China's access to advanced technologies. Finally, rebuilding power-projection capabilities to better protect U.S. friends, while providing the global public goods that ultimately advance U.S. interests and increase the legitimacy accruing to U.S. leadership, is indispensable. In short, if the United States is to protect its primacy in the face of continuing competition with China, it must behave like a responsible hegemonic power.

---

[118] Tellis, *Balancing Without Containment*; and Ashley J. Tellis, "The Geopolitics of TTIP and TPP," in *Power Shifts and New Blocs in the Global Trading System*, ed. Sanjaya Baru and Suvi Dogra, Adelphi Series 450 (New York: Routledge, 2015), 93–120.

EXECUTIVE SUMMARY

This chapter examines the impact of increasing U.S.-China competition on Japan's economic and security interests as well as on the U.S.-Japan alliance.

MAIN ARGUMENT

The rivalry between the U.S. and China will narrow Japan's strategic options. The Abe cabinet has sought to avoid zero-sum trade-offs by maintaining close relations with Washington while seeking to avoid a direct clash with Beijing. Within Japan, few advocate for strategic alignment with China; to the contrary, public opinion and the business community strongly favor deepening ties with the U.S. Growing hostility between the U.S. and China will lead Japan to work hard to ensure its strategic protection and has already begun to shape Japan's outreach to Indo-Pacific partners as a way of blunting Chinese influence. U.S. identification of China as a strategic challenge is positive for Japan as it binds the U.S. more deeply into offsetting China's regional influence. But open hostilities will severely compromise Japan's economic and security interests, making it likely that Tokyo could need to choose between Washington and Beijing at some point.

POLICY IMPLICATIONS

- The U.S. should do all it can to support and enhance the collective effort with Japan to check Chinese influence. Besides ensuring a robust military presence, the U.S. should strengthen regional trade and investment opportunities as well as increase development and infrastructure assistance.

- U.S. policymakers must continue to ensure that the U.S.-Japan alliance serves not only Japan's military interests but also its economic interests to promote Tokyo's continued alignment with Washington should the U.S.-China rivalry intensify.

- The U.S. must not allow Japanese leaders to doubt the strategic protection offered by the U.S.-Japan security treaty or otherwise weaken the strategic asset of the alliance. Japan's military capability and the bases the country offers are critical to deterring Chinese aggression.

Japan's Interests in an Era of U.S.-China Strategic Competition

Sheila A. Smith

Although China's rise has shaken the foundations of Japan's postwar confidence, it has yet to fundamentally alter Japan's strategy of seeking strategic protection from the United States while pursuing economic gains with China. The U.S.-Japan alliance has ensured Japanese security for over half a century, and continues to do so as Chinese military power has grown. Tokyo and Washington share concerns about Beijing's behavior, including predatory Chinese trade practices and increasingly assertive maritime activities. Japanese leaders continue to try to shape Chinese preferences, emphasizing their mutual economic interest in free trade and investment while deepening military cooperation with the United States. Prime Minister Shinzo Abe has actively sought to develop and implement a regional strategy across the Indo-Pacific as an additional hedge against the uncertainty of both China's growing power and U.S. strategic leadership.

Should tensions between the United States and China grow, Japan's choices will narrow and its leaders could confront greater demand from either Washington or Beijing to take sides as Japan pursues its economic and defense interests. Abe has done all that he can to avoid zero-sum choices as the United States and China intensify their trade dispute. But that is less about choosing sides than it is about Japan's own interests in the global liberal trading order. As the Trump administration threatens to reorganize global trade along national lines, the Abe cabinet has deepened its trade ties with others that have similar interests in global free trade, including the eleven remaining members of the original Trans-Pacific Partnership (TPP) as well as the European Union. However, as Prime Minister Abe seeks to find steadier ground with

Sheila A. Smith is a Senior Fellow for Japan Studies at the Council on Foreign Relations. She can be reached at <ssmith@cfr.org>.

President Xi Jinping for bilateral relations, he is unlikely to accommodate Beijing's maritime ambitions in the East China Sea or to renounce Japan's sovereignty claim over the Senkaku Islands (which China calls the Diaoyu Islands). The alliance with the United States remains Japan's primary route to deter military pressure on its defenses, and China has emerged as one of Japan's greatest security concerns. Neither Abe nor his successors will want that alliance to weaken, even as Tokyo's decision-makers straddle these two critical partnerships. Nor has Abe been willing to accept China's stance on regional security, including the country's assertiveness in the South China Sea or its behavior toward other, smaller maritime partners in the region. Instead, Japan has begun to support capacity building for these nations' maritime defenses, breaking from its long-standing policy of providing solely economic assistance to the region. The Japan Self-Defense Forces (JSDF) now regularly tour Indo-Pacific countries to demonstrate Japan's interests across the region. The JSDF also has increased its participation in U.S.-led maritime presence operations, adding its largest ships to offer asset protection for U.S. aircraft carrier task forces.

Open hostility between the United States and China will force harder choices on Japan and limit its ability to mitigate strategic risk. A retreat to autarky, for example, would deeply harm the Japanese economy, as the postwar global trading order has been the foundation of Japanese wealth. Without a doubt, an all-out military competition between the United States and China would involve Japan, given that 50,000 U.S. forward-deployed forces as well as a significant portion of the U.S. Pacific Fleet are based there. In the case of a conflict, Japan would have to increase its military capability rapidly and integrate its military operations with U.S. and other allied forces. Should China succeed in pushing U.S. forces from the region, Japan would be left vulnerable to Chinese military power, including its strategic forces.

Shy of military conflict, sustained rivalry between the United States and China could have a more gradual impact, forcing Japan to compromise its economic interests to align more fully with the United States. The current adjustments in the U.S.-Japan relationship suggest how these tensions might evolve. Washington could demand greater economic and military benefits from Tokyo in exchange for strategic protection; Beijing could offer alternatives to the regional order that include economic gains for Tokyo in exchange for limiting or even ending Japan's strategic relationship with the United States. While an either/or choice between the United States and China seems unlikely, the Abe cabinet is already diversifying its diplomatic options in the hope that Tokyo, along with other stakeholders in the region, can persuade Washington and Beijing of the folly in committing to an all-out confrontation. But the costs of continued alliance with the United States may rise. Washington's support for free trade and U.S. alliances had been a given until the Trump administration openly questioned their value to the United States. Strategic protection may not be rescinded, but Washington may ask more for it. Similarly, continued access to China's market may also come at a price. Economic coercion—by either China or the United States—could force Japan's hand.

This chapter analyzes the domestic constituencies that shape Japan's decision-making on the U.S.-China rivalry. It then examines the sustainability of U.S. strategic protection in the face of China's rise, and how Japan is increasing attention to building a network of strategic collaborators across the Indo-Pacific. Finally, the chapter examines the benefits and the downsides to Japan's interests from an intensifying U.S.-China rivalry.

Japan's Domestic Interests and U.S.-China Rivalry

The domestic alignments that might be affected by U.S.-China rivalry are difficult to predict, but Japanese businesses and the general public see much at stake in Japan's relationship with both powers. Over the past decade, the rise in Chinese influence over Japanese choices has been discernible, as greater tensions on a variety of issues have soured Sino-Japanese ties. Few in Tokyo doubt that it is China that poses the greatest long-term strategic challenge to Japanese interests. The rise in Chinese power and the use of that power to challenge Japanese interests have already resulted in a far more cautious diplomatic approach to Beijing. Economic ties, traditionally seen as the foundation of mutual interest, have recently been used by Beijing to demonstrate political displeasure. Diplomatic tensions over islands in the East China Sea have provided fodder for popular nationalism. Japanese and Chinese visions of Asian regionalism are far more competitive than complementary.

Tensions between Tokyo and Beijing will grow if Sino-U.S. competition continues to escalate. Already, the U.S.-Japan alliance has adjusted to the growing military pressures on Japan from the People's Liberation Army (PLA) Navy as well as from the growing presence of Chinese air forces in and around Japanese airspace. The legacy of Japan's clash with China over the Senkaku/Diaoyu Islands has been profound. Neither Tokyo nor Beijing has backed away from competing sovereignty claims, even as they both have attempted to reduce the risk of a reoccurrence of the crisis of 2012. The Chinese Ministry of National Defense's announcement in 2014 that it was establishing an air defense identification zone (ADIZ) across the East China Sea, including over the disputed islands, signaled open military competition. Even before the territorial dispute erupted, increasing numbers of Chinese forces had been reported in waters between the Chinese mainland and Japan, as the PLA Navy began operating through Japanese straits on its way to the western Pacific. The two sides tried to overcome their different interpretations of their maritime boundary through an agreement on joint energy development in 2008, but there are no signs yet that Beijing would be willing to go back to work on an implementation agreement. Indeed, if its approach to sovereignty claims in the South China Sea serves as any sort of reference for the future resolution of differences on the maritime boundary in the East China Sea, there may be further contest ahead.

These concerns for Tokyo would only grow in the context of escalating U.S.-China strategic rivalry. Tokyo could easily find itself being tested in an effort by Beijing to demonstrate the costs of Japan's reliance on the United States. Washington may be hard-pressed to defend every dispute between its allies and China. Both Presidents Barack Obama and Donald Trump have declared that the United States will defend the Senkaku/Diaoyu Islands if necessary, but operationalizing that commitment in an era of greater strategic tensions could prove difficult.[1] Japanese perceptions of the United States' reliability would be sensitive to any shift in Washington's view of the value of the alliance.

Japan's economic stake in China is considerable, and economic confrontation between the United States and China is most worrisome for Japanese businesses. Economic ties with China have not been static, however, as tensions between the two have grown. Nonetheless, Japan depends just as much on the fate of the Chinese economy as China depends on Japan's continued trade and investment (see **Table 1**).

Whereas Japanese businesses once relied on access to inexpensive Chinese labor, today it is the behavior of the middle class or wealthy Chinese consumers that attracts Japanese businesses. Japan remains a valued economic partner for China, but it is now one of China's many potential sources of foreign direct investment and trade. China no longer needs the overseas development assistance (ODA) from the Japanese government that funded the domestic infrastructure development critical to China's economic growth (see **Tables 2, 3,** and **4**). Instead, it now is a net exporter of development assistance, which is aimed primarily at building low-cost infrastructure across Asia. Chinese consumers also now have choices. Whereas the promise of Japanese investment once tempered the postwar legacy of anti-Japanese sentiment, today there are other options for Chinese looking for foreign investment.

The coincidence of Japan's economic stagnation with China's accelerated economic growth had a significant impact on how the Japanese viewed

---

[1] See the Treaty of Mutual Cooperation and Security between Japan and the United States of America, available at https://www.mofa.go.jp/region/n-america/us/q&a/ref/1.html.

TABLE 1   Japan's trade in goods with China, 2005–18 ($ billion)

	Total trade in goods with China			Year-to-year change			Share of Japan's total trade	
	Exports	Imports	Balance	Exports (%)	Imports (%)	Balance	Exports (%)	Imports (%)
2018	143.9	173.5	-29.6	8.5	5.6	2.0	19.5	23.2
2017	132.7	164.3	-31.6	16.5	5.0	11.0	19.0	24.5
2016	113.9	156.4	-42.6	4.2	-2.6	8.8	17.7	25.8
2015	109.3	160.7	-51.4	-14.0	-11.8	3.6	17.5	24.8
2014	127.1	182.1	-55.0	-2.1	-0.1	-2.6	18.3	22.3
2013	129.9	182.2	-52.3	-10.3	-3.6	-8.0	18.1	21.7
2012	144.7	189.0	-44.3	-10.4	3.0	-22.3	18.1	21.3
2011	161.5	183.5	-22.0	8.3	20.1	-18.3	19.7	21.5
2010	149.1	152.8	-3.7	36.0	24.7	9.2	19.4	22.1
2005	80.3	109.1	-28.8	8.8	15.8	-8.4	13.4	21.0

SOURCE: Japan External Trade Organization (JETRO), https://www.jetro.go.jp/en/reports/statistics.html.

TABLE 2   Japan's official development assistance to China, 1989–99 ($ million)

Year	Total official development assistance
1989	833
1990	740
1991	618
1992	1,131
1993	1,489
1994	1,645
1995	1,604
1996	1,103
1997	824
1998	1,423
1999	1,596

SOURCE: Ministry of Foreign Affairs (Japan), https://www.mofa.go.jp/mofaj/gaiko/oda/shiryo/jisseki/kuni/asia.html.

TABLE 3   Japan's outward FDI flow to China, based on net balance of payments

Year	Japan outward FDI to China ($ billion)	Japan FDI stock in China ($ billion, measured at year end)
2018	10.8	123.8
2017	11.1	119.0
2016	9.5	108.7
2015	10.0	108.9
2014	10.9	104.4
2013	9.1	98.1
2012	13.5	93.2
2011	12.6	83.4
2010	7.3	66.5
2005	6.6	24.7
2000	0.9	8.7

SOURCE: JETRO, https://www.jetro.go.jp/en/reports/statistics.html.

TABLE 4   China's top ten inward direct investment sources, 2017 ($ million)

Investment source	Inward direct investment
World	2,688,470
China and Hong Kong	1,242,441
British Virgin Islands	285,932
Japan	164,765
Singapore	107,636
Germany	86,945
South Korea	72,690
United States	72,202
Cayman Islands	49,250
Netherlands	36,593
Taiwan	32,657

SOURCE: International Monetary Fund (IMF), IMF Coordinated Direct Investment Survey, http://data.imf.org/regular.aspx?key=61227424.

their future. Throughout the first decade of the 21st century, Japanese increasingly felt the impact of China's rising influence on their daily lives. According to public polling, the result was a concomitant rise in skepticism about the Chinese government's intentions toward Japan (see **Figure 1**). As more and more Japanese companies moved offshore to China, Japanese consumers became concerned about the quality of goods that were exported back to Japan. Opinion polling conducted over the last few decades reveals that Japanese public opinion did not change perceptibly even when the two governments managed to find common ground. Fewer Japanese saw an

FIGURE 1   Japanese and Chinese impressions of the other country

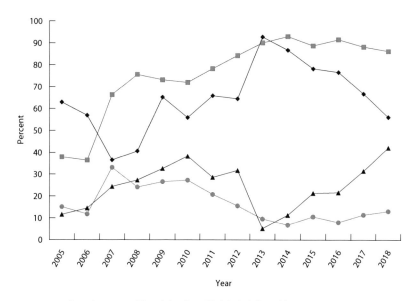

- ● — Japanese public opinion: favorable/relatively favorable
- ■ — Japanese public opinion: unfavorable/relatively unfavorable
- ▲ — Chinese public opinion: favorable/relatively favorable
- ◆ — Chinese public opinion: unfavorable/relatively unfavorable

SOURCE: "Japan-China Public Opinion Survey 2018," Genron NPO and China International Publishing Group, October 11, 2018, http://www.genron-npo.net/en/archives/181011.pdf.

advantage in closer ties with China, and many more worried that the Chinese government had hostile intentions toward Japan.[2]

In contrast to the souring of Japanese attitudes toward China over the past decade, the Japanese public continues to have a favorable view of the United States and its reliability as a strategic partner. In its annual global attitudes survey, conducted every spring since 2004, the Pew Research Center revealed that the majority of Japanese have a favorable opinion of the United States. Following the Great East Japan Earthquake in 2011, this percentage jumped to 85%. Conversely, after the United States elected Trump as president in 2017, there was a conspicuous drop from 72% to 57%, before increasing to 67% in 2018. While Japanese attitudes toward the United States do shift, they are generally far more positive than they are toward China.[3]

Business elites are also deeply supportive of Japan's relationship with the United States. But that favorable view is not simply a reflection of the economic trends. In terms of trade, the United States and China are both critical markets for Japanese products. Over the past decade, Japan has exported roughly the same amount to the United States in value terms as it has to China (see **Table 5**). Imports from the United States remain lower than from China, however (see **Table 6**). The United States continues to be a priority destination for Japanese FDI, representing almost one-third of Japan's total FDI in 2017. China received under a tenth of Japan's global FDI, or one-fourth the amount that went to the United States (see **Table 7**).

It is too early to tell whether—and how—the Trump administration's new approach to trade will affect Japanese business preferences. The bilateral U.S.-Japan trade deal was a relief to Keidanren, the Japan Business Federation, but considerable concern remains over how U.S. politics will affect the global supply chain, and in particular the global automobile industry.[4] Since Trump was elected president, senior Japanese corporate executives have joined with their prime minister to demonstrate to the American people the value of

---

[2] This growing public concern over the Chinese government's behavior toward Japan is reflected in the polling of Genron NPO. See polls from 2004 onward at "Opinion Polls," Genron NPO, http://www.genron-npo.net/en/opinion_polls.

[3] Pew Research Center, Global Indicators Database, https://www.pewresearch.org/global/database/indicator/1/country/JP.

[4] On September 26, 2019, Keidanren chairman Hiroaki Nakanishi issued a statement welcoming the outcome: "The imposition of tariffs by major economic powers has made the future of the global economy uncertain. Yet in the midst of this, we welcome the fact that the United States and Japan, representing one-third of the global economy, have managed to negotiate in good faith over a relatively short time, not even half a year, a balanced agreement that will lead to a stable U.S.-Japan trading relationship" (translation by author). The press release is available at https://www.keidanren.or.jp/speech/comment/2019/0926.html.

TABLE 5   Japan's exports to selected countries (free on board, $ million)

	China mainland	United States	Euro area
2018	143,998	140,616	61,617
2017	132,817	135,075	56,229
2016	113,877	130,428	53,319
2015	109,215	126,372	49,933
2014	126,346	130,571	54,223
2013	129,052	134,398	54,255
2012	144,202	142,053	60,895
2011	161,818	127,773	70,487
2010	149,626	120,483	64,164
2009	109,632	95,343	53,636

TABLE 6   Japan's imports from selected countries (cost, insurance, and freight; $ million)

	China mainland	United States	Euro area
2018	173,537	83,586	70,555
2017	164,354	73,835	62,563
2016	156,560	69,303	60,563
2015	160,598	68,322	57,405
2014	180,888	73,056	62,981
2013	180,784	71,939	64,097
2012	188,495	78,230	67,965
2011	183,902	76,172	65,418
2010	153,368	69,026	53,468
2009	122,536	60,486	47,823

TABLE 7   Japan's outward investment ($ million)

	World	United States	China mainland [Hong Kong]
2016	1,315,221	445,854	108,230 [27,539]
2015	1,228,766	413,342	107,576 [23,908]
2014	1,152,006	375,621	103,165 [22,231]
2013	1,118,010	331,659	98,197 [19,833]
2012	1,037,698	285,767	92,967 [18,334]
2011	962,790	274,972	83,218 [17,094]
2010	831,076	251,991	66,527 [15,554]
2009	740,925	231,123	55,087 [13,058]

SOURCE: IMF, "IMF Total End-Year Reporting on Inward and Outward Investments: Japan."

their investments in the U.S. economy and the impact of their presence in the U.S. market.[5]

At home, Japanese business leaders have become far more sensitive to the growing complexity of domestic politics. Tensions with China, in particular, have muted the public voice of individual executives, especially on issues such as Yasukuni Shrine visits and other war-legacy issues. Their conspicuous advocacy of the importance of the U.S.-Japan relationship has far more popular traction.[6] Thus, the political foundation of Japan's strategic alignment with the United States remains firm, while domestic skepticism of China would make it difficult for elected leaders to make concessions to Beijing, even if they were so inclined.

Ensuring U.S. Strategic Protection

Japan's relationship with the United States remains the foundation of its national strategy. Both security and trade relations have been adapted in response to the U.S.-China rivalry and U.S. doubts about the strategic value of alliances.

Security Relations

The U.S.-Japan alliance remains the primary mechanism for Japan's strategic response to China's military challenge. Tokyo's deepening concerns over Chinese military intentions led to a renewed effort to clarify the U.S. commitment to Japan's defenses, especially with respect to the Senkaku/Diaoyu Islands. During the Cold War, and even for some time after, most military planners in Japan assumed that a conflict in Northeast Asia would begin elsewhere. There was little doubt that the United States would respond to a Korean contingency or even to a Taiwan Strait crisis. But for the most part, the division of labor between U.S. and Japanese forces relegated the

---

[5] Japan's business leaders have actively sought to highlight Japan's value to U.S. workers and local communities, traveling across the United States annually. When the United States was preparing to join the TPP, for example, the Keidanren initiated a series of high-profile visits to the United States beginning in 2015. See "Report on the Keidanren Mission to the United States," Keidanren, July 21, 2015, https://www.keidanren.or.jp/en/policy/2015/069.html.

[6] Indeed, Japanese executives have supported the Abe cabinet's efforts to demonstrate the value of Japanese investment in the U.S. economy, meeting with Trump during his visit to Japan and increasing their investments in the United States. Abe has frequently shared data with Trump on the growing number of Japanese private-sector investments in the United States and the jobs created as a result. In the beginning of his relationship with Trump, Abe reportedly drafted a document entitled the "U.S.-Japan Growth and Employment Initiative," which proposed creating 700,000 jobs in the United States and new markets worth $450 billion over the next decade. For more information, see Mitsuru Obe, "Abe to Tout Japan's U.S. Investment Plans in Trump Meeting," *Wall Street Journal*, February 6, 2017, https://www.wsj.com/articles/abe-to-tout-japans-benefits-to-u-s-in-trump-meeting-1486373098.

JSDF to a supporting role. Indeed, much of Japanese military planning revolved around these flashpoints elsewhere. But the territorial dispute with China offered a different prospect. Japan itself could be the target of Chinese military action, and this would require Tokyo to ask the United States for aid. Tokyo worried that Washington may not see a conflict with China as in its interests. Japan has often wondered if the United States would really come to its aid in the event of a conflict, given that this premise of the alliance has never been tested. But in 2012, when the Chinese government ordered its coast guard forces to the Senkaku/Diaoyu Islands to defend its sovereignty claim, the prospect of a military clash seemed far more real. A crisis below the level of the use of military force could challenge Japan's ability to demonstrate its sovereignty, creating a scenario that both Tokyo and Washington want to avoid.[7]

Reassurance took the form of an explicit U.S. statement that, should China attempt to assert its claim to the islands by military force, the United States would assist in defending Japan. As noted earlier, Obama himself offered this assurance on a trip to Tokyo in 2014, stating that the protections under Article 5 of the Treaty of Mutual Cooperation and Security extended to the Senkaku/Diaoyu Islands. Washington and Tokyo also agreed to an alliance-coordination mechanism to address any future tensions in the region, institutionalizing the commitment to manage crises together. Abe understood that Japan needed to offer more to offset the changes in the regional military balance. In 2014, he reinterpreted the Japanese constitution to allow for "collective self-defense"—paving the way for Japan's military to operate alongside other national militaries and to use force if necessary. The United States had long wanted Japan to play a more active military role in maritime security operations. Since 2006, Japan has been part of trilateral security consultations with the United States and Australia largely designed to improve maritime cooperation in the western Pacific, and in 2015 the JSDF joined the U.S.-India Malabar exercises on a permanent basis. The decision to reinterpret Article 9 cost Abe in the short term, as many in Japan worried that their prime minister may be too ready to take Japan to war. A long list of security reforms, however, had been in the works prior to his return to office. His ruling coalition managed to maintain a

---

[7] Japan's Ministry of Defense has developed a considerable doctrine based on the threat of "gray zone" maritime activities by Chinese forces. See, for example, Ministry of Defense (Japan), *2016 Defense of Japan* (Tokyo, 2016), https://www.mod.go.jp/e/publ/w_paper/pdf/2016/DOJ2016_Digest_part1_web. pdf. More recently, Chinese gray-zone "coercion" has been identified as a challenge in additional domains of U.S.-Japan security cooperation, including the cyber and space domains. See, for example, Scott Harold et al., "The U.S.-Japan Alliance and Deterring Gray Zone Coercion in the Maritime, Cyber and Space Domains," RAND Corporation, 2017, https://www.rand.org/content/dam/rand/pubs/conf_proceedings/CF300/CF379/RAND_CF379.pdf.

supermajority in the Diet, making policy change far easier than it had been for his predecessors.[8]

The change in U.S. leadership in January 2017 brought renewed effort by the Abe cabinet to confirm U.S. military protection for the Senkaku/Diaoyu Islands. The presidential election campaign surprised many in Tokyo as Trump questioned not only the U.S. role in international trade but also defense assistance to U.S. allies. In an interview with the *New York Times*, he went so far as to suggest that Japan and South Korea should defend themselves with nuclear weapons if necessary against North Korea, prompting a statement by Japan's foreign minister to the effect that Japan remained strongly committed to its non-nuclear status. When Trump won the election, Abe moved quickly to reach out to the new president-elect, and arranged an unconventional pre-inauguration meeting at Trump Tower. Abe's political gamble paid off, and he continued to work hard at building his personal relationship with Trump after he took office.

The Trump administration's more forceful articulation of the United States' strategic contest with China eased Japanese fears that the United States would accommodate China. In Trump's first meeting with Abe, the two leaders reaffirmed that Article 5 of the U.S.-Japan security treaty covers the Senkaku/Diaoyu Islands. More importantly, the emphasis of the new U.S. National Security Strategy on the broader systemic challenges of China and Russia brought Japanese and U.S. assessments more into alignment. The new priorities in U.S. military planning displayed in the 2018 National Defense Strategy and the Nuclear Posture Review reassured Tokyo that the United States would not stand by as China sought to revamp the regional military balance.[9]

---

[8] The ruling coalition of the Liberal Democratic Party (LDP) and Komeito was well positioned to pass new legislation, having garnered two-thirds of the lower house seats and a majority of upper house seats. For an excellent analysis of the ramifications of Japan's most recent election, see Robert J. Pekkanen et al., eds., *Japan Decides 2017: The Japanese General Election* (New York: Palgrave Macmillan, 2018).

[9] See "Joint Statement from President Donald J. Trump and Prime Minister Shinzo Abe," White House, Press Release, February 2017, https://www.whitehouse.gov/briefings-statements/joint-statement-president-donald-j-trump-prime-minister-shinzo-abe; White House, *National Security Strategy of the United States of America* (Washington, D.C., December 2017), https://www.whitehouse.gov/wp-content/uploads/2017/12/NSS-Final-12-18-2017-0905.pdf; and U.S. Department of Defense, *Nuclear Posture Review* (Washington, D.C., February 2018), https://media.defense.gov/2018/Feb/02/2001872886/-1/-1/1/2018-NUCLEAR-POSTURE-REVIEW-FINAL-REPORT.PDF. The U.S. Department of Defense began reporting on China's growing military prowess in 2002. For the most recent report, see U.S. Department of Defense, *Annual Report to Congress: Military and Security Developments Involving the People's Republic of China 2019* (Washington D.C., 2019), https://media.defense.gov/2019/May/02/2002127082/-1/-1/1/2019_CHINA_MILITARY_POWER_REPORT.pdf. Japan's National Institute for Defense Studies, the research arm of the Ministry of Defense, followed suit in 2010. For its annual reports, see "China Security Report," National Institute for Defense Studies (Japan), http://www.nids.mod.go.jp/english/publication/chinareport/index.html.

Tokyo and Washington have found ample ground for strategic collaboration, from enhancing their military capabilities in Asia and denying Beijing advantage across the first island chain, to working together with Europe to strengthen oversight of Chinese efforts to purchase strategic industries. Even the Trump administration's emphasis on strengthening allied military contributions finds some purchase in this new strategic alignment on China. Japan's 2018 National Defense Program Guidelines clearly identified strategic competition with China as a driver of enhanced defense spending to modernize Japan's air force as well as to propel greater cooperation between the U.S. and Japanese militaries in space. Alongside the ten-year defense plan was a five-year procurement plan that committed around $250 billion to modernizing fighters in the Japan Air Self-Defense Force, making a significant upgrade in the country's ballistic missile defenses, and continuing ongoing efforts to strengthen the Japan Maritime Self-Defense Force (JMSDF). Japanese hard-power investment is aimed not only at improving defense capabilities but also at making it possible for the JSDF to contribute to a regional maritime response to Chinese military power.[10]

Trump's ambition to reset the U.S.-Japan alliance may not yet be fully realized, however. Upcoming negotiations over Japan's five-year host-nation support agreement with the United States, which are due to begin in 2020, could exacerbate political friction between Tokyo and Washington. If the Trump administration's approach to burden-sharing in other alliances offers a precedent, then Japanese officials should worry. NATO allies were the first to feel the brunt of the U.S. president's ire over the inadequacy of their defense efforts. At his first NATO summit in 2017, Trump suggested that the United States could withhold Article 5 protections for NATO members and berated longtime allies, especially Germany, over their low spending on defense, while rewarding regimes he saw as more responsive to his demands (such as Poland) with upgrades in U.S. military assistance.

U.S. allies in Asia historically have responded to burden-sharing differently, choosing to increase their spending on U.S. forces stationed in their countries. South Korea was the first country to renegotiate its host-nation support agreement in 2018, but the initial talks ended in disarray. In December 2018, the press reported that the government in

---

[10] Japan will acquire additional F-35s and the Aegis Ashore ballistic missile defense system and give continued attention to its surface and submarine fleet, including hardening the decks of destroyers to carry short take-off and vertical landing (STOVL) F-35Bs. For further details, see Ministry of Defense (Japan), *National Defense Program Guidelines for FY19 and Beyond* (Tokyo, December 2018), https://www.mod.go.jp/j/approach/agenda/guideline/2019/pdf/20181218_e.pdf; Ministry of Defense (Japan), *Medium Term Defense Program (FY 2019–FY 2023)* (Tokyo, December 2018), https://www.mod.go.jp/j/approach/agenda/guideline/2019/pdf/chuki_seibi31-35_e.pdf; and Sheila A. Smith, "Japan's Active Defenses," Council on Foreign Relations (CFR), Asia Unbound, December 20, 2018, https://www.cfr.org/blog/japans-active-defenses.

Seoul had been asked by Washington to increase its spending on U.S. forces by 50%. Needless to say, the South Korean government rejected this, despite the ongoing alliance coordination on North Korea. But by early February, both governments stated that an interim one-year agreement would increase South Korean spending by 8.2% while talks continued. This precedent does not bode well for Japan, which today offers anywhere from 50% to 75% of the costs associated with basing U.S. forces in the country, depending on how the costs are calculated.[11]

Trade Relations

In addition to their disagreement on burden-sharing, the United States and Japan have parted ways on regional trade. More than on any other shared priority, Abe and Trump have failed to overcome their divergence on economic strategy toward China. Trump withdrew the United States from the TPP early in his presidency, and while Abe attempted to persuade him of the strategic benefits of multilateral agreements, the president has insisted on bilateralizing U.S. trade relations. The Abe cabinet has wrestled not only with the United States' abandonment of the TPP but also with the tariff war unleashed by the Trump administration on China. Just as Abe's friendly relationship with Trump has not inoculated the U.S.-Japan relationship from tensions over burden-sharing, trade continues to be a source of tension in the alliance. In repeated visits to Tokyo, Trump has scolded Japanese business for exploiting the openness of the U.S. market and called for greater investment in the United States.[12] Neither trade disputes nor burden-sharing pressures are new to the U.S.-Japan relationship, but the Trump administration has rattled Tokyo at precisely the time when Japan's security concerns are becoming more acute.

---

[11] "Highlights: In Brussels, Trump Scolds Allies on Cost-Sharing, and Stays Vague on Article 5," *New York Times*, May 25, 2017, https://www.nytimes.com/2017/05/25/world/europe/trump-brussels-nato.html. For reports on U.S. demands during negotiations with South Korea, see "Trump Wants South Korea to Pay More for U.S. Troop Presence," *Wall Street Journal*, December 7, 2018, https://www.wsj.com/articles/trump-wants-south-korea-to-pay-more-for-u-s-troop-presence-1544221727. According to a 2019 Congressional Research Service report, there is a wide range of estimates for what proportion of expenses for U.S. bases is covered by the Japanese government: "In January 2017, Japan's defense minister told Japanese parliamentarians that the Japanese portion of the total cost for U.S. forces stationed in Japan was more than 86%. Other estimates from various media reports are in the 40%–50% range. Most analysts concur that there is no authoritative, widely shared view on an accurate figure that captures the percentage that Japan shoulders." Emma Chanlett-Avery, Caitlin Campbell, and Joshua Williams, "The U.S.-Japan Alliance," Congressional Research Service, CRS Report for Congress, RL33740, June 13, 2019, 22, https://fas.org/sgp/crs/row/RL33740.pdf.

[12] "Remarks by President Trump to U.S. and Japanese Business Leaders," White House, Press Release, November 2017, https://www.whitehouse.gov/briefings-statements/5769. Trump repeated similar themes in a more recent meeting. See "Remarks by President Trump at a Reception with Japanese Business Leaders," White House, Press Release, May 2019, https://www.whitehouse.gov/briefings-statements/remarks-president-trump-reception-japanese-business-leaders-tokyo-japan.

In March 2018 the United States imposed tariffs on steel and aluminum imports, including those from Japan. Despite Abe's efforts to develop a close relationship with Trump, Tokyo received little advance warning and was stunned to find that Japanese exports were deemed a threat to U.S. national security. More alarming was the Trump administration's announcement on May 17, 2019, that the Commerce Department's investigation into automobile imports determined that there were similar national security concerns, again under Section 232 of the Trade Expansion Act of 1962. This was widely seen in Tokyo as a means of increasing U.S. leverage in bilateral negotiations with Japan.

Tokyo initially resisted the U.S. call for a bilateral free trade agreement, but in September 2018 it agreed to begin talks. Abe argued that the negotiations would culminate in a trade agreement in goods only, limiting the scope of negotiations to agricultural market access and digital trade. The United States was interested in greater access for agricultural goods and had already negotiated access under the TPP. Abe suggested that the United States could gain access on levels similar to other partners in the original TPP, even though it did not ratify the treaty. But the automobile tariffs continue to hang over talks, and the Trump administration's aims are still unclear. Just how tolerant the Abe cabinet will be of U.S. protectionism remains to be seen. The first in a series of bilateral agreements was announced on September 25, 2019. Abe was roundly criticized for his compromises, especially since he did not come home with a promise from Trump to exclude Japan from any future automobile tariffs.[13]

North Korea and Iran

Beyond the two bilateral issues of trade and burden-sharing, Japan has other global interests in which it conflicts with the United States. Perhaps most worrisome for Tokyo is Trump's handling of talks with Kim Jong-un. From a year of rising regional tensions in 2017 to a shift to dialogue in 2018, the Abe cabinet has struggled to keep pace with the Trump administration's thinking on North Korea. Abe had spent considerable time and effort in the first year of the Trump administration advocating for sustaining maximum pressure on Pyongyang, not only in Washington but also at the United Nations

---

[13] The U.S. and Japanese governments released their own announcements. For the Japanese government's announcement, see "Joint Statement of Japan and the United States," Ministry of Foreign Affairs (Japan), September 25, 2019, https://www.mofa.go.jp/files/000520821.pdf. For the U.S. Trade Representative's fact sheet, see Office of the U.S. Trade Representative, "U.S.-Japan Trade," Fact Sheet, September 2019, https://ustr.gov/about-us/policy-offices/press-office/fact-sheets/2019/september/fact-sheet-us-japan-trade-agreement. For Japanese criticism of the deal, see "Nichibei Boueki kyoutei no goi uin-uin towa iienai" [Japan-U.S. Trade Agreement Cannot Be Described as Win-Win], *Mainichi Shimbun*, September 27, 2019.

and in capitals across the world. As Trump's strategy shifted to summitry with Kim in early 2018, Abe continued to advocate for maintaining a tough line with Pyongyang. After the Singapore summit in June, the Japanese government continued to affirm its support for Trump's efforts to persuade Kim to negotiate a path to dismantling his nuclear program. But after the Hanoi summit ended in failure in February 2019, Abe argued that the time had come for his own meeting with Kim, a meeting "with no preconditions."[14] Kim has yet to agree to direct talks with Japan, and in 2019 continued to worry Tokyo with short- and medium-range missile tests. Trump's insistence that these missile tests would not impede future U.S. diplomacy with North Korea exacerbated the sense in Tokyo that the U.S. president could make a deal with Kim that would compromise Japanese security.[15]

Another source of tension is Iran. Iran has often presented a quandary for Japan, which has long sought close ties with the country, largely but not exclusively because of oil. When Iranian forces damaged a Japanese-owned oil tanker in the Gulf of Oman in June 2019, differences resurfaced. The Japanese company disputed the U.S. government's announcement that the damage was the result of a mine, and Japan's foreign minister did not share the attribution made by Secretary of State Mike Pompeo that it was the work of Revolutionary Guards.[16] In response to the Iranian attacks on civilian tankers, the Trump administration called for an allied maritime coalition to escort these tankers through the strait. Dubbed Operation Sentinel, the effort struggled to generate much support. The United Kingdom decided to develop its own task force with European allies. Abe was initially reluctant, and when national security adviser John Bolton traveled to Tokyo and Seoul to discuss the coalition, Abe demurred, suggesting that a new law would need to be drafted for parliamentary approval should Japan seek to participate. In the end, Abe decided that Japan would send the JMSDF for "research and cooperation" activities, demonstrating that Tokyo continues to view its interests with Iran differently from Washington. Thus, while the U.S.-Japan alliance remains Japan's paramount source of managing regional

---

[14] See Sheila A. Smith, "Hanoi Setback and Tokyo's North Korea Problem," CFR, Asia Unbound, March 1, 2019, https://www.cfr.org/blog/hanoi-setback-and-tokyos-north-korea-problem.

[15] Abe's differences with Trump on North Korea's missile tests were publicly visible at the G-7 meeting in August 2019. For more information, see "Trump, Abe at Odds on North Korea Missile Launches," *Asahi Shimbun*, August 26, 2019, http://www.asahi.com/ajw/articles/AJ201908260012.html.

[16] Simon Denyer and Carol Morello, "Japanese Ship Owner Contradicts U.S. Account of How Tanker Was Attacked," *Washington Post*, June 14, 2019, https://www.washingtonpost.com/world/japanese-ship-owner-contradicts-us-account-of-how-tanker-was-attacked/2019/06/14/7ea347d0-8eba-11e9-b6f4-033356502dce_story.html. Foreign Minister Taro Kono stated at a press conference that Japan has no evidence that supports the U.S. claim. See Tim Kelly, "Japan Defense Minister: Not Aware of Any Iran Involvement in Saudi Attacks," Reuters, September 18, 2019, https://www.reuters.com/article/us-saudi-aramco-attacks-japan/japan-defense-minister-not-aware-of-any-iran-involvement-in-saudi-attacks-idUSKBN1W30KV.

tensions, Japanese leaders—even the more assertive Abe—wield their military carefully as an instrument of foreign policy and not always in concert with the United States.

In summary, Japan's strategic dependence on the United States requires careful management of relations at the top. Abe pivoted quickly to the new U.S. president-elect after the 2016 election, and despite some serious policy differences, he has succeeded in forging a close working relationship with Trump. While this seemed to mitigate some of the president's criticism of the alliance, these personal ties did not preclude renegotiating trade relations nor have they protected Japan from Trump's growing demand for greater military burden-sharing. Trump's public suggestion that the bilateral security treaty ought to be renegotiated so that Japan would have more reciprocal defense obligations made headlines in Tokyo. The breakdown of U.S. negotiations with the Republic of Korea (ROK) over a new special measures agreement only heightened Japanese concerns. But the larger question that continues to worry Japanese decision-makers is whether U.S. and Japanese strategic interests will diverge or further converge as U.S.-China strategic rivalry intensifies.

Japan's Indo-Pacific Balancing

The Abe cabinet has not limited itself to strengthening the U.S.-Japan alliance. Building a network of economic and security partners in Asia that share Tokyo's concerns about China's growing assertiveness has also been a priority. Japanese diplomats have largely seen this as an integral extension of Japan's alliance with the United States. But whereas the Obama administration embraced Asian regionalism, the Trump administration has not made it a priority. Japan has been forced to articulate more clearly its commitment to liberal norms and the rule of law against the challenge from China, while the policies pursued by the Trump administration have created an impetus to ensure that, with or without the United States' full engagement, Japan's preferred vision of regionalism wins out in Asia.[17]

Tokyo and Beijing have been at odds over the legitimacy of using international law to resolve Asia's maritime disputes. Japan strongly supported the decision by the Philippines to use international law to cope with China's challenge to the status quo in the South China Sea. The United Nations Convention on the Law of the Sea (UNCLOS) provides

---

[17] In a speech to the UN General Assembly, Abe said that Japan would be a flag-bearer for a free, open, and rules-based international economic order. Shinzo Abe (speech delivered to UN General Assembly, New York, September 25, 2018), https://www.mofa.go.jp/fp/unp_a/page3e_000926.html. The Ministry of Defense's National Defense Program Guidelines state that "in line with the vision of [a] free and open Indo-Pacific, Japan will strategically promote multifaceted and multilayered security cooperation." See Ministry of Defense (Japan), *National Defense Program Guidelines for FY19 and Beyond*.

for the use of tribunals to arbitrate maritime disputes. Frustrated with the lack of progress in the China-ASEAN negotiations on a maritime code of conduct, then Philippine president Benigno Aquino III sought UNCLOS adjudication to deal with both China's increasingly antagonistic presence in the Philippines' exclusive economic zone and the growing role of Chinese maritime forces in and around contested islands in the South China Sea. Despite its membership in UNCLOS, China chose not to participate in the arbitration organized in April 2013 by the International Tribunal for the Law of the Sea and reacted negatively to the role played by the Japanese president of the international tribunal who appointed the judges. The outcome of the arbitration, which was largely in favor of the Philippines' assertion of its maritime boundary and understanding of the sovereignty status of the reefs that China claimed, was highly welcome in Tokyo. China, however, decried the tribunal as biased and has ignored the UNCLOS judgment.[18] Beijing continues to insist on bilateral negotiation of any disputes in the South China Sea.[19]

Japan is also wary of China's efforts to build new regional economic initiatives. Japan did not join the Asian Infrastructure Investment Bank (AIIB) created by China in 2016, citing skepticism about the governance standards. While Ministry of Finance officials have pointed out the benefits of membership, the Ministry of Foreign Affairs has largely seen it as a negative for Japan. Nonetheless, as the AIIB considered its first round of loans, consultations were held between the president of the AIIB, Jin Liqun, and the president of the Asian Development Bank (ADB), Takehiko Nakao, to identify projects in which the two regional development banks could complement each other.[20]

---

[18] See "Statement of the Ministry of Foreign Affairs of the People's Republic of China on the Award of 12 July 2016 of the Arbitral Tribunal in the South China Sea Arbitration Established at the Request of the Republic of the Philippines," Ministry of Foreign Affairs (PRC), Press Release, July 12, 2016; and "Statement by Foreign Minister Fumio Kishida," Ministry of Foreign Affairs (Japan), Press Release, July 12, 2016. See also "Failing or Incomplete? Grading the South China Sea Arbitration," Center for Strategic and International Studies, Asia Maritime Transparency Initiative, July 11, 2019.

[19] For context, see Tan Dawn Wei, "ASEAN and China Should Aim to Conclude Talks on Maritime Code of Conduct in 3 Years: PM Lee," *Straits Times*, November 14, 2018, https://www.straitstimes.com/singapore/asean-and-china-should-aim-to-conclude-talks-on-maritime-code-of-conduct-in-3-years-pm-lee.

[20] In May 2016, Nakao of the ADB and Jin of the AIIB signed a partnership agreement, following a similar AIIB agreement with the World Bank, which allowed the two institutions to co-finance and offer joint technical assistance to recipient countries. Their first project was a 64-kilometer road in Punjab Province in Pakistan. Lean Alfred Santos, "ADB, AIIB Sign Landmark Partnership Deal in Show of Cooperation," *Devex*, May 3, 2016, https://www.devex.com/news/adb-aiib-sign-landmark-partnership-deal-in-show-of-cooperation-88112. At the opening of the ADB's annual meeting in May 2017, Nakao emphasized that the ADB and AIIB would cooperate rather than compete with each other. See Tetsushi Kajimoto, "ADB Chief Seeks to Cooperate, Not Compete, with China-Led OBOR, AIIB," *Reuters*, May 4, 2017, https://www.reuters.com/article/us-adb-asia-nakao/adb-chief-seeks-to-cooperate-not-compete-with-china-led-obor-aiib-idUSKBN1800AS.

Similarly, Tokyo has been skeptical of China's ambitions in its Belt and Road Initiative (BRI), yet has sent high-level delegations to participate in BRI meetings. During a meeting in Beijing in October 2018, Xi and Abe agreed to cooperate on infrastructure projects that each could claim were deserving of support as a means of demonstrating the possibility that Chinese and Japanese standards for infrastructure development projects could be aligned.[21]

The Abe government has spent most of its energy advocating for its alternative to China's efforts, the "free and open Indo-Pacific" vision. This conception relies partly on giving priority to other Asian democracies, but the scope extends expansively to "three continents, two oceans," referencing the need to build ties between Asia, Australia, and Africa and to connect the many ports of the Pacific and Indian Oceans. Economic investment in infrastructure building across Southeast Asia by the Japanese government continues to top that from China, and the Abe cabinet has worked to offer an alternative, reliably high-quality infrastructure option for nations looking for development assistance.[22] In this effort, Japan's long-standing ties to Southeast Asia have served it well. Australia and India, in addition to the United States, are seen as Japan's primary co-architects of an Indo-Pacific that seeks to deepen economic, digital, and energy ties—what leaders in all of these countries now refer to as connectivity. Moreover, all four countries emphasize liberal norms and the rule of law.[23]

---

[21] In 2015, Minister of Finance Taro Aso argued that Asian infrastructure development was "not a zero-sum game" and that the ADB and AIIB could work together. See Tetsushi Kajimoto, "Japan Finance Minister Says Would Be Desirable for AIIB to Work with ADB," Reuters, March 23, 2015, https://www.reuters.com/article/us-asia-aiib-japan/japan-finance-minister-says-would-be-desirable-for-aiib-to-work-with-adb-idUSKBN0MK07T20150324. When Abe visited China in 2018, the Japan-China Forum on Third Country Business Cooperation met for the first time and produced over 50 memoranda of cooperation. For reference, see "52 MOCs Signed in Line with Convening of First Japan-China Forum on Third Country Business Cooperation," Ministry of Economy, Trade and Industry (Japan), Press Release, October 26, 2018, https://www.meti.go.jp/english/press/2018/1026_003.html.

[22] In June, private-sector analysts reported that Japan's infrastructure in Southeast Asia leads that of China, noting that Japanese-backed projects are valued at $367 billion, while Chinese-backed projects total $255 billion. See Michelle Jamrisko, "China No Match for Japan in Southeast Asia Infrastructure Race," Bloomberg, June 22, 2019, https://www.bloomberg.com/news/articles/2019-06-23/china-no-match-for-japan-in-southeast-asia-infrastructure-race.

[23] The free and open Indo-Pacific vision has been supported in joint statements between Abe and Indian prime minister Narendra Modi and between Abe and Australian prime minister Scott Morrison. See, for example, "Japan-India Joint Statement," Ministry of Foreign Affairs (Japan), November 11, 2016, https://www.mofa.go.jp/files/000202950.pdf; and "Joint Press Statement—Visit to Darwin by Japanese Prime Minister Abe," Ministry of Foreign Affairs (Japan), November 16, 2018, https://www.mofa.go.jp/files/000420402.pdf. For an overview of the U.S. Indo-Pacific strategy, see Mike Pompeo, "Remarks on America's 'Indo-Pacific Economic Vision'" (speech delivered at the U.S. Chamber of Commerce's Indo-Pacific Business Forum, Washington, D.C., July 20, 2018), https://www.state.gov/remarks-on-americas-indo-pacific-economic-vision. See also Sheila A. Smith, "Japan's Security Identity in the Indo-Pacific," in "Implementing the Indo-Pacific: Japan's Region Building Initiatives," ed. Kyle Springer, Perth USAsia Centre, August 2019, https://perthusasia.edu.au/events/past-conferences/defence-forum-2019/2019-indo-pacific-defence-conference-videos/keynotes-and-feature-presentations/pu-134-japan-book-web.aspx.

While military cooperation is not at the forefront in Japan's depictions of its Indo-Pacific vision, Abe has not been reticent in expanding the role of the JSDF across the region in support of this strategy. Alongside the U.S. military, the JMSDF has participated in exercises and planning with the Royal Australian Navy and the Indian Navy and has observed bilateral U.S.-Philippine Balikatan exercises. The JMSDF also has visited Vietnam, and in 2018 it announced an annual Indo-Pacific tour to multiple nations in South and Southeast Asia, including India, Sri Lanka, Indonesia, Singapore, and the Philippines. The Ministry of Defense also began to offer military assistance for maritime capacity building to the Philippines and signed a defense equipment transfer agreement in 2016. Under the agreement, Tokyo has provided retired coast guard vessels and training to improve the Philippines' ability to defend its waters.[24]

Japan has sought maritime partners as it seeks to cope with the changing military balance in Asia. The JMSDF continues to expand its regional cooperation with the United States. With the reinterpretation of Article 9, the JMSDF has been able to send its newest destroyers to participate in U.S. carrier taskforce operations across the Pacific, including exercises in the South China Sea.[25] But the JMSDF has also played a growing role in working with other global navies that share Japan's interests. For example, it has welcomed the role of NATO powers in helping monitor UN sanctions compliance in the waters surrounding the Korean Peninsula. As countries with Indo-Pacific interests, the UK, France, and Canada have all cooperated with Japan in ensuring maritime security as an important demonstration of the global security interests increasingly at stake in the region.

---

[24] See "Agreement between the Government of Japan and the Government of the Republic of the Philippines Concerning the Transfer of Defense Equipment and Technology," Ministry of Defense (Japan), February 29, 2016, https://www.mofa.go.jp/mofaj/files/000152490.pdf. For more details about the JMSDF's 2018 Indo-Pacific deployments, see Ministry of Defense (Japan), "Indo Southeast Asia Deployment 2018 (ISEAD2018)," https://www.mod.go.jp/msdf/en/operation/operation2018.html; and Ministry of Defense (Japan), "Indo-Pacific Deployment 2019 (IPD2019)," https://www.mod.go.jp/msdf/operation/cooperate/IPD19.

[25] In June 2019, for example, the JS *Izumo* joined the USS *Ronald Reagan* on a deployment to the South China Sea. See "USS *Ronald Reagan*, JS *Izumo* Sail Together in the South China Sea," U.S. 7th Fleet, Press Release, June 11, 2019, https://www.c7f.navy.mil/Media/News/Display/Article/1872904/uss-ronald-reagan-js-izumo-sail-together-in-the-south-china-sea. Regarding Japan's involvement in a U.S.-Australia bilateral exercise in July 2019, see "Talisman Sabre 2019—Largest Ever Bilateral Defense Exercise Begins," Department of Defence (Australia), Press Release, July 7, 2019, https://www.minister.defence.gov.au/minister/lreynolds/media-releases/talisman-sabre-2019-largest-ever-bilateral-defence-exercise-begins.

U.S.-China Rivalry: Opportunity or Setback?

In the past, Japan's leaders have tended to worry more about Washington and Beijing growing too close than about them competing for dominance. Japan's confidence in the reliability of the United States was shaken badly in the 1970s by the Nixon administration's opening to China, which Washington had negotiated in secret without consulting Tokyo. This left a lasting impression that U.S. strategic calculations could shift when opportunity arose.[26] More recently, President Bill Clinton's visit to China in 1998 that bypassed Japan gave rise to the phrase "Japan passing," reinforcing the perception that the United States could be fickle when it comes to China. In 2012, concerns about collusion between Washington and Beijing in forming a G-2, or group of two, resurfaced when the Obama administration seemed receptive to Xi Jinping's desire to build "a new type of great power relationship—one that avoided strategic competition and conflict."[27]

Past U.S. confrontations with China have also proved to be worrisome for Japan. In particular, crises across the Taiwan Strait have raised the specter of war very close to Japanese territory. While Tokyo supports Taiwan's independence, it has not been willing to support Taiwan's defenses directly. Only in 2005, when the United States and Japan announced that the alliance had "common strategic objectives," did Taiwan emerge on the strategic agenda at their 2+2 meeting.[28] Even then, however, the objective noted in the joint statement was simply put: the United States and Japan shared the objective of a peaceful resolution of differences between China and Taiwan. Japanese leaders have also been reluctant to confront China on its human rights record. Tokyo and Washington, for example, diverged in their responses to the 1989 Tiananmen Square crackdown. Tokyo did freeze loans to China initially, but it also sought to persuade other members of the G-7 that the long-term outlook for human rights would be more favorable once economic development was achieved. While Tokyo today still does not directly support Taiwan, it has become far more supportive of Taipei in the face of Beijing's increasing hostility. Similarly, while hesitating to intervene in domestic issues within

---

[26] Gerald L. Curtis, "U.S. Policy toward Japan from Nixon to Clinton," in *New Perspectives on U.S.-Japan Relations*, ed. Gerald Curtis (Tokyo: Japan Center for International Exchange, 2000), 23, http://www.jcie.org/researchpdfs/NewPerspectives/new_curtis.pdf.

[27] The Obama administration viewed this approach differently. At the top of the agenda for Obama was cooperation on North Korea, but he also expressed concern over China's maritime ambitions and the rising tensions with its neighbors over maritime boundaries and territorial claims. "Remarks by President Obama and President Xi Jinping of the People's Republic of China after Bilateral Meeting," White House, Office of the Press Secretary, June 8, 2013, https://obamawhitehouse.archives.gov/the-press-office/2013/06/08/remarks-president-obama-and-president-xi-jinping-peoples-republic-china-.

[28] "Joint Statement U.S.-Japan Security Consultative Committee," February 19, 2005, https://www.mofa.go.jp/region/n-america/us/security/scc/joint0502.html.

China, the Abe cabinet has not hesitated to emphasize the rule of law and Japan's identity as a democratic society.

To date, Japanese strategic planners and political leaders have interpreted the United States' shift to identifying China as a strategic competitor as a positive development for Japan. The Abe cabinet sees the Trump administration as being more willing to confront China and use its hard power to limit Chinese maritime ambitions. Meanwhile, Abe has also sought to steady Japan's relationship with China. In 2014, Abe's national security adviser Shotaro Yachi visited Beijing to work out the basis for the first meeting with Xi at the Asia-Pacific Economic Cooperation (APEC) summit. Four basic issues became the starting point for restoring government-to-government ties. The most important was the recognition that the risk of conflict between Japanese and Chinese forces in the East China Sea needed to be reduced.[29] Xi and Abe once more allowed economic ties to lead a process of diplomatic rapprochement.[30] Diplomatic recovery has been slower than in the past, though, as a result of the undercurrent of strategic tension that now characterizes Sino-Japan relations. In 2018, Abe visited Beijing for the first time since returning to the prime minister's office, and in 2019 Xi visited Japan for the G-20 meeting in Osaka. At the time of writing, Xi's first state visit to Japan is planned for 2020 and will coincide with the cherry blossom season.[31]

Yet this summitry has failed to reduce public suspicion of Beijing,[32] suggesting that unlike in past periods of tension, economic interests alone will be insufficient to rebuild trust. Current tensions in the Sino-U.S. relationship will also likely temper Abe's enthusiasm for a grand strategic gesture when Xi visits Japan. Tokyo is sensitive to Xi's new emphasis on techno-nationalism,

---

[29] For further discussion, see Smith, *Intimate Rivals*, 188–236.

[30] In May 2015 the deputy secretary general of the LDP, Toshihiro Nikai, led a delegation of three thousand Japanese business representatives to China. During one of their meetings, Xi made a surprise appearance. Nikai returned the following year as secretary general of the LDP to attend Xi's conference on BRI, carrying a letter from Abe to Xi. For an overview of the meeting, see "Xi Tells LDP's Nikai He Wants to Move Bilateral Relations in 'Right Direction,'" *Japan Times*, May 16, 2017, https://www.japantimes.co.jp/news/2017/05/16/national/politics-diplomacy/xi-tells-ldps-nikai-wants-move-bilateral-relations-right-direction/#.XcRv80VKhxg.

[31] According to a Ministry of Foreign Affairs readout of the Abe-Xi summit in Osaka, Xi accepted "in principle" an invitation to visit Japan in spring 2020. For the full readout, see "Japan-China Summit Meeting and Dinner," Ministry of Foreign Affairs (Japan), June 27, 2019, https://www.mofa.go.jp/a_o/c_m1/cn/page3e_001046.html.

[32] According to the 2019 Japan-China Joint Opinion Survey conducted by Genron NPO and China International Publishing Group, 45.9% of Chinese respondents hold a positive view of Japan, an all-time high since the survey started in 2005, while Japanese positive opinion toward China grew at a much slower pace to 15.0%. In comparison, in 2013, Chinese favorability toward Japan was 5.2%, while Japanese favorability toward China was 9.6%. See "The 15th Joint Public Opinion Poll: Japan-China Public Opinion Survey 2019," Genron NPO, October 24, 2019, http://www.genron-npo.net/en/archives/191024.pdf.

and in December 2018, following the United States, the Abe cabinet prohibited government purchase of Huawei and ZTE products due to security risks.[33] The arrest of Japanese citizens charged with spying in China also undoubtedly will create caution among Japanese companies operating there.[34]

Abe's summitry with Xi depends on the United States' military role in the Indo-Pacific. The Trump administration's emphasis in both the National Security Strategy and the National Defense Strategy on the threat posed by China, combined with the increased presence of the U.S. Navy and U.S. Coast Guard, has been reassuring.[35] The U.S. consideration of land-based intermediate-range missiles is also welcome news for Japanese defense planners, although the proposal has already drawn criticism from local officials in Okinawa.[36] The U.S. military's lead in the collective maritime response to China's assertiveness in the South China Sea expands the opportunities for the JSDF to build its professional experience with other regional militaries. Networked security cooperation helps Japan contribute to the regional military balance without raising fears about its intentions. Collective action, in other words, is not only an effective operational concept for balancing China's growing military reach, but it also provides a context within which Japan can apply military power to ensure regional security.

Conversely, rising tensions between China and the United States have Beijing more interested in repairing its ties with Tokyo. Diplomatic relations among the United States, China, and Japan have long exhibited a complex triangular dynamic. When U.S.-China ties are good, Japan struggles in its

[33] "Japan Bans Huawei and Its Chinese Peers from Government Contracts," *Nikkei Asian Review*, December 10, 2018, https://asia.nikkei.com/Economy/Trade-war/Japan-bans-Huawei-and-its-Chinese-peers-from-government-contracts.

[34] China has detained Japanese citizens, often for alleged spy activities. On May 22, 2019, Chinese courts sentenced a Japanese citizen charged with spying to six years imprisonment. Detentions continue despite the recent warming in diplomatic ties. Japanese were shocked by the revelation that a Japanese professor from Hokkaido University had been arrested in China and charged with spying in September 2019. Chief cabinet secretary Yoshihide Suga on October 21 stated that the Japanese embassy in Beijing had confirmed his arrest, and called on China to desist from these detentions of Japanese in China. For reporting on the incident, see "China Arrests Japanese Professor on Suspicion of Spying," *Guardian*, October 21, 2019, https://www.theguardian.com/world/2019/oct/21/china-arrests-japanese-professor-on-suspicion-of-spying.

[35] For a complete list of U.S. freedom of navigation operations conducted in 2018, see U.S. Department of Defense, *Annual Freedom of Navigation Report* (Washington, D.C., December 2018), https://policy.defense.gov/Portals/11/Documents/FY18%20DoD%20Annual%20FON%20Report%20(final).pdf?ver=2019-03-19-103517-010. See also White House, *National Security Strategy of the United States of America*, 2, 45, https://www.whitehouse.gov/wp-content/uploads/2017/12/NSS-Final-12-18-2017-0905.pdf; and U.S. Department of Defense, "Summary of the 2018 National Defense Strategy of the United States of America: Sharpening the American Military's Competitive Edge," January 2018, 1–2, https://dod.defense.gov/Portals/1/Documents/pubs/2018-National-Defense-Strategy-Summary.pdf.

[36] "Okinawa Governor Denny Tamaki Warns of Strong Resistance to U.S. Missiles in Japan," *Straits Times*, November 3, 2019, https://www.straitstimes.com/asia/east-asia/okinawa-governor-denny-tamaki-warns-of-strong-resistance-to-us-missiles-in-japan.

relations with China, and when U.S.-China ties are strained, Japan has often been at an advantage in its diplomacy with China. Today, it would seem that Xi is far more open to greater Sino-Japanese collaboration, despite the countries' serious differences over the Senkaku/Diaoyu Islands as well as competing interests elsewhere in maritime Asia.

Finally, Abe has been adroit at welcoming other countries into the Asian security equation. NATO allies such as the UK and France now work closely with Japan in the waters off China's coast to monitor UN sanctions compliance, but their navies are also present for some of the region's maritime exercises and dialogues. Bringing Europe into the conversation on maritime security in the Indo-Pacific offers added ballast to Japan's argument that the rule of law and freedom of navigation must remain core values not only in Asia but also around the globe. These opportunities for Japan to expand its security cooperation with other Indo-Pacific and global powers have been welcomed by the United States and have few downsides for Japanese diplomacy with China.[37]

Nonetheless, Japan faces considerable risk as the U.S.-China rivalry continues to escalate, and Abe's approach to the region has prioritized mitigating that risk. The Abe cabinet has diversified its strategic partnerships, deepening its strategic cooperation with other democracies in Asia while navigating this unpredictable moment in U.S. politics. As much as China's newfound power challenges Japan's strategic thinking, it has yet to alter the country's preferences. Several aspects of the U.S. confrontation of Chinese trade practices are welcome in Tokyo. For example, Japan hopes for a more unified position with the United States and European nations on monitoring the purchase of strategic technologies and encourages reform of the practice of requiring technology transfers by foreign firms that invest in China. However, Japanese investment in China exceeds that of the United States and Europe, and thus Japanese companies are far more exposed should increased U.S. trade pressure result in a backlash against all FDI.[38]

But the larger question of the systemic cost of rising U.S. protectionism is what worries Tokyo the most. A U.S. retreat from the premise of open global markets would be anathema to Japanese economic interests, and the political costs of acquiescing to a far more predatory U.S. approach to trade with Japan would be high for any Japanese politician. A scenario in which trade tensions between Washington and Beijing could devolve into open competition and

[37] "Seven Countries Join to Hunt Ships Smuggling Fuel to North Korea," *Wall Street Journal*, September 14, 2018, https://www.wsj.com/articles/new-u-s-led-coalition-to-track-illicit-fuel-shipments-to-north-korea-1536922923.

[38] FDI stock in China is compared using data from the Organisation for Economic Co-operation and Development (OECD). See "Outward FDI Stocks by Partner Country," OECD, https://data.oecd.org/fdi/outward-fdi-stocks-by-partner-country.htm#indicator-chart.

force Tokyo to put all of its eggs in one basket remains unlikely but is no longer inconceivable.[39] Should tensions continue to escalate between China and the United States, the risk to Japanese interests will only increase.

Japan's greatest risk is that the United States will step back from its long-standing offer of strategic protection. The territorial dispute over the Senkaku/Diaoyu Islands has brought this possibility to the fore. While alliance managers on both sides of the Pacific recognize the need for closer strategic cooperation, broader and sustained hostilities between China and the United States would inevitably force Tokyo's hand. Greater military effort and deeper operational integration of forces would be required. Short of military conflict, however, there are other security risks for Japan in an environment of heightened U.S.-China rivalry. Already apparent are differences in how China and Japan view the Korean Peninsula. China has teamed up with Russia to argue for an end to ballistic missile defenses in Asia, fearing that the United States, Japan, and South Korea will integrate their capabilities to reduce the value of the nuclear arsenals of both powers. Washington's decision to deploy more intermediate-range nuclear forces to the region will also increase the political pressure on Tokyo.

The growing rift between Tokyo and Seoul on their longer-term strategic futures may offer Beijing a greater opportunity to split these two U.S. allies.[40] Once again the legacy of World War II has become fodder for political discord. In late 2018 the South Korean supreme court ruled on several cases that involved plaintiffs who had been forcibly mobilized for Japan's war effort and ordered the companies involved to compensate Korean workers. The Abe cabinet argues that this violates the bilateral normalization agreement concluded in 1965 in which all claims were settled. The dispute between the Moon and Abe governments deepened in June 2019 when Japan served notice to South Korea that it was considering removing the country from its preferential list of trade partners due to concerns over lax export restrictions on chemicals and technology related to semiconductor production. In response, Seoul threatened to abandon a military information-sharing agreement, the General Security of Military Information Agreement (GSOMIA), that was set to expire in November. By the year's end, however, this downward spiral had been halted, as both governments sought to find

---

[39] At a Keidanren forum in July 2018, Japanese business leaders expressed concerns about the U.S.-China trade war and the possibility of automobile tariffs. For reporting on the forum, see "Kawaru Keidanren, kawaranu Keidanren" [A Changing Keidanren, An Unchanging Keidanren], *Nikkei Shimbun*, July 17, 2018.

[40] For background on the tense Japan-ROK relationship, see Brad Glosserman and Scott Snyder, *The Japan–South Korea Identity Clash: East Asian Security and the United States* (New York: Columbia University Press, 2017); and Sheila A. Smith, "Seoul and Tokyo: No Longer on the Same Side," CFR, Asia Unbound, July 1, 2019, https://www.cfr.org/blog/seoul-and-tokyo-no-longer-same-side.

ways to manage their differences. Nonetheless, divergent perspectives on the shape of Asia's future and on the longer-term strategic interests of Seoul and Tokyo have raised questions about whether these two U.S. allies still value their strategic cooperation.[41]

U.S. decision-making could also weaken the trilateral allied military cooperation. Trump gave credence to a far different arrangement of U.S. forces in Northeast Asia after his first meeting with Kim Jong-un, when he agreed that U.S.-ROK military exercises were provocative and that they cost too much money. A Korean Peninsula without the presence of U.S. forces would leave Japan more exposed militarily as the only Northeast Asian country with U.S. forces on its soil.[42] Furthermore, U.S. troop levels may be affected by the ongoing tensions between the U.S. and South Korean governments over cost sharing for U.S. troops in South Korea. If the Trump administration were to ever withdraw forces as a signal of displeasure, it would bode ill for Japan. Not only would the Abe cabinet worry about such a move reducing the deterrent value of trilateral military ties, but it also would worry that a similar threat of reducing U.S. strategic protection might hang over Japan's host-nation support talks with the United States.

Conclusion

The alliance with the United States has been Japan's preference for over 70 years, and rarely has its strategic benefit been called into question by either ally. The United States and Japan have weathered far more serious trade disputes without the security alliance being undermined. Similarly, Washington and Tokyo have debated and revised burden-sharing arrangements before, although not at a time of heightened military tensions in the region. But with a U.S. president openly criticizing the lack of reciprocity in the military roles of the alliance, the time may be at hand when Japanese strategic planners must decide how much they can do to ensure continued U.S. support for their defenses.

---

[41] See the following articles in the September 2019 issue of *Global Asia*: Sheila A. Smith, "Post-war Calm Can't Hold amid Present-Day Politics," 100–105; Cheol Hee Park, "The Destructive Escalation of Conflict Must Cease," 106–9; and Yoshihide Soeya, "How Ideological Differences Drove a Downward Spiral," 110–15.

[42] "China and Russia Close Ranks against U.S. Missile-Defence System," *South China Morning Post*, October 12, 2016, https://www.scmp.com/news/china/diplomacy-defence/article/2027171/china-and-russia-close-ranks-against-us-missile-defence; and Jina Kim, "China and South Korea's Simmering THAAD Dispute May Return to the Boil," East Asia Forum, February 2019, https://www.eastasiaforum.org/2019/02/22/china-and-south-koreas-simmering-thaad-dispute-may-return-to-the-boil. Trump referred to U.S.-ROK exercises as "war games" in a press conference following his summit with Kim Jong-un in Singapore. See "Press Conference by President Trump," White House, June 12, 2018, https://www.whitehouse.gov/briefings-statements/press-conference-president-trump.

At the end of the day, Japan expanding its military role within the alliance is far more likely than the country going it alone. Nonetheless, U.S. and Japanese planners must consider the worst-case scenario. If the United States were to choose to rescind its offer of strategic protection, Japan's options would then be far from desirable, both for planners and for the public. Three main options present themselves. The first option would be to develop an indigenous capability to deter aggression, including the acquisition of nuclear weapons. Japanese governments in the past have reviewed the decision to remain a non-nuclear state and continue to conclude that the nuclear option would likely reduce rather than enhance Japanese security. Two considerations inform this conclusion. The first is the likelihood that in exercising the nuclear option, Japan would increase its neighbors' perceptions that it is a threat and stimulate even further armament against it. Second, due to Japan's geographic location and topography, a survivable nuclear arsenal would be difficult to deploy. But should U.S. extended deterrence no longer be available, Tokyo may have no choice but to consider this option, even if it had to rely only on a submarine-launched force. Whether it would keep the Japanese people safe, however, can and should be debated.[43]

Should the United States prove unreliable, a second option would be for Japan to pursue even deeper strategic cooperation with other countries in Asia. The Indo-Pacific vision already lays out this premise of shared interest in democratic values, economic connectivity, and the implied commitment to collective action in the service of regional maritime security. Making this vision a full-bodied strategy could shift China's calculus. The question is whether partners like Australia and India would be willing to cooperate on containing China in the absence of U.S. military power. The Southeast Asian nations would most likely not see their interests best served by aligning militarily against China.

In the event that China creates sufficient disincentive for this type of concert of Indo-Pacific powers, Japan might have to consider some sort of strategic accommodation with China as a third option. A fully integrated military alliance may not be necessary, but acquiescence to a certain degree of Chinese dominance in the region would likely be required. Japan and China might reach an arms-control accord that limits the threat of the use of force in exchange for a division of labor in sustaining regional economic growth. In the absence of a United States willing and able to sustain its alliances, a

---

[43] For the Japanese debate surrounding the nuclear option, see Sheila A. Smith, "Realists, Not Rightists, Shape Japan's (Non) Nuclear Choice," Nonproliferation Policy Center, Working Paper, 2017; and Sheila A. Smith, *Japan Rearmed: The Politics of Military Power* (Cambridge: Harvard University Press, 2019). For a recent exploration of the steps it would take for Japan to develop nuclear weapons, see Mark Fitzpatrick, "How Japan Could Go Nuclear," *Foreign Affairs*, October 3, 2019, https://www.foreignaffairs.com/authors/mark-fitzpatrick.

reduction of military risk might be preferable to attempting an arms race with China. The economic payoffs could prove to be sufficient incentives, but the idea that Japanese decision-making could be fully subordinated to China's preferences seems inconceivable. That calculus might change, however, in what would be Japan's worst-case scenario for the future of Asia.

Both Washington and Beijing can impose significant costs on Tokyo—the former through disengaging from the U.S.-Japan alliance and the latter by its increasing ability to threaten Japanese interests. Open hostility between the United States and China would have systemic consequences, and Japan, given its proximity and economic vulnerability, would not be able to avoid paying a heavy price. Navigating this potential risk is what Japanese political leaders will have to do, however. Mitigating it will require responsive and nimble strategic leadership.

EXECUTIVE SUMMARY

This chapter analyzes South Korea's responses to the U.S.-China competition for global influence and discusses the drivers of South Korean foreign policy that intersect with U.S. and Chinese interests and strategic goals.

MAIN ARGUMENT

As the U.S. and China present competing visions of international order and strive for greater global influence, South Korea finds itself in a difficult position and is worried that its coping reflex of strategic nondecision may no longer be sustainable. At least four factors—North Korea, the domestic political divide between progressives and conservatives, economic interests, and Korean identity and desire for autonomy—explain why South Korea has so far adopted a policy of remaining indecisive in its relations with the U.S. and China. It has done so in large part to avoid the potentially unacceptable costs associated with choosing between the two rivals. As U.S.-China strategic competition intensifies in the future, South Korea will need to focus on building a solid geopolitical alliance with the U.S. that emphasizes political, rather than military, relations. At the same time, it must take care to ensure that its alliance with the U.S. does not contribute to negative spirals of Sino-U.S. tension.

POLICY IMPLICATIONS

- South Korean society as a whole should develop a vision for its place in the newly emerging international order and carefully examine its strategic priorities in the face of U.S.-China competition.

- Washington should not force a choice but should instead help empower Seoul politically to deal with Beijing's increasing influence on the Korean Peninsula.

- South Korea and the U.S. should emphasize the alliance's political, as opposed to military, value in shaping a new international order. At the same time, they must continually communicate what this alliance is and is not with China.

South Korea's Strategic Nondecision and Sino-U.S. Competition

Ji-Young Lee

As Washington has stepped up its hedging efforts vis-à-vis Beijing, these efforts to maintain U.S. global primacy have brought to the fore the role of the Republic of Korea (ROK) as an ally of the United States in its rivalry with China. Broadly speaking, the United States' strategic goals vis-à-vis South Korea have evolved. Responding to the changing international security environment, the United States now expects more from the alliance to help uphold a U.S.-centered global order. With Seoul's decision to accept the deployment of the Terminal High Altitude Area Defense (THAAD) system in South Korea, China began using its economic leverage to prevent South Korea from becoming more integrated into the United States' hedging efforts.

The United States' alliances with Asian powers have been at the heart of the postwar U.S.-led international order. The escalating Sino-U.S. competition for global influence poses particularly difficult foreign policy questions for South Korea, which has been an important member of the U.S. alliance system. Stephen Walt has argued, for example, that "a powerful China will not want the United States to have close alliances and a large military presence near its borders."[1] President Xi Jinping's "new Asian security" concept calls for "the people of Asia to run the affairs of Asia, solve the problems of Asia and

---

Ji-Young Lee is the Korea Policy Chair at the RAND Corporation and an Associate Professor of International Relations at American University. She can be reached at <lee@rand.org>.

[1] Stephen M. Walt, "Dealing with a Chinese Monroe Doctrine," *New York Times*, August 26, 2013, https://www.nytimes.com/roomfordebate/2012/05/02/are-we-headed-for-a-cold-war-with-china/dealing-with-a-chinese-monroe-doctrine.

uphold the security of Asia."[2] China's bold international undertakings such as the Asian Infrastructure Investment Bank (AIIB) and the Belt and Road Initiative (BRI) all speak to the new reality that "the possibility of systemic change is serious,"[3] thus presenting South Korea with new challenges as well as opportunities.

The questions that arise include the degree to which Seoul is willing to go along with Beijing's and Washington's aims, whether China is increasingly using its economic clout to weaken the U.S.-ROK military alliance, and how South Korea is responding to these early manifestations of the changing face of the international order. Both the Park Geun-hye and Moon Jae-in administrations responded to China's invitation to rewrite the rules of the international order with a mixture of interest and caution. However, even as Japan, another close Asian ally of the United States, has decided to align its strategy with the United States' Indo-Pacific strategy, South Korea to this day has adopted a strategy of avoiding these questions.

Seoul's overall response has focused on maintaining good relations with both Washington and Beijing in pursuit of two primary goals related to North Korea: denuclearization, on the one hand, and inter-Korean reconciliation and unification, on the other. To a certain degree, South Korea has always tended to approach relations with the United States and China through the lens of its relationship with Pyongyang, which is a cornerstone of its regional strategy. Under the progressive Moon government, the strong desire for a breakthrough in inter-Korean reconciliation has led Seoul to pursue rapprochement with Beijing after the deployment of THAAD in South Korea. At the same time, Seoul also endeavored to win Washington's support for a Korean Peninsula peace process—an effort that received unconventional and unexpected support from President Donald Trump. Despite President Moon's endorsement of the United States' Indo-Pacific strategy, South Korea's decision in August 2019 not to renew the General Security of Military Information Agreement (GSOMIA) with Japan because of deteriorating bilateral relations between the two countries and then to reverse its decision three months later just before the agreement deadline points to the lack of a clearly defined regionwide strategy rather than an outcome of a China policy per se. Overall, South Korea has been avoiding publicly spelling out how it feels about the rise of Chinese power even after China's economic retaliation over THAAD.

---

[2] Xi Jinping, "New Asian Security Concept for New Progress in Security Cooperation" (remarks at the Fourth Summit of the Conference on Interaction and Confidence Building Measures in Asia, Shanghai, May 21, 2014), https://www.fmprc.gov.cn/mfa_eng/zxxx_662805/t1159951.shtml.

[3] Ashley J. Tellis, "Pursuing Global Reach: China's Not So Long March toward Preeminence," in *Strategic Asia 2019: China's Expanding Strategic Ambitions*, ed. Ashley J. Tellis, Alison Szalwinski, and Michael Wills (Seattle: National Bureau of Asian Research [NBR], 2019), 4.

This chapter analyzes how the security competition with North Korea and pursuit of reunification, the internal divide between progressives and conservatives, economic interests, and the question of national identity all leave South Korean policymakers with important and yet often conflicting incentives in their dealings with Washington and Beijing. The first section discusses what U.S. and Chinese aims are vis-à-vis South Korea and whether they are compatible with those of South Korea in the geopolitical, economic, and military arenas. The next section then addresses how U.S. and Chinese goals are linked to key constituencies within South Korea, while the third section presents an analysis of South Korea's responses to U.S.-China competition for global influence. The chapter concludes by considering policy options.

South Korea's Place in the U.S.-China Rivalry

To understand Beijing's and Washington's aims and expectations regarding South Korea, it is necessary to first consider how structural factors such as geography and the U.S.-centered alliance system guide and constrain U.S. and Chinese approaches to South Korea. Specifically, this section will focus on how geopolitics, the dynamics of U.S.-China military competition over North Korea's actions, and the possible role of AIIB and BRI projects in advancing China's preferred rules for global governance all give South Korea a pivotal role in U.S.-China competition for greater global influence.

Geopolitics

In the words of Andrew Nathan and Andrew Scobell, "a country's geographical position is less malleable than its economic strategy, but it too produces a distinctive combination of security advantages and vulnerabilities."[4] Observers have typically characterized Korea as a "shrimp among whales," being caught between the strategic interests of China, Russia, Japan, and the United States. As misused as this phrase has often been, it is true that the Korean Peninsula's location is an enduring structural factor in the geostrategic calculations of both the United States and China. The peninsula creates a bridge or buffer between China and maritime powers such as the United States and Japan. Whenever there has been a major war in Northeast Asia that involved clashes between continental and maritime powers—from the Japanese invasions of Korea in 1592–98, to the First Sino-Japanese War in 1894–95, to the Korean War in 1950–53—it

---

[4] Andrew J. Nathan and Andrew Scobell, *China's Search for Security* (New York: Columbia University Press, 2012), 13.

either took place on or included competition for the Korean Peninsula. It is important to remember that the Korean War inflamed hostilities between the United States and China. The United States entered the war to aid South Korea as a principal participant of the UN force, and China entered to aid North Korea. An armistice agreement was signed but not a permanent peace treaty, and it is no coincidence that nearly 70 years later these same countries are dealing with North Korea's nuclear weapons and missile programs.

To the United States, the U.S.-ROK alliance is critical in terms of the United States' power projection in Asia. In 1953, the two sides signed a mutual defense treaty with one clear strategic rationale in mind—"to defend themselves against external armed attack."[5] Broadly speaking, the basic bargain between Washington and Seoul was one that exemplified the postwar U.S. liberal international order. The United States provided South Korea with security protection and market access in return for basing rights on the peninsula.[6] During much of the Cold War, South Korea's intense military confrontation with North Korea and the United States' strategy to contain the spread of Communism aligned the two allies' strategic interests, setting North Korea, the Soviet Union, and China on the opposite side of the regional security architecture.

The U.S.-ROK alliance is unique today in that North Korea remains an active security threat, even after the end of the Cold War. This threat has only increased with Pyongyang's programs to develop weapons of mass destruction and their delivery systems, as well as conventional capabilities. In 2009, Washington and Seoul adopted the Joint Vision for the Alliance of the United States of America and the Republic of Korea and sought to expand the alliance's scope to address regional and global challenges, such as peacekeeping, counterterrorism, nonproliferation, energy security,

---

[5] For the literature on the origins, role, and evolving nature of the U.S.-ROK alliance, see Ralph A. Cossa and Alan Oxley, "The U.S.-Korea Alliance," in *America's Asian Alliances*, ed. Robert D. Blackwill and Paul Dibb (Cambridge: MIT Press, 2000), 61–86; Katharine H. Moon, *Sex among Allies: Military Prostitution in U.S.-Korea Relations* (New York: Columbia University Press, 1997); Gi-wook Shin, *One Alliance, Two Lenses: U.S.-Korea Relations in a New Era* (Stanford: Stanford University Press, 2010); and Victor D. Cha, *Powerplay: Origins of the American Alliance System in Asia* (Princeton: Princeton University Press, 2016).

[6] On the U.S.-centered hegemonic order in postwar East Asia, see G. John Ikenberry, "American Hegemony and East Asian Order," *Australian Journal of International Affairs* 58, no. 3 (2004): 353–67; Evelyn Goh, *The Struggle for Order: Hegemony, Hierarchy, and Transition in Post–Cold War East Asia* (Oxford: Oxford University Press, 2013); Amitav Acharya, "Norm Subsidiarity and Regional Orders: Sovereignty, Regionalism, and Rule-Making in the Third World," *International Studies Quarterly* 55, no. 1 (2011): 95–123; and Ji-Young Lee, "Contested American Hegemony and Regional Order in Postwar Asia: The Case of Southeast Asia Treaty Organization," *International Relations of the Asia-Pacific* 19, no. 2 (2019): 237–67.

climate change, and development assistance.[7] In June 2017, Presidents Trump and Moon agreed to advance the comprehensive strategic alliance as global partners.[8]

It is important to note, however, that geopolitical considerations such as deterring North Korean provocations and pursuing denuclearization have continued to be the *raison d'être* of the U.S.-ROK alliance and its management. Consider, for example, North Korea's sinking of the South Korean navy vessel *Cheonan* in March 2010 and shelling of Yeonpyeong Island in November that same year. In September 2010, Seoul placed sanctions on Iran as part of the U.S.-led global nonproliferation effort, despite the fact that Iran was South Korea's largest export market in the Middle East. This decision was made in consideration of the strength of the U.S.-ROK alliance against the backdrop of its own effort to lead the international community toward pressuring North Korea after the *Cheonan* incident.[9] To this day, the Mutual Defense Treaty "remains the cornerstone of the U.S.-ROK security relationship," as the joint vision document released in 2009 describes it.[10]

China is located at the center of the Asian continent and neighbors several countries with which it has had military conflicts, including Japan, South Korea, India, Vietnam, Russia, and Taiwan. This geographic position explains much of China's Korea policy, which prioritizes stability over other objectives.[11] First, China's policies toward the Korean Peninsula are often an outcome of its strategies toward another great power, the United States. What this means is that Beijing's frustrations with Pyongyang's provocative behavior, which has destabilized the region and resulted in international criticism directed at China, have not translated into policy changes that increase pressure on North Korea and are not likely to do so, at least not to the extent that will risk destabilizing North Korea. From Beijing's geostrategic point of view, economic dependence by North Korea on China today can be used as future political leverage when Beijing seeks to influence Pyongyang's

---

[7] "Joint Vision for the Alliance of the United States of America and the Republic of Korea," White House, Office of the Press Secretary, Press Release, June 16, 2009, https://obamawhitehouse.archives.gov/the-press-office/joint-vision-alliance-united-states-america-and-republic-korea.

[8] "Joint Statement between the United States and the Republic of Korea," White House, Press Release, June 30, 2017, https://www.whitehouse.gov/briefings-statements/joint-statement-united-states-republic-korea.

[9] Choe Sang-hun, "South Korea Aims Sanctions at Iran," *New York Times*, September 8, 2010, https://www.nytimes.com/2010/09/09/world/asia/09korea.html; and Victor Cha and Ellen Kim, "Smooth Sailing in the Wake of the *Cheonan*," *Comparative Connections* 12, no. 3 (2010): 41–48.

[10] "Joint Vision for the Alliance of the United States of America and the Republic of Korea."

[11] See, for example, Cui Liru, "Chaoxianbandao anquan wenti: Zhongguo de zuoyong" [The Question of Security of the Korean Peninsula: The Role of China], *Xiandai guoji guanxi* 9 (2006): 42–47; and Nathan and Scobell, *China's Search for Security*, 15–18.

behavior in its favor.[12] Beijing will likely endeavor to maintain good political relations with North Korea as an insurance policy for any future developments concerning the Korean Peninsula, especially in its dealings with Washington.

Second, China has consistently expressed its opposition to the presence of U.S. forces in Asia as a sign of the United States' pursuit of hegemony in a challenge to China's sovereignty. The view that China's strategy is to kick the United States out of Asia has been gaining more currency in the last decade or so. It is worth remembering, however, that despite its growing economic and military capabilities, China's overall approach to South Korea's security ties with the United States has so far rested on the policy of noninterference, due in large part to the U.S.-ROK alliance's contribution to the stability of the Korean Peninsula against North Korea's provocations.[13] However, if the Sino-U.S. rivalry intensifies further, this may no longer be the case. Among other factors, whether China may try to actively weaken and even dismantle the United States' alliance with South Korea, and when it may choose to do so, depend in part on how vulnerable China feels from its geographic proximity to the Korean Peninsula. China would regard a scenario in which U.S. Forces Korea are stationed in a unified Korea, especially on the northern part of the peninsula, as hostile to its strategic interests.

North Korea's Challenges and the United States' Pursuit of Global Military Primacy

According to the U.S. Department of Defense's *Indo-Pacific Strategy Report* published in June 2019, the United States' commitment to the stability and prosperity of the region will be made through preparedness, partnerships, and the promotion of a networked region.[14] The Trump administration's expectations for South Korea as an ally are contained in the Indo-Pacific strategy concept, which is focused on maintaining global military primacy vis-à-vis China and Russia. In support of this goal, in December 2018 President Trump signed the Asia Reassurance Initiative Act (ARIA) "to develop a long-term strategic vision and a comprehensive, multifaceted, and principled United States policy for the Indo-Pacific region." ARIA assessed that North Korea's acceleration of its nuclear and ballistic

---

[12] This logic can be found in Albert O. Hirschman, *National Power and the Structure of Foreign Trade* (Berkeley: University of California Press, 1945).

[13] Robert Sutter, "China's Approach to the U.S.-ROK Alliance—Background, Status, Outlook," *International Journal of Korean Studies* 10, no. 2 (2006): 125–42.

[14] U.S. Department of Defense, *Indo-Pacific Strategy Report: Preparedness, Partnerships, and Promoting a Networked Region* (Washington, D.C., June 2019), https://media.defense.gov/2019/Jul/01/2002152311/-1/-1/1/DEPARTMENT-OF-DEFENSE-INDO-PACIFIC-STRATEGY-REPORT-2019.PDF.

missile capabilities challenges "the core tenets of the United States–backed international system."[15] According to the Department of Defense report, North Korea is a rogue state in the Indo-Pacific strategic landscape and possesses missiles "capable of striking the continental United States with a nuclear or conventional payload."[16]

One of the core elements of the Indo-Pacific strategy is to reinforce the United States' commitment to developing its alliances into a networked security architecture while sharing more costs and responsibilities with its allies. As an established ally, South Korea is an important part of the United States' force multiplier that can improve and complement the U.S. ability to deter North Korea's nuclear and missile capabilities by "leveraging [their] complementary forces, unique perspectives, regional relationships and information capabilities."[17] This emphasis on alliances, the U.S.-ROK-Japan trilateral security partnership, and a regionalized deterrence structure itself is not new. The broad range of deterrence challenges that U.S. policymakers saw as coming from North Korea—including provocations and low-level conflicts, combat operations by countries exploiting newly acquired nuclear and missile capabilities, and potential nuclear attacks on the homeland of the United States or its allies—compelled the Obama administration to deploy regional ballistic missile defense assets at various points in the missiles' potential trajectories across the region.[18] This policy materialized in the form of efforts to integrate air and missile defense capabilities and information sharing with U.S. partners in the region, including the deployment of THAAD in South Korea and the joint development of the SM-3 interceptor with Japan. The United States' missile defense systems in East Asia are, therefore, directly linked to the strengthening of the U.S. alliance system.

The Trump administration differs from the previous administrations in that the United States now explicitly labels China as a revisionist power that uses economic means to advance its strategic interests. North Korean provocations have increasingly had the effect of shifting the status quo of U.S.-China relations for the worse. The controversy surrounding the deployment of the THAAD system in South Korea and China's response can be understood in this broader context of North Korea's actions and U.S.-China military competition. Beijing views the system as a network

---

[15] U.S. Congress, Senate Foreign Relations Committee, *Asia Reassurance Initiative Act of 2018*, 115th Cong., 2nd sess., 2018, https://www.govinfo.gov/content/pkg/BILLS-115s2736enr/pdf/BILLS-115s2736enr.pdf.

[16] U.S. Department of Defense, *Indo-Pacific Strategy Report*, 12.

[17] Ibid., 16.

[18] Brad Roberts, "On the Strategic Value of Ballistic Missile Defense," Institut Français des Relations Internationales (IFRI), IFRI Proliferation Papers, no. 50, June 2014.

of sensors and interceptors deployed across the region and is wary of its potential future uses against China. The United States, by contrast, sees THAAD as a limited deployment of ballistic missile defenses and emphasizes the system's inability to intercept all of China's nuclear-armed intercontinental ballistic missiles.

Concurrently, the United States has been raising its expectations for its South Korean ally to join its hedging efforts against China, which are designed to preserve the U.S. military and geopolitical primacy in Asia. China believes that if the Korean Peninsula were to fall under the military influence of another great power, various strategic points in China would be vulnerable to foreign pressure, narrowing the range of choices available to it. Chinese strategists further argue that the Korean Peninsula is on the front line of the United States' strategy of containing China in geographic terms.[19]

From the perspective of ROK relations with China, a South Korean decision to fully join the United States' Indo-Pacific strategy could have the following implications. First, depending on the intensity of the U.S.-China competition, the geostrategic proximity of China to North Korea could further heighten China's sense of vulnerability to U.S.-ROK alliance activities. Beijing may be incentivized to tighten relations with Pyongyang to have more leverage over its behavior. Second, when the United States and South Korea conduct joint exercises and combined operations designed to deter North Korea, China would likely increase its criticism of the U.S.-ROK alliance as attempting to encircle China—especially if these activities are conducted with Japan.

The AIIB and BRI

The AIIB and BRI are multilateral development initiatives that can possibly complement other postwar U.S.-led multilateral institutions such as the World Bank. However, the decisions by South Korea and other U.S. allies regarding whether to join these initiatives must be understood in a highly politicized context in part because of China's change in its approach to international affairs. Institution building is a clear signal of China's aspirations to play a more prominent role in global governance. Both BRI and the AIIB are part of President Xi Jinping's "striving for achievement" strategy, designed

---

[19] Liu Xuelian and Huo Xuehui, "Zhongguo zai Chaoxian bandao de diyuan anquan zhanlue fenxi" [An Analysis of China's Geopolitical Security Strategy in the Korean Peninsula], *Dongbeiya Luntan* 16, no. 5 (2007): 50–56. On China's strategy of dealing with the U.S. alliance system in East Asia, see Zhou Jianren, "Dongmeng lilun yu meiguo chongfan yatai tongmeng zhanlüe yingdui" [Coping with America's Alliance Strategy within the Context of the Rebalancing to Asia and the Pacific], *Dangdai Yazhou* 4 (2015): 26–54; and Zhou Fangyin, "Meiguo de Yatai tongmeng tixi yu Zhoungguo de yingdui" [The U.S. Asia-Pacific Alliance System and China's Policy Options], *Shijie jingji yu zhengzhi* 11 (2013): 4–24.

to shape the international environment into one conducive to realizing "the great renewal of the Chinese nation."[20] Shortly after the launch of the AIIB in 2016, he stated that "one of [China's] priorities is to take an active part in global governance, pursue mutually beneficial cooperation, assume international responsibilities and obligations, and expand convergence of interests with other countries and forge a community of shared future for mankind."[21]

President Xi invited South Korea to join the AIIB during his first visit to Seoul in July 2014. This state visit had a high degree of symbolism because it was the first time that a Chinese president had visited South Korea before visiting North Korea. The itinerary also included only one country, showing the rapport between Presidents Xi and Park Geun-hye at that time. The ROK did not immediately join the bank, but when it did, the country announced that through its membership it would help the AIIB set "high level standards that are in line with those of existing multilateral development banks in responsibility, transparency, governance, and debt sustainability."[22] Within South Korea, those who were in favor of joining the AIIB understood the benefit of membership in terms of supporting South Korean companies' bids on Asian infrastructure projects in the communications, construction, and transportation sectors. Membership could also help the country prepare for future unification with North Korea, which would require a large amount of funding for infrastructure.[23] Reportedly, North Korea's application to join the AIIB was rejected by the Chinese authorities.[24]

Originally called One Belt, One Road (OBOR), BRI is primarily an ambitious infrastructure investment initiative. Northeast Asia, at least for now, is not very much in the picture.[25] Officially, BRI highlights connectivity through building infrastructure networks and coordinating economic development strategies and policies, with the AIIB as one of the institutions in support of financing the initiative. Both BRI and the AIIB are international

---

[20] Jae Ho Chung, "Views from Northeast Asia: A Chinese-Style Pivot or a Mega-Opportunity?" *Global Asia* 10, no. 3 (2015): 22–26.

[21] Xi Jinping, "Work Together for a Bright Future of China-Arab Relations" (speech at the Arab League Headquarters, Cairo, January 22, 2016), http://www.chinadaily.com.cn/world/2016xivisitmiddleea st/2016-01/22/content_23191229.htm.

[22] "S. Korea Decides to Join China-Proposed AIIB," Consulate General of the People's Republic of China (PRC) in New York, Press Release, March 27, 2015, https://www.fmprc.gov.cn/ce/cgny/eng/ xw/t1249164.htm.

[23] Ko Chang-nam, "Asian Infrastructure Investment Bank and Korea's Position," *Korea Times*, August 4, 2014, http://www.koreatimes.co.kr/www/news/opinon/2015/01/197_162280.html.

[24] "Hanguk AIIB chamyeo uimineun?" [What Is the Meaning of South Korea's Participation in AIIB?] Radio Free Asia, April 3, 2015, https://www.rfa.org/korean/weekly_program/news_analysis/ sisakorea-04032015103216.html.

[25] Kevin G. Cai, "The One Belt One Road and the Asian Infrastructure Investment Bank: Beijing's New Strategy of Geoeconomics and Geopolitics," *Journal of Contemporary China* 27, no. 114 (2018): 832.

manifestations of Beijing's desire to provide an alternative to U.S. dominance and increase its own influence in the regional and global economic fields. The initiatives are also partly understood as a response to the Obama administration's strategy of rebalancing to Asia, which China viewed as aimed at both strengthening and expanding the U.S. alliance system in East Asia.[26]

South Korea has yet to join BRI. In 2013, around the time of the announcement of the initiative under the OBOR banner, the Park administration announced the Eurasia Initiative. This initiative was intended to build a network of infrastructure for transportation, goods, and energy to create new business opportunities and cultural exchanges from South Korea's southern port city Pusan to North Korea, Russia, China, and Central Asia. Initially the Park government was interested in pursuing this initiative jointly with BRI.[27] However, the political circumstances surrounding North Korea's provocations, the chilling effect that the decision to deploy THAAD had on the ROK's relations with China, and the changes in political leadership in South Korea all led to a different initiative under the Moon Jae-in government called the New Northern Policy. Amid worsening political ties, Chinese news media announced that South Korea had agreed to join BRI, but the Moon government denied these reports, further complicating the bilateral relationship.[28]

In sum, South Korea's strategic choices are relevant in multiple areas of the U.S.-China competition, encompassing geopolitics, the international economic system, and military affairs, among others. Specifically, Beijing's and Washington's aims in South Korea are conditioned by certain structural factors such as the geostrategic location of the Korean Peninsula, North Korea's

---

[26] Cai, "The One Belt One Road and the Asian Infrastructure Investment Bank." For more on China's responses to the United States' pivot, see Christopher P. Twomey and Kali Shelor, "U.S.-China Strategic Dialogue, Phase III: The Role of National Perceptions of Security Environments in Shaping Sino-American Nuclear Affair," Naval Postgraduate School, January 2008; Ralph Cossa, Brad Glosserman, and Matt Pottinger, "Progress Despite Disagreements: The Sixth China-U.S. Strategic Dialogue on Strategic Nuclear Dynamics," Pacific Forum CSIS, Issues and Insights, November 2011; Eben Lindsey, Michael Glosny, and Christopher P. Twomey, "U.S.-China Strategic Dialogue, Phase VI; An NPS and Pacific Forum Conference," Naval Postgraduate School, January 2012; and Michael Glosny, Christopher P. Twomey, and Ryan Jacobs, "U.S.-China Strategic Dialogue, Phase VII," Naval Postgraduate School, May 2013.

[27] Chorong Park, "Han yurasia inisyeotibeu, jung ildaeillo hamkke chujin handa" [Korea and China Will Pursue Jointly Eurasia Initiative and One Belt and One Road], Yonhap, October 31, 2015, https://www.yna.co.kr/view/AKR20151031044300002.

[28] "Chinese President Receives Credentials of 7 Ambassadors," Xinhua, May 28, 2019, http://www.xinhuanet.com/english/2019-05/28/c_138097429.htm; Soo-jin Chun, "Janghaseong, ildaeillo chamyeo uisae hwadeuljjak, han jang daesa anya" [China, Jang Ha-sung Says South Korea Intends to Participate in Belt and Road, and South Korea, Taken Aback, Denies That Jang Said So], Joongang Ilbo, May 29, 2019, https://news.joins.com/article/23483226; and John Power, "What Does South Korea Think of China's Belt and Road?" South China Morning Post, June 1, 2019, https://www.scmp.com/news/asia/southeast-asia/article/3012713/what-does-south-korea-think-chinas-belt-and-road-its.

growing military capabilities, and South Korea's status as an established ally in the U.S.-centered alliance system, making the future course of South Korean action pivotal for this rivalry. In the realm of Sino-U.S. military competition, North Korea presents a source of vulnerability to both sides due in large part to geographic proximity for Beijing and the threat of Pyongyang's nuclear weapons and their delivery systems to the nonproliferation regime for Washington. The degree to which South Korea will implement the United States' Indo-Pacific strategy or participate in China's BRI could facilitate or slow down these two rivals' pursuit of their own vision of international order in Asia.

Drivers of South Korea's Strategic Choices

Many factors determine South Korea's strategic choices when it comes to U.S.-China competition. According to Colin Dueck, a country's grand strategy is a "calculated relationship of ends and means…in the face of one or more potential opponents" that "involves the prioritization of foreign policy goals, the identification of existing and potential resources, and the selection of a plan or road map that uses those resources to meet those goals."[29] South Korea's prioritization of foreign policy goals and strategy for achieving them have lacked consistency due to four main factors that are not mutually exclusive: the sensitivity of public opinion to North Korea's actions, domestic political cleavages, economic interests, and the emphasis on South Korean sovereignty and identity. While the South Korean public generally favors Washington over Beijing, Seoul faces both split interests (i.e., a difficult choice has to be made about whether to prioritize national defense or the economy) and split politics (i.e., South Korean policymakers and political constituencies are divided between conservatives and progressives over foreign policy goals and priorities).[30] South Korea's articulation of its national interests in any given period tends to hinge not only on top policymakers' dominant ideological leanings but also on public opinion about North Korea's actions. A net assessment of all four factors suggests that Seoul is not likely to make the choice to take a decisively pro-China alignment against Washington but will continue to maintain a strong alliance with the United States, especially when taking into account other considerations such as South Korean views of democracy and U.S. and Chinese systems of government.

---

[29] Colin Dueck, *Reluctant Crusaders: Power, Culture, and Change in American Grand Strategy* (Princeton: Princeton University Press, 2006), 10, 1.

[30] The author gratefully acknowledges an anonymous reviewer's comments, including the terms "split interests" and "split politics," which helped her frame South Korea's incentives this way.

Public Perception and North Korea

South Korean public perceptions of the United States and China are an important driver of Seoul's strategic choices vis-à-vis Washington and Beijing. Public surveys show that South Koreans tend to determine whether China and the United States are friends to South Korea through the lens of North Korea. First, in surveys conducted by Seoul National University's Institute for Peace and Unification Studies, an overwhelming majority of South Koreans (73.8% in 2016, 74.1% in 2017, and 72.5% in 2018) answered that the United States was the regional country to which they felt closest. South Korean public support for the alliance with the United States has not been affected much by the transition from the Obama to the Trump administration (see **Table 1**). While the three major political groups—conservatives, progressives, and centrists—differ in their degree of support for the alliance, the difference is over whether to strengthen or maintain the alliance as it is rather than over whether to have the alliance at all.[31]

Second, differences in South Korean public opinion about the United States and China are in large part a product of how the two countries have responded to North Korea's actions in consideration of their own national security. The same survey shows that in 2018 66.1% of South Koreans believed that the United States would support South Korea in the event of war on the Korean Peninsula, while 29.7% answered that the United States would act in its own self-interest, an increase from around 22% during the Obama presidency (see **Table 2**). By contrast, South Korean perceptions of China have deteriorated after North Korean provocations due to differences regarding how to deal with North Korea. On the question of China's likely actions in the event of war on the Korean Peninsula, there is a prevailing notion among South Koreans that Chinese policy toward the peninsula favors North Korea. The percentage of South Koreans who believe that China would support North Korea in the event of war increased significantly from 30.4% in 2008 to 55.5% in 2010 and 62.8% in 2011, reflecting South Korean public disapproval of China's handling of the North Korean attack on the *Cheonan* in March 2010 and the shelling of Yeonpyeong Island in November 2010 (see **Table 3**). The percentage of those who answered that China would maintain neutrality decreased from 13.0% in 2008 to 2.8% in 2012. Likewise, South Korean perceptions of China were negatively affected by its handling of the deployment of THAAD. In 2017 and 2018, the percentage of South Koreans who thought that China would support South Korea in

[31] Haesook Chae, "South Korean Attitudes toward the ROK-U.S. Alliance: Group Analysis," *PS: Political Science and Politics* 43, no. 3 (2010): 493–501.

TABLE 1   The country to which South Koreans feel closest (%)

	2008	2009	2010	2011	2012	2013	2014	2015	2016	2017	2018
United States	60.7	68.3	70.7	68.8	65.9	76.2	74.9	78.3	73.8	74.1	72.5
Japan	9.4	8.6	9.5	9.1	6.8	5.1	4.3	3.9	5.2	8.3	4.5
North Korea	20.4	16.0	14.8	16.0	20.6	11.0	8.9	8.1	10.8	11.3	19.1
China	7.8	6.1	4.2	5.3	5.8	7.3	10.3	8.8	9.7	5.0	3.7
Russia	1.7	1.0	0.8	0.8	0.9	0.5	1.0	0.9	0.4	1.1	0.1

TABLE 2   South Korean perceptions of what the United States would do in the event of war on the Korean Peninsula (%)

	2008	2009	2010	2011	2012	2013	2014	2015	2016	2017	2018
Support South Korea	57.4	65.1	74.7	72.4	72.8	75.2	74.0	70.5	74.1	67.8	66.1
Support North Korea	1.4	0.7	0.7	1.6	1.8	1.6	1.8	4.9	2.4	3.4	2.4
Act in its own interests	37.4	32.3	23.0	24.1	23.8	20.9	22.6	22.6	22.1	26.2	29.7
Maintain neutrality	3.8	2.0	1.7	1.9	1.6	2.3	1.6	2.0	1.4	2.7	1.7

TABLE 3   South Korean perceptions of what China would do in the event of war on the Korean Peninsula (%)

	2008	2009	2010	2011	2012	2013	2014	2015	2016	2017	2018
Support South Korea	4.5	3.1	3.3	2.4	1.3	3.3	5.2	5.8	5.3	1.2	1.2
Support North Korea	30.4	38.5	55.5	62.8	58.3	49.7	42.9	46.3	46.0	53.0	51.7
Act in its own interests	52.2	50.8	37.4	31.0	37.5	41.4	46.0	43.4	42.9	39.7	41.4
Maintain neutrality	13.0	7.7	3.8	3.8	2.8	5.6	5.9	4.5	5.9	6.1	5.6

SOURCE: Dong-jun Chung et al., *2018 Tongil uisik josa* [2018 Unification Perception Survey] (Seoul: Seoul National University Institute for Peace and Unification Studies, 2018), 123, 142, 148.

the event of war on the Korean Peninsula was at a record low due to China's economic retaliation.[32]

The Conservative-Progressive Divide

A second driver is the political split between conservatives and progressives.[33] According to Bobbi Gentry, political identity is defined as "an inner narrative of one's political self. Identity is the story that we tell ourselves and others about who we are, who we were, and who we foresee ourselves to be."[34] The conservative-progressive divide in South Korea is multifaceted and has evolved in a manner that is interlocked with South Koreans' perceptions of the role that the United States has played in the contemporary history of the two Koreas. In general, when it comes to foreign policy issues, government officials, political parties, and individuals on the left with progressive ideological leanings have been more critical of the United States while being sympathetic toward North Korea as South Korea's counterpart for national reconciliation. Those with more conservative leanings have tended to prioritize the alliance with Washington and the upgrading of deterrence vis-à-vis Pyongyang over inter-Korean reconciliation.

South Korea's conservatives posit that the United States is an upholder of a liberal international order, a benign hegemon, and a provider of security against North Korea's hostile plans to unify the peninsula by force. Scholars like Cha Sang-cheol have argued that one of the greatest accomplishments of the first president of South Korea, Syngman Rhee, was to sign the U.S.-ROK

---

[32] Dong-jun Chung et al., *2018 Tongil uisik josa* [2018 Unification Perception Survey] (Seoul: Seoul National University Institute for Peace and Unification Studies, 2018), 122–24.

[33] The discussion in this section draws generally on the following works that discuss the topic in foreign policy. Sang-sook Jeon, "Chinmi wa banmi ui inyeom galdeung: Banmi reul tonghae bon inyeom galdeung ui yeoksajeok giwon gwa gujo" [Ideological Conflicts between Pro-Americanism and Anti-Americanism: Historical Origins and Structure], *Review of Korean and Asian Political Thoughts* 11, no. 1 (2011): 147–71; David Steinberg, *Korean Attitudes toward the United States: Changing Dynamics* (London: Routledge, 2015); Thomas Kern, "Anti-Americanism in South Korea: From Structural Cleavages to Protest," *Korea Journal* 45, no. 1 (2005): 257–88; Haesook Chae, "South Korean Attitudes toward the ROK–U.S. Alliance: Group Analysis," *PS: Political Science and Politics* 43, no. 3 (2010): 493–501; Byong-kuen Jhee, "Anti-Americanism and Electoral Politics in Korea," *Political Science Quarterly* 123, no. 2 (2008): 301–18; Kang-ro Lee, "Hanguk nae banmi juui ui seongjang gwajeong bunseok" [Analysis of the Development of Anti-Americanism in South Korea], *Korean Journal of International Studies* 44, no. 4 (2004): 239–61; Junkab Chang and Kun Kim, "1980nyeon dae choban hanmi gwangye ikgi" [Reading of South Korea–America Relations in the Early 1980s], *Korean Journal of American Studies* 38 (2013): 191–218; Jung-in Cho, "Sources of Korean Public Attitudes toward the U.S. and the Impact of Anti-American Sentiment in Electoral Politics," *Ewha Journal of Social Sciences* 25 (2011): 93–124; Kim Yong Cheol and Choi Jong Ku, "Hangugin ui banmi haengdong uido e daehan ingwa bunseo" [Analysis of Causes of Anti-American Behavior], *Korean Journal of International Studies* 45, no. 4 (2005): 123–43; and Jang-jib Choi, "Hanmi gwangye ui mirae: Banmi gamjeong e daehan dansang" [Future of South Korea–U.S. Relations: Thoughts on Anti-American Sentiments], *Journal of Asiatic Studies* 46, no. 1 (2003): 97–104.

[34] Bobbi Gentry, *Why Youth Vote: Identity, Inspirational Leaders, and Independence* (New York: Springer International Publishing, 2018), 19.

Mutual Defense Treaty in 1953.[35] This view is found mostly among those who tend to view North Korea as the South's main enemy, one posing an existential threat. The alliance with the United States is considered to be the backbone of both the country's national defense and the peace and security of the Korean Peninsula, a position that all administrations have maintained since the formation of the alliance. This position is common among the generation that experienced the Korean War and its aftermath because of the role that the United States played in the defense of South Korea during that period.

On the other hand, progressives embrace North Korea as a "brother" and often portray the United States as an outsider meddling in inter-Korean affairs. The emergence of progressives in South Korean politics has much to do with the working relationships that the United States had with military dictators such as Park Chung-hee and Chun Doo-hwan before the June 1987 democratization movement. These authoritarian leaders used anti-Communism as a weapon against the groups that challenged their dictatorships during the Cold War, leading many college students, political leaders, and individuals who fought for democracy to associate the United States with repressive authoritarian regimes. Specifically, anti-Americanism became a force in the South Korean political scene after the Gwangju Uprising in May 1980 when the authoritarian government used force against civilians in Gwangju with the alleged tacit approval of the United States, which had held operational control over the combined forces since the Korean War.

The "386 generation" (comprising Koreans who were in their thirties in the 1990s, attended college in the 1980s, and were born in the 1960s) first became a prominent political force during the Roh Moo-hyun government on the wave of anti-U.S. sentiments in the early 2000s. Some progressive groups argued that the United States was an obstacle to reunification and reconciliation with North Korea and that South Korea's military alliance with the United States could undermine the ROK's sovereignty and autonomy. After democratization, they maintained that the question of unification should be decided by the two Koreas without "interference from an outside force," a position that is also held by some who are identified as pro–North Korean (*chinbuk*).[36]

Whereas the conservative-progressive divide in South Korean attitudes toward the United States has ideological and historical roots, this is not so much the case with China. According to Cha Jung-mi's study on the impact of political ideology on South Korean perceptions of China, progressive governments tend to be more amicable to China than do conservative

[35] Bak Ji-hyang et al., eds., *Haebang jeonhusa ui jaeinsik 2* [Reconsidering the History of Post-Liberation 2] (Seoul: Chaeksesang, 2006), 288–92.

[36] Jeon, "Chinmi wa banmi ui inyeom galdeung."

administrations because their policy preferences on North Korea converge rather than because progressives are generally favorable toward China. She argues that those policy elites who hold anti-U.S. sentiments do not necessarily share a pro-China outlook on foreign relations but instead often share a focus on Korean autonomy from an outside power. If Sino-U.S. competition intensifies and Chinese power further grows, the domestic divide within South Korea will likely be more along the lines of what Cha describes as "autonomy versus anti-Chinese sentiments."[37]

For example, President Roh Moo-hyun, a progressive who prioritized engagement and reconciliation with Pyongyang over other policy goals, advocated a "balancer" policy—the idea that "the map of power in Northeast Asia could shift, depending on what choice we [South Korea] make."[38] This position was largely interpreted as friendly toward China and was also criticized by the opposition conservative party leader Park Geun-hye for damaging the alliance with Washington.[39] It is worth remembering, however, that before the THAAD issue, South Korea's relations with China during the Park administration were considered so strong that some policymakers and pundits in the United States and Japan were worried about the possibility that Seoul could be leaning toward Beijing.

To the extent that U.S. and Japanese policies toward North Korea focus on the strengthening of a trilateral defense cooperation with the ROK, South Korea's split politics have implications for the country's relations with Japan as well. In recent years, relations have tended to improve following North Korean provocations, as Tokyo, Seoul, and Washington increase their level of policy coordination to strengthen deterrence.[40] As will be discussed below, the worsening of bilateral relations in 2018 and 2019 has largely been caused by disagreements over identity and historical issues. However, recent disputes over radar lock-on, a South Korean court ruling on forced labor, Japan's export controls, and South Korea's position on the GSOMIA suggest that a North Korean provocation might no longer put a brake on disputes over history.

---

[37] Cha Jung-mi, "Hanguk ui dae jungguk insik e daehan inyeom ui yeonghyang: jinbo bosu ui dae jungguk insik chai wa inyeomhwa ui teukjing eul jungsim euro" [The Role of Ideology in Korean Perception toward China: Focusing on the Peculiarity of Korean Ideological Conflicts on Perceptions toward China], *Journal of Asiatic Studies* 60, no. 2 (2017): 46–80.

[38] Choe Sang-hun, "South Korea's 'Balancer' Policy Attacked," *New York Times*, April 9, 2005, https://www.nytimes.com/2005/04/09/world/asia/south-koreas-balancer-policy-attacked.html.

[39] For the former view, which is shared by Chinese analysts, see Jae-ho Chung, "China's Evolving Views of the Korean-American Alliance, 1953–2012," *Journal of Contemporary China* 23, no. 85 (2014): 425–42. For the latter view, see Choe, "South Korea's 'Balancer' Policy Attacked."

[40] See, for example, David Kang and Ji-Young Lee, "*Cheonan* Incident Overshadows Everything," *Comparative Connections* 12, no. 2 (2010): 127–34.

Economic Interests

South Korea's concern for its economic future is one of the biggest incentives for Seoul to maintain good relations with Beijing. As unpopular as China has become over its response to the deployment of THAAD in South Korea (see Tables 1 and 3), the two countries' economic interdependence will likely continue to make Seoul very reluctant to join any U.S.-led coalition designed to openly balance against China's power. Even before the normalization of diplomatic relations between Beijing and Seoul in the early 1990s, commercial interests and economic development provided both sides with strong incentives to keep good relations. South Korean business leaders were the ones to advocate closer Sino-Korean relations.

When President Park entered office, her first state visit to China in 2013 marked a change from the Lee Myung-bak administration's focus on the alliance with the United States and opened new opportunities for bilateral relations. The conservative Park administration joined the AIIB in 2014 and agreed to a free trade agreement (FTA) with China in 2015, despite deciding not to join negotiations for the U.S.-led Trans-Pacific Partnership (TPP). As noted above, some in the United States and Japan worried that Seoul was tilting toward Beijing at the expense of the U.S.-ROK alliance, especially after President Park attended China's Victory Day celebration in September 2015.[41]

Notwithstanding the rapport between Presidents Park and Xi, Sino-Korean relations deteriorated rapidly after Seoul's decision to deploy THAAD. China's retaliatory measures included canceling the simplified visa application procedures and reducing the number of Chinese tourists visiting South Korea. The airing of popular Korean programs was prohibited in Chinese studios. Individual companies such as Lotte, Amore Pacific, LG Cosmetics, and Hyundai Motors were targeted.[42] With Beijing's banning of Chinese tourist visits to South Korea on March 15, 2017, there was a 39% decline in March compared to a month earlier in February 2017.[43] According to reports by Hyundai Research Institute, South Korea would

---

[41] See, for example, Tom Wright, "South Korea Looks to Prosper in China While Staying Close to U.S.," *Wall Street Journal*, November 25, 2014; and Yong-in Yi, "U.S. Government Not Thrilled with Park's Attendance at Beijing Military Parade," *Hankyoreh*, September 5, 2015, http://english.hani. co.kr/arti/english_edition/e_international/707572.html. For a good discussion on this assessment, see Jae Ho Chung and Jiyoon Kim, "Is South Korea in China's Orbit? Assessing Seoul's Perceptions and Policies," *Asia Policy*, no. 21 (2016): 123–45.

[42] Jae Ho Chung, "South Korea's Strategic Approach to China (or Lack of It)," in *A Whirlwind of Change in East Asia: Assessing Shifts in Strategy, Trade, and the Role of North Korea*, ed. Gilbert Rozman (Washington, D.C.: Korea Economic Institute of America, 2018), 71–90.

[43] Adriana Diaz and Shuai Zhang, "Angered by U.S. Anti-Missile System, China Takes Economic Revenge," CBS News, April 7, 2017, https://www.cbsnews.com/news/china-retaliates-south-korea-us-thaad-missile-defense-lotte-and-k-pop.

have lost 400,000 jobs in 2017 as a result of these measures.[44] South Korea is far more dependent on trade with China than China is on trade with South Korea. In 2017, China accounted for 22.8% of South Korea's total trade, whereas China's trade dependence on South Korea that same year was only 5.8%. China is South Korea's top trading partner.[45]

South Korea's actions to mend relations with China after the THAAD controversy deserve special attention. First, President Xi's peripheral diplomacy on helping "turn China's neighborhood areas into a community of common destiny," based on the formula of distributing China's economic benefits to its Asian neighbors, is part of the strategic use of economic power to achieve foreign policy goals.[46] This offers a glimpse of the expected gains and costs of aligning with or against China. China's 2017 white paper conditions the economic benefits for small and medium-sized neighboring countries generated through economic relations with China on the expectation that they "need not and should not take sides among big countries."[47] From the Chinese point of view, South Korea's decision to accept THAAD is an example of Seoul siding with Washington against Beijing. More likely than not, China's use of sanctions was designed to prevent the ROK from being further integrated into the U.S.-led alliance structure in Asia.

When the Moon Jae-in government came into office, it sought rapprochement with Beijing, leading to a truce but not to the degree that Seoul had hoped. In October 2017, an effort to restore relations between the ROK and China resulted in "the Chinese side express[ing] its positions and concerns regarding MD [missile defense], additional THAAD deployment, Korea-U.S.-Japan military cooperation, and so on."[48] Seoul pursued what is often termed balanced diplomacy intended to create space for independent decision-making by forging friendly relations with both Washington and Beijing. Shortly thereafter, in an interview with international media, President Moon stated:

---

[44] Lee Seung-yoon, "Korea's '17 Financial Toll from THAAD Row with China to Near $16 Billion in Tourism Revenue Loss," *Pulse*, September 15, 2017, https://pulsenews.co.kr/view.php?year=2017&no=621635.

[45] Chung, "South Korea's Strategic Approach to China," 73.

[46] "The Central Conference on Work Relating to Foreign Affairs Was Held in Beijing," Ministry of Foreign Affairs (PRC), November 29, 2014, http://www.fmprc.gov.cn/mfa_eng/zxxx_662805/t1215680.shtml.

[47] "China's Policies on Asia-Pacific Security Cooperation," Ministry of Foreign Affairs (PRC), January 11, 2017, www.fmprc.gov.cn/mfa_eng/zxxx_662805/t1429771.shtml.

[48] For a good analysis, see Bonnie S, Glaser and Lisa Collins, "China's Rapprochement with South Korea: Who Won the THAAD Dispute?" *Foreign Affairs*, November 7, 2017, https://www.foreignaffairs.com/articles/china/2017-11-07/chinas-rapprochement-south-korea; and Chung, "South Korea's Strategic Approach to China," 82.

> For South Korea, the alliance with the U.S. is more important than anything in safeguarding our security....The relationship with China has become more important not only in terms of economic cooperation, but also for strategic cooperation for the peaceful resolution of the North Korean nuclear issue. That is why I am pursuing a balanced diplomacy with the U.S. as well as China.[49]

President Moon subsequently clarified that by "balanced diplomacy" he meant a more balanced approach by diversifying and expanding diplomatic efforts, including those vis-à-vis the United States and China.[50] Yet President Moon's pursuit of denuclearization and inter-Korean relations with both Beijing and Washington continued to prove difficult and signaled that his brand of balanced diplomacy has its limits.

His summit meetings with both Presidents Trump and Xi a few months earlier in 2017 illustrate South Korea's dilemma and responses vividly. On June 30, Presidents Moon and Trump agreed that the THAAD deployment was a joint U.S.-ROK decision that would be implemented. Four days later, North Korea launched a ballistic missile on July 4, leading South Korea to announce that THAAD would not be withdrawn. When Presidents Moon and Xi met two days after Pyongyang's missile launch, President Xi demanded that China's core interests be respected and that Seoul remove the key obstacle to restoring Sino-Korean bilateral ties. But Moon, having already decided that South Korea would keep the THAAD system and confirmed this position with President Trump, did not agree to this request. Instead, the Moon administration tried to delay the final decision on the deployment of the THAAD system by conditioning it on a general environmental assessment of the deployment site, while continuing to operate those batteries that had been deployed. Seoul knew that this measure was only a stopgap for a truce with Beijing to buy time to find a permanent solution.

South Korean Identity and Sovereignty

Finally, the historical narratives and public sentiments surrounding the issues of South Korean sovereignty and identity have a significant impact on South Korea's ties with both the United States and China. These have also been decisive factors affecting South Korea's relations with Japan, which in turn has implications for the United States' Indo-Pacific strategy. Earlier controversies over the deaths of two Korean girls who were hit by a U.S.

---

[49] Lim Yun Suk, "Cooperation with the U.S., Japan Important to Deal with Tension with Pyongyang: South Korea's Moon," Channel News Asia, November 3, 2017, https://www.channelnewsasia.com/news/asia/cooperation-with-the-us-japan-important-to-deal-with-tension-9373348.

[50] "Remarks by President Trump and ROK President Moon in Join Press Conference," U.S. Embassy and Consulate in Korea, November 7, 2017, https://kr.usembassy.gov/110717-remarks-president-trump-rok-president-moon-joint-press-conference.

military vehicle in 2002 or China's Northeast Project suggest that the South Korean desire for autonomy not only temporarily affects public opinion but also can result in more enduring perceptions of threats to Korean identity. With other conditions being equal, a future event that seriously threatens South Korea's sense of agency could be a game changer in Seoul's calculation of its strategic choices between the United States and China.

South Korea's responses to the United States and China tend to vacillate because North Korea's actions at any given moment can invoke two different conceptions of North Korea in the minds of South Koreans—as an existential threat and as a counterpart for reunification. Overall, perceptions of U.S. power and the alliance with the United States remain positive among South Korean policymakers and the public, particularly in the aftermath of North Korean provocations. However, as seen above, events and popular discourse that frame the alliance as eroding South Korean sovereignty and autonomy and impeding inter-Korean reconciliation can provoke anti-U.S. sentiments.

For members of South Korean society, unification is a national goal that they are socialized to take for granted. The ROK constitution states that "the Republic of Korea shall seek unification and shall formulate and carry out a policy of peaceful unification based on the principles of freedom and democracy (Article 4)." The constitution further stipulates that South Korean presidents "shall have the duty to pursue sincerely the peaceful unification of the homeland (Article 66)." Both progressives and conservatives embrace unification despite their differing views of how reliable and trustworthy North Korea is. According to the 2018 Unification Perception Survey conducted by Seoul National University's Institute for Peace and Unification Studies, between 2014 and 2017 approximately 30% of progressives, 20% of centrists, and 20% of conservatives responded affirmatively when asked whether North Korea can maintain dialogue and compromise as South Korea's counterpart in reunification. In 2018, after the 2018 Winter Olympics in Pyeongchang, support increased to 60% of progressives, 56% of centrists, and 40% of conservatives.[51]

Understanding the complexities of unification and other North Korea–related issues within South Korea enables us to see why Seoul prefers not to choose between Washington and Beijing and has opted instead for nondecision. On the one hand, the emphasis on autonomy is at the heart of the Korean discourse when discussing reunification. The July 4 South-North Joint Communiqué of 1972 stated that reunification should be achieved through the independent efforts of the two Koreas, peaceful means, and the promotion of national unity that transcends the differences

---

[51] Chung et al., *2018 Tongil uisik josa*, 74–75.

in ideologies and systems. On the other hand, Korean policymakers are well aware that reunification not only is a matter of inter-Korean reconciliation but also requires a security environment in which other powers such as the United States, China, Japan, and Russia do not assess that a unified Korea will undermine their own national security interests.

The desire for reunification with North Korea will continue to incentivize South Korea to be on good terms with Beijing as well as with Washington. At the same time, the Koguryo dispute in 2004 was perhaps the first significant instance in which South Korea began to seriously consider what a future with a rising China as a neighbor that shares its border might look like. Koreans have long considered Koguryo—an ancient kingdom that existed across Manchuria and the northern part of the Korean Peninsula from 37 BC to 668 CE—as the precursor to a fiercely independent Korean state. Chinese claims that Koguryo was a provincial vassal kingdom of China had a direct impact on South Korean threat perceptions.[52] Before the flare-up over Koguryo, a poll in late April 2004 showed that 63% of South Korea's elected ruling party members thought that China was South Korea's most important diplomatic partner. After the dispute, however, only 6% of South Korea's National Assembly lawmakers regarded China as the most important diplomatic partner.[53]

National identity and public sentiment in South Korea have implications for its relations with Japan as well. The nationalist tendency of the Shinzo Abe administration and some comments about Japan's imperial past made by Prime Minister Abe and his cabinet members have been perceived by Seoul not only as insensitive to the tremendous suffering that imperial Japan inflicted on Korea but also as threatening to South Korea's national security. Many South Koreans believe that Tokyo's real future intention is reflected in these Japanese political elites' remarks and actions over such issues as the Yasukuni Shrine, the so-called "comfort women," the Dokdo/Takeshima Islands, Japanese history

---

[52] For more on China's claims and South Korea's threat perceptions, see Peter Gries, "The Koguryo Controversy: National Identity, and Sino-Korean Relations Today," *East Asia* 22, no. 4 (2005): 3–17; Choe Sang-hun, "Tussle over a Vanished Kingdom; South Korea–China Dispute Could Affect Future Borders," *International Herald Tribune*, October 13, 2006; "The 2011 Survey of Public Awareness of Unification," Seoul National University, Institute for Peace and Unification Studies, 2011; and "South Korea in a Changing World: Foreign Affairs," Asan Institute for Policy Studies, April 2013, http://asaninst.org/eng/03_publications/report_detail.php?seq=100740. For discussion of an important earlier event, see Jae Ho Chung, "From a Special Relationship to a Normal Partnership? Interpreting the 'Garlic Battle' in Sino–South Korean Relations," *Pacific Affairs* 76, no. 3 (2004): 549–68; and Hwy-tak Yoon, "China's Northeast Project: Defensive or Offensive Strategy?" *East Asia* 16, no. 4 (2004): 99–121.

[53] "China or the United States?" *Korea Herald*, April 28, 2004; Lee Joo-hee, "Lawmakers Pick U.S. as Top Ally; Many Pessimistic on Economic Outlook for Second Half; *Herald* Survey," *Korea Herald*, August 16, 2004; Scott Snyder, "A Turning Point for China-Korea Relations?" *Comparative Connections* 6, no. 3 (2004): 109–16, http://csis.org/files/media/csis/pubs/0403qchina_korea.pdf; and Cha, "Hanguk ui dae jungguk insik e daehan inyeom ui yeonghyang," 73.

textbooks, and forced labor during Japan's colonial rule of Korea in 1910–45.[54] Historical considerations will continue to make Seoul wary of tighter trilateral security cooperation with Tokyo and Washington.

From the United States' point of view, however, how well South Korea and Japan can forge security partnerships and enhance interoperability as part of a regional security network will have a direct impact on how successful the U.S. Indo-Pacific strategy will be in dealing with the rise of Chinese power in Asia. Now more than ever, Japan-ROK relations are becoming a major stumbling block for the United States. Consider the fact that the implementation of the Indo-Pacific strategy rests on building a regional security network that connects existing allies. Precisely at a time when the need for close ties between South Korea and Japan is high, these U.S. allies are engaging in yet another round of bilateral diplomatic rows. What is new about the recent developments is that the disputes over history have spilled into the security and economic arenas, thus erasing the traditional boundaries of cooperation and changing the status quo for the worse.

Bilateral conflict between Japan and South Korea has far-reaching implications for the future regional order in Asia. First, diplomatic and political crises about history weaken the policy coordination efforts of Seoul, Tokyo, and Washington over North Korea's denuclearization. Second, never before in the recent history of Japan-ROK relations have the two countries used economic interdependence as a tool of politics to hurt each other to such a degree that they will also hurt themselves. But in July 2019 the Japanese government imposed export restrictions on three chemicals critical to South Korean high-tech manufacturing, and South Korea responded with retaliatory economic measures. Despite South Korea's desire to handle relations with Japan separately from relations with the United States, their sharp clashes on issues related to history have spilled over to create tension in the U.S.-ROK alliance.

South Korea's Response to U.S.-China Competition

Despite escalating U.S.-China competition at the geopolitical, economic, military, and institutional levels, South Korea has not actively debated or pursued a strategy designed to prepare itself for a post–U.S. primacy era. Its security competition with North Korea, its national goal of reunification, and

---

[54] In October 2018, South Korea's Supreme Court ordered Japanese companies to compensate South Koreans who had been forced into labor during Japan's occupation of the Korean Peninsula from 1910 to 1945. Soon thereafter, the Moon administration decided to formally dissolve the foundation that was set up based on the two countries' 2015 "comfort women" agreement. By the year's end in December 2018, Japan and South Korea were engaged in a dispute over the radar lock-on incident, which led to the suspension of all senior-level defense exchanges for the first half of 2019.

questions of national identity, geopolitics, and the internal divide between progressives and conservatives all leave South Korean policymakers feeling conflicted in their dealings with Washington and Beijing.

Broadly speaking, the continued centrality of the U.S.-ROK alliance, combined with the absence of a consistent China policy, suggests that strategic nondecision remains South Korea's primary response to the growing Sino-U.S. competition. Seoul has embraced the Indo-Pacific strategy, but without adopting a clear stance on issues such as the South China Sea and in areas like trilateral defense cooperation with the United States and Japan where it might appear to be taking sides between Washington and Beijing. President Trump, during his summit meeting with President Moon in November 2017, said that the US-ROK alliance is "a linchpin for security, stability and prosperity in the Indo-Pacific."[55] In July 2019, President Moon likewise stated, "We've reached a consensus to put forth further harmonious cooperation between South Korea's New Southern Policy and the United States' Indo-Pacific Strategy."[56]

Seoul is aware of the political significance of being part of the Indo-Pacific strategy, which designates China as a revisionist power, yet it has supported the initiative in consideration of the alliance. Further, the Moon administration has received unexpected help for its progressive agenda of reconciliation with North Korea from President Trump's unconventional style of negotiation. Leading up to the Olympic Games in February 2018, for example, Presidents Trump and Moon agreed to halt joint U.S.-ROK military exercises, which aids President Moon's efforts to improve his relations with Kim Jong-un. The Moon administration has thus been incentivized to support President Trump's agenda in the hopes of keeping the momentum of dialogue between Trump and Kim.

But the United States during the Trump presidency may not be viewed as a reliable enough partner for Seoul to fully implement the Indo-Pacific strategy and align with Washington more decisively. Such a decision would likely involve high political and economic costs for Seoul vis-à-vis Beijing. As unsustainable as strategic nondecision may be, especially in the event of intensified competition between China and the United States, South Korean policymakers and experts worry that Washington will withdraw U.S. forces or act in ways that ignore or harm South Korea's strategic interests. Not long

[55] "Joint Press Release by the United States of America and the Republic of Korea," White House, November 8, 2017, https://www.whitehouse.gov/briefings-statements/joint-press-release-united-states-america-republic-korea; and Sarah Kim, "Moon Signs onto Trump Indo-Pacific Strategy," *Korea Joongang Daily*, July 2, 2019, http://koreajoongangdaily.joins.com/news/article/article.aspx?aid=3064972.

[56] Jung Da-min, "South Korea Responds to U.S. Call for Support on Indo-Pacific Strategy," *Korea Times*, July 10, 2019, http://www.koreatimes.co.kr/www/nation/2019/07/356_272049.html.

ago, President Trump argued that maintaining troops in South Korea was too expensive and declared that he would like to bring them home. His "America first" strategy prioritizing alliance burden-sharing and the renegotiation of the Korea-U.S. (KORUS) FTA has created greater uncertainty in the U.S.-ROK alliance.

The Moon administration's response has so far been to seek to accommodate the Trump administration's requests as much as possible, believing that this is the best policy in the circumstances. President Trump's role in restarting the Korean Peninsula peace process vis-à-vis Pyongyang provided further incentive for President Moon to accommodate the United States' alliance demands. At the request of the United States, the KORUS FTA was renegotiated and updated in 2018 to allow U.S. carmakers to double the number of vehicles that they could sell in South Korea to 50,000 cars per year without having to satisfy local safety standards. After ten rounds of talks, South Korea agreed to pay $920 million for cost sharing in February 2019 for a one-year agreement, and there is currently no concrete plan to withdraw U.S. forces. But President Trump's demand that Seoul pay about $5 billion to share the cost of maintaining 28,500 U.S. troops puts strain on the alliance. If the mood of the U.S.–North Korea dialogue changes and relations cool again, with no prospect for mending, the idea that U.S. allies have to pay more for their own defense will shadow the progressive Moon administration, negatively affecting bilateral relations.

The United States has been pushing for a trilateral military partnership with the ROK and Japan since before the Trump administration, but without much success, due in large part to Seoul's reluctance. Washington expressed disappointment over South Korea's initial decision to withdraw from the intelligence-sharing agreement with Japan and encouraged the Moon administration to reconsider this decision. Although Seoul eventually decided to renew the agreement, mistrust between the ROK and Japan will likely continue to be a major factor in alliance management.

Second, an analysis of South Korean behavior with respect to the AIIB, BRI, and THAAD shows that South Korea is worried about both the actual and the potential risks to its economy should its relations with China sour again. For example, members of the Federation of Korean Industries who advocate free trade with China would not support policies that could reduce business opportunities with China. In May 2019, Huawei, a Chinese telecommunications equipment and technology company, was placed on the U.S. Department of Commerce's blacklist of foreign companies with which U.S. companies are prohibited from doing business. The Trump administration suspects that Huawei, in cooperation with the Chinese government, can plant malicious software to steal information from its users in the United States.

The United States began pressuring its allies in Asia to ban Huawei technology from their networks. Beijing, for its part, has requested South Korea not to sever trade with the company, while also urging Seoul to make the "right judgment" with regard to Chinese interests and security.[57]

More broadly, the export-driven South Korean economy is likely to undergo a big setback from the trade war between the United States and China as a result of increasing tariffs.[58] According to the Hyundai Research Institute, a 10% decrease in U.S. imports from China could mean a $28.26 billion decrease in South Korea's exports to China. The Ministry of Trade, Industry and Energy has downplayed the immediate impact of the dispute for the Korean economy based on an assessment that the dispute would not significantly affect Korean exports to either China or the United States.[59] Some of the options available to South Korean companies include moving production to other countries like Canada, Mexico, or even the United States.[60] South Korean companies have also considered Vietnam as an alternative because of its low labor costs or India to reduce dependence on China.[61]

Thus far, South Korea has not taken steps to comply with the U.S. requests related to Huawei in consideration of its economic relations with China. Although KT Corporation and SK Telecom have ruled out working with Huawei, the company still conducts business with Samsung, SK Hynix, and other Korean companies. LG U+ is one company that even uses Huawei for its 5G infrastructure.[62] The Moon administration takes the position that it respects corporate autonomy and that Huawei's role in South Korea's 5G network would not likely pose a threat to national security.[63]

---

[57] Jun-yong Ahn, "China Warns Korea to Make 'Right Judgment' in Trade Wars," *Choson Ilbo*, June 5, 2019, http://english.chosun.com/site/data/html_dir/2019/06/05/2019060501240.html; and Soon-chan Park, "China Warns Korean Firms over Huawei Boycott," *Choson Ilbo*, June 10, 2019, http://english.chosun.com/site/data/html_dir/2019/06/10/2019061001338.html.

[58] Shin Ji-hye, "U.S.-China Trade Disputes Weigh on Export-Reliant South Korea," *Korea Herald*, May 12, 2019, http://www.koreaherald.com/view.php?ud=20190512000164.

[59] Choi Ha-yan, "Trade Minister Says U.S.-China Trade War's Immediate Impact on South Korea Will Be Minimal," *Hankyoreh*, July 7, 2019, http://english.hani.co.kr/arti/english_edition/e_international/852314.html.

[60] Seunghyun Han, "South Korea's Options amidst a U.S.-China Trade War: Opportunities and Risks," *Journal of International Affairs*, November 19, 2018, https://jia.sipa.columbia.edu/online-articles/south-koreas-options-admidst-us-china-trade-war.

[61] Choi Hyun-june and Hong Dae-seon, "South Korean Industries Look to India as New Export Market amid U.S.-China Trade War," *Hankyoreh*, June 10, 2018, http://english.hani.co.kr/arti/english_edition/e_international/852719.html.

[62] Song Gyung-hwa, Hong Dae-sun, and Park Min-hee, "China Issues Warning to S. Korean Companies to Maintain Trade with Huawei," *Hankyoreh*, June 10, 2019, http://english.hani.co.kr/arti/english_edition/e_business/897311.html; and Kim Eun-jung, "Huawei Opens Its First 5G Lab in Seoul in Low-Key Ceremony," Yonhap, May 30, 2019, https://en.yna.co.kr/view/AEN20190530008500320.

[63] Kim Ji-eun, "S. Korea Decides to 'Respect Corporate Autonomy' in Response to U.S. Anti-Huawei Pressure," *Hankyoreh*, June 14, 2019, http://english.hani.co.kr/arti/english_edition/e_international/897954.html.

Conclusions

South Korea's foreign and security policy choices, despite having the potential to have a direct impact on U.S.-China security competition and to shape the future of the Asian regional order, have not led to the formation of a clear South Korean strategy for Asia. This strategic nondecision reflects Seoul's concerns that making a clear strategic choice between Washington and Beijing will come with unacceptable costs to its national security, relations with North Korea, and economy. Given that the U.S.-China strategic rivalry is expected to intensify for the foreseeable future, Seoul's strategic nondecision will not likely be sustainable. What, then, are the best policy options for South Korea and the United States?

First, South Korea should take a more proactive yet gradual approach to the shifting security environment in Asia and clearly articulate what its strategic choices are on important issues in U.S.-China relations. South Korea's strategic nondecision was designed to create room for Seoul to alter its decision-making depending on changes in the power balance and other circumstances in Northeast Asia. The risk of this strategy, however, is that South Korea could be marginalized or left out altogether from the process of shaping a new order in Asia. Further, this strategy works well only when both Washington and Beijing do not believe their national interests are negatively affected by Seoul's refusal to take sides.

Second, as Seoul works to make this policy change on its own, Washington should not force a choice but instead work with South Korean policymakers by empowering them politically, especially in their pursuit of the goals related to reunification and peace on the peninsula. Typically, alliances are stronger when allies identify the same country as their common enemy. However, due to the phenomena of split interests and split politics in South Korea, a U.S.-ROK alliance that focuses only on the military role of deterring and defending against North Korea as an enemy will turn the alliance into a crisis-management mechanism. Alliance managers should discuss the broader role that the alliance can play in creating peace and security in the region while promoting reunification and the peace process on the peninsula, in addition to the denuclearization and deterrence of North Korean military power.

It is important for U.S. policymakers to remember that the kind of threats that South Koreans feel from China are political rather than military in nature. One of the strongest arguments that can be made in support of South Korea's embrace of the alliance with the United States is geopolitical.[64] That is, the

---

[64] This idea can be found in Victor Cha, "What's Next for the U.S.-Korea Alliance," statement before the House Committee on Foreign Affairs, Subcommittee on Asia and the Pacific, June 6, 2012.

alliance is best understood as a mechanism to enhance South Korea's position and political leverage to deal with its neighbors, including China. Seoul and Washington could redefine and reinterpret the concept of a comprehensive strategic alliance by making it a geopolitical alliance tailored to the Korean context. This would be a reasonably good option for the United States, which could rely on Seoul as a solid, as opposed to a reluctant, partner in Sino-U.S. strategic competition without excessively provoking China. This approach would also take full advantage of the South Korean public's and policymakers' natural affinity toward the United States over China. This soft power–based approach is more likely to succeed and would be more sustainable than focusing only on approaching South Korea in a military sense, especially given the public's strong desire for autonomy and sovereignty.

Third, and related, the United States should understand that given the country's split politics, it is not politically sustainable for South Korea to join hands with Japan and other countries to form an explicitly anti-China coalition that is military in nature. Geographic proximity to China, the national goal of reunification, and economic considerations will likely prevent the ROK from openly pursuing this option, especially given that the United States may reverse its course of action when a new administration enters office. By the same token, South Korea is not likely to support China's regional and global ambitions. Beijing's response to North Korea's conventional provocations, economic retaliation for the deployment of THAAD, and identity-related bilateral rows have led South Koreans to be increasingly suspicious of China's intentions and to even conclude that the country would take sides with North Korea or act in its own interests in the event of a war between the two Koreas.

EXECUTIVE SUMMARY

This chapter examines how India manages the tensions between the U.S. and China vis-à-vis its own independent efforts of balancing China while maintaining some form of cooperation.

MAIN ARGUMENT

The intensification of the rivalry between the U.S. and China does not change the nature of the challenges to India's interests. It does, however, exacerbate the tensions and potential contradictions within Indian foreign policy. This is particularly true with regard to India's relations with China. China's growing rivalry with the U.S. does not substantially alter its differences with India, but in a context of growing polarization, this rivalry tends to transform those differences into leverage points for China to try to weaken the links between India and the U.S. Similarly, it does not affect the congruence between U.S. and Indian objectives but does strain the condition under which this congruence could be translated into actual cooperation.

POLICY IMPLICATIONS

- India's strategic, political, and economic interests converge with those of the U.S., and New Delhi will not do anything that may undermine Washington's position vis-à-vis China so long as U.S. policies will not affect major Indian interests. It could therefore be counterproductive for the U.S. to be excessively transactional or try to coerce India into policies that are detrimental to its regional interests.

- Possible U.S. frustration will be subtly compensated for by India mobilizing capacity around U.S. objectives in places where the U.S. is quasi-absent. The inclusion of the East African shores in the Indian concept of the Indo-Pacific should be understood in this perspective.

- The slow pace of Indian economic reforms generates questions regarding India's ability to manage its power asymmetry with China. The U.S. should therefore manage its own expectations and incentivize, rather than coerce, India to reform.

Managing U.S.-China Rivalry: India's Non-escalatory Reinforcement

Frédéric Grare

Despite a long tradition of nonalignment, India has never been a neutral observer of U.S.-China strategic competition but has concerns of its own vis-à-vis China. Persisting territorial disputes and painful memories of the 1962 Sino-Indian War make the prospect of being left alone to face Beijing particularly daunting. Moreover, the spectacular increase of China's power following the reforms initiated in the early 1980s led New Delhi to worry about the possibility of a Chinese-led regional order. The fear of a powerful and potentially hegemonic China therefore has been a strong motivation for India to look for new partnerships, including with the United States. Yet rapprochement would have been impossible without the United States having similar concerns that Chinese hegemonic designs in Asia constitute a challenge to U.S. interests in the region.

Such a challenge remained a distant prospect when the rapprochement was initiated, and it competed in U.S. political thinking with the perception that an increasingly prosperous China could be socialized over time into Western norms and values. Moreover, because the idea that a strong India served the strategic interest of the United States prevailed at the time, Washington was willing to support it without expectations of reciprocity. India thus could maintain a carefully calibrated public posture vis-à-vis China while growing closer to the United States. In such a context, India became the desired yet inaccessible prize in U.S.-China strategic competition. This enabled the country to simultaneously engage and balance China, including in military matters, while maintaining a strong degree of political and strategic autonomy.

Frédéric Grare is a Nonresident Senior Fellow in the South Asia Program at the Carnegie Endowment for International Peace. He can be reached at <fgrare2@gmail.org>.

However, the increasingly open and intensifying competition between the United States and China has altered the strategic environment in which India has defined its foreign policy since the end of the Cold War. U.S. economic disillusion with China as a result of its unfair trade practices, intellectual property theft, and forced technology transfer policies, combined with China's aggressive behavior, malicious cyberactivities, and influence operations overseas, has led the United States to openly "take up the challenge of the long-term strategic competition with China."[1] The resulting regional polarization tends to turn every relationship with the two giants into a zero-sum game and affects every partner of India in Asia, thereby limiting New Delhi's own space to maneuver and eroding some of the pillars of its regional policy.

This chapter examines how India manages the growing tensions between the United States and China vis-à-vis its own independent efforts of balancing China while maintaining some level of economic cooperation. It argues that the new intensity of the U.S.-China competition does not fundamentally change India's foreign policy. Instead, India must continue to carefully manage its complicated relations with China, now more than ever, while developing even closer cooperation with the United States. Indian foreign policy will therefore need to become more flexible, even as it continues to adhere to a policy of strategic autonomy. The next section discusses U.S. and Chinese aims in India. The subsequent two sections then assess the intersection of U.S. and Chinese interests with Indian interests and consider India's options for responding to the intensifying Sino-U.S. rivalry. The chapter concludes by drawing implications for U.S. and Indian policy.

U.S. and Chinese Aims in India

India has never been the primary focus of either China or the United States. China was relatively unconcerned about threats from India until the latter's rapprochement with the United States in the late 1990s. During the Cold War, the United States and India were estranged, and even before then, neither country saw a close relationship as vital.[2] India's closed economy and preferential trade system with the Soviet Union preserved it from the

---

[1] Satoru Mori, "U.S.-China: A New Consensus for Strategic Competition in Washington," *Diplomat*, January 30, 2019, https://thediplomat.com/2019/01/us-china-a-new-consensus-for-strategic-competition-in-washington. See also Jean-Baptiste Jeangène Vilmer et al., *Les manipulations de l'information: Un défi pour nos démocraties* [Information Manipulation: A Challenge for Our Democracies] (Paris: Institute for Strategic Research at the Military School, 2018).

[2] Stephen P. Cohen, "India and America: An Emerging Relationship" (paper presented to the Conference on the Nation-State System and Transnational Forces in South Asia, Kyoto, December 8–10, 2000).

need to adjust to the constraints of international markets and did not make a relationship with the United States necessary. Similarly, U.S. and Chinese aims in India have never been determined exclusively by the evolution of Sino-U.S. competition, nor has India's positioning played a role in this rivalry. Instead, both countries pursue bilateral objectives with India unrelated to their rivalry but which overlap with and sometimes contradict their strategic aims vis-à-vis one another. Washington looks at India as a potential balancer against China, whereas Beijing is trying to neutralize India. In that sense, with the exacerbation of U.S.-China rivalry, India has become the prize of a zero-sum game.

U.S. Aims

The United States pursues two sets of objectives with India. First, it seeks greater and easier access to the Indian market, which it hopes will become more open. Second, the United States encourages India to play a more active role in regional security and assume a balancing role vis-à-vis China in the Indo-Pacific. Successive U.S. administrations since Bill Clinton have so far maintained a delicate balance between these two sets of objectives. But the risk exists that the relationship will become excessively transactional, which could in turn become a source of tension, and possibly of uncertainty.

The 1990s were indeed an age of transformation for U.S. policy toward South Asia in general and toward India in particular. India's liberalization of its economy and, paradoxically, its decision to conduct nuclear tests were strong factors in rapprochement. After the nuclear tests in 1998, Prime Minister Atal Bihari Vajpayee made clear to President Clinton that India's nuclear weapons were potentially aimed at China, with which deep mistrust persisted.[3] The message was not lost on the United States. U.S. and Indian national interests did suddenly overlap even though both countries were still committed to engagement with China during that period.

In the following decade, however, the relationship experienced its most spectacular development. Following the September 11 terrorist attacks, a sudden (though perhaps superficial) convergence of interests in the war on terrorism cemented the relationship even though it also generated mutual frustration as neither India in Afghanistan nor the United States with Pakistan were, for different reasons, capable of fulfilling each other's expectations. Economically, India experienced an average growth rate of 7.6% for most of the decade, despite a downturn in 2008 and 2009, peaking at 10.3% growth in 2010 and generating new expectations for U.S. and

---

[3] "Nuclear Anxiety; India's Letter to Clinton on the Nuclear Testing," *New York Times*, May 13, 1998.

international investors.[4] The relationship reached a qualitative high point in November 2008 with the signing of the civil nuclear agreement at the end of the Bush presidency. Although the actual strategic impact of the agreement has been the object of considerable debate, in particular vis-à-vis Beijing, the political intent was clear. The agreement put India on a par with other nuclear powers, including China.

Successive administrations have had similar expectations vis-à-vis India. But as expectations about India assuming a greater share of the regional security burden and opening up its market grew, so did the frustration. The Obama administration repeatedly stated that it saw India as part of its "rebalance to Asia" strategy, but the tone had changed. Speaking in Chennai in July 2011, Secretary of State Hillary Clinton signaled U.S. impatience by asking India "not just to look east, but to engage east and to act east as well."[5] Similarly, India was not included in the negotiations for the Trans-Pacific Partnership, a free trade agreement signed (but not ratified) in 2016 by the United States and eleven other countries, most of which are located in Asia.

This trend has accelerated under the Trump administration. The administration has not questioned the fundamentals of the relationship, and it even gave India pride of place in national security planning. In May 2018, U.S. Pacific Command was renamed U.S. Indo-Pacific Command in recognition of the importance of the Indian Ocean region. In addition, some of the administration's policies vis-à-vis Pakistan and China have been welcomed in New Delhi. The challenge, however, is balancing this approach with President Donald Trump's focus on bilateral trade issues. He has made his dissatisfaction with India's lack of economic openness clear, describing the country as the "tariff king" and making derisive comments on its policy in Afghanistan. As provocative as this characterization of India's economic and foreign policies may be, it nevertheless reflects overall U.S. frustration.

Chinese Aims

In contrast to the United States' objectives in India, China's aims are a consequence of its grand strategy in Asia. They have varied over time according to the phases of China's own development, reflecting its threat perception as well as its expanding strategic ambitions. As a developing country, China competed successfully with India for the leadership of the Non-Aligned Movement. The rivalry ended with the Chinese victory in the

---

[4] International Monetary Fund (IMF), "Real GDP Growth," IMF DataMapper, https://www.imf.org/external/datamapper/NGDP_RPCH@WEO/OEMDC/ADVEC/WEOWORLD/IND.

[5] Hillary Rodham Clinton, "Remarks on India and the United-States: A Vision for the 21st Century" (remarks in Chennai, July 20, 2011), https://2009-2017.state.gov/secretary/20092013clinton/rm/2011/07/168840.htm.

1962 war and has been followed by a prolonged period of peace, which lasts to this day, even though the two countries came close to a confrontation in 1987 over Arunachal Pradesh and despite occasional border skirmishes since then.[6]

As an emerging power, China also has sought alliances with other dissatisfied emerging countries, including India. The 1990s saw a drastic change in China's strategic environment. The collapse of the Soviet Union relieved China of its most immediate threat, but it still faced domestic legitimacy problems combined with new external vulnerabilities. The 1990s was the decade during which China was dependent on the outside world for several vital resources necessary for sustainable economic development. It became a net oil importer in 1993, exposing the country to internal threats of subversion as well as external disruptions, in particular from the United States.[7] In this context, the success of the Indian reforms initiated at the beginning of the decade heightened India's expectations and raised the possibly of a renewal of Sino-Indian rivalry. These factors made it imperative for Beijing to neutralize the emerging rapprochement between New Delhi and Washington by exploiting the former's aspiration to become a major player on the world stage. China hoped that India would help keep the United States in check.[8]

However, this policy failed spectacularly. Important factors were China's spectacular rise and increasingly assertive policies and Xi Jinping's ascent to the head of both the Chinese Communist Party and the Chinese state. The persistence of the territorial disputes between the two sides also contributed to worsening Sino-Indian relations.

As a global power, China seeks to limit or prevent altogether India's influence in Asia while trying to discourage the country from partnering with the United States. In regional and international organizations, China maneuvers—although not always successfully—to prevent the accession of India to membership and associated status, thus limiting its potential international influence. Beijing could not prevent India from becoming a member of the East Asia Summit, for example, but it has so far successfully blocked the country's accession to membership in the Nuclear Suppliers Group.

As China identifies itself alternately, but sometimes simultaneously, with each of these three roles (developing country, emerging power, and

---

[6] Ashley J. Tellis, "Pursuing Global Reach: China's Not So Long March toward Preeminence," in *Strategic Asia 2019: China's Expanding Strategic Ambitions*, ed. Ashley J. Tellis, Alison Szalwinski, and Michael Wills (Seattle: National Bureau of Asian Research [NBR], 2019), 3–46.

[7] John Lee, "China's Geostrategic Search for Oil," *Washington Quarterly* 35, no. 3 (2012): 76.

[8] M. Taylor Fravel, "China Views India's Rise: Deepening Cooperation, Managing Differences," in *Strategic Asia 2011–12: Asia Responds to Its Rising Powers—China and India*, ed. Ashley J. Tellis, Travis Tanner, and Jessica Keough (Seattle: NBR, 2011).

global power), the hierarchy of its aims, which sometimes balance one another, shifts over time. Its policies combine balancing support to Pakistan and increasingly all of India's immediate neighbors—through political and economic engagement and deterrence—while maintaining pressure on disputed territories. Directly or indirectly, Beijing thus possesses several options for exercising leverage whenever it feels the relation between New Delhi and Washington becomes too close.

How U.S. and Chinese Interests and Ambitions Intersect with Indian Interests

The intensification of the rivalry between the United States and China has not changed the nature of the challenges to India's interests. It does, however, exacerbate the tensions and potential contradictions within Indian foreign policy. This is particularly true with regard to India's relations with China. Although this growing rivalry does not substantially alter China's differences with India, in a context of growing polarization it tends to transform them into leverage points for China to try to weaken the links between India and the United States. Similarly, the rivalry does not affect the congruence between U.S. and Indian objectives, but it does strain the conditions under which this congruence could be translated into actual cooperation. It should also be noted that the actual impact of the U.S.-China rivalry is often difficult to distinguish from the effects—both positive and negative—of India's own rise on its bilateral relations with China as well as the United States. Moreover, the perception of actual and potential conflicts of interest varies according to the position of decision-makers in each sector of activity. It is therefore necessary to deconstruct this perception per category.

Foreign Policy Interests

Prevent a Chinese-led regional and international order. China is seen as a major obstacle to Indian foreign policy ambitions, which have both positive and negative dimensions. India is determined to recover its status as a leading Asian nation and project itself as a major power on the international scene. Its desire to become a permanent member of the UN Security Council and application to become a member of the Nuclear Suppliers Group have crystalized the country's global ambitions, which have been constantly frustrated by China's opposition. India's membership in the Nuclear Suppliers Group in particular is being held hostage by the Sino-U.S. rivalry.

In the past, however, China was less successful in blocking India on the regional scene. India's courting of regional organizations was always focused on preventing the region from falling under the influence of any one major power. The Association of Southeast Asian Nations (ASEAN) has been India's institution of choice for its Look East and Act East policies since the early 1990s because ASEAN's consensus-based decision-making process has discouraged hegemonic aspirations.

The U.S.-China rivalry does weaken some of the pillars of India's foreign policy and complicates its relationships with both countries. ASEAN's autonomy is eroding due to a deep and effective penetration of both ASEAN institutions and their member states by China, which has invested substantial financial and human resources in the institution. The volume of China-ASEAN trade, which amounted to $514.8 billion in 2017; the importance of China's direct investment in member states; and the density of the formal exchanges between Beijing and ASEAN have further undermined the organization's already relative autonomy.[9] The situation has so far been met with benign neglect by the United States, as both Washington (especially under the Trump administration) and Beijing are more comfortable with bilateral approaches.

Limit China's influence in India's neighborhood. Indian policymakers are also trying to limit China's influence in India's neighborhood, where Beijing is increasingly willing to play the role of an external balancer against New Delhi. Relations between India and its smaller neighbors have always been difficult. It is therefore easy for China to play on the resentment of the smaller South Asian states who fear the shadow of their Indian big brother.

Pakistan has long been China's major client state in South Asia. Based on a shared enmity toward India, China's backing has gone as far as providing Pakistan with the design and material necessary to build a nuclear bomb.[10] But Pakistan is no longer the only state on India's periphery receiving attention from China. Smaller countries in South Asia and the Indian Ocean are increasingly hedging between India and China. Almost every neighboring country, including Bangladesh, Maldives, Nepal, and Sri Lanka, has leveraged its enhanced relations with China to diminish India's influence. This trend has created a sense of unease in New Delhi.

China, for example, is now Bangladesh's largest bilateral trade partner. It has also strengthened Bangladesh's military capabilities and is the country's main provider of military hardware, including delivering two Ming-class submarines in 2014 and helping build a missile launch pad near Chittagong

[9] Sophie Boisseau du Rocher, "La Chine et les Institutions de l'ASEAN" [China and ASEAN Institutions], Institut Français des Relations Internationales (IFRI), March 2018, 10.

[10] Andrew Small, *The China-Pakistan Axis: Asia's New Geopolitics* (New York: Oxford University Press, 2015), 1.

in 2008.[11] Beijing has also broken India's monopoly in Nepal through a trade and transit protocol signed in 2008.[12] Although India is still by far Nepal's most significant trade partner, China is rapidly increasing its market share. In 2018, Nepal announced that it would conduct a joint military exercise with China just days after backing out of a joint military exercise organized by the Bay of Bengal Initiative for Multi-Sectoral Technical and Economic Cooperation, a move viewed by most observers as anti-India.[13] In Sri Lanka and Maldives, where China has invested massively and created long-term dependence, Beijing and New Delhi have been competing for political influence through their respective proxies.[14]

In this context, the Belt and Road Initiative (BRI) has raised alarm in the Indian capital. Many of the projects that today constitute BRI were launched as bilateral initiatives before it was announced in 2013 (under the name One Belt, One Road). Their inclusion contributes nevertheless to shaping India's perception of BRI as a Chinese grand strategy. India is indeed concerned about the strategic implications of some specific projects.[15] Four projects, detailed below, stand out in this regard.

The China-Pakistan Economic Corridor (CPEC), which intends to link Kashgar in China's Xinjiang Uighur Autonomous Region and the port of Gwadar in Pakistan's Baluchistan Province through a network of railways, highways, pipelines, ports, and information technology parks along the route is one such example. The project has been criticized primarily on the grounds that it crosses disputed territories in Gilgit-Baltistan, but Indian concerns go beyond this legal dispute. Despite real tensions between China and Pakistan over many related issues, CPEC epitomizes the deepening relationship between the two countries. (See the Appendix for a brief analysis of Pakistan and the U.S.-China rivalry.) Moreover, it provides China with an outlet to the Arabian Sea and the Indian Ocean and as such creates an additional security dilemma for India. Other examples are the trans-Himalayan economic corridor, a railway cutting through the

---

[11] Asma Masood, "India-Bangladesh-China Relations: A Complex Triangle," Chennai Centre for China, March 2, 2015, https://www.c3sindia.org/archives/india-bangladesh-china-relations-a-complex-triangle-by-asma-masood.

[12] Nicola P. Contessi, "China Opens Border Connections to Nepal," YaleGlobal Online, January 31, 2019, https://yaleglobal.yale.edu/content/china-opens-border-connections-nepal.

[13] "Nepal to Join Military Drill with China after Snubbing India; Move Likely Aimed at Ending Indian Monopoly," Firstpost, September 11, 2018, https://www.firstpost.com/india/nepal-to-join-military-drill-with-china-after-snubbing-india-move-likely-aimed-at-ending-indian-monopoly-5159431.html.

[14] Vivek Mishra, "China Is Moving into the Indian Ocean," National Interest, April 14, 2018, https://nationalinterest.org/print/feature/china-moving-the-indian-ocean-25380.

[15] Darshana M. Baruah, "India's Answer to the Belt and Road: A Road Map for South Asia," Carnegie India, Working Paper, August 2018, https://carnegieendowment.org/files/WP_Darshana_Baruah_Belt_Road_FINAL.pdf.

Himalayas and linking China's Gansu Province to Kathmandu in Nepal, and the Bangladesh-China-India-Myanmar economic corridor. The latter proposal predates the Xi Jinping era and aims to connect the Chinese city of Kunming to the Indian city of Calcutta through Dhaka in Bangladesh and Mandalay in Myanmar with transportation infrastructure.[16]

Indian decision-makers are also deeply worried that China may establish a presence in the Indian Ocean from which it can challenge India's position in the region. Not only have Chinese submarines docked in Pakistan and Sri Lanka, but China also opened its first overseas base in Djibouti in 2017. This dimension is progressively commanding India's attention as China develops its influence all over the Indian Ocean region, in particular on the East African coast, using BRI north-south corridors such as CPEC and the Bangladesh-China-India-Myanmar corridor.

India's anxieties about its periphery ultimately reflect a deep awareness of its own financial, technological, and administrative limitations, which prevent the country from either addressing its neighbors' concerns or imposing its will. But the neighborhood is not viewed by New Delhi solely through the lens of the China question. The United States' partnership with Pakistan has weakened since the Trump administration has toughened its position vis-à-vis Islamabad as a result of Pakistan's policies in Afghanistan and use of terrorist groups as a tool of foreign policy. Any advantage to India, however, has been dampened by the U.S. decision to withdraw from Afghanistan, which raises the prospect of Kabul, sooner or later, falling under Pakistani control. Moreover, India fears that Washington's toughness may be only temporary as the United States needed Pakistan's help to facilitate the conclusion of an agreement with the Taliban. With Trump's decision to de facto stop the dialogue, this fear disappeared, but the possible collapse of Afghanistan did not.

Limit the potential for conflict. For the Indian foreign policy elite, painful memories of 1962 and the still unsettled border disputes with China in Aksai Chin and Himachal Pradesh make the possibility of conflict quite real. No fewer than five agreements on border management have been signed since 1993, the last one in 2013 during Prime Minister Manmohan Singh's final official visit to China. Yet violations of the demarcation line between the two countries in Himachal Pradesh have been recurrent since 1962. They remain manageable and not a single bullet has been shot since 1975. But the number of incidents that could have led to a confrontation, such as in the Depsang Plains in 2016 and Doklam in 2017, has increased since the beginning of the rapprochement between India and the United States.

---

[16] See Baruah, "India's Answer to the Belt and Road," 17–25.

China is indeed perceived as a direct military threat to India. With 1.15 million troops, it still has fewer ground forces than India, which has 1.20 million troops. The terrain in the contested areas, however, favors China, as does the superior transportation infrastructure in Tibet.[17] In addition, China has an advantage in conventional and strategic missile capabilities, which have forced India into a defensive position. Similarly, in the Indian Ocean, China's willingness to project power through increasing its naval presence and building a base in Djibouti is creating a security dilemma for India, heightening its sense of insecurity and leading to an arms race. In this context, the ongoing reorganization of the People's Liberation Army (PLA) and its modernization through the accelerated development of access-denial capabilities (including in cyberspace and outer space), the enhancement of power-projection capabilities, and the spectacular development of the PLA Navy are of particular concern to India, which lacks the financial and organizational capabilities to respond at the required pace.[18]

Preserve India's strategic autonomy. The growing polarization of the strategic situation in Asia tends to turn every relationship with China or the United States into a zero-sum game, a choice between us and them. India has always tried to avoid situations that threaten its cherished strategic autonomy. This essentially means that it has refused to join formal alliances and accept the obligation of intervention, including armed intervention, that they may imply. This specific dimension remains. Indian decision-makers welcome U.S. support but have no intentions of fighting U.S. wars and are trying not to be dragged into the current tensions between China and the United States. Multiplying partnerships with Asian and European middle powers, a policy of relative appeasement vis-à-vis China, and the use of multilateral institutions such as ASEAN where India could not be coerced into specific positions have so far been its favorite instruments to maintain Indian autonomy. However, as the power gap with China increases, and with it India's fear of Chinese hegemony in Asia, Indian decision-makers have needed to rely increasingly on the United States in order to acquire sufficient capabilities to manage this asymmetry. India's situation is further complicated by the United States' growing transactionalism. India will have to deliver—in whatever the field in question may be—if it wants the dynamic of the rapprochement with the United States to continue unabated. This could have positive consequences

---

[17] Rajesh Rajagopalan, "India's Strategic Choices: China and the Balance of Power in Asia," Carnegie India, September 2017, https://carnegieindia.org/2017/09/14/india-s-strategic-choices-china-and-balance-of-power-in-asia-pub-73108.

[18] See Vinod Anand, "Trends in Chinese Military Modernization: Implications and Responses," Vivekananda International Foundation, Occasional Paper, February 2016.

for India in the longer term but may come at a social and potentially political cost in the short term.

De-ideologize nonalignment. Until the end of the Cold War, nonalignment was an untouchable principle of India's foreign policy. It lost most of its significance with the collapse of the Soviet Union but seems to be re-emerging as a consequence of the current polarization of U.S.-China relations. Sino-U.S. competition has indeed strengthened the arguments of both those advocating a closer relationship with the United States and the proponents of a renewed nonalignment strategy. In its manifesto for the 2019 Lok Sabha (lower house) elections, the Congress party stated, for example, "its firm belief in the continued relevance of the policy of friendship, peaceful coexistence, non-alignment, independence of thought and action, and increased bilateral engagement in its relations with other countries of the world."[19]

The idea that India does not need the United States is another frequent theme in the domestic political debate. This position reflects more hubris than ideology, but it is strengthened by the fact that India is courted by many actors in the international system. The argument has been echoed in defense-related research organizations with often dubious results. Nonetheless, the debate about nonalignment is mostly rhetorical. With the exception of the Communist Party of India, which is traditionally soft on China, ambiguity is the rule when it comes to election manifestos. While no party advocates complete alignment, the relationship with the United States is instrumental even in the version of nonalignment to which the Congress party seems to be referring.

Moreover, the concept of nonalignment itself has evolved. Nonalignment is now conceived of as encompassing "a deep and wide engagement with as many powers as are willing to engage with" India.[20] Under this policy, India could manage the rivalry between great powers thanks to its economic attractiveness, engaging with China economically while leaning on the United States for security. This form of nonalignment says little about the actual proximity between India and its potential partners and leaves a large margin of maneuver for the ruling government. The policy is mainly a warning about the consequences of alliances. From this perspective, it is indeed significant that Narendra Modi's government, although determined to make the best of its proximity to the United States, is as wary of being dragged into U.S. wars as nonalignment proponents would recommend

---

[19] Indian National Congress, "Congress Will Deliver," 2019, https://manifesto.inc.in/pdf/english.pdf.

[20] Sunil Khilnani et al., *Nonalignment 2.0: A Foreign and Strategic Policy for India in the Twenty First Century* (New Delhi: Centre for Policy Research, 2012), https://www.cprindia.org/research/reports/nonalignment-20-foreign-and-strategic-policy-india-twenty-first-century.

it be.[21] Nonalignment in today's India is a political marker that has lost a substantial part of its ideological content and survives at best as a *quid pro quo* for the country's consensus on the need to preserve India from falling into the trap of Sino-U.S. polarization.

India's Economic Interests

Improving the economy has always been a major concern of India's foreign policy. India is highly dependent on trade with both China and the United States. Bilateral trade with China reached $87 billion in 2017–18, whereas trade with the United States was $88 billion during that period. However, comparable global figures hide vast qualitative differences. India's export deficit with China has grown exponentially over the past few years and now stands at just under $54 billion, whereas the country still has a large export surplus with the United States (around $18 trillion), which is also a valuable technology provider.[22] Thus, India can only benefit from the ongoing trade war between Beijing and Washington should it result in a greater opening up of the Chinese market—an outcome that remains uncertain. Indian firms find it difficult to enter China, but the Indian government only has a limited margin of maneuver. As Indian manufacturing depends on cheap Chinese imports of electronic and information technology products, any retaliatory move by India to restrict imports of Chinese goods would be counterproductive.[23] A report from the UN Conference on Trade and Development projected that Indian exports should grow by 3.9% as a consequence of U.S. and Chinese tariffs on each other's products.[24]

India may have reasons for concern with respect to its trade relationship with the United States. The opening up of the U.S. market to Indian goods, transfers of U.S. technology to India, and nuclear and military cooperation were based on the assumption that India had the potential to become a balancer to China and a profitable market for U.S. companies. Yet the Indian economy is still perceived in the United States as too closed. Repeated threats by Trump related to India's high tariffs have been made credible by the recent revocation of its preferential trade treatment under the Generalized System of Preferences (GSP) program.[25] The question for India is whether this action

---

[21] Rajagopalan, "India's Strategic Choices," 11.

[22] Ministry of Commerce and Industry (India), Export Import Data Bank, https://commerce-app.gov.in/eidb/default.asp.

[23] Kashyap Arora and Rimjhim Saxena, "India-China Economic Relations: An Assessment," South Asian Voices, April 21, 2018, https://southasianvoices.org/india-china-economic-relations-an-assessment.

[24] "Trade Wars: The Pain and the Gain," UN Conference on Trade and Development, February 4, 2019.

[25] "U.S. Ends Special Trade Treatment for India amid Tariff Dispute," BBC, June 1, 2019, https://www.bbc.com/news/world-asia-india-48482988.

is only a temporary phase linked to the current administration and can be expected to be reversed over time or whether it reflects a deeper trend that portends a more turbulent economic relationship. Even as pro-Indian sentiments still prevail in the United States due to the China factor, there is a sense in certain U.S. quarters that India has been given advantages that it never really reciprocated. In 2008 the Bush administration had justified its decision to sign the civil nuclear agreement on the basis that civil nuclear trade with India would create jobs in the United States. These jobs are still awaiting realization.

When examined from the perspective of business elites, the outlook for these same issues varies greatly depending on both the sector considered and China's dependence on specific products or materials. Indian producers of diamonds, cotton yarn, iron ore, copper, and organic chemicals, all of which are among India's top exports to China, are not surprisingly great supporters of deeper economic relations.[26] On the contrary, producers of electrical machinery or fertilizers, sectors that suffer from Chinese competition, are more protectionist or call for greater market access in China. Even in sectors where India has a comparative advantage, such as IT, pharmaceuticals, or agriproducts, Indian companies find it difficult to enter Chinese markets. Like the Indian government, business elites in these sectors believe that Beijing's protectionist policies have hindered the ability of Indian companies to compete with their Chinese counterparts on a level playing field. U.S. efforts to force China to grant access to its market are therefore seen positively. Yet companies involved in the production of goods such as medical devices, dairy products, and agricultural goods—all of which are affected by Trump's decision to remove India from the list of GSP beneficiary countries—fear that the United States may also turn against India at a later stage to pressure it to open its own domestic market.

Other issues confront India with a separate dilemma. The development of 5G networks has created a divide between domestic vendors and the government, and within the latter, between the institutions in charge of security and the economy. In early July a high-level committee on 5G recommended that "India should go for trial immediately with all except for Chinese vendors."[27] This finding was based on the fear that equipment sold by Huawei might include a backdoor that could allow the Chinese government to access data from 5G networks. The Indian government now finds itself under

---

[26] Ministry of External Affairs (India), "India-China Bilateral Relations," October 2017, https://mea.gov.in/Portal/ForeignRelation/China_October_2017.pdf.

[27] "5G Panel Wants India to Start 5G Mobile Network Trials without Chinese Vendors, Including Huawei," News18, July 2, 2019, https://www.news18.com/news/tech/5g-panel-wants-india-to-start-5g-trials-without-chinese-vendors-including-huawei-2212963.html.

pressure in one direction from the United States to end cooperation with Huawei on 5G and in the opposite direction from Indian telecommunications providers that use Huawei equipment.[28]

It remains to be seen whether the Bharatiya Janata Party's large political victory in the May 2019 national election will translate into decisive reforms of the Indian economy or whether India will keep responding cautiously and in an ad hoc manner to U.S. pressures, careful as always not to alienate the most fragile segments of society. Modi's governance has so far been characterized by a reformist agenda, though one more focused on issues relevant to the daily lives of Indian citizens. But the question of his willingness to open the Indian economy in a significant way is still unanswered.

Military Interests

India's military interests reflect its major policy concerns, particularly its perception of China and Pakistan. Pakistan both is a problem in itself and heightens India's concerns about encirclement by China. But despite a long history of hostility with Pakistan, China is the main reason for India's rapprochement with United States.

Indeed, from a military perspective, growing Sino-U.S. competition has brought benefits to India. China's rise has been a key driver of U.S.-India defense relations, which have improved significantly since the early 2000s. In 2002 the two sides signed the General Security of Military Information Agreement, followed in 2005 by the New Framework for the India-U.S. Defense Relationship and in 2012 by the Defense Technology and Trade Initiative. The increasingly competitive nature of the Sino-U.S relationship has accelerated defense and security ties between the United States and India. As underlined by Indian analyst Vivek Mishra, the U.S.-India Joint Strategic Vision for the Asia-Pacific and Indian Ocean Region, announced in January 2015 during Barack Obama's last official visit to India, as well as the rebranding of the Look East policy as the Act East policy as a way of signaling New Delhi's intent to demonstrate greater voluntarism in Asia, "made the fault lines of what some refer to as the Asian Great Game…more perceptible than ever."[29] Later in 2015, the two countries also renewed the Framework for the U.S.-India Defense Relationship.

---

[28] Amy Kazmin and Stephanie Findlay, "Washington Warns India over Using Huawei for 5G," *Financial Times*, October 4, 2019, https://www.ft.com/content/4181ee4e-e5de-11e9-9743-db5a370481bc.

[29] "U.S.-India Joint Strategic Vision for the Asia-Pacific and Indian Ocean Region," White House, Office of the Press Secretary, January 25, 2015, https://obamawhitehouse.archives.gov/the-press-office/2015/01/25/us-india-joint-strategic-vision-asia-pacific-and-indian-ocean-region; and Vivek Mishra, "India-U.S. Defence Cooperation: Assessing Strategic Imperatives," *Strategic Analysis* 42, no. 1 (2018): 1–14.

The joint strategic vision was followed in 2016 by the signing of the Logistics Exchange Memorandum of Agreement, which marked a new phase in India-U.S. cooperation in the Indian Ocean as both countries opened their naval facilities in the area to each other. The two countries took another qualitative step in strategic and defense cooperation in 2018 with the signing of the Communications Compatibility and Security Agreement and the launching of a regular 2+2 dialogue. At the operational level, their armed forces are actively working on interoperability through a series of bilateral exercises—Cope India (air force), Yudh Abhyas (army), and Vajra Prahar (special forces)—as well as multilateral exercises—Malabar, Red Flag, and the Rim of the Pacific (RIMPAC).[30] Moreover, India has been able to purchase nearly $18 billion of arms from the United States since 2008. Items include C-17 and C-130J transport planes, P-8I maritime reconnaissance aircraft, Harpoon missiles, AH-64E and CH-47F helicopters, and M777 howitzers.[31]

Paradoxically, this spectacular increase in defense cooperation also has collateral benefits for India's military relations with China. India and China have entertained a strategic dialogue since 2008 as well as specific security mechanisms, such as the meeting of special representatives on the boundary question and the high-level dialogue mechanism on counterterrorism and security. Since 2013, they also have held regular joint military exercises in Chengdu in Sichuan Province. Although these exercises remain limited in scope and amount mostly to confidence building, they are nevertheless significant in a context of recurrent border tensions between the two countries. These exercises do not eliminate the source of friction, particularly in the Indian Ocean where the rivalry is growing, but they could help prevent differences from escalating into a conflict.[32]

The more important question, however, is whether the pace of U.S.-India cooperation matches the speed of China's own military expansion. The gap has widened between India's commitments and capabilities. The 2019 budget had the lowest defense allocation since 1962, despite the country being in a "readiness crisis caused by shortfall," according one U.S. defense analyst.[33] Still, as a result of heavy bureaucratic procedures and slower economic growth,

---

[30] Sujan R. Chinoy, "Indo-U.S. Defence Partnership: Future Prospects," Institute for Defence Studies and Analyses (IDSA), IDSA Comment, June 26, 2019, https://idsa.in/idsacomments/indo-us-defence-partnership-srchinoy-260620.

[31] Ibid.

[32] Kristin Huang, "Rivals and Neighbours: China and India Count Down to Joint Military Drill," *South China Morning Post*, December 10, 2018, https://www.scmp.com/news/china/diplomacy/article/2177319/rivals-and-neighbours-china-and-india-count-down-joint-military.

[33] Benjamin E. Schwartz, "From Inertia to Integration: Getting Serious about U.S.-India Defense Cooperation," *American Interest*, January 24, 2019, https://www.the-american-interest.com/2019/06/24/from-inertia-to-integration-getting-serious-about-u-s-india-defense-cooperation.

the situation is unlikely to improve soon. This only reinforces New Delhi's dilemma. Indian decision-makers from all sides of the political spectrum know that they need the United States. But India also cannot afford U.S. policies that are likely to destabilize the fragile regional equilibrium that it is constantly trying to restore and reinvent.

India's Response to the Evolving U.S.-China Competition

India's response to the evolving U.S.-China competition differs depending on the issue but is somewhat inconsistent. Even though the Sino-Indian rivalry remains manageable, India's challenges vis-à-vis China are becoming more and more intractable with each passing year. The military gap in particular is expected to continue to widen, which will increase the need for U.S. technology and support. But India also desires to avoid antagonizing China unnecessarily, which will require maintaining the right distance with the United States. In effect, India can exploit the Sino-U.S. rivalry to its own benefit only if it can avoid the two extreme poles of Sino-U.S. confrontation or a group of two relationship that would make India irrelevant.

Carefully Managing the Relationship with the United States

The history of the U.S.-India relationship since the end of the Cold War is a history of constant, sometimes spectacular, often complex, but always cautious rapprochement between the two countries. Successive Indian prime ministers since the late 1990s have all contributed, in various degrees, to the development of a closer partnership with Washington. All of them understood Washington's "centrality in New Delhi's external balancing of Beijing."[34] None of them, however, even toyed with the idea of a complete alignment with the United States for reasons that have to do with the perceived unreliability of the United States as well as domestic insecurities.

Similar considerations inform Modi's foreign policy and are unlikely to change in the foreseeable future. Following the 1998 Indian nuclear tests, Prime Minister Vajpayee initiated the dialogue which led to Clinton's visit to India in March 2000, followed by Vajpayee's reciprocal visit to Washington six months later. His successor, Singh, is credited with the most significant achievement to date in the U.S.-India relationship—the signing of the civil nuclear agreement in 2008, which opened the possibility of full civil nuclear cooperation between the two countries. Since his election in 2014, Modi has

---

[34] Ashley J. Tellis, "Troubles Aplenty: Foreign Policy Challenges for the Next Indian Government," Carnegie Endowment for International Peace, May 20, 2019, https://carnegieendowment. org/2019/05/20/troubles-aplenty-foreign-policy-challenges-for-next-indian-government-pub-79161.

navigated the challenges of two different U.S. administrations. The Obama and Trump administrations are radically different in their outlooks but are both trying to rethink the United States' role in the world, although neither administration has questioned the U.S. partnership with India.

China's growing superiority justifies India's need for a closer strategic relationship with the United States in order to receive desired military and technological support. India-U.S. cooperation has so far brought substantial benefits to India, in particular with regard to access to advanced technology. However, the country is now facing a different United States, even though the fundamentals of the relationship have so far not been affected.

Defense and political cooperation remain strong. Speaking at the 2+2 ministerial meeting with the United States on September 6, 2018, Indian defense minister Nirmala Sitharaman declared that defense cooperation was "the most significant dimension of [the] strategic partnership and a key driver of [the] overall bilateral relationship."[35] Logistics support agreements, unthinkable a decade ago, have now been signed. Moreover, New Delhi appreciates U.S. pressure on Pakistan and feels comfortable with the trade war between China and the United States, given that India is among the countries most likely to benefit from it. More generally, New Delhi is comfortable with any U.S. pressure on China that is likely to increase Beijing's vulnerability and make it more amenable to dialogue.

But the idea that the two sides' contributions to the relationship can remain asymmetrical because a strong India is in the United States' interests has been considerably weakened. The relationship has become significantly more transactional under the Trump administration, which in exchange for its support is demanding a price that may occasionally prove economically and politically costly for India. The question that India is now facing in its relationship with the United States is how to keep benefitting from U.S. support while avoiding U.S. arm twisting when the two countries' interests differ.

The Indian debate on the United States' Countering America's Adversaries Through Sanctions Act (CAATSA), enacted in August 2017, illustrates this point. Section 231 allows the United States to impose sanctions on entities engaging in business transactions with the Russian defense sector. As the largest buyer of Russian weapons, India is particularly vulnerable. The problem became acute when the United States imposed CAATSA sanctions on the Equipment Development Department of China's Central Military

---

[35] Jim Garamone, "U.S.-India Defense Cooperation a 'Key Driver' of Overall Relationship," U.S. Department of Defense, September 6, 2018, https://dod.defense.gov/News/Article/Article/1622396/us-india-defense-cooperation-a-key-driver-of-overall-relationship.

Commission and on its director in September 2018.[36] The move should have pleased New Delhi, given that ties between Russia and China are of particular concern. But when India formally signed a $5.2 billion deal with Russia for the acquisition of the S-400 missile defense system in October 2018, Trump made his displeasure clear by stating that India would soon find out whether the United States would impose punitive sanctions.[37] Similarly, the Trump administration's decision not to extend waivers for Iran sanctions to countries that needed to find alternative suppliers of crude oil did not go down very well with Indian decision-makers.

India has so far responded quite deftly to the new situation with a mix of compliance, diplomatic know-how, and firmness. It did comply, for example, with the U.S. injunction on oil and gas imports from Iran.[38] India also could obtain a waiver from the United States for its defense relations with Russia thanks to its diplomatic efforts, and the country should not be too affected by Trump's decision to withdraw it from the list of GSP beneficiaries.[39] India's relative confidence seems to be grounded in the belief in its own indispensability in the Indian Ocean. Accordingly, New Delhi has framed its priorities in U.S. terms. Although the recent decision to create an Indo-Pacific wing in the Ministry of External Affairs does address the need for better coordination in the area, and most of its activities are centered on the Indian Ocean, the decision is unmistakably an official endorsement of the U.S. Indo-Pacific vision.

As the prospect of a return to the *status quo ante* if a new U.S. administration is elected in 2020 is uncertain at best, India is likely to remain cautious. Cooperation with the United States will continue to go as far as possible in all fields that are likely to guarantee Indian security, but India will also resist the United States where its own interests dictate. Strategic autonomy will remain a driver of India's foreign policy.

---

[36] G. Balachandran, "CAATSA Sanctions on India," IDSA, IDSA Comment, September 26, 2018, https://idsa.in/idsacomments/caatsa-sanctions-and-india-gbalachandran-260918.

[37] Rakesh Krishnan, "Countering CAATSA: How India Can Avoid American Arm Twisting," *Business Today*, March 6, 2019, https://www.businesstoday.in/opinion/columns/caatsa-how-india-can-avoid-us-arm-twisting/story/286653.html.

[38] "India Will Stop Importing Crude Oil from Iran after U.S. Ends Sanction Waiver: Official," *Livemint*, April 23, 2019, https://www.livemint.com/industry/energy/india-will-stop-importing-crude-oil-from-iran-after-us-ends-sanction-waiver-1556008925244.html.

[39] "S-400: India Meets U.S. Waiver Criteria, Can't Wish Away Russia Ties, Say Sources," *Livemint*, June 25, 2017, https://www.livemint.com/news/india/s-400-india-meets-us-waiver-criteria-can-t-wish-away-russia-ties-say-sources-1561480410207.html; and "U.S. President Trump to End Preferential Trade Status for India under GSP on June 5," Press Trust of India, June 1, 2019, https://yourstory.com/2019/06/trump-terminate-trade-status-india-gsp.

Maintaining Cooperation with China

The closer the desired rapprochement with the United States, the more necessary it is for India to remain insulated as much as possible from the confrontation between the two superpowers. Geographic contiguity, asymmetrical power, uncertainty regarding the U.S. commitment to Indian security, and caution, combined with a strong desire to remain independent, dictate that India conducts its China policy on its own terms. Maintaining dialogue with China and managing the relationship bilaterally in order to avoid being ensnared by the zero-sum relationship that is currently developing between the United States and China is therefore a necessity for India. Any direct U.S. support would inevitably be interpreted by Beijing as a sign of open hostility.

China is indeed the main strategic challenge confronting India for the foreseeable future. Moreover, the asymmetry of power between the two countries is only likely to grow.[40] New Delhi can therefore ill afford to make an enemy out of a more powerful China. It does maintain annual political and security dialogues with Beijing, despite the fact that other significant issues such as the border dispute and the long-standing Pakistan-China partnership remain unresolved. India has also progressively become more economically enmeshed with China.

Although India does stand up to Chinese pressure on occasion, it attempts to avoid tension as much as possible, and whenever friction occurs, works to mitigate the situation diplomatically and peacefully. Two border incidents, both of which took place after Modi's ascent to power, illustrate this point. On September 10, 2014, during Xi Jinping's visit to India, an Indian patrol discovered that Chinese troops had deployed heavy machinery to build a road inside Indian territory. Indian forces moved immediately and were stationed opposite Chinese forces. The standoff lasted until September 26, several days after the Indian and Chinese leaders had officially resolved the matter. A year later, Indian Armed Forces and the PLA faced one another again over the construction of a road in Doklam near the border area between China, India, and Bhutan. The standoff, which started on June 16, 2017, lasted roughly 70 days.[41] It is worth noting that Washington offered New Delhi support in the crisis. Yet, as noted by Ashley Tellis, after the Doklam crisis

---

[40] Addressing the Lok Sabha Committee on External Affairs in February 2018, Foreign Secretary S. Jaishankar declared that "after China's modernization, its economy today is five times the size of the Indian economy, with its consequent capabilities, economic, military and political." "Sino-India Relations Including Doklam, Border Situation and Cooperation in International Organizations," Committee on External Affairs, Sixteenth Lok Sabah, September 2018.

[41] Prabhash K. Dutta, "How India, China Compromise: A Look at How Standoffs before Doklam Were Resolved," *India Today*, August 31, 2017, https://www.indiatoday.in/india/story/doklam-standoff-india-china-compromise-demchok-chumar-daulta-beg-oldi-1034861-2017-08-31.

"Modi became more cautious about visibly tilting toward the United States and publicly confronting China."[42] The informal summit in Wuhan was, for different reasons, an attempt by both India and China to keep the United States out of their disputes. Taking place a few months after the standoff, the summit was meant to mitigate tension between the two countries at a time when China had already entered a trade war with the United States and was trying to prevent the emergence of a common U.S.-India front. Protocol and appearances mattered more than substance, and no joint communiqué was released at the end of the summit. The summit did, however, provide a pretense for a new phase in the Sino-Indian relationship and was for that reason qualified as a "reset."

Significantly, India has since adopted a more conciliatory and cautious approach regarding Tibet and maintains official distance from the Tibetan government in exile.[43] Similarly, the Indian government has toned down its opposition to BRI.[44] At the Wuhan summit, Xi and Modi also reaffirmed the necessity for India and China to strengthen their economic cooperation. India is also willing to continue developing alternative economic partnerships, such as the Regional Comprehensive Economic Partnership (RCEP) with China, in order to avoid being marginalized in its relationship with the United States.

Even if the goodwill demonstrated by Xi and Modi in Wuhan still needs to be translated into action, the summit undoubtedly helped ease some tensions between the two sides. China and India resumed border negotiations, a joint military exercise called Hand-in-Hand 2018, and a maritime dialogue that was originally scheduled for 2017. They also created the China-India High Level Mechanism on Cultural and People-to-People Exchanges.[45] But more than ever, they compartmentalized negotiations so as to prevent difficulties on one issue from blocking progress on another. India's boycott of BRI, for example, does not affect its trade ties with China.[46]

---

[42] Tellis, "Troubles Aplenty."

[43] Aakriti Bachhawat, "India Should Play the Tibet Card with China," Australian Strategic Policy Institute, Strategist, April 2, 2019, https://www.aspistrategist.org.au/india-should-play-the-tibet-card-with-china.

[44] Atman Trivedi, "One Year On, Should India Rethink Its Reset with China?" War on the Rocks, April 17, 2019, https://warontherocks.com/2019/04/one-year-on-should-india-rethink-its-reset-with-china.

[45] Siwei Liu, "What Will the China-India Relationship Look Like in 2019?" Eurasia Review, February 10, 2019, https://www.eurasiareview.com/10022019-what-will-the-china-india-relationship-look-like-in-2019-analysis.

[46] "India's Boycott of BRI Not to Affect Trade Ties with China: Indian Envoy," Economic Times, May 3, 2019, https://economictimes.indiatimes.com/news/economy/foreign-trade/indias-boycott-of-bri-not-to-affect-trade-ties-with-china-indian-envoy/articleshow/69162769.cms.

In effect, the summit helped create a favorable narrative for the leaders of both countries.[47]

However, the Indian government is aware of the limits of such engagement. The Wuhan summit was a tactical move for both countries. Thanks to its economic might, China keeps developing its influence and exerts pressure on India's immediate neighborhood, from Bhutan and Nepal to Sri Lanka and Maldives. U.S. administrations come and go, and with them come various degrees of reassurance to India, but China is and will remain a structural problem. New Delhi sees no option but to continue treading carefully in its diplomacy with Beijing.

Partnering with Middle Powers

As relations with China become more complicated and relations with the United States become more difficult, India has built up a web of relationships with middle powers. These relationships vary according to a set of factors including relations with Beijing as well as the availability of military, financial, and economic development capabilities. None of these partnerships are decisive for India, but all of them contribute to mitigating and balancing the China threat, as well as mitigating India's dependence—actual and potential—on any single partner. The articulation of these relationships defines the nature of the cooperation between India and its partners.

France and Japan, for example, share perceptions of China that are compatible with India's, are capable of providing the country with advanced technology, and are willing to help it redefine relations with China in the Indo-Pacific. Historically an arms supplier and provider of advanced military technology to India, France became one of India's major defense partners in the early 1980s. However, it was only in the late 1990s that New Delhi's perception of France's role in the region changed significantly. Cooperation between the two sides improved dramatically after the 1998 nuclear tests, with France being one of the only two countries that did not condemn India. Their strategic and political interactions intensified in the following years. Increasingly concerned about the Chinese presence in the Indian Ocean, the Indian security establishment gradually woke up to the complementarity of French and Indian interests and approaches, as well as to the potential of maritime security cooperation with France, which has been traditionally

---

[47] "Sino-India Cooperation on a Fast Track after Wuhan Summit: China," *Economic Times*, January 4, 2019, https://economictimes.indiatimes.com/news/defence/sino-india-cooperation-on-a-fast-track-after-wuhan-summit-china/articleshow/67383713.cms.

present and active in the Indian Ocean.[48] As the two countries deepened their relationship, they also developed highly comparable—both geographically and conceptually—approaches to the Indo-Pacific.

Since the beginning of the second prime ministerial term of Shinzo Abe, Japan—with which India's relations had taken a turn for the better at the beginning of the century—has been India's partner of choice in Asia. The relationship is multidimensional and includes a strong economic component. Yet security concerns about China are increasingly central. Military and industrial defense cooperation are important components of the relationship. These concerns, however, find their expression mostly in cooperation in third countries where India and Japan try jointly to dispute China's monopoly in infrastructure building through BRI. The Asia-Africa Growth Corridor, which aims at developing connectivity between Asia and Africa, is one such project.[49]

Yet India's building up of partnerships with like-minded middle powers remains cautious. Similar threat perceptions do not mechanically generate strong strategic cooperation. The economic importance of Australia for India is growing, but despite their very real convergence of strategic interests, India remains skeptical about partnering on security issues. Although it does acknowledge the tensions in the Australia-China relationship, India considers Australia to be too structurally dependent on the Chinese economy and insufficiently involved in the Indian Ocean to be a reliable and useful partner. The two countries find it difficult to define a meaningful strategic complementarity. India remains centered on the Indian Ocean, whereas Australia, though active in the northeast of the Indian Ocean, looks primarily toward the Pacific. This difference, in turn, determines the nature of their cooperation. It provides a strong incentive for intelligence sharing but partly inhibits operational cooperation.

India also maintains a relationship with Russia, based on past dependence and the need to neutralize potential nuisance capabilities. Russia remains an essential spare-parts provider for the Indian Air Force, whose fighter aircraft fleet is still around 65% of Russian origin. However, this once privileged partnership between India and Russia has changed. Moscow is no longer New Delhi's best protection against Beijing. Although still characterized by mutual suspicion, the relationship between Russia and China has become gradually closer since the beginning of the

---

[48] C. Raja Mohan and Darshana M. Baruah, "Deepening the India-France Maritime Partnership," Carnegie India, February 23, 2018, https://carnegieindia.org/2018/02/23/deepening-india-france-maritime-partnership-pub-75630.

[49] "Asia Africa Growth Corridor: Partnership for Sustainable and Innovative Development," African Development Bank Meeting, Ahmedabad, May 22–26, 2017, http://www.eria.org/Asia-Africa-Growth-Corridor-Document.pdf.

rapprochement between India and the United States. As a result, China is now more important than India for Russia. Nonetheless, New Delhi still desires to prevent a de facto alliance between Beijing and Moscow that would leave India isolated in Asia and give China a decisive advantage in the disputed border area. In this context, arms procurement remains one of the few tangible results of the relationship—one that, despite pressure from the Trump administration, is unlikely to disappear soon as long as India is also Russia's main client.

Managing Coalitions

Previous considerations explain why, of all India's predicaments, managing coalitions is likely to be the most difficult. The term coalition itself remains anathema in India's political language, as it de facto implies a delegation of power to other members of the coalition and a subsequent loss of sovereignty. India does indeed remain cautious vis-à-vis every grouping likely to be perceived as an anti-China coalition. It is at once actively seeking the political and strategic reassurances that could emerge from such groupings while trying to minimize the potential political cost of an overtly hostile posture toward China.

The Quad, which was formed in 2006 as the Quadrilateral Security Dialogue as a result of the close coordination among the governments of India, Japan, Australia, and the United States during the devastating tsunami of December 2004, illustrates this point. But although the Quad did emerge at the first meeting as no more than a promising consultative forum "for regular exchange of views on regional challenges, in particular dealing with maritime emergencies and security threats such as piracy,"[50] at the joint secretary level it soon fell victim to the tactical compulsions of some of the participants. Even though the participating countries had made clear that it would not take on a military dimension and was not directed at any third country, China criticized the grouping as a potential Asian NATO.[51] As the United States needed China's and Russia's support on the Iran and North Korea issues, the Quad soon disappeared from the agenda, while Australia made it clear that India was not part of its security arrangements.

The Quad was reactivated ten years later at a meeting of senior officials on the sidelines of the ASEAN summit in Manila in November 2017, following the announcement by the Trump administration that it sought

---

[50] Shyam Saran, "The Quadrilateral: Is It an Alliance or an Alignment?" *Hindustan Times*, November 25, 2017, https://www.hindustantimes.com/analysis/the-quadrilateral-is-it-an-alliance-or-an-alignment/story-16CvgQjKHWaayoQjaOl2kM.html.

[51] Ibid.

a free and open Indo-Pacific with the objective of containing Chinese maritime expansionism. India participated in the November 2017 and June 2018 meetings of the Quad. In the aftermath of the 2017 Doklam standoff, however, the China-centered narrative of the Quad generated nothing but caution in New Delhi, with India being the only country in the group sharing a land boundary with China. India also rejected Australia's request to participate in the Malabar military exercise along with the United States and Japan for the fourth year in a row. Although some interpreted this decision as being the result of the Wuhan summit between Xi and Modi,[52] it seems to primarily reflect India's unwillingness to transform the Malabar exercise into a Quad exercise and the country's rejection of anti-Chinese coalitions. This move, though seemingly inconsistent with India's interest in countering China's plans for maritime expansion, is fully consistent with its concept of the Indo-Pacific, specifically as articulated in Modi's keynote address at the Shangri-La Dialogue in June 2018.

The Indian prime minister used the term Indo-Pacific, which he characterized not as a strategy or a club of limited members "and by no means…directed against any country," no fewer than ten times but omitted the term Quad.[53] On the contrary, Modi insisted strongly on the inclusivity of the Indian concept, signaling his willingness to maintain some balance between China and the United States. As discussed earlier, India has historically been averse to multilateral arrangements that could be construed as alliances. Therefore, although the term Indo-Pacific de facto recognizes India's growing influence and hopes for "cooperation in upholding freedom of navigation and overflight,"[54] New Delhi remains wary of its endorsement of the concept creating unnecessary hostility vis-à-vis China. Like that of a number of other countries, India's official rhetoric refuses the competitive dimension implicit in the concept of the Indo-Pacific and redefines the concept in a way that allows New Delhi to avoid choosing between the United States and China. This reticence also signals India's skepticism regarding the value of a partnership whose backbone—U.S. commitment to the security of the region—is uncertain.

Finally, unlike other Quad participants, India's vision of the Indo-Pacific is focused on the Indian Ocean rather than the Pacific. This vision reflects India's actual interests and strategy (in particular, the need to take East

---

[52] Derek Grossman, "India Is the Weakest Link in the Quad," *Foreign Policy*, July 23, 2018, https://foreignpolicy.com/2018/07/23/india-is-the-weakest-link-in-the-quad.

[53] Narendra Modi (keynote address at Shangri-La Dialogue, Singapore, June 1, 2018), available at https://www.mea.gov.in/Speeches-Statements.htm?dtl/29943/Prime+Ministers+Keynote+Address+at+Shangri+La+Dialogue+June+01+2018.

[54] Rahul Roy-Chaudhury and Kate Sullivan de Estrada, "India, the Indo-Pacific and the Quad," *Survival* 60, no. 3 (2018): 181–94.

African littoral states of the Indian Ocean into account) and is more in line with its actual capabilities. As rightly observed by Rahul Roy-Chaudhury and Kate Sullivan de Estrada, "in terms of declaratory policy and defense diplomacy, India is certainly looking beyond the Indian Ocean, which helps explain why it is amenable to participating in the Quad even if it is reluctant to call it that."[55] However, India's capabilities in the Pacific do not allow the country to be a significant military actor there. This limits its capacity to act autonomously and implies a level of dependence vis-à-vis its partners that is too high for India to be comfortable with.

Implications for Indian and U.S. Policy

The Indian responses to the U.S.-China rivalry examined in the previous section are unlikely to change the nature of India's dilemma. India will still need to avoid antagonizing China unnecessarily while increasing cooperation—including military cooperation—with the United States. On the contrary, closer cooperation with the United States will make it even more indispensable for New Delhi to carefully manage its relationship with Beijing. The growing polarization between the United States and China will, however, exacerbate the tensions among the various constraints that structure Indian foreign policy. But India is unlikely to question the fundamentals of this foreign policy unless these constraints become irreconcilable. Until then, it will try to manage these existing contradictions as well as possible.

The United States will draw India into U.S. competition with China whenever U.S. policies strengthen the deterrence dimension of India's own China policy, helping India both structure regional architectures to its benefit and peacefully dilute the impact of China's presence in its neighborhood. India is therefore likely to increase cooperation in the larger Indian Ocean region, including military cooperation.

Conversely, India will choose not to cooperate with the United States when U.S. policies are perceived as leading to a more confrontational posture vis-à-vis China or will alter the political and strategic regional equilibrium to India's detriment. New Delhi will not participate, for example, in any policy targeting Russia, not only because India is heavily dependent on Russian military hardware but also because it fears that any such move would draw Moscow closer to Beijing—and to a lesser extent Islamabad—with undesirable consequences such as additional technology transfers to China and a loss of political support. From that perspective, it is ironic that India

---

[55] Roy-Chaudhury and Sullivan de Estrada, "India, the Indo-Pacific and the Quad," 189.

initially welcomed the election of Trump as president on the expectation that he would normalize U.S. relations with Russia.

Last, India will remain ambivalent on issues where it cannot play a significant role but that may positively affect its own standing. The ongoing trade war between China and the United States is one example. India will stay away as much as possible from such bilateral disputes and will opportunistically try to benefit from the polarization. The extent to which the emerging polarization is likely to facilitate the success of U.S. or Chinese strategic aims is unclear. India has been so far a net beneficiary of the current tensions. Its strategic, political, and economic interests clearly converge with those of the United States, and it will not do anything that may undermine the U.S. position as long as U.S. policies do not affect major Indian interests. India's posture reflects pragmatism and caution rather than ideology. Moreover, conflictual rivalry with the United States is only likely to push China to be more accommodating of India's demands.

India's position on the Indo-Pacific concept illustrates this point and constitutes a subtle expression of both autonomy from and closeness to the United States. New Delhi has endorsed the concept of the Indo-Pacific and given the region its own geographic definition that encompasses the shores of East Africa. Yet it has also welcomed the ASEAN Outlook on the Indo-Pacific, which insists on dialogue and cooperation rather than rivalry and reasserts ASEAN's centrality—a pillar of India's foreign policy in Southeast Asia.[56] In doing so, India states its global convergence with the United States. But it also asserts its own specificities in the process, taking along a number of Indian Ocean littoral states that are too weak to be significant players but are unwilling to be left out. These states are ready to be part of some Indo-Pacific dynamics, a move that should ultimately politically benefit the United States. Strategic dynamics will only push India and the United States closer. Two factors could, however, lead India to diversify its options: a U.S. approach to the region that is too narrowly transactional; and India's incapacity to reform its economy at a pace sufficient to reverse, or at least stabilize, the power gap with China. In both cases, India may have to look for alternative policies and search for greater accommodation with China.

Although India would benefit from continued U.S. pressure to reform, both Indian and U.S. decision-makers will have to keep their respective expectations in check to ensure that the transition costs of reforms remain socially bearable and politically acceptable. From that perspective, the Trans-Pacific Partnership was an interesting model. India was not part of

---

[56] ASEAN, "ASEAN Outlook on the Indo-Pacific," June 2019, https://asean.org/storage/2019/06/ASEAN-Outlook-on-the-Indo-Pacific_FINAL_22062019.pdf.

negotiations and, until the Trump administration's decision not to ratify the treaty, feared being left out of the emerging dynamic. But the potential benefits that the signatories could have expected from the United States were powerful incentives for India to continue, even if only incrementally, to modernize its economy. By contrast, in the context of large asymmetry between the U.S. and Indian economies, coercion alone is unlikely to deliver reforms and will only complicate the relationship.

Finally, India's contribution to the overall balance between China and the United States should be reassessed. Furthermore, it should be analyzed in political and diplomatic terms as much as in military and economic terms. With the exception of the late 1950s and early 1960s, India has historically always managed its relations with China deftly, including in the context of growing asymmetry of power, and thereby has significantly contributed to Asia's stability. This political capacity should be understood by future U.S. administrations as a valuable resource at a time when the United States is determined to constrain China to play by established international rules but is equally reluctant to engage in new military adventures. Such considerations would not preclude the United States from helping India mitigate its power asymmetry with China. They would, however, re-establish some balance in U.S.-India relations as well as a level of trust that will be important for future developments in the relationship. An India that is confident in itself and in its relationship with the United States is more likely to accept playing a significant balancing role vis-à-vis its northern neighbor.

Appendix

Pakistan and U.S.-China Competition

The growing U.S.-China rivalry is as much a problem for Pakistan as it is for India, although for different reasons. Historically, Pakistan has always been able to maintain a balance between China and the United States. China has delivered political and military support as well as providing security guarantees against India. The United States, on the other hand, has been a traditional provider of military technology and financial support. As long as a relative stability prevailed between the two countries, Islamabad was able to maintain a subtle balance between them and use the implicit threat to move toward Beijing as a way of signaling its discontent with U.S. policies or pressure.

The intensification of the U.S.-China rivalry partly altered the existing balance by exasperating this specific dilemma in Pakistan's foreign policy. On the one hand, it did tighten the bonds between Beijing and Islamabad. Under pressure from Washington regarding both Pakistan's Afghanistan policy and use of terrorism as a tool of foreign policy, Islamabad benefited from Beijing's political protection and relative support. China used, for example, some political capital to protect Pakistan in the Masood Azhar case. Even though Beijing ultimately had to accept the registration of the leader of the Pakistani terrorist group Jaish-e-Mohammed on the UN terrorist list, it did prevent Pakistan's name from appearing in the resolution, an outcome that Islamabad presented as a diplomatic victory over India.

On the other hand, Pakistan has felt increasingly uneasy over its increased dependence on China, especially given the ambiguity of Beijing's expectations. If China is willing to use Pakistan as leverage against India, it is unwilling to let Pakistan dictate the terms of its own relationship with India. China is also not willing to support Pakistan's adventurism and will protect the country only as long as China's own interests are not affected. Pakistani officials realize that this asymmetry of power can ultimately lead to a relationship of domination, including in the security domain, where the convergence of the two countries' interests is only partial and characterized by a deep mistrust. Last but not least, the military, which dominates Pakistan's political life, is culturally much closer to the United States than it is to China.

Launched in April 2015, the China-Pakistan Economic Corridor (CPEC) exemplifies the complexity of the Sino-Pakistani relationship as well as China's ambiguity about its own expectations for Pakistan's role vis-à-vis India. The corridor was supposed to build transportation and energy infrastructure and transfer dying industries that would have found a new life in Pakistan thanks to lower labor costs. Islamabad also expected security guarantees vis-à-vis India from China's military presence in Pakistan. China, on the other hand, intended to consolidate its strategic position in the Indian Ocean and the Strait of Hormuz and find an alternative to its Malacca dilemma, an objective for which the control of the Gwadar port was central. But Pakistani officials' optimism could not mask the deeper malaise generated by overdependence on China, reinforced by the opacity of the project, while Beijing soon understood that the conditions for CPEC's economic success were not met.

As a result, Islamabad realized that it needed to get out of the zero-sum game it had fallen into and mend relations with Washington. The intensity of the relationship between China and Pakistan has grown considerably since the rapprochement between the United States and India, but Washington remains Islamabad's partner of choice, despite a complex and sometimes difficult relationship. Whatever their political reservations about U.S. policies, Pakistan's civilian and military elites are deeply aware that China will never provide them with the same level of technological and financial support as the United States has. The Afghan peace process has recently provided Pakistan with a temporary opportunity to achieve this objective. Yet it remains to be seen how far the rapprochement can go.

EXECUTIVE SUMMARY

This chapter examines Taiwan's options in navigating the growing rivalry between China and the U.S. and what its choices reveal about Taiwanese assessments of U.S. credibility and Chinese intentions.

MAIN ARGUMENT

As the rivalry between China and the U.S. intensifies, the Taiwan Strait remains one of the most important arenas of competition. The double bind of trying to preserve a strong Taiwanese identity against increasing Chinese pressure, while integrating more closely with the Chinese market to address the severe economic problems produced by Taiwan's high-income trap, has made China both an increasingly important economic partner to Taiwan and a dangerous existential threat. As a new democracy, Taipei sees the U.S. as a natural ideological ally as well as a security partner, but it also worries about Washington's unreliability as China grows stronger. This complex situation leaves Taiwan with three main options: moving closer to the U.S. to balance China, accommodating Beijing, and hedging.

POLICY IMPLICATIONS

- The U.S. must review its "one China" policy in light of changes in both cross-strait and U.S.-China relations and reassess whether and how to pursue its traditional interest in preserving a future for Taiwan that is prosperous, democratic, peaceful, and secure.

- The U.S. must increase its attractiveness as an economic partner and investment base for Taiwanese firms that may otherwise feel that they have no choice but to work more closely with China as it becomes the world's largest economy and the center of global supply chains.

- The U.S. must demonstrate the effectiveness of market economics and democratic institutions based on individual freedom in order to reinforce Taiwan's commitment to these models.

How Taiwan's High-Income Trap Shapes Its Options in the U.S.-China Competition

Syaru Shirley Lin

Since the Taiwan Relations Act was passed 40 years ago, U.S.-China relations have changed from a cooperative to a competitive relationship, while Taiwan has transformed itself from an authoritarian regime to a free and democratic nation. This means that the values of the United States and Taiwan are increasingly aligned. However, rising pressure from Beijing for unification may require the United States to re-examine its strategy toward Taiwan.[1] As the U.S.-China rivalry intensifies, there is now some reason to question whether the United States would welcome Taiwan's socioeconomic integration with China, let alone unification with the mainland, even if those developments were to occur peacefully and voluntarily. All three governments have begun to challenge the status quo. With the tension between the United States and China rising and Taiwan's interest in unification decreasing, Taiwan remains one of the most important issues in U.S.-China relations.

After Xi Jinping became China's leader in 2012, and especially after the two-term limit for the presidency was lifted in 2017, Beijing has intensified its efforts to persuade Taiwan to agree that it is part of "one China" and ultimately to accept unification on Beijing's terms. But Beijing has not been able to increase support among the Taiwanese people for unification, and few endorse Xi's insistence on the "one country, two systems" model as practiced in Hong Kong, especially after the 2019 protests.

Syaru Shirley Lin is Compton Visiting Professor in World Politics at the Miller Center of Public Affairs at the University of Virginia. She can be reached at <shirley@virginia.edu>.

[1] Russell Hsiao, "U.S.-Taiwan Relations: Hobson's Choice and the False Dilemma," in *Strategic Asia 2014–15: U.S. Alliances and Partnerships at the Center of Global Power*, ed. Ashley J. Tellis, Abraham M. Denmark, and Greg Chaffin (Seattle: National Bureau of Asian Research [NBR], 2014), 266.

In response to Beijing's more assertive and provocative posture on Taiwan, and in competition with China on economic and military issues, the U.S. government has also changed course under the Trump administration. Together with an increasingly unified Congress, the administration has focused on balancing, or even restricting, the rise of China's comprehensive national power. Under Trump, the United States has also adopted several pieces of legislation to strengthen ties with Taiwan and has approved four arms sales packages containing advanced weapons.

But perhaps more important than the policy changes in China or in the United States have been the profound changes that have occurred in Taiwan since its democratization in the late 1980s. Although the Kuomintang (KMT) and the Democratic Progressive Party (DPP) have alternated in occupying the presidency since the first free election in 1996, 2016 was the first time that the DPP won both the presidency and the legislature. This prompted Beijing, which sees the DPP as promoting independence, to immediately cut off all official dialogue with Taipei. Taiwan has responded to this growing pressure by diversifying its economy away from China and working more closely with the United States not only in defense but in other areas of foreign policy as well. In addition to unveiling a new de facto embassy building in Taipei that cost $255 million and expanding exchanges of both civilian and military officials, the United States is collaborating with Taiwan on several initiatives to elevate Taiwan's role in the region as part of a new "free and open Indo-Pacific" strategy.

The nomination process leading up to the January 2020 presidential election revealed deep divisions within both major parties and intense debate over Taiwan's policy toward the United States and China. The two leading nominees, current president Tsai Ing-wen of the DPP and Kaohsiung mayor Han Kuo-yu of the KMT, represented two starkly contrasting foreign policy positions. Beijing continues to support the KMT and openly punishes the DPP and its supporters, hoping to project the inevitability of unification. The United States will need to decide how to respond.

This chapter analyzes the objectives and strategies of the United States and China with regard to Taiwan as well as their appeal to Taiwan's major parties, political leaders, the Taiwanese business community, the military, and other interest groups. It then identifies three long-term options available to Taiwan and assesses their costs and benefits. Finally, the chapter concludes by examining the implications of this analysis for Taiwan and the region and considering policy options for the United States.

U.S. and Chinese Aims in Taiwan

Changing U.S. Strategy within Consistent Historical Objectives

In most ways, official U.S. objectives toward Taiwan have remained the same since normalization: to assure a future for Taiwan that is peaceful and acceptable to both sides of the strait without expressing a preference for the final outcome. But the United States' strategies for advancing those objectives are changing, largely in response to China's growing power and assertiveness.[2] Washington is upgrading its relationship with the island, which has been hailed as "one of the world's great trading economies and beacons of Chinese culture and democracy" by Vice President Mike Pence.[3] Under the Trump administration, the implementation of the United States' one-China policy has become more favorable to Taiwan than ever, and there seems to be greater consensus on Taiwan policy between Congress and the White House.[4] So far, the U.S. approach to Taiwan has arguably remained within the one-China framework. However, some in the United States and Taiwan, as well as in Beijing, are concerned that these changes will threaten stability in the Taiwan Strait and in the broader Asia-Pacific region.[5] Others, such as President Donald Trump's adviser Peter Navarro, have argued that the one-China policy is obsolete and needs careful review and possible revision.[6]

As part of its closer security relationship with Taiwan, the United States and its allies are conducting an increasing number of freedom of navigation operations in both the Taiwan Strait and the South China Sea to counter Chinese encroachment and to balance against increasing Chinese threats.[7] Some critics of this policy in the United States say that supporting Taiwan's security is becoming too costly and risky, while, more recently, others argue that upgrading U.S. defense relations with Taiwan is impeding a resolution

---

[2] Harry Harding, "Change and Continuity in American Policy toward Taiwan," in *Taiwan's Economic and Diplomatic Challenges and Opportunities*, ed. Dafydd Fell (London: Routledge, forthcoming); and Evan S. Medeiros, "The Changing Fundamentals of U.S.-China Relations," *Washington Quarterly* 42, no. 3 (2019): 93–119.

[3] Mike Pence (remarks at the Frederic V. Malek Memorial Lecture, Washington, D.C., October 24, 2019), https://www.whitehouse.gov/briefings-statements/remarks-vice-president-pence-frederic-v-malek-memorial-lecture.

[4] Dean P. Chen, "The Trump Administration's One-China Policy: Tilting toward Taiwan in an Era of U.S.-PRC Rivalry?" *Asian Politics and Policy* 11, no. 2 (2019): 250–78.

[5] See, for example, Richard N. Hass, "Asia's Scary Movie," Project Syndicate, July 17, 2019, https://www.project-syndicate.org/commentary/asian-stability-in-jeopardy-by-richard-n-haass-2019-07?barrier=accesspaylog.

[6] Peter Navarro, "America Can't Dump Taiwan," *National Interest*, July 19, 2016, https://nationalinterest.org/feature/america-cant-dump-taiwan-17040?page=0%2C1.

[7] Karen Leigh and Dandan Li, "Taiwan Sees Most U.S. Navy Sail-Bys Since Trump Took Office," Bloomberg, July 25, 2019, https://www.bloomberg.com/news/articles/2019-07-25/u-s-warship-sails-through-taiwan-strait-ahead-of-trade-talks.

of the trade dispute with China.[8] However, Taiwan's geostrategic importance as part of the first island chain is a cornerstone of U.S. efforts to balance or contain Chinese power projection in the Pacific.[9] There is bipartisan support to provide more advanced weapons, including the $8 billion sale of 66 new F-16 fighter jets and the $2.2 billion sale of Abrams main battle tanks and Stinger missiles to Taiwan in 2019.[10] There is also more engagement between defense officials from the two sides, presumably to discuss the further upgrading of Taiwan's defense capabilities and coordination of strategy in the event of a Chinese attack. These developments have been accompanied by the passage of the Taiwan Travel Act, the National Defense Authorization Act, and the Asia Reassurance Initiative Act (ARIA), as well as the introduction of the proposed Taiwan Assurance Act and the Taiwan Allies International Protection and Enhancement Initiative (TAIPEI) Act. All these initiatives reflect greater U.S. support for Taiwan. With Trump's approval, Tsai Ing-wen visited the United States in July 2019, making stops in New York and Denver. She also met with the representatives of Taiwan's diplomatic allies in the United Nations, and received perhaps the warmest welcome given to any leader of Taiwan. In the past, the United States seemed more concerned about Taiwanese leaders who might provoke Beijing by showing sympathy for formal independence. Now, however, it is increasingly worried about leaders who might be too accommodating to China.

The United States is also helping Taiwan create a more innovative and dynamic economy by working with civil-society organizations to promote innovation, women's empowerment, and entrepreneurship. Under the Global Cooperation and Training Framework, which was created during the Obama administration, and the new Consultations on Democratic Governance in the Indo-Pacific Region, Washington is also helping Taiwan share its development experience with countries in Southeast Asia. The joint efforts to promote entrepreneurship are important for reversing Taiwan's brain drain, particularly to China. Through these efforts, the United States is trying to reduce the international marginalization of Taiwan and enhance its relations

---

[8] Ted Galen Carpenter, "Taiwan's Growing Political Turbulence Creates a Problem for Washington," Cato Institute, May 15, 2019, https://www.cato.org/publications/commentary/taiwans-growing-political-turbulence-creates-problem-washington.

[9] Robert D. Kaplan, "The Geography of Chinese Power: How Far Can Beijing Reach on Land and at Sea?" *Foreign Affairs*, May/June 2010, 22–41.

[10] Chris Horton, "Taiwan Set to Receive $2 Billion in U.S. Arms, Drawing Ire from China," *New York Times*, July 9, 2019, https://www.nytimes.com/2019/07/09/world/asia/taiwan-arms-sales.html; and Ryan Browne, "Trump Admin Formally Approves Fighter Jet Sale to Taiwan amid China Trade Fight," CNN, August 21, 2019, https://edition.cnn.com/2019/08/20/politics/taiwan-fighter-jet-sales/index.html.

with the region by leveraging Taiwan's position as an advanced economy with an open market and a democratic system.

The weakest link in the U.S.-Taiwan relationship is trade and investment, which, unless repaired, may steer Taiwan more toward the Chinese market in the long term.[11] There has been little progress in negotiating a trade and investment framework agreement or a bilateral free trade agreement, given Taiwan's lack of resolve to lift restrictions on pork imports from the United States.[12] More recently, Taiwan has become an unintended victim of changing U.S. trade policy under the Trump administration. First, the United States withdrew from the Trans-Pacific Partnership (TPP), which Taiwan had hoped to join in the future. Then, the U.S. trade war against China hurt Taiwanese exporters, initially by subjecting their steel and aluminum exports to higher global tariffs. Taiwan's economy is also particularly vulnerable to Washington's threat to raise tariffs on Chinese information and communications technology, since so much of that technology is produced by Taiwanese-owned firms.[13]

One of the United States' key objectives in its rivalry with China is to maintain U.S. technological superiority, and Taiwan plays a particularly important role in that regard because of its leadership in semiconductor fabrication. Even the most advanced Chinese companies such as Huawei still cannot make cutting-edge chips.[14] The United States is pressuring Taiwan to refrain from being a conduit of advanced technology to China and is promoting cooperation between U.S. and Taiwanese technology companies, especially in semiconductor manufacturing, to fend off technology theft by China.[15]

Xi Jinping's Accelerating Progress toward Unification

Beijing's policy toward Taiwan remains within the strategy set by Deng Xiaoping but exhibits a greater sense of urgency. Like previous Chinese leaders, Xi continues to stress that unification with Taiwan is one of China's

---

[11] Ashley J. Tellis, "Sign a Free-Trade Deal with Taiwan," *Wall Street Journal*, December 2, 2018, https://www.wsj.com/articles/sign-a-free-trade-deal-with-taiwan-1543786364.

[12] "Taiwan's Ban on American Beef, Pork a Trade Barrier: U.S. Report," Taiwan News, March 30, 2019, https://www.taiwannews.com.tw/en/news/3669693.

[13] Tariffs that could significantly hurt Taiwan's economy have not been implemented yet. For more information, see Ralph Jennings, "Trade War: Why Next U.S. Tariffs on China Could Halve Taiwan's Growth," *South China Morning Post*, May 17, 2019, https://www.scmp.com/news/article/3010524/trade-war-why-next-us-tariffs-china-could-halve-taiwans-growth.

[14] James A. Lewis, "Learning the Superior Techniques of the Barbarians: China's Pursuit of Semiconductor Independence," Center for Strategic and International Studies (CSIS), January 2019, https://csis-prod.s3.amazonaws.com/s3fs-public/publication/190115_Lewis_Semiconductor_v6.pdf.

[15] Heather Timmons, "The U.S.'s Newest Partner in Fighting Chinese Intellectual Property Theft Is Taiwan," Quartz, November 2, 2018, https://qz.com/1447913/the-us-is-partnering-with-taiwan-to-fight-chinas-intellectual-property-theft.

core interests.[16] But Chinese objectives regarding Taiwan are now being stated more explicitly and pursued more aggressively than ever, backed by bigger sticks and sweeter carrots.[17] On January 1, 2019, Xi explicitly demanded that Taiwan agree to eventual unification on the basis of the same one country, two systems framework that Beijing has applied to Hong Kong, perhaps with some as yet unspecified variations.[18] While this position was implicit in Beijing's previous interpretation of the 1992 Consensus—the tacit agreement that each side is committed to eventual unification—it is now being stated more unequivocally. Moreover, Xi's demand that the Taiwan issue not be passed "from generation to generation" suggests a deadline that many interpret as being during his leadership.[19]

Moreover, Beijing has repeated that it will not renounce the use of military force against Taiwan to achieve unification and has dispatched naval and air forces in and around the Taiwan Strait to demonstrate its ability to use force. In China's white paper on national defense released in July 2019, the language on the United States and Taiwan is aggressive and unambiguous. Secessionist movements in Taiwan, and also those in Xinjiang and Tibet, are listed as leading security threats, and unification with Taiwan is identified as one of China's primary goals. Compared with the 2015 white paper, this report devotes greater attention to Taiwan, emphasizes the potential use of force, and openly states that drills in the Taiwan Strait are stern warnings against secessionists:[20]

> To solve the Taiwan question and achieve complete reunification of the country is in the fundamental interests of the Chinese nation and essential to realizing national rejuvenation. China adheres to the principles of "peaceful reunification," and "one country, two systems," promotes development of cross-Strait relations, and advances peaceful reunification of the country. Meanwhile, China resolutely opposes any attempts or actions to split the country and any foreign interference to this end. China must be and will be reunited....We make no promise to

[16] Michael S. Chase, "A Rising China's Challenge to Taiwan," in *Strategic Asia 2019: China's Expanding Strategic Ambitions*, ed. Ashley J. Tellis, Alison Szalwinski, and Michael Wills (Seattle: NBR, 2019), 113–19.

[17] Syaru Shirley Lin, "Xi Jinping's Taiwan Policy and Its Impact on Cross-Strait Relations," Hoover Institution, China Leadership Monitor, June 1, 2019, https://www.prcleader.org/lin.

[18] Xi Jinping, "Working Together to Realize Rejuvenation of the Chinese Nation and Advance China's Peaceful Reunification" (speech, Beijing, January 2, 2019), http://www.gwytb.gov.cn/wyly/201904/t20190412_12155687.htm.

[19] For Chinese articles on Xi's Taiwan policy, see Zhou Zhihuai, "Xi Jinping de guojia tongyiguan yu duiTai gongzuo lunshu de hexin lilun chuangjian" [Xi Jinping's View on Reunification and His Insightful Theorization of Taiwan-Related Initiatives], *Cross–Taiwan Strait Studies*, no. 2 (2019): 1–7; and Teddy Ng, "Xi Jinping Says Efforts Must Be Made to Close the China-Taiwan Political Divide," *South China Morning Post*, October 6, 2013, https://www.scmp.com/news/china/article/1325761/xi-jinping-says-political-solution-taiwan-cant-wait-forever.

[20] Helena Legarda, "China Global Security Tracker, No. 5," International Institute for Strategic Studies, August 1, 2019, https://www.iiss.org/blogs/research-paper/2019/08/china-security-tracker-jan-to-june.

renounce the use of force, and reserve the option of taking all necessary measures....The PLA will resolutely defeat anyone attempting to separate Taiwan from China and safeguard national unity at all costs.[21]

In response, the United States, sometimes joined by France, Canada, and Australia, has conducted regular freedom of navigation operations through the Taiwan Strait, which have further angered Beijing. China conducted three more sets of drills off the coast of Taiwan after the July and August announcements of arms sales and the U.S. Navy's transit through the Taiwan Strait.[22]

As part of a strategy to isolate Taiwan internationally, Beijing has persuaded several of the island's longtime diplomatic allies, such as Panama, El Salvador, and the Solomon Islands, to sever ties with Taipei after Tsai Ing-wen became president. This campaign has left only fifteen states that recognize Taipei. Taiwan's participation in international organizations has also been severely restricted. Furthermore, multinational corporations with a presence in China are under pressure from Beijing to describe Taiwan on their websites and printed materials as part of China rather than as a separate country.[23]

On an individual level, China is punishing Taiwanese whom it regards as hostile by denying them visas to visit China, blocking their access to Hong Kong, and even arresting some of those who traveled to China.[24] This hard-line strategy has been reinforced through the exercise of "sharp power" to infiltrate and influence Taiwanese society and "sticky power" to provide the Taiwanese people with economic incentives and create dependence.[25] In an attempt to influence the 2018 local elections and the 2020 presidential and legislative elections, China augmented its traditional "united front" strategy through friendly media and civil-society

---

[21] State Council Information Office of the People's Republic of China, *China's National Defense in the New Era* (Beijing, July 2019), http://english.www.gov.cn/archive/whitepaper/201907/24/content_WS5d3941ddc6d08408f502283d.html.

[22] Laura Zhou, "Chinese Military Starts Taiwan Strait Drills amid Rising Tension with U.S. over Island," *South China Morning Post*, July 29, 2019, https://www.scmp.com/news/china/military/article/3020544/chinese-military-starts-taiwan-strait-drills-amid-rising.

[23] See, for example, "Three Biggest U.S. Airlines Bow to China Taiwan Demand as Deadline Passes," BBC, July 25, 2018, https://www.bbc.com/news/world-asia-china-44948599; and "China Fines Retailer Muji for Listing Taiwan as a Country," BBC, May 24, 2016, https://www.bbc.com/news/world-asia-china-44234270.

[24] Brian Hioe, "China Retaliates against Continued Advocacy for Lee Ming-Che's Release," New Bloom, February 4, 2019, https://newbloommag.net/2019/02/04/lee-ming-che-retaliate.

[25] For a definition of sharp power, see Christopher Walker and Jessica Ludwig, "The Meaning of Sharp Power: How Authoritarian States Project Influence," *Foreign Affairs*, November 16, 2017. For a definition of sticky power, see Walter Russell Mead, "America's Sticky Power," *Foreign Policy*, March 2004, 46–53.

organizations and disinformation campaigns.[26] These efforts have focused on supporting pro-Beijing individuals as well as friendly political parties such as the KMT. In 2017, Xi enacted 31 preferential policies for Taiwanese "compatriots," allowing Taiwanese to work and live in China with the same privileges as Chinese nationals. These incentives targeted Taiwanese who have traditionally not supported the KMT or closer relations with China, including farmers, doctors, PhD students, and young people, as well as small and medium-sized business owners and other professionals.[27] Chinese investment in Taiwan, while still largely prohibited by Taipei, is increasingly taking place through proxy individuals and pro-Beijing offshore and onshore companies.

The Convergence of Taiwanese Interests with U.S. and Chinese Interests

As the rivalry between the United States and China increases, the challenges that Taiwan faces in navigating between the two countries become greater. China has become more attractive as a partner that can provide solutions to Taiwan's slowing economic growth, even though China's own growth rates are also experiencing a gradual decline. The United States is still viewed by most Taiwanese as an irreplaceable security partner, but some doubt its reliability under the Trump administration and its credibility as China becomes more powerful. For many Taiwanese leaders, working more closely with the United States militarily and politically, but maintaining or even increasing economic and societal ties with China, is a necessary balancing act. It is within this context that the preferences of Taiwan converge or diverge with the interests of the two rivals.

As Taiwan faces the severe socioeconomic challenges typical of any high-income economy, it is caught in a double bind that is difficult for its leaders to resolve. The first imperative is to preserve a strong Taiwanese identity with democratic values against increasing Chinese pressure to

---

[26] Gary Schmitt and Michael Mazza, "Blinding the Enemy: CCP Interference in Taiwan's Democracy," Global Taiwan Institute, October 2019, http://globaltaiwan.org/wp-content/uploads/2019/10/GTI-CCP-Interference-Taiwan-Democracy-Oct-2019-final.pdf; and Sonny Shiu-Hing Lo, "Co-opting Individuals with External Implications: Business Elites, Democrats, Civil Servants, Educators and Taiwanese," in China's New United Front Work in Hong Kong: Penetrative Politics and Its Implications, ed. Sonny Shiu-Hing Lo, Steven Chung-Fun Hung, and Jeff Hai-Chi Loo (London: Palgrave Macmillan, 2019), chap. 10.

[27] See "Huitai 31 tiao quanmian luoshi tongdeng daiyu" [31 Preferential Measures: Full Implementation of Equal Treatment], China Times, May 2, 2019, https://www.chinatimes.com/newspapers/20190502000129-260301?chdtv; and Ralph Jennings, "China Stockpiles Options for Taiwan Charm Offensive," Voice of America (VOA), September 11, 2019, https://www.voanews.com/east-asia-pacific/china-stockpiles-options-taiwan-charm-offensive.

restore a Chinese identity. The second is to integrate more closely with the Chinese market to alleviate the economic problems associated with the high-income trap. The dilemma created by this double bind partly explains the political debates and the resulting oscillations in Taiwan's policies in the last three decades.

The Double Bind of Strong Taiwanese Identity and the High-Income Trap

The first half of the double bind is the need to defend a consolidated Taiwanese identity, which has sharply diverged from the Chinese identity that the Nationalist government tried to impose on Taiwan and that Beijing wishes to promote. Although it was taboo to question Chinese identity under the previous dictatorship, soon after the lifting of martial law in 1987 the residents of Taiwan became able to explore what it meant to be Taiwanese and began to develop a distinctive political culture of their own. Ironically, Beijing's attempts to use its own definition of a Chinese identity to replace the one promoted by the Nationalists accelerated Taiwan's search for its own identity. What emerged was a way of life rooted in civic nationalism and democratic values that has become very difficult to reverse, despite Beijing's painstaking efforts, especially among younger generations that have grown up in a democracy.[28]

Surveys and polls that began three decades ago demonstrate this consolidation of a Taiwanese identity. That identity can be measured in two ways: as self-identification and as a preference regarding Taiwan's future political status. Self-identification is usually gauged through a three-way question: are you Chinese, Taiwanese, or both? In 1989, over half of the respondents called themselves exclusively Chinese. That figure has fallen to around 4% for over a decade, replaced by identities that have a Taiwanese component. In terms of preference for Taiwan's political future, respondents can select from a range of options on the spectrum from independence to unification. Support for the most extreme option (immediate unification), which implies absorption into China, has hovered around 1%–3% for decades. Conversely, for more than a decade, over 85% of Taiwanese have supported some other form of autonomy.[29] In recent years, Taiwanese have rejected

[28] Syaru Shirley Lin, *Taiwan's China Dilemma: Contested Identities and Multiple Interests in Taiwan's Cross-Strait Economic Policy* (Stanford: Stanford University Press, 2016); and Syaru Shirley Lin, "Analyzing the Relationship between Identity and Democratization in Taiwan and Hong Kong in the Shadow of China," *ASAN Forum*, December 20, 2018, http://www.theasanforum.org/analyzing-the-relationship-between-identity-and-democratization-in-taiwan-and-hong-kong-in-the-shadow-of-china.

[29] "Trends of Core Political Attitudes (1992/06~2019/06)," National Chengchi University, Election Study Center, July 10, 2019, https://esc.nccu.edu.tw/course/news.php?class=203.

leaders whose cross-strait economic policies they perceived as allowing the mainland to threaten or undermine Taiwan's identity and values. While older generations remain focused on economic prosperity and have strong views on China, whether favorable or unfavorable, young people are pragmatic about seizing opportunities in China without sacrificing Taiwan's autonomy. They prefer leaders who are firmly Taiwanese, have progressive values, and can effectively manage both domestic governance and cross-strait relations.

The second half of the double bind is to find a solution to Taiwan's high-income trap. At the same time that it liberalized politically, Taiwan also attained the status of a high-income economy, joining the ranks of Japan, South Korea, Singapore, and Hong Kong as well as the advanced economies of Western Europe and North America. The rise in Taiwanese living standards was achieved after decades of double-digit growth fueled by the export of higher value–added products. But as soon as Taiwan reached high-income status, it faced fierce competition from lower-cost manufacturing economies, especially China, and its position in the global value chain deteriorated. Taiwan entered a trap whereby society expects higher standards of living and increasing welfare entitlements, but those expectations become more difficult to meet as growth rates decline and painful trade-offs must be made.[30]

Like other East Asian economies caught in the high-income trap, Taiwan's interrelated symptoms include slower growth, stagnating wages, demographic decline, a high youth unemployment rate, and the inequalities and risks produced by financialization. These structural issues are hard to resolve. The Ma Ying-jeou administration attempted to do so between 2008 and 2016 by relying on China to stimulate growth while maintaining cross-strait stability. After several years of closer integration, including increased Taiwanese investments in China, in Ma's last full year as president Taiwan's GDP growth rate dropped to less than 1% and Taiwan's trade surplus with China fell to a nine-year low. As growth stagnated, average real wage levels for Taiwanese workers in nine out of nineteen sectors also declined after 2000, especially in export-oriented manufacturing.[31] Although business and political elites benefited from closer integration with China, workers suffered and inequality grew. While many in high-income societies blame the trap on globalization, Taiwanese, especially the younger generations, have identified China and cross-strait economic liberalization as the more specific culprits for job losses,

---

[30] Syaru Shirley Lin, "Taiwan in the High Income Trap and Its Implications for Cross-Strait Relations," in Fell, *Taiwan's Economic and Diplomatic Challenges and Opportunities.*

[31] Earnings Exploration and Information System database, Directorate-General of Budget, Accounting and Statistics, Executive Yuan (Taiwan), https://earnings.dgbas.gov.tw.

wage stagnation, and inequality.[32] Therefore, while some people view China as a solution to the high-income trap, many young people and marginalized groups see it as exacerbating the problem.

This double bind—the tension between efforts to consolidate Taiwanese identity threatened by China and the perception that China can help Taiwan escape the high-income trap—has had far-reaching political consequences. In 2014 the student-led Sunflower Movement successfully blocked the ratification of an agreement that would have allowed greater Chinese investment in Taiwan. Subsequently, the DPP won a landslide victory in the local midterm elections in late 2014 and in the presidential and legislative elections in 2016. The expectation was high that the DPP would better safeguard Taiwan's values, invigorate the economy, and escape the high-income trap, which had been aggravated, rather than alleviated, by further integration with the Chinese economy. Since 2016, the DPP government under Tsai Ing-wen has tried to pursue this agenda by moving beyond the lower-end consumer electronics industry that has dominated Taiwan's export economy for decades and promoting higher value–added software and manufacturing. However, the higher costs of a wide range of inputs, excessive financial regulation, lack of innovation, and increasing competition from emerging markets are creating what seem to be insurmountable obstacles to these policies. In response, Tsai has tried to diversify Taiwan's foreign trade and investment by adopting the New Southbound Policy to encourage trade and investment with the Association of Southeast Asian Nations (ASEAN) members and South Asian countries as well as a set of painful domestic structural reforms.[33] Because many of these reforms were poorly conceived and executed, the DPP lost the midterm local elections in 2018 in a landslide defeat to the KMT, which regained all the seats it had lost in the previous election cycle.[34]

Just as economic policy toward China has fluctuated, Taiwan's political parties have traded places three times, from the KMT to the DPP in 2000, to the KMT in 2008, and back to the DPP in 2016. The victory of the KMT and its relatively pro-China candidates in the local midterm elections of 2018 boosted its confidence regarding the national elections in 2020. However, neither party has been able to permanently convince Taiwanese voters that it can simultaneously promote economic prosperity and national security, and

[32] Thung-hong Lin, "Ni shi 1977 nianhou chusheng dema? Kuayue 25 nain shuju da diaocha 30 duosui yishi shouru gaofeng, cisheng buhui zai zhuangengduo" [Are You Born after 1977? Survey Data for 25 Years Show That You Will Peak at Age 30 and Never Make More], *Business Today*, July 31, 2019.

[33] Bonnie S. Glaser et al., "The New Southbound Policy: Deepening Taiwan's Regional Integration," CSIS, January 19, 2018, https://www.csis.org/analysis/new-southbound-policy.

[34] Richard C. Bush, "Taiwan's Local Elections, Explained," Brookings Institution, December 5, 2018, https://www.brookings.edu/blog/order-from-chaos/2018/12/05/taiwans-local-elections-explained.

subsequent developments make a KMT victory increasingly improbable as of the time of writing.

Taiwan's Political Parties and the Double Bind

After three decades of democratization, the two leading political parties and several smaller ones allied with them dominate Taiwan's politics, even though third-party candidates continue to emerge during every presidential election, including James Soong, who ran for the fourth time in the 2020 election.[35] The two major parties serve as interest aggregators, advocating distinctive policies on issues ranging from international relations and economic reform to social justice and environmental sustainability. Historically, they have been divided over national identity and Taiwan's future political status. The DPP had an emerging Taiwanese identity and leaned toward independence, while the KMT was led by elites from the mainland who were more sympathetic to a Chinese identity and unification. Over time, however, this distinction began to blur as all presidential candidates embraced Taiwanese identity and promoted Taiwan's autonomy to varying degrees.

On economic policies, the two parties' more recent strategies for lifting Taiwan out of the high-income trap have differed because of their other domestic priorities. The DPP has upheld labor rights, social welfare, and environmental sustainability and prioritized safeguarding Taiwan's sovereignty. To the DPP, therefore, distributional issues are far more important than economic growth, although the two DPP presidents—Chen Shui-bian and Tsai Ing-wen—have often been criticized as too accommodating to businesses and as failing to carry out important reforms. In contrast, the KMT has focused on improving economic growth and the business climate. The DPP has enjoyed strong grass-roots ties, especially in southern Taiwan, whereas the KMT has been elite-led but maintained a strong network of specific interest groups across the island.

On foreign policy, both parties have acknowledged the importance of the United States, but they have differed on policy toward the mainland, specifically on how much to integrate with the Chinese economy. But the elite-led KMT has been far more adept at dealing with both the United States and China than its rival. This is because the KMT has strong links to Washington dating back to World War II. Both popularly elected KMT presidents—Lee Teng-hui and Ma Ying-jeou—were U.S.-educated, and KMT-trained officials, often educated in the United States, have dominated

---

[35] Kharis Templeman, "The Dynamics of Taiwan's Party Politics" (conference presentation, Nottingham, June 27–28, 2019), https://www.kharistempleman.com/uploads/1/5/8/5/15855636/templeman. dynamics_of_taiwans_party_system.20190614.pdf.

the foreign ministry and intelligence bureaucracies. Although staunchly anti-Communist, the party ironically has shared a common vision of Chinese nationalism and eventual unification with the Chinese Communist Party (CCP). They also share common Leninist roots, at least before Taiwan's democratization. In 1992, the KMT resumed communication with the CCP on a party-to-party basis after a gap of over four decades.

For its part, the DPP was a newly formed party with personal ties to Japan and the United States, especially the Taiwanese diaspora, but with limited institutional ties abroad.[36] The DPP's first president, Chen Shui-bian, pushed the issue of Taiwanese sovereignty and was therefore regarded as a troublemaker by Washington and *persona non grata* by Beijing. Thus, the KMT was preferred by both the United States and China for maintaining predictability and stability in the Taiwan Strait until the KMT lost control of the legislature and presidency in 2016. Beijing then realized that it could no longer count on the KMT to defeat the DPP, let alone deliver unification,[37] and the United States realized that the KMT might move closer to China than Washington preferred.

The KMT Turns Populist and Favors Relying on Beijing

Today's political map has been significantly redrawn, in large part due to changes in Washington and Beijing. KMT president Ma Ying-jeou's eight years of détente with Beijing were welcomed by the United States and lauded as promoting regional stability.[38] But Ma's cross-strait policies did not resonate with Taiwanese voters, especially the youth and the working class, who believed that economic dependence on China exacerbated Taiwan's inequality and diluted its democratic values. Furthermore, Ma failed to meet Beijing's expectation of opening political negotiations. After the KMT's humiliating defeat in the 2016 presidential and legislative elections, a new group of populist leaders replaced Ma and the mainstream old guards who had been familiar to both the United States and China. The most prominent of these was the KMT's 2020 presidential nominee Han Kuo-yu, a charismatic outsider and second-generation mainlander, who in 2018 won the mayorship of Kaohsiung, a former DPP stronghold. Without any formal U.S. education,

---

[36] Shelley Rigger, *From Opposition to Power: Taiwan's Democratic Progressive Party* (Boulder: Lynne Rienner, 2001).

[37] Chen Hongjin, "Xi Jinping miandui de shi yige shenmeyangde Guomindang?" [What Kind of Kuomintang Is Xi Jinping Faced With?] Initium Media, November 1, 2016, https://theinitium.com/article/20161101-taiwan-KMT.

[38] Yu-Shan Wu, "Pivot, Hedger, or Partner: Strategies of Lesser Powers Caught between Hegemons," in *Taiwan and China: Fitful Embrace*, ed. Dittmer Lowell (Berkeley: University of California Press, 2017), 197–220.

Han often cites Chiang Ching-kuo, Lee Kuan-yew, and Deng Xiaoping as his heroes, appealing to a nostalgic authoritarian past where stability and growth were the primary goals along with a strong sense of Chinese identity.[39]

Han's main popular appeal is on economic issues, and he presents deeper integration with China as the key to continued economic growth. He has proposed creating a free economic pilot zone in Kaohsiung to attract more Chinese investment. Although Han has agreed to the 1992 Consensus, he and other leaders supportive of the KMT all eventually rejected unification under Beijing's one country, two systems formula, with Han colorfully saying that Taiwan would accept it "over my dead body."[40] However, Han has yet to articulate a coherent cross-strait policy.[41] So the double bind—to promote the economy while preserving Taiwan's autonomy and identity—is reflected in the ambiguity of Han's policy toward China. Nonetheless, Han's presidential campaign was supported by pro-Beijing media, and there were allegations that the CCP invested heavily in his campaign.[42] Although business elites with ties to China (who have traditionally supported the KMT) welcomed his more accommodative approach to Beijing, they have also been concerned that Han is an inexperienced populist who may harm their interests in the end.

Furthermore, most Taiwanese businesses want to maintain good relations with both parties and tend to keep a low profile during elections. Taiwanese firms that operate in China and Southeast Asia (*taishang*) are in a particularly awkward position because their business has depended on exports to the United States, which makes both U.S.-Taiwan and U.S.-China relations important. Taiwanese technology companies, especially the semiconductor leaders Taiwan Semiconductor Manufacturing Company (TSMC) and United Microelectronics Corporation (UMC) that manufacture products in Taiwan and China for U.S., European, and Chinese clients such as Huawei, face conflicts of interest and evidence of intellectual

---

[39] Han Kuo-yu, "Wei Zhonghua Minguo buxi fenshen suigu" [Smashed into Pieces without Regret for the Republic of China], *China Times*, June 1, 2019, https://www.chinatimes.com/realtimenews/20190601002380-260407?chdtv.

[40] Minnie Chan, Kristin Huang, and Matt Ho, "How the Storm over Hong Kong's Extradition Bill Battered Beijing's 'One Country, Two Systems' Ambitions for Taiwan," *South China Morning Post*, June 22, 2019, https://www.scmp.com/news/china/politics/article/3015578/how-storm-over-hong-kongs-extradition-bill-battered-beijings.

[41] "Tongpi Tsai bitan Zhonghua Minguo, Han Kuo-Yu: Wo yeyou henshen de wangguogan" [Criticizing Tsai's Refusal of Mentioning the Republic of China, Han Kuo-Yu Said He Deeply Felt the Downfall of the Nation], *China Times*, October 10, 2019, https://www.chinatimes.com/realtimenews/20191010001176-260407?chdtv.

[42] Kathrin Hille, "China Is Influencing Taiwan's Elections—Through TV," OZY, July 26, 2019, https://www.ozy.com/fast-forward/china-is-influencing-taiwans-elections-through-tv/95666; and Paul Huang, "Chinese Cyber-Operatives Boosted Taiwan's Insurgent Candidate," *Foreign Policy*, June 26, 2019, https://foreignpolicy.com/2019/06/26/chinese-cyber-operatives-boosted-taiwans-insurgent-candidate.

property theft among these customers, making producing for them more problematic than ever.[43] A China-friendly government can provide some assistance to these businesses but may not be able to eliminate the growing risks of manufacturing in China. Furthermore, few businesses, especially taishang, are interested in asserting themselves politically and becoming active in Taiwan's domestic politics out of fear that they will be scrutinized at home by the DPP or penalized in China by the CCP.[44] While some business groups are openly supportive of Beijing, the business community as a whole welcomes promoting a closer relationship with the United States without provoking China.

The DPP Turns Technocratic and Favors Closer Ties with the United States

The double bind also puts the DPP in a difficult position. The DPP has traditionally appealed to native Taiwanese, many of whom have been sympathetic to Taiwan's independence for decades and oppose dealing with China in any form, and to working-class families who have been the losers in globalization and in "mainlandization." Many DPP leaders began their careers as activists under the KMT's authoritarian rule and care deeply about transitional justice, progressive social values, and environmental sustainability. However, the DPP has been commonly viewed as hostile to China and unfriendly to business; therefore, some voters have doubted that it could effectively deal with Taiwan's economic challenges.

Tsai Ing-wen is a technocrat who was deeply involved in Taiwan's accession to the World Trade Organization and a moderate who has demonstrated restraint by toeing the official one-China line rather than endorsing independence. But she has disappointed both Beijing and the deep blue by refusing to reaffirm the 1992 Consensus and the deep green who saw her election as an opportunity to move toward independence.[45] Compared with her provocative predecessors, the KMT's Lee Teng-hui and the DPP's Chen Shui-bian, Tsai is a voice of moderation and reason, while being far less enthusiastic about deepening relations with China than Ma Ying-jeou. Economically, she has a solid record of overseeing rising wages, the lowest unemployment rate in decades, and record-level exports. The Sino-U.S.

---

[43] Matthew Fulco, "Semiconductor Firms Strive to Contain Trade-Secret Theft," *Taiwan Business TOPICS*, September 19, 2018, https://topics.amcham.com.tw/2018/09/semiconductor-firms-strive-to-contain-trade-secret-theft.

[44] Gunter Schubert, Ruihua Lin, and Jean Yu-Chen Tseng, "Are Taiwanese Entrepreneurs a Strategic Group?" *Asian Survey* 57, no. 5 (2017): 856–84.

[45] "Blue" refers to individuals and parties supportive of the KMT and unification, while "green" refers to supporters of the DPP and an independence-leaning agenda.

trade war and China's economic slowdown have made China less appealing as an investment destination, and the DPP has had some initial success in helping taishang return to Taiwan or move to Southeast Asia through the New Southbound Policy.[46] Still, while Tsai has advocated the diversification of Taiwan's markets, its export and trade surplus with China actually reached an all-time high in 2018, and its investments in China have steadily increased as well.[47] Overall, Taiwan's economic growth in 2019 is estimated to outpace its high-income neighbors.[48]

However, Tsai's labor, pension, and energy reforms were viewed as badly designed and executed and were a primary reason for the DPP's abysmal performance in the 2018 local elections. Energy reform is an issue that illustrates the challenges facing Tsai in implementing structural changes. Although the DPP had promised for years to create a nuclear-free homeland, phasing out nuclear energy increased the use of fossil fuel, which worsened carbon emissions and air pollution as well as power outages, all of which led to mounting criticism.

Tsai has sought positive relations with both the United States and China, with mixed results. Beijing failed to accept Tsai's overtures and instead intensified its hard-line tactics, leaving her with little room to maneuver. However, Xi Jinping's pronouncement in January 2019 that reasserted China's right to use force to compel unification and equated the 1992 Consensus with acceptance of unification under the one country, two systems policy backfired badly and revived Tsai's popularity after the DPP's 2018 electoral defeat. Her support, particularly among young Taiwanese, was further enhanced by the enactment of same-sex marriage legislation in May 2019 and the mass antigovernment protests in Hong Kong that started in June 2019.[49] Beijing was seen as threatening Hong Kong's autonomy as well as its freedoms of speech, press, and assembly, and this united the city's students, professionals, and businesses in opposition. The protests only reinforced the long-standing view that China's one country, two systems formula is

---

[46] In January 2019, the government issued the "Action Plan for Welcoming Overseas Taiwanese Businesses to Return to Invest in Taiwan" to assist Taiwanese companies with reinvesting in Taiwan. By October 2019, NT$622.3 billion of Taiwanese reinvestment had been approved. For more details, see Elaine Huang and Liang-Rong Chen, "Made in Taiwan, Straight to the United States," *CommonWealth Magazine*, July 15, 2019, https://english.cw.com.tw/article/article.action?id=2471. For results of the New Southbound Policy, see data from Office of Trade Negotiations, Executive Yuan (Taiwan), https://www.ey.gov.tw/otn/52AE1A9E6029676F.

[47] For data related to cross-strait trade and investment, see "Cross-Strait Economic Statistics Monthly," Mainland Affairs Council (Taiwan), https://www.mac.gov.tw/en/Content_List. aspx?n=13E6E9C4BE15A3CA.

[48] Huang Tzu-ti, "Taiwan's Economy Grows by 2.91% in Third Quarter," *Taiwan News*, November 1, 2019, https://www.taiwannews.com.tw/en/news/3807881.

[49] Hilton Yip, "Xi Jinping Is Tsai Ing-wen's Best Poster Boy," *Foreign Policy*, July 10, 2019, https://foreignpolicy.com/2019/07/10/xi-jinping-is-tsai-ing-wens-best-poster-boy.

unacceptable to Taiwan.[50] The suppression of the protests by the Hong Kong police produced widespread outrage among Taiwanese, increasing opposition to this policy to an all-time high and boosting Tsai's support.[51]

As a result of the protests in Hong Kong, solving Taiwan's high-income trap through diversification of economic relations became more appealing, especially in light of the U.S.-China trade war. In July 2019, Tsai made several public speeches during transit stops in New York and Denver, clearly distinguishing herself from Han, who had visited the United States earlier but without high-profile appearances. Partly due to her cautious approach to cross-strait relations and her outreach to the United States, Tsai may be the Taiwanese president with the highest level of U.S. support since democratization.

Although Taiwan's military historically has been one of the island's most important interest groups, its political orientation has changed dramatically in recent decades. Traditionally a KMT stronghold, after democratization and the dismantling of much of the party's apparatus within both the government and society, the officer corps has made clear that it is faithful to the constitution and is no longer partisan, and some have even become more sympathetic to Tsai and the DPP. In part, this is because the KMT has an uneven record in supporting funds for the military. During the Chen presidency, KMT legislators obstructed approval of arms purchases from the United States, saying that they "opposed wasteful arms procurement" that appeared necessary only because Chen was provoking Beijing.[52] After the KMT returned to power in 2008, Ma also proposed to buy less advanced weapons in order to avoid irking Beijing. During the 2019 KMT primary, candidate Terry Gou argued that his pro-China policy would reduce conflict in the strait, and that Taiwan could stop purchasing arms from the United States.[53] The military has thus come to see the KMT as a less reliable ally. In contrast, the Tsai administration has endorsed the transformation of the military to increase its ability to defend Taiwan and deter Beijing's use of force.

---

[50] Chan et al., "Storm over Hong Kong's Extradition Bill."

[51] A record-high percentage of 89% of Taiwanese opposed the one country, two systems model as of October 2019, a 14% rise since January 2019. See surveys conducted in January, March, May, July, and October 2019 commissioned by the Mainland Affairs Council: "Taiwan zhuliu minyi jujue Zhonggong yiguoliangzhi de bilv chixu shangsheng, geng fandui Zhonggong duiwo junshi waijiao daya" [Taiwanese Mainstream Public View against One Country Two Systems by the Chinese Communist Party Keeps Rising, Objecting to the Chinese Communist Party's Military and Diplomatic Coercion], October 24, 2019, https://www.mac.gov.tw/cp.aspx?n=0E7480E052A6E5AA. Support for Tsai's presidency in the 2020 election rose from 15% in January to 52% in October 2019. See TVBS Poll Center, https://www.tvbs.com.tw/poll-center/1.

[52] Chen Kuan-Fu, "Meaningless Rhetoric by Gou, KMT on U.S. Arms," *Taipei Times*, May 12, 2019, http://www.taipeitimes.com/News/editorials/archives/2019/05/12/2003714979.

[53] Ibid.

The former chief of the General Staff, Admiral Lee Hsi-ming, emphasized the need to develop innovative asymmetric capabilities, improve mobility and survivability, and identify and maximize Taiwan's defensive advantages to deter a Chinese attack.[54] This requires a larger military budget and the acquisition of more advanced weapons systems from the United States and its allies.[55]

Voters Caught between a Rock and Hard Place

Opinion surveys show that most Taiwanese support the status quo and prioritize safeguarding Taiwan's freedom and democracy without necessarily supporting either unification or formal independence.[56] But for those still sympathetic to either unification or independence, particularly in the older generations, the two parties now offer completely different positions with little overlap. The KMT and its candidate Han Kuo-yu recognize the 1992 Consensus and want to work more closely with Beijing for the economic benefits it can provide. Han reflects the views of those who think accommodating Beijing is necessary to maintain peace in the Taiwan Strait, even if they do not support unification under one country, two systems. Furthermore, the Chinese economy seems to provide the answer for many individuals, entrepreneurs, organizations, and companies that want larger markets, faster growth, and better jobs.

However, economic growth is no longer the biggest issue for many Taiwanese voters, the majority of whom are not committed to either the DPP or the KMT.[57] A primary driver in Taiwanese politics is that the priorities of younger Taiwanese, more than a million of whom were eligible to vote in a presidential and legislative election for the first time in 2020, are quite different from those of their parents.[58] Surveys show that young voters, who have even lower levels of party affiliation, are presently drawn to the DPP because it is more committed than the KMT to equality, environmental

---

[54] Ministry of National Defense (Taiwan), *Guarding the Borders, Defending the Land: The ROC Armed Forces in View* (Taipei, December 2017), https://www.ustaiwandefense.com/taiwan-ministry-of-national-defense-reports.

[55] "Junfang guanyuan: Zhengqu tiaozeng guofang yusuan, dan nan yibu daowei" [Military Official Says Must Strive for Increase in Defense Budget, but Hard to Get It All at Once], *Liberty Times*, October 14, 2017, https://news.ltn.com.tw/news/focus/paper/1143250; and "Taiwan: Incremental Rises in Defense Spending," *Asia Times*, April 16, 2019, https://www.asiatimes.com/2019/04/article/taiwan-incremental-rises-in-defense-spending.

[56] "Objecting to the Chinese Communist Party's Military and Diplomatic Coercion."

[57] For reference, see "Party Preferences" chart in "Trends of Core Political Attitudes (1992/06~2019/06)."

[58] "Zhongxuanhui: 2020 xuanju renshu 1934 wanren, shoutouzu 118 wanren" [Central Election Commission: Number of Voters in 2020 General Election Is 19.34 Million, with 1.18 Million First-Time Voters], SET News, September 12, 2019, https://www.setn.com/News.aspx?NewsID=601301.

sustainability, and democracy.[59] But unlike some of their parents who are devoted to the DPP because of its historic commitment to independence, they also believe that Taiwan has already achieved de facto independence and does not need to run the risk of making any formal declaration to that effect.[60]

To be sure, the DPP's poor record in governance and economic planning may give these younger voters pause. With a youth unemployment rate over 12% (twice the national average), Taiwan's high-income trap has afflicted many young people who are unable to save and therefore are marrying later and not having children. Fewer of them are able to care for their parents in a super-aged society. Therefore, young professionals are tempted by the opportunities being offered to them in China, even though they prefer not to live there on a long-term basis. Although young entrepreneurs would like to raise capital from quality investors in U.S. markets, they have found China to be much easier to access due to policy incentives, high liquidity, and a similar culture.[61] Accordingly, the DPP still needs to prove to younger voters that it can not only defend Taiwan's democracy but also provide an economic future.

Taiwan's Response to the Evolving U.S.-China Competition

Taiwan faces three alternative strategies for navigating the intensifying U.S.-China rivalry, and consensus will be difficult to reach. Throughout the Cold War, Taiwan was allied with the United States to ensure its security against China. In recent decades, however, it has become increasingly dependent on China economically, and there is now a tendency in some quarters to see China as a successful model of effective authoritarian governance, as compared with the dysfunctionality of many Western democracies. Tilting away from the United States and toward China is therefore a second option—albeit one that so far has only received minority support from some in the business community or the KMT. Several other small states in Asia are trying to hedge against both the United States and

---

[59] For party affiliation by age group, see "Taiwan National Security Survey," Duke University, Asian Security Studies Program, https://sites.duke.edu/pass/taiwan-national-security-survey.

[60] Chen Fang-yu, "Taiwan nianqing shidai de zhengzhi taidu mindiao: Yuanwei Taiwan erzhan, zhichi minzhu, fandui tongyi" [Survey on the Political Attitudes of Younger Generation in Taiwan: Willing to Fight for Taiwan, Supporting Democracy and Opposing Unification], Initium Media, April 17, 2018, https://theinitium.com/article/20180417-opinion-chenfangyu-taiwan-teenagers. Also see polls commissioned by Taiwan Public Television Service Foundation, https://d1onng0u0flh7y.cloudfront.net/ourcountry/index.html and https://news.ltn.com.tw/news/politics/breakingnews/2942002.

[61] Ralph Jennings, "China Offers Special Breaks to Attract Taiwanese Startups, but Only 1% Find Success," Forbes, March 26, 2019, https://www.forbes.com/sites/ralphjennings/2019/03/26/china-offers-special-breaks-to-attract-taiwanese-startups-but-only-1-find-success.

China, and this third strategy is becoming more attractive for Taiwan as well. But Taiwan faces more intense security challenges from China than most other Asian countries do, and therefore it will be more difficult for Taiwan to exercise a hedging option successfully. Accordingly, the alliance with the United States is still widely regarded in Taiwan as indispensable, and therefore serves to some degree as the basis for the other two options.

Option One: Move Closer to the United States to Balance against China

Given the heightened threat from China and the deteriorating Sino-U.S. relationship, the first option is for Taiwan to move even closer to the United States to both ensure its autonomy and find solutions to its economic problems. As already noted, this option is supported by the military, a wide segment of the younger generation, and many interest groups that have been marginalized economically through Taiwan's closer integration with China. In part because of China's refusal to engage with the DPP, this also seems to be the course that Tsai Ing-wen has chosen. In line with this strategy, Taiwan is working more closely with both the United States and Japan and has been welcomed to participate in their vision of a free and open Indo-Pacific. The U.S. Department of Defense's June 2019 *Indo-Pacific Strategy Report* declared that "the United States has a vital interest in upholding the rules-based international order, which includes a strong, prosperous, and democratic Taiwan." The report also included Taiwan in a list of four countries that, though not formal allies, are described as "reliable and capable partners."[62]

Some in Taiwan hope that an extreme form of this option would include re-establishing official relations with the United States, gaining membership or observer status in major international organizations, or even achieving independence. Others, in contrast, including a majority of Taiwanese, probably consider any movement toward formal independence to be unnecessarily dangerous and provocative under foreseeable circumstances. Nonetheless, the small but committed group of Taiwanese advocating such a strategy are determined, and any further deterioration in U.S.-China relations could give them more hope of success.[63] Furthermore, this first option has many variants. Less extreme versions include more frequent meetings between

---

[62] U.S. Department of Defense, *Indo-Pacific Strategy Report: Preparedness, Partnerships, and Promoting a Networked Region* (Washington, D.C., June 2019), https://media.defense.gov/2019/Jul/01/2002152311/-1/-1/1/DEPARTMENT-OF-DEFENSE-INDO-PACIFIC-STRATEGY-REPORT-2019.PDF.

[63] Ralph Jennings, "Who's Behind the Quick Rise in U.S.-Taiwan Relations," VOA, March 27, 2019, https://www.voanews.com/east-asia/whos-behind-quick-rise-us-taiwan-relations.

national security and foreign affairs officials, enhanced military coordination, and further cooperation in international development efforts.

On the other hand, if Taiwan chooses any version of this option, it will potentially be penalized by China. Ever since the DPP was voted into power, Beijing has imposed economic sanctions by drastically reducing the number of group and individual tourists to Taiwan.[64] Beijing is on the alert for any signs of further upgrades in U.S.-Taiwan relations and vehemently protested when Taiwan's national security adviser met with U.S. officials in the United States in May 2019, the first time since derecognition in 1979.[65] For this option to be accepted by the Taiwanese public, it must also include signs that Taiwan is benefiting economically from closer cooperation with the United States, particularly through the conclusion of free trade and investment agreements, and is not simply enhancing its military security. As already noted, this may prove difficult.

A second risk produced by this option is that if tensions between the United States and China deepen, Taiwan will become entrapped in the Sino-U.S. rivalry, at some risk to its security. As the United States offers to sell larger numbers of more advanced arms to Taiwan, Taiwan will need to decide whether to increase its defense expenditures in order to purchase them. Opponents will argue that civilian needs should have priority, that the likelihood of a Chinese attack is low as long as Taiwan does not provoke Beijing, or that any resistance to a Chinese attack would be futile and that Taiwan should just rely on the United States. Taiwan already spends over 2% of its GDP on defense, equal to NATO's goals for 2024, and increasing the defense budget has been contentious.[66] Moreover, Tsai's expensive decisions to upgrade Taiwan's existing indigenous defense fighters, develop a sixth-generation stealth fighter, and build its own submarines have aroused public skepticism.[67] Taiwan is also transitioning from a conscription system

---

[64] Chinmei Sung, "Taiwan Set for First Tourist Drop since 2003 after China Ban," Bloomberg, October 28, 2019, https://www.yahoo.com/news/taiwan-set-first-drop-tourists-055928464.html.

[65] "Rare Meeting between Taiwanese, U.S. Security Officials Angers Beijing," Reuters, May 27, 2019, available at https://www.scmp.com/news/china/diplomacy/article/3011978/rare-meeting-between-taiwanese-us-security-officials-angers.

[66] Teng Pei-ju, "Defense Budget to Increase by NT$18.3 Billion in 2019: Taiwan Premier," Taiwan News, July 27, 2018, https://www.taiwannews.com.tw/en/news/3492793. For further analysis of Taiwanese attitudes on defense spending, see Wang Hong'en, "Guofang, Who Cares?—Cong mindiao taolun Taiwan guofang zhichu lunshu ying conghe zhuoshou" [National Defense, Who Cares?—How to Interpret Survey Results of Discussion about National Defense Budget], Voice Tank, May 2, 2019, https://www.voicettank.org/single-post/2019/05/02/050201.

[67] Lawrence Chung, "Taiwan Offers Glimpse of Home-Built Submarine Designed to Deter Beijing," South China Morning Post, May 9, 2019, https://www.scmp.com/news/china/military/article/3009573/taiwan-offers-glimpse-home-built-submarine-designed-deter; and Ministry of National Defense (Taiwan), Guarding the Borders, Defending the Land.

to an all-volunteer army, which is challenging given its declining birth rate and the increased personnel costs that this transition will entail.

Option Two: Accommodate China and Rely on It Economically

Given the rise of China economically and militarily and the uncertainties surrounding a continued U.S. commitment to the region, support for accommodating China is growing. The variants of accommodation run across a wide spectrum, but their common prerequisite is the reaffirmation of the 1992 Consensus or some other commitment to eventual unification. Accommodation might also require voting the DPP out of office because Beijing is highly suspicious of any DPP government, given the party's historic commitment to independence.

Accommodation is supported by the old guard within the KMT and by many mainlanders who see eventual unification as desirable and unavoidable. This option may also be supported by some Taiwanese multinational corporations, especially those with a strong Chinese presence. During his presidency, Ma Ying-jeou accepted the 1992 Consensus—but with the proviso that "each side has its own interpretation"—allowing him to claim that the 1992 Consensus means unification under the Republic of China.[68] But after Xi's pronouncement in 2019 that eventual unification means one country, two systems under the rule of the CCP, the KMT can no longer insist on its own interpretation. And given recent developments in Hong Kong, any version of unification under one country, two systems will be unlikely to gain the support of the majority of Taiwanese citizens.

The primary reasons to choose this option would be to strengthen the economy and alleviate the fear of U.S. abandonment, especially given the Trump administration's unpredictability. But Taiwanese people will be debating whether a recommitment to unification on China's terms would be an acceptable price to pay.

As with the first option of moving closer to the United States, the option of accommodating China has several variants. At one extreme, it could involve the negotiation of a peace agreement with China, as proposed by KMT chairman Wu Den-yih in early 2019.[69] A more moderate version could be attractive to the majority of Taiwanese who hope that there is a way to reap economic benefits from China and stabilize the Taiwan Strait without sacrificing Taiwan's autonomy and alliance with the United States. This might

---

[68] Yu-Jie Chen and Jerome A. Cohen, "China-Taiwan Relations Re-examined: The 1992 Consensus and Cross-Strait Agreements," *University of Pennsylvania Asian Law Review* 14, no. 1 (2019): 11.

[69] Shih Hsiao-kuan and Jonathan Chin, "Wu Den-Yih Says KMT Could Sign Peace Treaty If It Regains Presidency Next Year," *Taipei Times*, February 15, 2019, http://www.taipeitimes.com/News/front/archives/2019/02/15/2003709751.

include joining Chinese-led free trade agreements such as the Regional Comprehensive Economic Partnership (RCEP), participating in China's Belt and Road Initiative, and joining the Asian Infrastructure Investment Bank (AIIB), as many U.S. allies have already done. This would be especially important for Taiwan because it has been unable to join any free trade agreements due to Beijing's pressure and is less likely to join the successor to the TPP, the Comprehensive and Progressive Agreement for Trans-Pacific Partnership, as long as the United States is not a member. Furthermore, accommodating China economically could lead to more Chinese investment in Taiwan that could invigorate the economy by creating jobs and growth, as well as to increased Chinese agricultural imports from Taiwan. Another possibility would be to include Taiwanese technology companies in the Made in China 2025 project. Politically, accommodation could give Taiwan more international space to maneuver, as it did during Ma's eight years in office. Before 2016, Beijing allowed Taiwan to participate in certain international organizations on an ad hoc basis.

The costs and benefits of these various forms of accommodation are difficult to quantify. It is hard to predict whether accommodating China politically for greater economic and diplomatic benefits would weaken Taiwan's connection with the United States and whether even a vague commitment to unification could eventually be invoked to demand a nominally peaceful but involuntary absorption by an increasingly powerful China. Although this Faustian bargain has some supporters in the business community and among the mainlanders, there is no sign that this option has any appeal to the younger generations of Taiwanese.

Option Three: Join the Others and Hedge

The last option is what most small countries in Asia have been attempting: to hedge between China and the United States by building economic ties with the former while developing some form of security relations with the latter.[70] This corresponds with the meaning of hedging in the financial world, where it denotes employing two contradictory strategies to maximize gains and minimize risks. For Taiwan, hedging would mean a combination of the first two options. Advocates of hedging argue that it would be undesirable for Taiwan either to balance with the United States against China's rise or to bandwagon with China by voluntarily submitting to Beijing's demands.

[70] See, for example, Jürgen Haacke, "The Concept of Hedging and Its Application to Southeast Asia: A Critique and a Proposal for a Modified Conceptual and Methodological Framework," *International Relations of the Asia-Pacific* 19, no. 3 (2019): 375–417; and Kuik Cheng-Chwee, "Malaysia between the United States and China: What Do Weaker States Hedge Against?" *Asian Politics and Policy* 8, no. 1 (2016): 155–77.

It would also be infeasible to try to remain neutral by seeking parallel and balanced relations with both.

For Taiwan, hedging would entail further purchases of U.S. arms and even closer security relations through joint military exercises and coordination of defense policies, alongside increased two-way trade and investment with China and participation in the Belt and Road Initiative, RCEP, and the AIIB. Most Taiwanese presidents in the past have claimed to know how to walk this tightrope during their electoral campaigns, but in the end, each president alienated either Beijing or Washington or both.

Given the deterioration in U.S.-China relations, trying to improve relations with both superpowers while not crossing this red line may become even more difficult. If Taiwan accepts opportunities to solidify its economic relations with China, can it ever be certain that Washington will not abandon Taipei in order to maintain its own relations with Beijing? And if Taiwan can gain economic and political benefits from China, how can it be sure that China will not use the resulting economic dependence as leverage one day?

Another version of hedging is therefore to diversify Taiwan's international relations by seeking economic and security ties with other countries in the region that are facing the same threats and opportunities and are adopting similar hedging strategies. These would include South Korea, Japan, and the members of ASEAN. With the New Southbound Policy, Taiwan is in fact pursuing this form of hedging by promoting economic and social exchanges with like-minded democratic countries interested in enhancing their international relationships with Taiwan either officially or unofficially. But Tsai faces a serious challenge in this regard because both Beijing and the United States can exert great pressure on these countries to make a choice. While some proponents of a free and open Indo-Pacific strategy, such as the United States and Japan, may be willing to work more closely with Taiwan, other countries, such as India, will try to remain neutral; some like Australia and Vietnam will be guarded; and still others, like the Philippines, may choose to tilt toward China in their responses to Taiwan's overtures.

The dilemma for the Taiwanese public is that none of Taiwan's political parties has developed a clear strategy for navigating the U.S.-China rivalry, and their stated positions may actually be disingenuous. Tsai may appear to be a moderate who would prefer to hedge, but with the CPP stonewalling the DPP, she realistically can only adopt option one. Similarly, although the KMT may also claim to have adopted option three by trying to maintain its historical ties with the United States while moving toward China for economic benefits, it has actually been pursuing option two. The real concern of course is that both China and the United States may enforce certain red lines that would prevent Taiwan from hedging effectively.

The majority of Taiwanese people are undecided about their choice of leader and prefer a moderate who can deal with the United States and China on equal terms—a leader who can adopt option three and successfully hedge between the two superpowers. Furthermore, how Taiwan can walk this tightrope without Beijing accusing it of resisting unification and Washington of excessive accommodation of China is unclear. Both China and the United States will be tempted to press Taiwan to clarify its choice rather than allowing it to develop relations with both countries.

Conclusions and Implications

Both Taiwanese voters and leaders face the difficult challenge of finding effective solutions to Taiwan's high-income trap while defending the autonomy, identity, and values that the overwhelming majority of Taiwanese people hold dear. It will be difficult, if not impossible, for a mature economy like Taiwan's to maintain, let alone increase, its standard of living and level of social welfare as it faces growing competitive pressures from lower-cost economies and as its citizens demand greater fairness and environmental sustainability. Taiwan may simply need to adapt to slower growth and re-prioritize its economic goals according to the demands of younger generations, but with relatively fewer resources than in the past. At the same time, as the Sino-U.S. competition intensifies, Taiwan's leaders may find it more difficult to navigate this rivalry, especially if both China and the United States try to discourage, or even punish, smaller nations that try to hedge between them. Indeed, this situation will be just as challenging for Taiwan as managing the domestic double bind.

Taiwan Is an Important Litmus Test

Taiwan is an example of how a U.S. ally facing domestic economic problems can cope with a China that is economically attractive while simultaneously an existential threat. China's neighbors will be looking to see whether Taiwan can successfully rely on the United States for security as it becomes increasingly entangled with the Chinese economy, as well as whether it can engage with China without losing its identity and autonomy in the process. Taiwan is also a test of China's capabilities and intentions. Although China claims to be rising peacefully, its expansive geopolitical aims, increasing comprehensive national power, and growing national ambitions have challenged all of its neighbors. Hong Kong's unrest has also demonstrated China's inability to successfully implement the one country, two systems model that is supposed to be applied to Taiwan. If China ultimately chooses to use force against Taiwan to compel unification, that will be a more alarming sign to the region about its broader intentions.

Moreover, Taiwan's fate will test U.S. resolve in the region. A free and democratic Taiwan is an indispensable partner in any U.S. attempt to balance China and should have the full backing of the United States.[71] In addition, the region's stability depends on Taiwan's continued support of the United States' regional leadership. The U.S. response to a potential military attack across the strait has historically been characterized by "strategic ambiguity," whereby no unconditional commitment has been made.[72] But Beijing believes that such a position still enables Taiwan to resist unification and is the root cause of the tension across the strait. Conversely, some Americans are asking whether Taiwan is sufficiently important to warrant the risks and potential costs of a military confrontation with an increasingly powerful China. As such, Taiwan is in doubt as to whether the United States would come to its aid in the event of a Chinese attack, and that doubt has encouraged the rise of pro-Beijing political parties and politicians. How well the United States can manage the Taiwan issue will be an indicator of U.S. leadership in the region in the face of China's rise.

Implications and Policy Options for the United States

As the United States' tenth-largest trading partner and a crucial link in the global technology supply chain, and given its geostrategic position, Taiwan occupies an important place in the United States' Indo-Pacific strategy. The United States cannot afford to lose Taiwan's support, especially through any form of coercion from China. Given the growing awareness of the U.S.-China rivalry and the loss of confidence in the previous U.S. policy of engagement, there is bipartisan support in Congress for balancing China and safeguarding Taiwan. Yet the strategy for doing so remains largely unspecified.

It is important for the United States to help Taiwan escape the high-income trap so that it does not overly rely on China to address its socioeconomic problems. To this end, the United States should reach a mutually acceptable economic agreement with Taiwan, overcoming the objections by pork farmers and consumer groups in Taiwan and the high standards demanded by both the U.S. trade representative and Congress. The United States must also encourage Taiwanese entrepreneurship and innovation and promote the flow of capital between the two countries. In particular, the United States should help Taiwanese companies, especially

---

[71] Chris Horton, "Taiwan's Status Is a Geopolitical Absurdity," *Atlantic*, July 8, 2019, https://www. theatlantic.com/international/archive/2019/07/taiwans-status-geopolitical-absurdity/593371.

[72] Bill Sharp, "Whither Strategic Ambiguity," PacNet, Pacific Forum, July 30, 2019.

high-tech firms, move toward higher-end research and manufacturing and diversify Taiwan's industrial base.

Second, the United States should continue to reassure Taiwan militarily through arms sales and security coordination. But the United States must also pressure Taiwan to update its defense doctrine and be more self-reliant in weapons production. Washington needs to work with Taipei to develop a military deterrent that would greatly increase the costs of a Chinese invasion while also maintaining its own capabilities so as to preserve the credibility of a possible U.S. intervention. Since Taiwan will never be able to keep up with Chinese defense spending, the United States must help it develop asymmetric capabilities for responding to nontraditional threats, especially cyberwarfare. Supported by forward-thinking elements in the Taiwanese military, this effort will involve high-level exchanges and the re-examination of Taiwan's defense requirements to overcome the expected resistance from both traditional elements in the military and U.S. arms producers that remain committed to conventional approaches to the island's security.

Third, the United States should help the Taiwanese people protect and promote the values that have become important aspects of their new national identity, including democracy, political autonomy, social justice, and environmental sustainability. Taiwan's democracy is threatened not only by its own shortcomings but also by Chinese efforts to undermine it through pro-Beijing ownership of mainstream media and the spreading of misinformation through social media. These efforts require Taiwan and the United States to work more closely to identify and counter such efforts.

Given that China is attempting to present authoritarian and mercantilist alternatives to U.S. models of democratic politics and market economics, it is important for the United States to demonstrate the continued effectiveness of democratic institutions and the dynamism of market economies, as well as to show the compatibility of democracy with Chinese culture against Beijing's claims that democratic systems are suitable only for Western societies. Taiwan will be a key test of the United States' ability to do so. The two sides should further enhance their pursuit of common interests in such areas as women's empowerment, civil society, and governance. The United States should encourage more tourism, educational exchange, and understanding between the two democratic countries, especially among the younger generations.

Conversely, the United States must avoid giving the impression that its policies toward Taiwan are aimed solely at advancing its own interests while ignoring the Taiwanese people's will. China will be looking for any evidence that would support such a characterization, and Washington must demonstrate that it sees its relationship with Taipei as important in its own right and not merely as a card that it can either play or withhold in its interactions with Beijing.

Finally, the United States must review how to adapt its one-China policy to account for Beijing's changing attitudes and Taipei's evolving views on Taiwan's future relationship with the mainland. Abandoning this policy would remove one of the cornerstones of the U.S.-China relationship and would be provocative and unwise. However, some interpretations of it seem increasingly anachronistic. To imply, as the one-China policy may once have done, that unification is the inevitable future for Taiwan runs counter to the Taiwanese people's preference for continued autonomy. Similarly, while Bill Clinton's interpretation of the one-China policy may still prevent Washington from supporting Taiwan's formal membership in international institutions composed exclusively of sovereign states, the United States should actively promote Taiwan's meaningful participation in international forums where its involvement is important for success.[73] Nor should the absence of formal diplomatic relations with Taiwan preclude contacts between the two governments to manage their extensive bilateral relations.

The United States' Taiwan policy thus should recognize that Taiwan is an increasingly important part of the U.S. strategy in Asia, especially among the community of democracies that are facing ever greater threats from an ambitious China. The United States must help Taiwan deal with the growing challenges to its security, safeguard its future as a democracy, and stay deeply engaged in a globalized world. There is much at stake for U.S. leadership in the region in promoting values that matter to the liberal order. If the United States does not show leadership economically and politically, as well as militarily, China has a proven ability to use hard, sharp, sticky, and soft power against Taiwan and other countries in the region.

While Taiwan remains very reluctant to acquiesce to Chinese pressure and demands, the island is so vulnerable that, without U.S. support, it could be absorbed by China involuntarily after fighting so hard for democracy for many decades. The future of Taiwan is important for the Taiwanese people, for the stability of the region and the world, and for U.S. leadership in the liberal democratic order. What is at stake is ultimately which side will win the competition between two entirely different systems. Taiwan's vulnerability and importance make the country a priority as the United States develops strategies to compete with China and balance its rise.

---

[73] Clinton's "three no's" included no U.S. support for Taiwan's membership in international organizations where membership was restricted to sovereign states. For a critical analysis, see Stephen Yates, "Clinton Statement Undermines Taiwan," Heritage Foundation, Executive Memorandum, no. 538, July 10, 1998.

EXECUTIVE SUMMARY

This chapter argues that U.S.-China competition is reshaping international politics in the post-Soviet space as countries in the region look to play China and the U.S. off of each other.

MAIN ARGUMENT

U.S.-China competition has disparate impacts in different countries in the post-Soviet space. Russia is using the competition to bolster its own geopolitical competition against the U.S., hoping that China will work with it to degrade U.S. power. Eastern European countries such as Ukraine and Georgia want Chinese investment but realize that a close partnership with the U.S. remains their best hope for security against Russia. Central Asian countries also desire Chinese investment but are wary of the political strings that come attached. They hope that U.S.-China competition will encourage the U.S. to increase its economic and diplomatic engagement in Central Asia while convincing Washington to drop its demands for democratization. Most countries in the region, therefore, view U.S.-China competition as an opportunity to demand more support from both Beijing and Washington. Though countries in the post-Soviet space will argue that they are crucial to the outcome of U.S.-China competition, the region will ultimately remain a sideshow in this rivalry.

POLICY IMPLICATIONS

- In Central Asia, countries welcome more U.S. engagement but oppose U.S. pressure for the protection of human rights or democratization.

- In Eastern Europe, the U.S. must balance its desire to compete with China with the reality that countries such as Ukraine and Georgia could benefit economically from Chinese investment.

- Russia has a favorable view of U.S.-China competition because the Kremlin's overwhelming priority is to reduce U.S. power, even if this means an expansion of China's relative influence in Central Asia and Eastern Europe.

U.S.-China Competition in the Post-Soviet Space

Chris Miller

As the U.S.-China rivalry heats up, the two countries are competing not only in traditional spheres such as East Asia but also in new regions. The post-Soviet space—Russia, Central Asia, and parts of Eastern Europe—is increasingly seen in Beijing and Washington through the lens of U.S.-China competition. This is a marked change from even a decade ago. After the collapse of the Soviet Union in 1991, China ignored much of the region, focusing its foreign policy in the post-Soviet space primarily on maintaining stable relations with Russia. For the United States, the region has largely been seen through the lens of U.S.-Russia relations, which have become increasingly competitive and zero-sum.

This chapter charts the changing dynamics of U.S. and Chinese engagement with the post-Soviet space. The first section explains the two countries' aims in the region. The subsequent sections then explore how these aims interact with regional dynamics in Russia, Central Asia, and Eastern Europe and describe how countries there are reacting to U.S.-China competition. The conclusion draws implications for U.S. policymakers.

U.S. and Chinese Goals in the Post-Soviet Space

U.S. Goals

The United States' aims in the post-Soviet region in recent decades have focused almost exclusively on Russia and the threats it poses to U.S. allies.

Chris Miller is Assistant Professor of International History at the Fletcher School of Law and Diplomacy at Tufts University, where he co-directs the Russia and Eurasia Program. He is also Director of the Foreign Policy Research Institute's Eurasia Program. He can be reached at <christopher.miller@tufts.edu>.

This focus on threats from Russia has only intensified over the past five years. After the Soviet Union collapsed in 1991, the United States sought both to establish stable relations with Russia and to support the independence of the other fourteen states that emerged from the Soviet Union.[1] These two goals regularly come into conflict because Russia sees the region as its own sphere of influence and resents U.S. efforts to support the independence of countries on its border. Disagreements about whether Russia should have a sphere of influence have caused small wars—for example, between Russia and Georgia in 2008 and between Russia and Ukraine in 2014–15.[2] Russia and the United States have both concluded that they cannot establish stable relations, and each power is taking steps to weaken the other.

The current U.S. strategy toward Russia is to contain the Kremlin's influence in the region and to degrade the foundations of Russian power. Strict U.S. export controls limit Russia's ability to access high-tech U.S. goods or dual-use military technologies, while economic sanctions slow Russia's economic growth. U.S. diplomats undermine Russian-led institutions such as the Eurasian Economic Union and counter Russian soft power by criticizing Moscow in international arenas and ejecting it from Western-led institutions such as the G-8.[3] U.S. government policy on Russia during the Trump administration has not substantially deviated from the policy of the late Obama administration, even though Trump himself would like to take a far softer line.

At the same time that it works to constrain Russian influence, the United States seeks to bolster the independence of the countries that border Russia, hoping that fully independent states will be more stable than a persistent Russian empire. For close U.S. partners such as Georgia and Ukraine, Washington provides military technology and training as well as financial support. Other post-Soviet countries such as Armenia and Azerbaijan have taken intermediate positions between the United States and Russia, but Washington is nevertheless keen to bolster their autonomy.

In Central Asia, U.S. policymakers think not only about countries' relationships with Russia but also about issues that are less relevant in other post-Soviet countries. As long as the United States is fighting a war

---

[1] On U.S. policy, see Angela E. Stent, *The Limits of Partnership: U.S.-Russian Relations in the Twenty-First Century*, rev. ed. (Princeton: Princeton University Press, 2014); and Steven Pifer, *The Eagle and the Trident: U.S.-Ukraine Relations in Turbulent Times* (Washington, D.C.: Brookings Institution Press, 2017).

[2] On the war with Georgia, see Ronald Asmus, *A Little War That Shook the World: Georgia, Russia, and the Future of the West* (New York: St. Martin's Press, 2010). On the war with Ukraine, see Samuel Charap and Timothy Colton, *Everyone Loses: The Ukraine Crisis and the Ruinous Contest for Post-Soviet Eurasia* (New York: Routledge, 2017).

[3] Charles Clover, "Clinton Vows to Thwart New Soviet Union," *Financial Times*, December 6, 2012, https://www.ft.com/content/a5b15b14-3fcf-11e2-9f71-00144feabdc0.

in Afghanistan, it wants stable ties with Afghanistan's northern neighbors. Washington is also concerned about the risks of extremism in the region, which are relevant to both the war in Afghanistan and conflicts farther afield in the Middle East. Finally, in the past several years, the United States has begun to worry about China's role in Central Asia and Eastern Europe, a shift that began late in the Obama administration and has accelerated during the Trump administration. The 2017 National Security Strategy popularized the notion of great-power competition and characterized China and Russia as the United States' key rivals.[4] The United States is concerned about Chinese investments not only in neighboring Kazakhstan, Kyrgyzstan, and Tajikistan but also in countries such as Georgia and Ukraine, fearing that these investments give Beijing political leverage.[5]

Chinese Goals

China's aims in the post-Soviet space have expanded substantially in recent years, especially following the announcement in Kazakhstan's capital of plans for a "new Silk Road," a proposal that evolved into the Belt and Road Initiative (BRI).[6] China sees BRI as an initiative that will achieve multiple goals in Central Asia. First, it will bind these countries to China economically, providing an opening for Chinese firms. Second, as Central Asian countries become more dependent on China, Beijing hopes that it can convert this economic influence into political leverage. Third, there is

---

[4] White House, *National Security Strategy of the United States of America* (Washington, D.C., December 2017), 2, 25.

[5] For analysis of China's influence in Central Asia, see Marlene Laurelle and Sébastien Peyrouse, *The Chinese Question in Central Asia: Domestic Order, Social Change, and the Chinese Factor* (London: Hurst, 2012); and Sébastien Peyrouse, "Discussing China: Sinophilia and Sinophobia in Central Asia," *Journal of Eurasian Studies* 7, no. 1 (2016): 14–23. On China's presence in Georgia, see Yevgen Sautin, "China's Black Sea Ambitions," Foreign Policy Research Institute, December 11, 2018, https://www.fpri.org/article/2018/12/chinas-black-sea-ambitions; and Dong Yan, "China's Strategy in the Caucasus," Foreign Policy Research Institute, April 3, 2017, https://www.fpri.org/article/2017/04/chinas-strategy-caucasus. On China's economic ties with Ukraine, see Anton Troianovski, "At a Ukrainian Aircraft Engine Factory, China's Military Finds a Cash-Hungry Partner," *Washington Post*, May 20, 2019, https://www.washingtonpost.com/world/europe/at-a-ukrainian-aircraft-engine-factory-chinas-military-finds-a-cash-hungry-partner/2019/05/20/ceb0a548-6042-11e9-bf24-db4b9fb62aa2_story.html; and Dong Yan, "Ukraine and Chinese Investment: Caution Amid Potential?" Foreign Policy Research Institute, September 6, 2017, https://www.fpri.org/article/2017/09/ukraine-chinese-investment-caution-amid-potential.

[6] Wu Jiao and Zhang Yunbi, "Xi Proposes a 'New Silk Road' with Central Asia," *China Daily*, September 8, 2013, http://www.chinadaily.com.cn/china/2013xivisitcenterasia/2013-09/08/content_16952228.htm. On Chinese foreign and security policy, see Sulmaan Khan, *Haunted by Chaos: China's Grand Strategy from Mao Zedong to Xi Jinping* (Cambridge: Harvard University Press, 2018); M. Taylor Fravel, *Active Defense: China's Military Strategy since 1949* (Princeton: Princeton University Press, 2019); and M. Taylor Fravel, *Strong Borders, Secure Nation: Cooperation and Conflict in China's Territorial Disputes* (Princeton: Princeton University Press, 2008).

growing evidence that BRI opens the door to a Chinese security and military presence in the region.[7]

In the Eastern European countries of the post-Soviet space, China's aims are relatively limited, given that the region is more peripheral to China's foreign policy aims. Beijing hopes to use BRI to bolster China's economic presence and political influence in the region, but it is far from a top priority for Chinese policymakers. With respect to Russia, China's priority is to retain stable, cooperative relations. The two countries have similar views on the key question of international politics: both see the United States as a threat and hope for a decline in U.S. power. Beijing's main goal is to ensure that this convergence of interests with Russia persists. A return to the hostility of the 1960s and 1970s would be very dangerous for both countries.[8] As the rising power in the relationship, China believes that time is on its side. It has therefore sought to assuage Russian concerns about being the junior partner in the relationship via effective diplomacy. China also desires to buy energy from Russia, which has been its largest supplier of crude oil since 2016.[9]

In Central Asia, China's main concern is the security of its border region. Beijing worries about potential failed states, looking not only at Afghanistan but also at Tajikistan, which fought a civil war in the 1990s and remains a weak state.[10] Kyrgyzstan has also seen several riots and incidents of ethnic violence in recent decades. The Fergana Valley, a populous and diverse region shared by Tajikistan, Uzbekistan, and Kyrgyzstan, sits not far from the border with China.[11] Over the past three decades the valley has seen an array of riots, revolts, and alleged extremism, all of which worry Beijing. China has held counterterrorism drills with Central Asian countries for over a decade.[12] It has already begun deploying Chinese border guards along the Tajikistan-Afghanistan border, in accordance with an agreement between

---

[7] Nadège Rolland, ed., "Securing the Belt and Road Initiative: China's Evolving Military Engagement Along the Silk Roads," National Bureau of Asia Research (NBR), NBR Special Report, no. 80, September 2019.

[8] On the history of China-Russia relations, see Alexander Lukin, *The Bear Watches the Dragon: Russia's Perceptions of China and the Evolution of Russian-Chinese Relations since the Eighteenth Century* (Armonk: M.E. Sharpe, 2003).

[9] "Russia Seals Position as Top Crude Oil Supplier to China, Holds Off Saudi Arabia," Reuters, January 24, 2019, https://www.reuters.com/article/us-china-economy-trade-crude/russia-seals-position-as-top-crude-oil-supplier-to-china-holds-off-saudi-arabia-idUSKCN1PJ05W.

[10] Olivier Roy, "The Civil War in Tajikistan: Causes and Implications," United States Institute for Peace, 1993; and Tim Epkenhans, *The Origins of the Civil War in Tajikistan: Nationalism, Islamism, and Violent Conflict in Post-Soviet Space* (New York: Lexington Books, 2016).

[11] See S. Frederick Starr, *Ferghana Valley: The Heart of Central Asia* (Armonk: M.E. Sharpe, 2011).

[12] Bruce Pannier, "China/Kazakhstan: Forces Hold First-Ever Joint Terrorism Exercises," Radio Free Europe/Radio Liberty, August 24, 2006, https://www.rferl.org/a/1070801.html.

the Tajikistan and Chinese governments.[13] This concern is heightened by the links between China's far western region of Xinjiang and Kazakhstan and Kyrgyzstan. In Xinjiang, ethnic Uighurs and Kazakhs have a long history of seeking autonomy or even independence from China.[14] The Chinese Communist Party is determined to stamp out such movements and insists that Central Asian governments support it in doing so. As Beijing has expanded its repressive apparatus in Xinjiang in recent years, securing the support of Central Asian governments has only become more important.[15]

Russia's Approach to Sino-U.S. Competition

Russian Interests

Russia's elite sees U.S.-China competition as a trend that will provide substantial benefit to Russia. First, and most importantly, competition with China will distract Russia's primary rival, the United States, from containing Russian power in the region. Second, Russia hopes that Sino-U.S. rivalry will allow it to play other great powers off of one another, creating a more multipolar international political system. Russia's strategy is a bet that neither the United States nor China is likely to win the competition outright and that the Kremlin will retain freedom of maneuver. Indeed, the Kremlin thinks that the competition will increase, rather than decrease, its diplomatic possibilities by ensuring that U.S. and Chinese actions in the post-Soviet space face counteraction from other powers. This bet that U.S.-China competition is in Russia's interest seems plausible but risky. A more competitive multipolar order in Eurasia could expand Russia's room for maneuver, but it could also divide the region into two camps and force the Kremlin to take sides as the junior partner of one of the great powers.

Russia's foreign policy is shaped primarily by the elite, given that the general population plays little role in foreign policy formation.[16] Two core beliefs unite most of the country's elite. First is the belief that Russia is and ought to be a great power, treated on a par with the United States and China.

[13] Craig Nelson and Thomas Grove, "Russia, China Vie for Influence in Central Asia as U.S. Plans Afghan Exit," *Wall Street Journal*, June 18, 2019, https://www.wsj.com/articles/russia-china-vie-for-influence-in-central-asia-as-u-s-plans-afghan-exit-11560850203.

[14] On the history of Xinjiang, see James A. Millward, *Eurasian Crossroads* (New York: Columbia University Press, 2009); and Justin M. Jacobs, *Xinjiang and the Modern Chinese State* (Seattle: University of Washington Press, 2017).

[15] "'Eradicating Ideological Viruses': China's Campaign of Repression against Xinjiang's Muslims," Human Rights Watch, September 9, 2018, https://www.hrw.org/report/2018/09/09/eradicating-ideological-viruses/chinas-campaign-repression-against-xinjiangs.

[16] Jeffrey Mankoff, *Russian Foreign Policy: The Return of Great Power Politics* (New York: Rowman and Littlefield, 2009), chap. 2.

As early as 1999, when he first came to power, Vladimir Putin promised that Russia "will remain a great power. It is preconditioned by the inseparable characteristics of its geopolitical, economic and cultural existence."[17] Though most Russians recognize that their country is less influential than the United States by almost any metric, they nevertheless wish to be treated as a great power.[18] A second point of consensus among elites is that Russia has been treated unfairly by the West since the collapse of the Soviet Union, which is unbefitting of its status as a great power. Putin has stated his belief that "we are constantly proposing cooperation…and for our relations to be equal, open and fair. But we saw no reciprocal steps. On the contrary, they [the West] have lied to us."[19] This view is commonly stated by Russian foreign policy elites.

Within this consensus about Russia's great-power status, there is substantial variation of opinion among the elite about the foreign policy that the country should pursue, as well as about the tools it should use and the costs it should be willing to bear in order to achieve its goals. Many analysts divide the Russian elite into two groups: the economic bloc, which consists of the Ministries of Finance and Economic Development and key corporate leaders; and the *siloviki*, the leaders of the security services. On some issues, this divide makes sense. As a rule of thumb, the economic bloc is more concerned with maximizing economic well-being, more interested in economic rather than military tools, and more focused on stable relations with the West. Members of the siloviki, by contrast, are more inclined to use military tools and more suspicious of the West.

On many issues, however, describing the views of the Russian elite requires a more complicated schematic than a straightforward division between the economic bloc and the siloviki. One reason for this is that the siloviki have come to play an ever-larger economic role. The CEO of Rosneft, Russia's largest state-owned oil company, is also reportedly a former KGB agent and is widely seen as a leading silovik.[20] He therefore looks at sanctions against Rosneft through the lens of both economics and geopolitics. When his firm does business with China—as it does with

---

[17] Vladimir Putin, "Russia at the Turn of the Millennium," December 30, 1999, available at http://pages.uoregon.edu/kimball/Putin.htm.

[18] Sarah A. Topol, "What Does Putin Really Want?" *New York Times*, June 25, 2019, https://www.nytimes.com/2019/06/25/magazine/russia-united-states-world-politics.html.

[19] "Address by the President of the Russian Federation," President of Russia website, March 18, 2014, http://en.kremlin.ru/events/president/news/20603.

[20] Luke Harding, "Igor Sechin: Rosneft's Kremlin Hard Man Comes Out of the Shadows," *Guardian*, October 18, 2012, https://www.theguardian.com/business/2012/oct/18/igor-sechin-rosneft-kremlin-hard-man-shadows.

increasing frequency—this is also a matter both of politics and economics.[21] An additional category of Russian elite is made up of longtime friends of Putin who have become owners of major businesses, including Gennady Timchenko, Boris Rotenberg, and Arkady Rotenberg. The firms these businessmen own often work with Chinese firms, in which their main interests appear to be their personal finances rather than broader political and geopolitical considerations.[22]

The primary foreign policy concern of the elite is to retain and bolster Russia's geopolitical position, which the Kremlin sees as being most threatened by the United States.[23] Hence, they believe that the country has an interest in pursuing confrontation with the United States with the aim of weakening U.S. power. Russia hopes to achieve this by degrading U.S. alliances and by opposing the United States' efforts to expand its influence in the post-Soviet space. This goal of bolstering Russia's geopolitical position overlaps significantly with Chinese interests, at least for now. Russia welcomes China's desire for friendly bilateral ties, which are just as useful for its efforts to confront the United States as they are for China. Beijing and Moscow insist that they see eye to eye on nearly all major international political questions and that there are no important issues that divide them.[24] They certainly both agree that an expansion of U.S. influence in Central Asia is in neither country's interest.

A second key interest of Russia's elite is to retain power. Many elites, including by all accounts Putin, believe that the U.S. government is trying to push them from power. Putin regularly decries what he sees as the U.S. policy of "color revolutions," which are "used as a geopolitical instrument for remaking spheres of influence…[and are] a lesson and a warning."[25] Russia's official foreign policy concept document states that the country's goal is to "counter attempts to interfere in the domestic affairs of states with

[21] Shunsuke Tabeta and Tomoyo Ogawa, "China Strikes Oil and Gas Deals with Russia's Rosneft," *Nikkei Asian Review*, November 30, 2018, https://asia.nikkei.com/Business/Business-trends/China-strikes-oil-and-gas-deals-with-Russia-s-Rosneft.

[22] Katya Golubkova and Maria Kiselyova, "Russia's Novatek to Sell 20 Percent in Arctic LNG 2 to China," Reuters, April 25, 2019, https://www.reuters.com/article/us-russia-gas-novatek-cnodc/russias-novatek-to-sell-20-percent-in-arctic-lng-2-to-china-idUSKCN1S11WY.

[23] Angela Stent, *Putin's World* (New York: Twelve, 2019).

[24] "Xi Cherishes Close Friendship with Putin," TASS, June 4, 2019, https://tass.com/world/1061701; and Holly Ellyatt, "China's Xi Calls Putin His 'Best Friend' against a Backdrop of Souring U.S. Relations," CNBC, June 5, 2019, https://www.cnbc.com/2019/06/05/putin-and-xi-meet-to-strengthen-ties-as-us-relations-sour.html.

[25] Darya Korsunskaya, "Putin Says Russia Must Prevent 'Color Revolution,'" Reuters, November 20, 2014, https://www.reuters.com/article/us-russia-putin-security-idUSKCN0J41J620141120.

the aim of unconstitutional change of regime."[26] Elites place different levels of emphasis on the threat of regime change, but all agree that China prefers the continuation of authoritarian rule in Russia, whereas many see the West as a threat.

The Russian government generally treats economic aims as secondary to political aims. Its main economic interest is to reduce Russia's vulnerability to Western economic pressure, ensuring that the country can make geopolitical decisions independently of economic considerations. Putin has argued that Russia is "being threatened with sanctions," which are part of "the infamous policy of containment," because it has "an independent position."[27] In principle, Russia would also like to develop its economy so that it can compete in the long term, but in practice the government does not prioritize economic growth and has achieved little over the past decade, with the economy growing only 1.3% per year on average.[28]

Russia's Identity and Ideology

Russia is commonly described as a country torn between European and Eurasian identities.[29] Russians themselves have debated for centuries whether they are, or should become, European; whether they have a unique Russian or Slavic civilization; or whether they are in fact culturally closer to their Eastern neighbors. At times this debate about identity has shaped Russian foreign policy, encouraging the government, for example, to focus more on its Slavic neighbors than would otherwise be justified by national interests.[30] Russians often see themselves as culturally European, but there is a long tradition in Russia of distinguishing the country's European cultural heritage from any sort of political allegiance. The great Westernizer Peter the Great waged wars with other European powers, for example. There is also a long history in Russia of emphasizing cultural differences with China, and at times in the past several centuries Russians have been whipped up by fears of a "yellow peril,"

---

[26] "Foreign Policy Concept of the Russian Federation," Embassy of the Russian Federation to the United Kingdom of Great Britain and Northern Ireland, November 30, 2016, https://www.rusemb.org.uk/rp_insight.

[27] "Address by the President of the Russian Federation."

[28] Data is from Rosstat. On the Russian elite's prioritization of political imperatives over economic growth, see Chris Miller, *Putinomics: Power and Money in Resurgent Russia* (Chapel Hill: University of North Carolina Press, 2018).

[29] See, for example, Isabelle Facon, "Russian Strategic Culture in the 21st Century: Redefining the West-East Balance," in *Strategic Asia 2016–17: Understanding Strategic Cultures in the Asia-Pacific*, ed. Ashley J. Tellis, Alison Szalwinski, and Michael Wills (Seattle: NBR, 2016).

[30] Russia's intervention in Balkan politics in the 1870s is one example; Boris Yeltsin's desire to play a role in the Balkan wars in the 1990s is a second.

most notably around the turn of the twentieth century.[31] Yet neither a desire for Westernization nor a fear of Asia is central to Russian thinking today, though each is occasionally exploited for domestic political purposes.

More important than cultural or historical identity, however, is ideology. Some of the Russian elites—notably those aligned with former finance minister Alexei Kudrin—would prefer that the country have a more liberal and competitive political system, which they associate with the United States. "Russia needs free elections," Kudrin has argued, and "has to take a chance with more democracy."[32] This portion of the elite is less fearful of the United States and less suspicious of Western policies. Yet the more liberal-oriented Russian elites also see in China a potential model of a country that, unlike Russia, has focused on economic reform and growth and has become powerful as a result.

The far more common ideological position in Russia, however, sees Western liberalism as mostly pernicious. Opponents of liberal politics are impressed by China's authoritarian capitalism, whereby the state exercises strict political control and dominates portions of the economy. Putin has praised China's "stability and predictability," arguing that "stability guarantees the progressive development of China."[33] Russia's elites have plenty of reasons to fear liberal political ideas. In a free election, many of them might be cast out of power, while ideas about transparency and measures to limit corruption would threaten many elites' income streams.[34] China's ideological model—support for regime stability coupled with opposition to Western liberalism—is therefore more appealing.

Russia's two main foreign policy crises over the past fifteen years were wars with U.S.-supported countries—Georgia in 2008 and Ukraine in 2014. Both conflicts are now governed by ceasefires of varying efficacy, but the divergent interests that caused the wars remain unresolved. The key dispute was that Georgia and Ukraine wanted the ability to establish deep political and security ties with the United States in order to bolster their room for maneuver vis-à-vis Moscow. Russia, however, saw both states as falling within its sphere of influence and resented Georgia's and Ukraine's refusal to defer to it, as well as the United States for supporting these countries.

---

[31] David Schimmelpenninck van der Oye, *Toward the Rising Sun: Russian Ideologies of Empire and the Path to War with Japan* (DeKalb: Northern Illinois University Press, 2006).

[32] "We Have to Take a Chance with More Democracy," interview with Alexei Kudrin, *Der Spiegel*, January 23, 2013, https://www.spiegel.de/international/world/interview-with-putin-ally-alexei-kudrin-on-democracy-in-russia-a-878873.html.

[33] "Putin Praises Achievements of China's Reform and Opening Up," Xinhua, December 20, 2018, http://www.xinhuanet.com/english/2018-12/20/c_137687814.htm.

[34] On rent-seeking among Russia's elite, see Anders Åslund, *Russia's Crony Capitalism: The Path from Market Economy to Kleptocracy* (New Haven: Yale University Press, 2019).

Russia's wars with Georgia and Ukraine have reshaped Russia-U.S. relations and thus transformed how the Kremlin views Sino-U.S. competition. Particularly in Ukraine, the United States and Russia look likely to continue disagreeing about how to resolve the crisis. As long as Russian forces prevent the resolution of the conflict in Donbas, Ukraine, the United States will retain its tough sanctions that compel Russia to turn to other economic partners. In both Moscow and Washington, the war has poisoned attitudes and shredded trust, leaving each side convinced that the other is not a credible partner. China, by contrast, has studiously avoided taking stances. It abstained, for example, on the crucial UN resolution on Crimea.[35] The Ukraine war has therefore had little direct effect on Russia-China relations. But by ruining Russia's relations with the West, the annexation of Crimea has sharply reduced the prospects for constructive relations between Moscow and Washington.

Russia's Response to U.S.-China Competition

Given Russia's desire to assert its great-power status and its belief that the United States is the key threat to this status, Moscow believes that U.S.-China competition is beneficial to its interests. It is therefore pleased to see the two powers clash. Russian analysts believe that the competition will last for a generation and further intensify in the coming years.[36] Elites hope that Sino-U.S. tension will force China to adopt a more cooperative position vis-à-vis Russia in places such as Central Asia, thereby helping the country manage China's rise. Yet Moscow's main interest in U.S.-China competition is that it will distract the United States, reducing the U.S. ability to contain Russia and perhaps even convincing Washington to offer concessions to the Kremlin.

Russian elites see only limited risk of being harmed by U.S.-China competition, given that Russia would avoid participation in any open confrontation. They describe their position as one of not taking sides but rather intensifying cooperation with China while leaving the door open to a future rapprochement with the United States (on Russia's terms, of course). In practice, this currently means working with China to degrade U.S. power. As political analysts Sergei Karaganov and Dmitry Suslov have argued, "the U.S. has intensified containment vis-à-vis both China and Russia…pushing other countries to pick sides: Either they are with the U.S. as part of the

---

[35] "General Assembly Adopts Resolution Calling upon States Not to Recognize Changes in Status of Crimea Region," United Nations, Press Release, March 27, 2014, https://www.un.org/press/en/2014/ga11493.doc.htm.

[36] Vasily Kashin, "Edinstvo i bor'ba" [Unity and Struggle], *Russia in Global Affairs*, September 8, 2016, https://globalaffairs.ru/number/Edinstvo-i-borba-18346.

liberal order, or against it, together with Moscow and Beijing."[37] Unless the United States changes tack, most Russian analysts expect their country to stay closer to China.

This strategy faces two risks, both of which will materialize if Moscow fails to convince the West to offer concessions in exchange for improved relations. First, if the Russia-China axis fails to degrade U.S. power substantially and if Russia remains sundered from Western investment, the country will fall behind economically and find itself in an increasingly less advantageous place—economically backward and still locked in a geopolitical confrontation with the West. Second, if the Russia-China axis succeeds at reducing U.S. power but the United States nevertheless declines to offer concessions to Russia, the Kremlin could find itself next to an uncomfortably powerful Chinese neighbor. The West is trying to convince Russia via sanctions and diplomatic isolation that the first scenario is most likely. Moscow, for its part, hopes that the West will conclude that the Russia-China axis is sufficiently threatening to warrant a change in policy toward Russia before China's power continues to grow. Beijing prefers to keep Russia and the West far apart, with the Kremlin in its camp.

Russia's strategy for taking advantage of Sino-U.S. competition, therefore, is to side largely with China in the hopes that the two countries can together degrade U.S. power. Moscow has sided with Beijing in multiple ways. First, it has intensified diplomatic cooperation, with Putin and Xi Jinping meeting nearly 30 times in recent years.[38] Second, Russia has deepened military ties with China by selling it more advanced military equipment and conducting joint exercises in hot spots such as the Baltic Sea and the South China Sea.[39] Third, Russia is building international institutions with China, including the Shanghai Cooperation Organisation (SCO) and the BRICS grouping (Brazil, Russia, India, China, and South Africa), though the latter has been less substantive than Russia initially hoped.[40] Fourth, it is boosting bilateral trade, notably in energy, though whether higher trade volumes will have substantial political ramifications is still uncertain. Fifth, the Kremlin continues to work with China at the United Nations and in other venues

[37] Sergei Karaganov and Dmitry Suslov, "A New World Order: A View from Russia," *Russia in Global Affairs*, October 4, 2018, https://eng.globalaffairs.ru/pubcol/A-new-world-order-A-view-from-Russia--19782.

[38] Lionel Barber and Henry Foy, "Vladimir Putin: Liberalism Has 'Outlived Its Purpose,'" *Financial Times*, June 27, 2019, https://www.ft.com/content/2880c762-98c2-11e9-8cfb-30c211dcd229.

[39] Andrew Higgins, "300,000 Troops and 900 Tanks: Russia's Biggest Military Drills since Cold War," *New York Times*, August 28, 2018; and "Russia Completes Delivery of Su-35 Fighter Jets to China for $2.5Bln," *Moscow Times*, April 17, 2019.

[40] Alexander Cooley, "What's Next for the Shanghai Cooperation Organization?" *Diplomat*, June 1, 2018, https://thediplomat.com/2018/06/whats-next-for-the-shanghai-cooperation-organization.

to establish international norms on issues such as internet censorship that contradict Western preferences.[41]

Russia has also used the Sino-U.S. rivalry to guarantee that China does not side with the West in key disputes. For example, Chinese officials have supported Russian military efforts in Syria, praising them as "part of international counterterrorism efforts."[42] China has also voted in favor of Russian resolutions on Syria at the United Nations.[43] Likewise, on the most important question to Russia, the status of Crimea, Chinese representatives have avoided stating any opinions beyond calling for a "balanced approach" and reiterating that "China had always opposed intervention in the internal affairs of states, and respected the sovereignty and territorial integrity of all countries."[44] It is difficult to know whether China would have voted in this way in the absence of its growing competition with the United States. But the two countries' deteriorating relationship has underscored the importance to China of keeping Russia satisfied with their partnership.

Moreover, Russia has sought to take advantage of U.S.-China competition to reduce its vulnerability to Western pressure. In particular, it hopes that collaboration with China in spheres such as payment systems will improve its ability to withstand current and future U.S. sanctions. New business deals are not the only step that Russia has taken to insulate itself from Western sanctions. The country has shifted some of its foreign exchange reserves from dollars to Chinese yuan.[45] Moscow and Beijing have announced plans to create a yuan-denominated fund to invest in Russia, though whether these plans will actually materialize is not clear, as promises often exceed action in this sphere.[46] Russian officials have also discussed potentially issuing

[41] Daniel Oberhaus, "The UN Would Really Appreciate It If Countries Stopped Turning Off the Internet," Vice, July 3, 2016, https://www.vice.com/en_us/article/pgk3nn/the-un-would-really-appreciate-it-if-countries-stopped-turning-off-the-internet.

[42] Ben Blanchard, "China's New Syria Envoy Praises Russian Military Mission," Reuters, April 8, 2017, https://www.reuters.com/article/us-mideast-crisis-syria-china-idUSKCN0X50OP; and "Foreign Ministry Spokesperson Geng Shuang's Regular Press Conference on March 21, 2019," Ministry of Foreign Affairs of the People's Republic of China, March 21, 2019, https://www.fmprc.gov.cn/mfa_eng/xwfw_665399/s2510_665401/t1647428.shtml.

[43] "Security Council Fails to Adopt Three Resolutions on Chemical Weapons Use in Syria," UN News, April 10, 2018, https://news.un.org/en/story/2018/04/1006991.

[44] "General Assembly Adopts Resolution Calling upon States Not to Recognize Changes in Status of Crimea Region."

[45] "Russian Central Bank Lowers U.S. Dollars Share in Reserves Due to Possible Risks," Reuters, May 20, 2019, https://www.reuters.com/article/us-russia-cenbank-reserves/russian-central-bank-lowers-u-s-dollars-share-in-reserves-due-to-possible-risks-idUSKCN1SQ1CR; and Natasha Doff and Anna Andrianova, "Russia Buys Quarter of World Yuan Reserves in Shift from Dollar," Bloomberg, January 9, 2019, https://www.bloomberg.com/news/articles/2019-01-09/russia-boosted-yuan-euro-holdings-as-it-dumped-dollars-in-2018.

[46] "Russia, China to Announce Joint Yuan Fund to Invest in Russia: RDIF," Reuters, June 3, 2019, https://www.reuters.com/article/us-russia-china-fund/russia-china-to-announce-joint-yuan-fund-to-invest-in-russia-rdif-idUSKCN1T41LI.

government bonds denominated in yuan,[47] and leaders from both countries have expressed their desire to encourage bilateral trade in rubles and yuan. Although there has been little progress so far in either area, intensified U.S. economic pressure on Russia and China could change this.[48]

More generally, Russia has trumpeted its growing economic ties with China since 2014, when the West first imposed sanctions. Whenever there is talk of future sanctions, Russia highlights its economic relations with China. For example, in 2014 the two countries signed a deal to trade gas via the Power of Siberia pipeline, which was a signal to the world that Western sanctions would not limit Russia's international business deals.[49] Although Russia and China might have signed this gas deal at some point regardless of foreign policy considerations, Russia probably compromised on price to finalize an agreement quickly and declare a great foreign policy success.[50]

Moscow has also used U.S.-China competition to encourage greater Chinese investment in Russia, though this is a secondary goal. Attracting investment has never been a primary aim of the Russian government, which has always preferred to let elites extort businesses, even though this depresses investment.[51] This business climate has been a persistent drag on investment, regardless of the country of origin or the business climate of the investors. The Russian government would nevertheless be happy to receive an influx of Chinese funds, especially in nonsensitive sectors but also in sensitive areas such as the energy and telecommunications industries.[52] Yet compared with China's outward investment in other countries, the total amount going to Russia remains small. China has invested only twice as much in Russia as it has in Kazakhstan, despite the fact that the Russian economy is many times as large. In the sectors in which China often invests abroad, such as infrastructure, Russia struggles to get projects approved and started.

---

[47] Amanda Lee, "Russia Keen to Sell Yuan Bonds to Deepen Ties with China and Further Reduce U.S. Dollar Dependence," *South China Morning Post*, June 7, 2019, https://www.scmp.com/economy/china-economy/article/3013528/russia-keen-sell-yuan-bonds-deepen-ties-china-and-further.

[48] On Russian and Chinese leaders' plans, see "Dollar Dump? Russia and China Agree to Bilateral Trade in National Currencies during Putin-Xi Meeting," RT, June 5, 2019, https://www.rt.com/business/461147-russia-china-nuclear-reactors. On the reality, see "Dollar i yevro v pyat' raz prevzoshli natsvalyuty v torgovle Rossii i Kitaya" [The Dollar and Euro Five Times Exceed National Currencies in Russia-China Trade], RBC, May 31, 2019, https://www.rbc.ru/economics/31/05/2019/5cefb2a09a79472aaa9047e4.

[49] Elizabeth Wishnick, "The 'Power of Siberia': No Longer a Pipe Dream," PONARS Eurasia, Policy Memo, no. 322, August 2014, http://www.ponarseurasia.org/sites/default/files/policy-memos-pdf/Pepm332_Wishnick_August2014.pdf.

[50] Szymon Kardaś, "The Eastern 'Partnership' of Gas," Centre for Eastern Studies (OSW), OSW Commentary, June 16, 2014, https://www.osw.waw.pl/en/publikacje/osw-commentary/2014-06-16/eastern-partnership-gas-gazprom-and-cnpc-strike-a-deal-gas.

[51] For an overview, see Miller, *Putinomics*.

[52] "Russian Telecom Giant and China's Huawei Launch 5G Zones in Russian Cities," RT, August 30, 2019, https://www.rt.com/business/467619-mts-huawei-5g-russia.

For example, after several years of discussion about Chinese participation in building a high-speed railway from Moscow to the Russian city of Kazan, the project was canceled.[53]

When it comes to investment in sensitive sectors of the economy, Russia is more ambivalent. While the country has attracted substantial Chinese investments in the energy sector, it has also received major investments from India, Japan, and the United Arab Emirates, suggesting a desire for diversification.[54] Western oil companies retain major stakes in Russian energy projects as well, though new investments are limited by sanctions. China, for its part, values Russia as a source of energy that does not require transit through the Strait of Malacca, which could be closed during a crisis. Yet China buys energy from many countries, allowing it to diversify supply and extract better prices.[55] On the question of 5G networks, Russia has trumpeted its contracts with Huawei.[56] But it has also more quietly signed deals with Nokia and Ericsson, which provide evidence of diversification in the telecommunications sector, too.[57]

Even as Russia seeks to take advantage of Sino-U.S. competition by working with China to degrade U.S. power, it is cognizant of the long-term implications of China's rise. Its growing collaboration with Beijing amid rising Chinese power requires Moscow to take a sanguine view of the effects that China has on its own stature. Despite the expectations of many Western analysts, most Russian leaders see China's rise more as a geopolitical opportunity than as a threat, at least for the next decade. When asked whether China's rise threatens Russia's position in Central Asia, many Russian experts demur, either insisting that their country's position remains strong or asserting that Russia's pattern of collaboration with China will help establish

---

[53] Elena Gosteva, "Kazan' ne nuzhna: Putin razvernul VSM" [Kazan Is Unnecessary: Putin Turned Around the HSR], Gazeta.ru, April 16, 2019, https://www.gazeta.ru/business/2019/04/16/12303943.shtml; and Anastasia Vedeneeva and Natalya Skorlygina, "V skorosti i v radosti: Resheno vernut'sya k proyektu VSM Moskva–Sankt-Peterburg" [In Speed and in Joy: It Is Decided to Return to the Moscow–St. Petersburg High-Speed Rail Project], Kommersant, April 16, 2019, https://www.kommersant.ru/doc/3945517.

[54] Eric Ng, "China's Russian Buying Spree to Continue, Says Leading Moscow Investment Bank," South China Morning Post, November 19, 2017, https://www.scmp.com/business/companies/article/2120571/chinas-russian-buying-spree-continue-says-leading-moscow; Stephen Blank, "India's Arctic Energy Partnership with Russia," Lowy Institute, Interpreter, October 24, 2018, https://www.lowyinstitute.org/the-interpreter/indias-arctic-energy-partnership-russia; Jane Nakano, "Japan to Invest in the Latest Russian LNG Project," Center for Strategic and International Studies (CSIS), July 12, 2019, https://www.csis.org/analysis/japan-invest-latest-russian-lng-project; and "Gulf States Are Becoming More Adventurous Investors," Economist, June 15, 2019, https://www.economist.com/middle-east-and-africa/2019/06/13/gulf-states-are-becoming-more-adventurous-investors.

[55] "The Emerging Russia-Asia Energy Nexus," NBR, NBR Special Report, no. 74, December 2018, https://www.nbr.org/publication/introduction-the-emerging-russia-asia-energy-nexus.

[56] "Russian Telecom Giant and China's Huawei Launch 5G Zones in Russian Cities."

[57] Janis Kluge, "Sino-Russian Chimera," Berlin Policy Journal, June 27, 2019, https://berlinpolicyjournal.com/sino-russian-chimera.

rules that will constrain the country in the future, even if it grows substantially in power relative to Russia.[58]

It is difficult to imagine that a Russian effort to forge such rules in Central Asia will succeed. Perhaps over time cooperation between Russia and China will foster habits of behavior that begin to create the underpinnings of a durable partnership in their respective diplomatic cultures. Both governments certainly agree at a rhetorical level on the importance of state sovereignty. But in practice, each defines sovereignty in ways that bolster its own interests as a great power. Russia's hope that it can sufficiently institutionalize such practices to restrain China in case of a future disagreement will be tested by China's belief that, as a rising power, it deserves an ever-larger voice in international politics. Does it not then follow that, in the zero-sum world of international power politics, Russia will have to give way on certain issues?

Relations may be particularly zero-sum in Central Asia, which had been part of the Russian empire for a century and a half before the five regional countries gained independence in 1991. Since then, Russia has played a major role in politics in Kazakhstan, Kyrgyzstan, and Tajikistan, while Uzbekistan and Turkmenistan have sought to lock Russia out. All these countries now have substantial economic and political relationships with China, and Chinese forces are even deployed along the Tajikistan-Afghanistan border—a border that used to be the southern frontier of the Russian empire.[59]

In the long run, there are potential contradictions between China's aim of expanding influence along its Central Asian border and Russia's aim of keeping the region within its privileged sphere. For now, Russia's elite assesses that the United States is the main threat to Russian influence in Central Asia. If, however, Beijing and Moscow succeed in further limiting U.S. presence, and if China's power continues to grow, then Moscow's threat perceptions might shift. Although Russia's elite is resolutely focused on the United States, one can imagine a future in which, prodded by a growing Chinese presence in Central Asia, Moscow reassesses its view of China's rise as mostly benign.

Russian analysts close to the Kremlin rarely discuss such risks publicly, but Moscow is nevertheless sensitive to China's role in Central Asia. In June 2016, for example, the SCO invited India and Pakistan to become members on Russia's urging, which some analysts interpreted as a Russian effort to

---

[58] Author's participation in an off-the-record roundtable with Russian experts on Eurasia, March 2019.

[59] Catherine Putz, "China in Tajikistan: New Report Claims Chinese Troops Patrol Large Swaths of the Afghan-Tajik Border," *Diplomat*, June 18, 2019, https://thediplomat.com/2019/06/china-in-tajikistan-new-report-claims-chinese-troops-patrol-large-swaths-of-the-afghan-tajik-border; and Gerry Shih, "In Central Asia's Forbidding Highlands, a Quiet Newcomer: Chinese Troops," *Washington Post*, February 18, 2019, https://www.washingtonpost.com/world/asia_pacific/in-central-asias-forbidding-highlands-a-quiet-newcomer-chinese-troops/2019/02/18/78d4a8d0-1e62-11e9-a759-2b8541bbbe20_story.html.

balance against China dominating the forum.[60] Russia also values its ties with India and Vietnam, even though both are rivals of China, and sells advanced military equipment, potentially including S-400 surface-to-air missiles, to both countries.[61]

More broadly, Russia's position in Eurasia points to a second challenge amid growing U.S.-China competition: to ensure for Russia a voice among the great powers. Many Russians speak of the world as having three great powers today: China, the United States, and Russia.[62] Most non-Russian observers, however, would not put Russia in a position equivalent to that of either the United States or China, and many analysts might even challenge the notion that Russia is the world's third most powerful country, ahead of France, Germany, Britain, and Japan. Yet if the Sino-U.S. rivalry intensifies, and if the West declines to respond as Russia hopes—i.e., by offering concessions—the world could splinter into two camps, one more aligned with the United States and the other with China. As discussed earlier, this is a risk for Russia, because such an outcome would leave it as China's junior partner and provide limited room for maneuver. Russia is betting that this will not happen and that the United States will compromise before such a bipolar split in international politics occurs. Whether this bet will pay off is far from clear.

The Impact of Sino-Russian Competition Beyond Russia

Central Asia

Russia is the most important player in the post-Soviet space, both as a partner to China and as a rival to the United States. Yet it is not the only country finding that U.S.-China competition is creating new opportunities and challenges. The five countries of Central Asia are all close to China and share substantial economic and cultural ties with it. Kazakhstan, Kyrgyzstan, and Tajikistan also share a border with China. Intensifying competition provides the Central Asian states a chance to play the great powers off of

---

[60] Derek Grossman, "China Will Regret India's Entry into the Shanghai Cooperation Organization," *Diplomat*, June 24, 2017, https://thediplomat.com/2017/07/china-will-regret-indias-entry-into-the-shanghai-cooperation-organization.

[61] Andrew Desiderio, "Congress Lets Some U.S. Allies Buy Russian Weapons Despite Sanctions," *Daily Beast*, July 23, 2018, https://www.thedailybeast.com/congress-lets-some-us-allies-buy-russian-weapons-despite-sanctions; and Franz-Stefan Gady, "U.S. Defense Bill May 'Permit' India to Purchase S-400 Missile Air Defense Systems from Russia," *Diplomat*, July 24, 2018, https://thediplomat.com/2018/07/us-defense-bill-may-permit-india-to-purchase-s-400-missile-air-defense-systems-from-russia.

[62] See, for example, Tatiana Shakleina, "Russia in the Contemporary International Order," in *Russia and the United States in the Evolving World Order*, ed. Antoly Torkunov, Norma C. Noonan, and Tatiana Shakleina (Moscow: Moscow State Institute of International Relations, 2018).

each other, with the potential to receive a better deal not only from the United States and China but also from Russia.

Interests. It is not easy to generalize the main interests of the five countries given the differences between them. Kazakhstan and Turkmenistan are rich in energy, while the others are much less so. Kazakhstan is an urbanized and middle-income country, whereas Tajikistan is quite poor. Most people in Tajikistan speak a version of Persian, whereas Turkic languages such as that spoken in Kazakhstan predominate elsewhere in Central Asia. Some countries, notably Kazakhstan, retain large ethnic Russian populations, while others, such as Turkmenistan, have far fewer ethnic Russians.

Despite these differences, several interests unite most or all Central Asian states as they interact with the United States and China. First, all five states are keen to preserve their independence from Russia, which they received in 1991 amid the collapse of the Soviet Union. In Turkmenistan, this has led the country to adopt a policy of strict neutrality, while for Uzbekistan this has caused prickly relations with Russia. Even Kazakhstan, which maintains the best relations with Moscow of all the Central Asian states, was outraged in 2014 when Putin suggested that it had never had its own statehood before 1991.[63] The United States has vocally supported these states' independence from Russia since 1991, and China, too, has no interest in seeing Russia dominate the region.

Since the end of the Cold War, Central Asian states' relations with China have often been derivative of their relationships with Russia. When these countries want more autonomy from Russia, they tack closer to China—as Turkmenistan did, for example, by striking gas deals with China. They do so knowing that they can always tack back toward Russia, as Turkmenistan has recently begun to do.[64] Yet as Russia's power wanes and China's increases, Central Asian states are recalibrating their relations with both powers.

A second concern of Central Asian leaders is internal security. Tajikistan suffered a devastating civil war in the 1990s, and many of the region's countries have issues with terrorism or extremism. Since 2001, the United States and China have been broadly aligned on the need to oppose terrorism and religious extremism in the region, with the war in Afghanistan motivating U.S. counterterrorism efforts and with concerns about the Xinjiang region driving China's attention. Today, however, the overlap in how China and the United States view these local security conflicts is diverging. U.S. and

---

[63] Farangis Najibullah, "Putin Downplays Kazakh Independence, Sparks Angry Reaction," Radio Free Europe/Radio Liberty, September 3, 2014, https://www.rferl.org/a/kazakhstan-putin-history-reaction-nation/26565141.html.

[64] "Turkmen Gas Flows to Russia Again after Three-Year Standoff," Reuters, April 15, 2019, https://www.reuters.com/article/us-turkmenistan-russia-gas/turkmen-gas-flows-to-russia-again-after-three-year-standoff-idUSKCN1RR1Z0.

other Western experts are increasingly noting the extent to which Central Asian governments use the rubric of extremism to describe not only genuine extremists but also anyone who is dissatisfied with the government and inclined to protest.[65] China's crackdown in Xinjiang, meanwhile, is attracting increasing Western criticism. The United States, for its part, is likely to continue reducing its focus on Afghanistan, which will further limit the overlap between U.S. and Chinese priorities in Central Asia.

A third interest of Central Asian states is economic development, which poses increasingly complicated trade-offs in their relations with China. They realize that Russia's funds are limited and that the United States and other Western countries are uninterested in devoting substantial resources to economic development in the region. Private Western firms can be induced to invest, but only if they are given profitable opportunities with limited risk of expropriation. Outside of natural resource sectors, Western investment is likely to be limited. China's BRI, by contrast, appears to offer vast funds for the construction of infrastructure across the region—at least that is how Beijing has marketed the initiative thus far. Central Asian countries have few industries beyond commodities that attract substantial foreign investment, and the region's governments need funds to improve infrastructure. Yet these states also know that Chinese investment brings its own complications and are very sensitive about the political ramifications, despite their need for investment.[66] Even Turkmenistan, which shares no border with China, has had major disputes with China over the two countries' gas trade.[67] Concern over Chinese investment in Kazakhstan and Kyrgyzstan, meanwhile, has sparked protests in both countries over issues such as land ownership and the presence of foreign workers.[68] Central Asian governments are therefore trying to strike a balance between their desire for Chinese money and the potential risks that it poses.

---

[65] Noah Tucker, "Terrorism without a God," Central Asia Program (CAP), CAP Papers, no. 225, September 2019, https://centralasiaprogram.org/wp-content/uploads/2019/09/CAP-paper-225-September-2019-1.pdf; and Mariya Y. Omelicheva, Counterterrorism Policies in Central Asia (New York: Routledge, 2011).

[66] Jakub Jakóbowski and Mariusz Marszewski, "Crisis in Turkmenistan. A Test for China's Policy in the Region," OSW, OSW Commentary, August 31, 2018, https://www.osw.waw.pl/en/publikacje/osw-commentary/2018-08-31/crisis-turkmenistan-a-test-chinas-policy-region-0.

[67] Paolo Sorbello, "Turkmenistan's Ongoing Gas Quandary," Diplomat, April 25, 2017, https://thediplomat.com/2017/04/turkmenistans-ongoing-gas-quandary.

[68] "Kazakhstan's Land Reform Protests Explained," BBC, April 28, 2016, https://www.bbc.com/news/world-asia-36163103; "Kyrgyzstan: Another Week, Another Anti-China Rally," Eurasianet, January 17, 2019, https://eurasianet.org/kyrgyzstan-another-week-another-anti-china-rally; and Reid Standish and Aigerim Toleukhanova, "Kazakhs Won't Be Silenced on China's Internment Camps," Foreign Policy, March 4, 2019, https://foreignpolicy.com/2019/03/04/961387-concentrationcamps-china-xinjiang-internment-kazakh-muslim.

A fourth interest of Central Asian governments, and one that has emerged only recently, is devising a response to China's intensifying repression of Muslims in its Xinjiang region. Xinjiang borders Kazakhstan, Kyrgyzstan, and Tajikistan and is inhabited by ethnic Kazakhs, Kyrgyz, Tajiks, and Uighurs, the latter being the most numerous non–Han Chinese ethnic group in Xinjiang. Beijing sees the repression of minorities as crucial to retaining control over this region, but its actions have also swept up family members of citizens of the Central Asian countries, sparking discontent across the border. These countries have evidently concluded that they are unable to affect China's strategy. They not only have avoided making controversial public comments on the issue but have harassed their own citizens who have organized against China.[69] Balancing the desire to avoid angering China with the need to placate their populaces could be increasingly challenging for Central Asian leaders, especially as news of China's internment camps spreads.[70]

A final interest is regime stability. The United States' demands that Central Asian governments hold free elections or respect rights conflict with this goal. Except for Kyrgyzstan, the region has been ruled by a handful of strongmen since 1991. U.S. calls for political change have been deeply unpopular among the region's elite. Turkmenistan has aggressively censored its media and has long restricted the presence of U.S. groups that support civil society. Uzbekistan also began a crackdown on civil-society groups after being criticized by the United States in 2005 for violently suppressing what the Uzbek government described as a radical Islamist movement, but which human rights groups say was only a political dispute.[71] Central Asian elites, especially the countries' security services, much prefer China's ask-no-questions approach to regime stability over the United States' intrusive demands.

In particular, the demand by the United States and other Western countries that business transactions occur in a transparent and non-corrupt manner is interpreted by many Central Asian leaders as a potential threat to regime stability. Where corruption from business deals is a crucial source of the funding needed to glue together patron-client networks, demands for

---

[69] Reid Standish, "'Our Government Doesn't Want to Spoil Relations with China,'" *Atlantic*, September 3, 2019, https://www.theatlantic.com/international/archive/2019/09/china-xinjiang-uighur-kazakhstan/597106.

[70] On recent popular discontent in Kazakhstan over China, see Naubet Bisenov, "Kazakh President's Upcoming Beijing Trip Stokes Sino-Phobia," *Nikkei Asian Review*, September 10, 2019, https://asia.nikkei.com/Politics/International-relations/Kazakh-president-s-upcoming-Beijing-trip-stokes-Sino-phobia.

[71] "'Bullets Were Falling Like Rain,'" Human Rights Watch, June 6, 2005, https://www.hrw.org/report/2005/06/06/bullets-were-falling-rain/andijan-massacre-may-13-2005.

transparency can threaten elites' hold on power. Cooperation with the United States on economic projects, for example, usually requires commitments to transparency and anticorruption measures. U.S. firms are subject to legislation prohibiting corruption, which gives Central Asian elites an incentive to work with China, notwithstanding the risk of overdependence on Beijing.[72]

Response to U.S.-China competition. Central Asian countries see U.S.-China competition as an opportunity to attract more attention from the United States, which helps them balance against both Russia and China, while also insisting that U.S. engagement does not come with demands for democratization. In the past, these states at times viewed the United States as a problematic partner and feared U.S.-inspired political reform pressures more than they desired U.S. economic or diplomatic engagement. Now, however, U.S.-China competition is likely to allow Central Asian states to take advantage of U.S. engagement without worrying about demands for political reform. At a time when Russia and China are offering economic and political support without demanding domestic reform, Washington and its allies will likely conclude that to compete in Central Asia, they must downplay democracy—a change that regional governments will welcome. This shift was visible even during the Obama administration. When Secretary of State John Kerry visited Central Asia in 2015, he told the region's governments, "I'm not here to lecture you."[73] The Trump administration has further downplayed the role of democracy and human rights in U.S. foreign policy more generally.

In economic terms, Central Asian states plan to leverage U.S.-China competition to negotiate the best deals possible, while diversifying their economic relations to avoid becoming too reliant on either Russia or China. Uzbekistan's recent opening and partial liberalization were primarily driven by internal dynamics, but the new government is actively seeking U.S. and Chinese investment, recognizing that both great powers have goods to offer.[74] Uzbekistan is not alone. Across Central Asia, leaders are hoping that

[72] Jonathan Hillman, "1MDB Probe Shines Uncomfortable Light on China's Belt and Road," *Nikkei Asian Review*, January 18, 2019, https://asia.nikkei.com/Opinion/1MDB-probe-shines-uncomfortable-light-on-China-s-Belt-and-Road.

[73] David E. Sanger, "John Kerry Confronts Human Rights as He Zips through Central Asia," *New York Times*, November 3, 2015, https://www.nytimes.com/2015/11/04/world/asia/john-kerry-confronts-human-rights-as-he-zips-through-central-asia.html; and David E. Sanger, "John Kerry Is Cautious on Human Rights during Uzbekistan Visit," *New York Times*, November 1, 2015, https://www.nytimes.com/2015/11/02/world/asia/john-kerry-is-cautious-on-human-rights-during-uzbekistan-visit.html.

[74] China is reported to have invested $7.8 billion in Uzbekistan. See "China Becomes Largest Trade Partner of Uzbekistan Again," Xinhua Silk Road Information Service, November 16, 2018, https://en.imsilkroad.com/p/120030.html; and Edward Lemon, "Mirziyoyev's Uzbekistan: Democratization or Authoritarian Upgrading?" Foreign Policy Research Institute, Central Asia Papers, June 12, 2019, https://www.fpri.org/article/2019/06/mirziyoyevs-uzbekistan-democratization-or-authoritarian-upgrading.

U.S.-China competition will induce both countries—and Russia—to offer more aid and better business deals.

The challenge for Central Asian states in exploiting this rivalry is that China cares far more about the region than does the United States. For reasons of geography, economic interests, and Beijing's perception of a Uighur threat, the Chinese government is willing to devote far more resources to Central Asia than is the United States. Xi Jinping, for example, announced BRI in Kazakhstan's capital in 2013.[75] By contrast, no U.S. president has visited the region, while the last secretary of state to visit was John Kerry in 2015.[76] In the 2017 U.S. National Security Strategy, Central Asia was given only two stand-alone sentences and was otherwise lumped together with South Asia. The main policy goal that the document articulated in Central Asia was "to guarantee access to the region to support our counterterrorism efforts."[77] The Obama administration's 2015 National Security Strategy included only one mention of Central Asia.[78] Given the gap between U.S. and Chinese levels of interest in the region, Central Asian states realize that China will likely have more to offer, even if the United States remains more powerful in absolute terms. They will therefore focus more on playing the United States, China, and Russia off of one another.

Other States in the Post-Soviet Region

Outside Russia and Central Asia, the other states in the post-Soviet region have diverse interactions with U.S.-China competition. There is one key factor that unites how Ukraine, Georgia, Belarus, Armenia, Azerbaijan, and Moldova view China: China is a faraway country and is therefore not seen as a significant security risk.[79] All these countries see it instead as a source of investment and as a means of diversifying away from reliance on Russia. Each, by contrast, sees Russia as a major risk, though for some it is an unavoidable one. Countries that have close relationships with the United States, notably Georgia and Ukraine, face pressure from Washington to ensure that China's footprint does not grow too rapidly, especially in

---

[75] Jiao and Yunbi, "Xi Proposes a 'New Silk Road' with Central Asia."

[76] Luke Coffey, "Why Trump's Meeting with Kazakhstan's President Was So Important," Heritage Foundation, January 17, 2018, https://www.heritage.org/asia/commentary/why-trumps-meeting-kazakhstan-president-was-so-important; and Sanger, "John Kerry Confronts Human Rights."

[77] White House, *National Security Strategy of the United States of America* (2017).

[78] White House, *National Security Strategy of the United States of America* (Washington, D.C., February 2015), https://obamawhitehouse.archives.gov/sites/default/files/docs/2015_national_security_strategy_2.pdf.

[79] The Baltic states—Estonia, Latvia, and Lithuania—also have a complex view of China but are best analyzed in comparison with other European Union member states.

sensitive sectors. Belarus, by contrast, has strained relations with the West and sees China as crucial to its strategy of reducing dependence on Russia. Armenia and Azerbaijan are less affected by Sino-U.S. competition, though China's trade relations with both countries have expanded, while Moldova is too small to play anything beyond a bit role in either U.S. or Chinese thinking.

Belarus. Belarus is deeply intertwined with Russia in terms of security and economics, yet it is concerned that Russia might try to annex it by force in advance of 2024, when Putin's current presidential term ends. Some Russians have discussed integrating Russia and Belarus as part of a process to change Russia's constitution and extend Putin's time in power.[80] Belarus is therefore deepening ties with other partners. In recent years it has improved relations with the West slightly, though these efforts are limited by undemocratic rule at home.[81] Belarus also has welcomed investment from China, which raises no questions about President Alexander Lukashenko's strongman tactics. The biggest current project is the China-Belarus Great Stone Industrial Park, which was launched when Xi Jinping visited Minsk in 2010.[82] China describes the park as "the pearl of the Silk Road Economic Belt" and sees it as a gateway to Europe. It is on track to be China's largest industrial park in Europe, occupying 80 square kilometers and, according to Belarus's government, potentially employing 130,000 people by 2030.[83] China has provided $3 billion via the China Development Bank and the Export-Import Bank of China. Such development zones have a long track record of underperformance, and the projections for the industries that Belarus plans to target with tax benefits, including the biotechnology and electronics sectors, seem overly optimistic.[84] Yet even if this project

---

[80] Yaroslav Trofimov, "Belarus Comes In from the Cold as It Seeks to Distance Itself from Russia," *Wall Street Journal*, June 14, 2019, https://www.wsj.com/articles/belarus-comes-in-from-the-cold-as-it-seeks-to-distance-itself-from-russia-11560504604.

[81] Benno Zogg, "Belarus between East and West: The Art of the Deal," Center for Security Studies (CSS), CSS Analyses in Security Policy, no. 231, September 2018, https://css.ethz.ch/content/dam/ethz/special-interest/gess/cis/center-for-securities-studies/pdfs/CSSAnalyse231-EN.pdf.

[82] "China-Belarus Great Stone Industrial Park," CSIS, Reconnecting Asia, https://reconnectingasia.csis.org/database/projects/china-belarus-great-stone-industrial-park-construction/6b6fbeb0-7f10-4d8a-9935-11b75dfeb9dd; and "Industrial Park Great Stone," Republic of Belarus, https://www.belarus.by/en/business/business-environment/industrial-park-great-stone.

[83] "China-Belarus Industrial Park Makes Breakthrough in Attracting Investors," Xinhua, October 12, 2017, available at http://www.chinadaily.com.cn/business/2017-10/12/content_33154129.htm; "Interview: China-Belarus Industrial Park Propels Belarusian Economy," Xinhua, August 11, 2018, http://www.xinhuanet.com/english/2018-08/11/c_137383743.htm; and Chen Meiling, "Belarus, a Gateway to Europe," *China Daily*, March 4, 2019, http://www.chinadaily.com.cn/a/201903/04/WS5c7c9c5ca3106c65c34ec959.html.

[84] Jacob Mardell, "Big, Empty, but Full of Promise? The Great Stone Industrial Park in Minsk," Mercator Institute for China Studies (MERICS), April 29, 2019, https://www.merics.org/en/blog/big-empty-full-promise-great-stone-industrial-park-minsk.

disappoints, it is not the only major Chinese investment in Belarus. China has also funded the renovation of the Minsk airport and several other road and rail projects.[85] As long as Belarus worries about Russian pressure, it has an incentive to welcome Chinese investment, even when political strings are attached. Given its limited relations with the United States, Belarus faces little pressure from Washington to curtail ties with China.

Ukraine and Georgia. The primary foreign policy issue for Ukraine and Georgia is the threat posed by Russia, and they both interpret U.S.-China competition through this lens. Russia's wars with Georgia and Ukraine in 2008 and 2014, respectively, had little direct relevance for China, but these conflicts were crucial for the United States, which saw them as a challenge to European security. Washington is therefore working closely with Ukraine and Georgia to reduce Russian influence. Both countries, meanwhile, depend on the United States to support their sovereignty. Yet they have also been hit hard economically by the disruption of trade and investment flows with their largest neighbor, Russia.

Georgia and Ukraine thus face a growing dilemma. They welcome Chinese investment because it lets them diversify away from Russia, which was one of their long-term key trade and investment partners.[86] Yet they also face U.S. pressure to not welcome too substantial a Chinese presence. For example, Russia used to be one of the main export markets for the Ukrainian defense contractor Motor Sich, but the war has disrupted those trade ties. A Chinese firm has proposed buying the company, which could provide it new opportunities to integrate with Chinese customers. The United States, however, fears the transfer of sensitive technology to China and is seeking to block the sale.[87] Yet it is not clear whether the United States can offer an equally compelling business proposition.

---

[85] "Electrification of the Gomel-Zhlobin-Osipovichi Section," CSIS, Reconnecting Asia, https://reconnectingasia.csis.org/database/projects/electrification-of-railway-sections-gomel-zhlobin-osipovichi/013de91d-2794-4b2f-baaf-5e8ee4458934; "Electrification of Molodechno-Gudogay-State Border Line," CSIS, Reconnecting Asia, https://reconnectingasia.csis.org/database/projects/electrification-molodechno-gudogay-state-border-line/c01999f3-6ff1-42f8-87b1-17eb0c0ad09b; "Minsk-Grodno Highway," CSIS, Reconnecting Asia, https://reconnectingasia.csis.org/database/projects/minsk-grodno-highway/d4ad3247-8f54-4231-ad44-1f112a0308f6; and "Bobruisk-Zhlobin Highway," CSIS, Reconnecting Asia, https://reconnectingasia.csis.org/database/projects/bobruisk-zhlobin-highway/45093a69-c481-4fbfb985-a3b967e81bd5.

[86] Michael Cecire, "China's Growing Presence in Georgia," *Diplomat*, May 6, 2015, https://thediplomat.com/2015/05/chinas-growing-presence-in-georgia; and James Brooke, "With Russia on the Sidelines, China Moves Aggressively into Ukraine," Atlantic Council, January 5, 2018, https://www.atlanticcouncil.org/blogs/ukrainealert/with-russia-on-the-sidelines-china-moves-aggressively-into-ukraine.

[87] Brett Forrest, "U.S. Aims to Block Chinese Acquisition of Ukrainian Aerospace Company," *Wall Street Journal*, August 23, 2019, https://www.wsj.com/articles/u-s-aims-to-block-chinese-acquisition-of-ukrainian-aerospace-company-11566594485.

Other sensitive sectors have also received scrutiny; for example, China's role in building a port in Anaklia, Georgia, has drawn attention from U.S. policymakers, who have warned that it might create dependence on Beijing. For Georgia, this project offers not only a new port but also a chance to involve China in a major project, which Georgia hopes might deter Russia from future military incursions.[88] Similarly, Ukraine has faced U.S. pressure over a Chinese offer to finance a Huawei 5G network at a steep discount.[89] Ukrainian and Georgian government officials, seeing China more as an opportunity than as a threat, find U.S.-China competition frustrating when it forces them to decline trade and investment deals. Nevertheless, when forced to choose, they prioritize relations with Washington over Beijing.

Conclusions for U.S. Policymakers

U.S.-China competition will create opportunities for rulers in Russia and other countries in the post-Soviet space. Russia has welcomed growing Sino-U.S. competition. Moscow does not fear rising Chinese power in the short term and is focused instead on its goal of degrading U.S. influence. Beijing is a useful partner for Russia in this effort. In Central Asia, meanwhile, leaders hope that they can use Sino-U.S. competition to attract more attention from Washington, while continuing to receive investment from Beijing. Central Asian countries realize that engagement with China is unavoidable given their proximity, but they hope to take advantage of U.S., Chinese, and Russian engagement to ensure that no single power dominates the region. Indeed, U.S.-China competition is already allowing countries to attract more attention from the great powers and giving them opportunities to negotiate better deals as a result. At the same time, Central Asian governments will face less U.S. pressure to democratize. In Eastern Europe, countries such as Ukraine and Georgia have found U.S.-China competition more frustrating, especially when their key security partner, the United States, requests that they reject Chinese investment.

What does this mean for U.S. policymakers as they consider relations with countries in the post-Soviet space? With regard to Russia, Washington must recognize that U.S.-Russia antagonism substantially constrains U.S. policy in Central Asia in particular and in Eurasia more broadly. For example, it is very difficult for the United States to work with Russia in helping Central Asian countries diversify away from economic dependence on China.

---

[88] "On the Fault Line: Georgian Relations with China and the West," Foreign Policy Research Institute, September 2019, https://www.fpri.org/wp-content/uploads/2019/09/on-the-fault-line.pdf.

[89] Conversation with a Ukrainian official in Kiev, March 2019.

More generally, it is unclear how U.S.-Russia relations might be improved without offering Russia undesirable concessions, even though less antagonistic bilateral relations would certainly make it much easier for Washington to limit Chinese influence in the post-Soviet space.

With regard to the post-Soviet countries in Eastern Europe, U.S. policymakers must understand that these countries have very different threat perceptions about China. For countries such as Ukraine and Georgia, the overriding concern is Russia. China, by contrast, is generally seen as a country that is far away and therefore not a security threat. These countries have only limited experience in receiving Chinese investment, and unlike in the United States, there is relatively little skepticism about the benefits of Chinese funds. U.S. efforts to pressure them to limit or reject Chinese investment will face difficulty, given that these countries struggle to attract foreign investment and do not see Chinese funds as a substantial threat. Many people from Eastern Europe, by contrast, see a growing Chinese economic footprint as providing the resources needed to chart a course independent of Russia.

In Central Asia, meanwhile, the U.S.-China competition is likely to induce Washington to limit its strategic aims and demand fewer domestic political changes in the region. Washington is also likely to devote relatively few resources to containing Russia while devoting more toward containing China. Central Asian countries are deeply concerned about China's growing power, even more than they worry about Russia. For Kazakhstan and Kyrgyzstan, for example, Russia is at times a problematic partner, but Chinese dominance could well be worse. Russia's presence, in other words, can in some instances help countries balance against China. Ultimately, however, the United States should focus far more on Eastern Europe and on Russia than on Central Asia, which plays a peripheral role in U.S. national interests. Eastern Europe matters because of its proximity to key U.S. allies in Europe. Russia matters because it is a great power. Central Asian countries, though they are most influenced by China, are far less important to the United States. To be sure, the United States has powerful tools, and governments in the region are keen for more U.S. engagement to balance China and Russia. But Washington ultimately will devote only limited resources to the region and must craft its aims accordingly. This may mean taking a more disinterested view of Chinese influence. If Central Asia is a low priority for the United States, it should continue to get limited resource allocations from Washington, even if Chinese influence increases.

During the Cold War, the United States tolerated Russian dominance of Central Asia, preferring to focus on pushing against Russian influence in regions that were more important for U.S. interests, such as Europe and East Asia. Now, as then, it is difficult to imagine that the post-Soviet space will play anything more than a marginal role in shaping the outcome of the U.S.-China competition. Of all parts of the post-Soviet space, therefore, Washington would be well advised to focus its attention on Eastern Europe and Russia, even though this means playing a less substantial role in Central Asia, the region that faces the most substantial growth in Chinese influence.

EXECUTIVE SUMMARY

This chapter examines the competition between the U.S. and China in Oceania and finds that it is greatly complicating regional relationships and power dynamics.

MAIN ARGUMENT

The growth in China's presence and influence in Oceania has led to both alarm and opportunity in this normally uncontested region. While Pacific Island leaders see the economic and diplomatic benefits of engaging with China, the Australian and New Zealand governments worry about the prospects of Chinese bases so close to their shores. The U.S., Australia, and New Zealand have responded by refocusing their attention on the island states of the South Pacific, seeking both to compete directly with China's initiatives and to raise regional concerns about the dangers of China's presence. Most of the island states have refused to accept this polarizing logic and instead have seen China's presence and the greater U.S., Australian, and New Zealand attention that it has spurred as an advantage. Moreover, they have insisted on pursuing their own alternative nontraditional security agenda that is heavily focused on addressing climate change.

POLICY IMPLICATIONS

- Escalating rivalry in Oceania could have polarizing effects both domestically and intraregionally, leading to a destabilization of the region that is in no country's interests.

- For commercial, diplomatic, and military reasons, China is in Oceania to stay. The South Pacific's traditional partners should accept this and work to build the capacity of island states to manage multiple relationships that are in their own and the region's interests.

- The U.S., Australia, and New Zealand should not exaggerate China's advantages in the region. Beijing has made significant mistakes and faces considerable suspicions, and the South Pacific's traditional partners should seek to build on their traditional connections and reputational advantages.

Oceania: Cold War Versus the Blue Pacific

Michael Wesley

The strategic significance of Oceania (comprising the island states of the southwest Pacific, New Zealand, and Australia) arises from its position at the end of the world's longest archipelago, stretching along Asia's eastern coast from the Sakhalin and Kuril Islands in the north; continuing down through Japan, Taiwan, the Philippines, Indonesia, New Guinea, Australia, and New Zealand; and reaching out to Fiji, Samoa, and Tonga. The greater the strategic competition is for the northern and middle reaches of this archipelago, the more the rivalries spill into Oceania.

Imperial Japan first used this archipelago during World War II for its southern lightning strike, which pushed out British, French, Dutch, and U.S. spheres of influence and briefly established Japanese hegemony. The Allied counterattack began in Oceania, on the island of Guadalcanal, and drove the Japanese back up the archipelago in the famous island-hopping campaign of the Pacific War. During the early stages of the Cold War, the United States designated the island chain as a strategic perimeter beyond which it would not permit the expansion of Communist influence. Chinese strategists referred to the archipelago as the "first island chain" and saw it as a rampart of U.S.-allied or -aligned states that were blocking China's egress into the Pacific and beyond. They thus oriented the country's maritime strategy toward solving the dilemma of the first island chain. This strategy became particularly acute after 1993 when China became a net energy importer and was increasingly reliant on seaborne supplies of oil from the Persian Gulf, thus rendering it ever more dependent on sea lanes dominated by the U.S. Navy in the Indian and Pacific Oceans.

Michael Wesley is Deputy Vice-Chancellor International at the University of Melbourne in Australia. He can be reached at <michael.wesley@unimelb.edu.au>.

China's growing strategic interest in the Indian Ocean, its increasing naval might, and other Asian states' investments in their own maritime weapons systems have brought about an Indo-Pacific strategic system that includes Oceania. All the major industrial states of Northeast Asia rely on seaborne energy that passes through the Indo-Pacific archipelago via the Malacca, Lombok, or Sunda Strait. All these straits would become the focus of blockade operations in the event of conflict in the Pacific. Consequently, all the major powers in the Pacific have shifted their strategic focus toward Southeast Asia, investing heavily in building partnerships with South and Southeast Asian states.[1] At the same time, there has been significant investment in military equipment in the region. In the quarter century since the end of the Cold War, China's arms spending has increased by 875%, Indonesia's by 210%, India's by 176%, Malaysia's by 170%, Singapore's by 165%, Vietnam's by 135%, and South Korea's by 119%.[2] Most of these investments have been in maritime weapons systems, including ships, submarines, missiles, surveillance systems, and jet fighters. As a consequence, the Indo-Pacific has shifted from being a maritime system dominated by U.S. sea control to being one of multiple interlocking zones of sea denial.[3] The increasing congestion of Southeast Asia's strategic waterways has resulted in rivalries spilling over into Oceania as various powers look for alternative points of advantage, resulting in the most sustained strategic competition in the region since 1942.

This chapter examines the effects of growing Sino-U.S. competition in Oceania on the foreign policies and domestic politics of the region's states. It argues that competition between Washington and Beijing in Oceania is an extension of their competition for influence across the Indo-Pacific. It has particular implications for the regional posture of the United States' treaty ally Australia and security partner New Zealand, both of which view China's growing presence in Oceania with the same alarm as Washington. China has chosen to emphasize the mutual benefits of its engagement with Pacific Island states, in contrast to the United States and its allies. Most Pacific Island leaders have refused to buy in to the strategic competition, instead focusing on the benefits of engaging with all sides. They have also advanced their own, alternative security agenda, which prioritizes addressing climate change and other transnational threats.

---

[1] For example, China's Belt and Road Initiative, South Korea's New Southern Policy, Japan's Vientiane Vision (for new defense diplomacy in Southeast Asia), Taiwan's New Southbound Policy, and India's Act East policy all have a maritime component.

[2] Data is taken from the Stockholm International Peace Research Institute (SIPRI), SIPRI Military Expenditure Database, https://sipri.org/databases/milex.

[3] For the shift in maritime dominance, see Michael Wesley, *Restless Continent: Wealth, Rivalry and Asia's New Geopolitics* (Melbourne: Black, 2015), 136–37.

The chapter begins by examining the policies of the United States, Australia, New Zealand, and China toward Oceania. It examines the complex alliance considerations that explain the intense focus of Australia and New Zealand on the region. The chapter then explores Pacific Island states' responses, discussing points of solidarity and division both among the states and between elites and populations. The new security agenda in the Pacific, as advanced by Pacific Island leaders, is contrasted with the geopolitical agendas of the United States and its allies. The chapter concludes by outlining policy implications for the United States, Australia, and New Zealand.

Competing U.S. and Chinese Interests in Oceania

U.S. Aims

The United States has traditionally factored Oceania into its broader Pacific strategy. Maintaining exclusive sea control of the Pacific Ocean was an essential part of U.S. Cold War strategy. The United States used island bases in Japan, Guam, and the Philippines, as well as aircraft carriers, to project power onto the Eurasian landmass.[4] While Oceania was never at the front lines of this strategy, keeping the region free of hostile interests that could threaten or distract the main thrust of U.S. efforts farther north was an important secondary interest. After signing the Australia, New Zealand, United States (ANZUS) Security Treaty in 1951, Washington was comfortable outsourcing the management of Oceania to Canberra and Wellington on behalf of the Western alliance system. The treaty committed the countries to "consult together whenever in the opinion of any of them the territorial integrity, political independence or security of any of the Parties is threatened in the Pacific."[5] The same year, the three allies signed the Radford-Collins Agreement, which created a joint zone of maritime responsibility across Oceania, Southeast Asia, and the eastern Indian Ocean. A third element of U.S. outsourcing evolved from the 1948 UKUSA agreement, which committed the United States, the United Kingdom, Canada, Australia, and New Zealand to sharing signals intelligence. The agreement divided up the responsibilities for collecting signals intelligence among the five allies: Britain would collect in Africa and in Eastern Europe, Canada in northern Europe and Russia, Australia in the eastern Indian Ocean as well as in parts of Southeast Asia and the southwest Pacific, New Zealand in the South Pacific,

---

[4] Samuel P. Huntington, "National Policy and the Transoceanic Navy," *Proceedings of the U.S. Naval Institute* 80, no. 3 (1954): 483–93.

[5] See art. 3 of the ANZUS Treaty.

and the United States in all other designated places.[6] From this specific responsibility for collecting intelligence across Oceania, Australia and New Zealand slowly assumed responsibility for managing the region on behalf of the Western alliance.

For most of the postwar period, allied strategy in Oceania has rested on an alignment between U.S. strategic interests and those of Australia and New Zealand. The United States has seen Oceania as a region of secondary strategic importance, and has increasingly trusted its antipodean allies to keep it that way. Since the mid-nineteenth century, a deep motivation for Australia's and New Zealand's foreign policies had been to maintain Oceania's freedom from interests that were hostile to their own. Indeed, frustration with Britain's willingness to allow potentially hostile French, U.S., and German interests to intrude into the region provided significant impetus for the Australian colonies to unite in a federation and push for constitutional independence from Britain.[7] The seizure of German colonies in New Guinea and Samoa during World War I established Australia and New Zealand, respectively, as colonial powers, while the sudden appearance of Japanese forces in Papua New Guinea and the Solomon Islands in World War II only heightened Australia's and New Zealand's sensitivity to the vulnerability of small island states to the ingress of hostile interests. Finally, as the Cold War progressed, both Oceanian powers had the chance to realize their visions of a region free of hostile interests: the entire Pacific was dominated by their major ally, the United States; Japan had been decisively defeated and absorbed into the U.S. alliance system; and France, although maintaining its Pacific colonies, had become a member of NATO.

Subsequently, policing Oceania became part of the alliance deal with the United States. As the island states of the Pacific were decolonized, Australia and New Zealand worked to build access and influence with their governments. They became the region's major aid providers, served as the metropolitan members of fledgling regional organizations such as the Pacific Islands Forum, and ensured that the newly decolonized states had no reason to be attracted to the more radicalizing influences that were sweeping the Afro-Asian grouping at the United Nations. The United States relied on Canberra and Wellington to represent its interests in Oceania, devoting few resources and scant attention to the region.

For Australia and New Zealand, preserving the balance between their alliance responsibilities of maintaining access and influence in the region

---

[6] Jeffrey T. Richelson and Desmond Ball, *The Ties That Bind: Intelligence Cooperation between the UKUSA Countries*, 2nd ed. (Sydney: Unwin Hyman, 1990), 143.

[7] Neville Meaney, *The Search for Security in the Pacific, 1901–1914*, vol. 1, *A History of Australian Defence and Foreign Policy 1901–1923* (Sydney: Sydney University Press, 1976).

and their alliance commitments to support U.S. strategic policy could be difficult at times. When the Pacific Island states began to mobilize against nuclear testing in Oceania and move toward signing the 1985 South Pacific Nuclear Free Zone Treaty that would create a nuclear-free zone in Oceania, Australia and New Zealand were placed in a difficult position. On the one hand, their alliance responsibilities to maintain access to and influence in the Pacific Island governments suggested that they should show solidarity with the region's anti-nuclear sentiments. On the other hand, their alliance commitments to support U.S. sea control in the Pacific mandated that they should support the rights of nuclear-armed U.S. Navy vessels to operate in Oceania. New Zealand chose to show solidarity with the Pacific Island states and exited from the ANZUS Treaty in the 1980s, whereas Australia supported both U.S. access and the Pacific's nuclear-free goals and remained inside the alliance.

The alliance deal was built into Australia's own strategic planning. During the 1980s, Canberra replaced its old "forward defence" doctrine, in which it committed to expeditionary coalitions to defeat aggression on the Asian mainland, with the new "defence of Australia" doctrine, which would invest heavily in air and maritime assets capable of defeating possible adversaries in the "air-sea gap" to Australia's north and northwest.[8] Central to this strategy were three concentric circles of strategic priorities: the Australian continent, an inner arc encompassing maritime Southeast Asia and the South Pacific, and an outer arc stretching to continental Southeast Asia and the western Indian Ocean. Thus, the strategic denial of access to the South Pacific to hostile interests served both national defense planning and alliance obligations. This strategy has since remained central to Australian defense planning for over 40 years.

For New Zealand, regardless of whether it was formally inside or outside the ANZUS Treaty, the limited scale of its defense force has meant that it has prioritized responding to security challenges as part of coalitions, which of necessity requires a fairly close adherence to Australian and U.S. strategic objectives. The most recent Strategic Defence Policy Statement, for example, echoes Australian and U.S. pessimism about China's growing role in the broader region and makes a significant decision to bolster New Zealand's maritime power through the purchase of Boeing P-8A Poseidon maritime patrol aircraft.[9] New Zealand has aligned its strategic policy with those of the United States and Australia for much of this century so far—for example,

---

[8] Commonwealth of Australia, *The Defence of Australia 1987* (Canberra, 1987).

[9] On New Zealand's defense policy, see Robert Ayson, "The Domestic Politics of New Zealand's Defence," Lowy Institute, Interpreter, July 9, 2018, https://www.lowyinstitute.org/the-interpreter/domestic-politics-new-zealand-defence.

by making contributions to allied operations in Iraq and Afghanistan and counterpiracy missions in the Indian Ocean. It has taken similar positions on the South China Sea and blocking Huawei from its telecommunications infrastructure as Canberra and Washington. Further, its response to China's role in the Pacific has been highly consistent with those of Australia and the United States.

The island countries of Oceania were given no voice in this strategic framing of their region. Only three Pacific Island countries—Papua New Guinea, Fiji, and Tonga—had armed forces. However, the Papua New Guinea Defence Force was preoccupied between 1989 and 1999 with fighting separatists in Bougainville Province, while the Fijian and Tongan militaries had mainly been involved in UN peacekeeping. In the case of Fiji, the military also launched several coups. The only two times during the Cold War period that the island states became involved in broader strategic issues were during their anti-nuclear campaign and in Vanuatu's membership of the Non-Aligned Movement. Vanuatu has periodically caused the greatest concerns in Canberra, Wellington, and Washington, such as when the country negotiated a fisheries access agreement with the Soviet Union or when it allowed a Libyan People's Bureau to open in its capital, Port Vila, in the 1980s. But beyond these brief forays into broader geopolitics, the island states remained focused on intraregional relations and rivalries for much of the first quarter century of their independence. Although quick to observe that they are never consulted in the development of allied strategy toward Oceania, Pacific Island leaders quietly endorse the role of the United States and its allies in the region. Too small to defend themselves, most Pacific Island states have been the beneficiaries of the strategic stability brought by U.S. primacy in the Pacific. However, this has not stopped these states from also being critical of specific U.S. actions, such as nuclear testing in the Marshall Islands or the withdrawal from the Paris climate change agreement.

The strategic objectives of the United States in Oceania center on ensuring that the southern end of the Pacific Island chain does not become host to hostile interests. While Oceania has been of secondary importance to the United States, the United States has been willing to allow its ally Australia and security partner New Zealand to maintain stability and an absence of rival interests in Oceania. Washington has relied on Canberra and Wellington to represent its interests in Oceania and has only become more attentive to the region since China has started to build a significant presence there.

Wesley – Oceania • 197

Chinese Aims

China's interests in Oceania are varied and have evolved through several phases. Australia and New Zealand are important suppliers of minerals, energy, and food to the fast-developing Chinese economy, and China's goods and services trade with these two countries has been expanding rapidly. Developing close relations with Australia and New Zealand became important to China in the two decades after its economic opening, as they became strong supporters of China's entry into regional and global trade organizations such as the Asia-Pacific Economic Cooperation (APEC) and the World Trade Organization (WTO), respectively. Australia and to a lesser extent New Zealand are also important to China's strategic aims as allies of the United States. As Beijing tries to weaken the U.S. role in the western Pacific, it has used a variety of tactics to try to loosen U.S. allies' commitments to the United States. For example, the Chinese telecommunications firm Huawei has spent resources trying to gain access to the Australian and New Zealand markets that are well beyond what such modest markets would return, arguably for the psychological effect of having close U.S. allies partner with a Chinese company in ways objected to by Washington.[10]

Increasingly, the deepening economic complementarities that China has with the economies of Australia and New Zealand have emerged as a possible lever for China to weaken Australia's commitment to the U.S. alliance and New Zealand's general alignment with Western liberal democratic causes. China's recent imposition of trade and investment restrictions on Japan, South Korea, and the Philippines has made Australia and the United States anxious about the aggregate effect on their own economies if China were to decide to take similar measures against them.[11] Washington has also voiced concerns that Australia's and New Zealand's trade dependence on China will cause them to equivocate in their commitments to their strategic partnerships with the United States. Such concerns were heightened in 2004 when the Australian foreign minister denied that the ANZUS Treaty obliged Australia to join with the United States in the event of war with China and in 2014 when the defense minister said the same thing.[12] However, to date there is no evidence that considerations of trade ties to China have caused

---

[10] Jennifer Duke, "Fighting the 'Domino Effect': Why Huawei Is Doubling Down on Australia," *Sydney Morning Herald*, June 29, 2019.

[11] Richard McGregor, "Trade Deficits: How China Could Punish Australia," *Australian Foreign Affairs*, no. 7 (2019): 54–74.

[12] Brendan Taylor, "Australia and the United States in Asia," in *Australia's American Alliance*, ed. Peter J. Dean, Stephan Frühling, and Brendan Taylor (Melbourne: Melbourne University Press, 2016), 256–58.

either Australia or New Zealand to distance itself from U.S. strategy in the region.[13]

China's initial interest in the South Pacific began through the lens of its diplomatic rivalry with Taiwan. Currently five of the seventeen states that recognize Taiwan as a sovereign state are Pacific Island countries. At times of particularly intense rivalry with Taiwan, Beijing has stepped up its attempts to persuade these countries to switch their recognition to China. A more recent wave of Chinese interest has occurred as a consequence of the rapid development and evolution of the Chinese economy. Chinese economic influence has increased throughout the Pacific Island countries as a result of the uncoordinated activities of thousands of Chinese migrants who have relocated to Oceania and established small businesses. Across the region, these migrants have started to dominate local economies, particularly in the retail sector.[14]

More recently, a third phase of Chinese interest in the islands of the South Pacific has emerged as a result of the deepening rivalry with the United States and its allies in the Indo-Pacific. Oceania has begun to play into Beijing's strategic planning in this regard due to two considerations. The first is China's continuing concern about the ability of its nuclear submarine fleet to maneuver from bases on Hainan Island, past the first island chain, and into the Pacific. Having bases in the Pacific outside the first island chain would enable the People's Liberation Army (PLA) Navy to increase the U.S. Navy's strategic uncertainties, while providing its own fleet with substantially greater freedom of navigation. The second impulse relates to what President Hu Jintao termed China's "Malacca dilemma"—the possible blockade of the transit routes through which the country's energy supplies transit Southeast Asia. While considerably longer, a transit route that runs to the south of Australia and north through the South Pacific would free Chinese shipping of chokepoints; moreover, a permanent PLA Navy presence would make this route much more secure for China than the crowded and contested waters of maritime Southeast Asia.

Beijing has consequently deployed in the South Pacific the same playbook that it has used to build influence in other developing regions.[15] Proclaiming "South-South cooperation," Beijing has directed increasing amounts of development assistance to the Pacific Islands. One credible estimate calculates

---

[13] Shannon Tow, *Independent Ally: Australia in an Age of Power Transition* (Melbourne: Melbourne University Press, 2017).

[14] Kathryn Hille, "Pacific Islands: A New Arena of Rivalry between China and the U.S.," *Financial Times*, April 9, 2019.

[15] On China's "playbook," see Avery Goldstein, "A Rising China's Growing Presence," in *China's Global Engagement: Cooperation, Competition and Influence in the 21st Century*, ed. Jacques deLisle and Avery Goldstein (Washington, D.C.: Brookings Institution Press, 2017), 1–34.

that, since 2006, Beijing has provided $632 million in aid to Papua New Guinea, $359 million to Fiji, $243 million to Vanuatu, $230 million to Samoa, and $172 million to Tonga. The assistance, predominantly in the form of concessional loans, has been directed across a range of sectors, including infrastructure, communications, mining and forestry, and health and education.[16] China has financed large infrastructure projects in small nations; promised new forms of connectivity to isolated island societies, ranging from telecommunications infrastructure to markets to tourism; and rolled out its own forms of imperial diplomacy, including two leaders' summits between the Chinese president and the leaders of the Pacific Islands. Beijing's strategy appears to be evolutionary rather than declaratory, seeking to build influence and access in the present as a precursor to greater political and strategic influence in the future.

China's objectives in Oceania are several. It continues to compete for diplomatic recognition with Taiwan in the region, where five states still recognize Taipei. Beijing also has an interest in building a greater presence in Oceania as a consequence of its expanding global status as a great power. More recently, China has developed a focused strategic interest in the South Pacific. It feels that a base in the region would ease its challenges in developing and maintaining naval access to the Pacific Ocean outside the first island chain. As noted above, the South Pacific also has strategic value as a possible maritime route to the western Indian Ocean if the narrow and contested straits through Southeast Asia become too dangerous.

Increasing Sino-U.S. Competition in the South Pacific

In response to China's growing influence in the South Pacific, the United States has become less willing to outsource its strategic interests to Australia and New Zealand. Responding both to their own concerns and to the growing discomfort of the United States, the two U.S. allies have unveiled major increases to their aid to and activities in the South Pacific. Australia's policy shift, labeled the "Pacific step-up," involves a range of initiatives from training security officials across the region to major infrastructure investments, such as building undersea internet cables between Solomon Islands, Vanuatu, and Australia in order to prevent Huawei from doing so. New Zealand's policy has been christened the "Pacific reset" and involves an additional NZ$714 million in aid to the South Pacific.

The logic of both Australia's and New Zealand's policies seems to be to reduce the need for and attraction of Chinese initiatives and assistance among Pacific Island countries. Initiatives such as the Australian Infrastructure

---

[16] "Chinese Aid in the Pacific," Lowy Institute, https://chineseaidmap.lowyinstitute.org.

Financing Facility for the Pacific appear to be directly countering China's most prominent activities in the region. Conversely, both New Zealand's and Australia's intensified capacity-building activities in the security sectors of Pacific countries appear to be aimed at depriving China of any strategic advantage that it might have hoped to derive from its largesse in the South Pacific through fostering greater alignment with its security goals. Canberra and Wellington have been vocal in warning their Pacific neighbors of the dangers of becoming too involved with China. Concetta Fierravanti-Wells, then Australian minister for international development and the Pacific, warned Pacific Island countries of Beijing's "debt-trap diplomacy" whereby it offers concessional loans that are beyond the capacities of the receiving countries to repay and then demands debt-for-equity swaps of strategic real estate.[17] The then Australian foreign minister Julie Bishop was unequivocal in her pledge to "compete with China's infrastructure development spree in Australia's neighborhood to help ensure that small nations are not saddled with debt that threatens their sovereignty."[18] The sudden counter-bid for Australia to build the Solomon Islands' internet cable rather than Huawei also carried clear implications that Canberra believed that such infrastructure could be used by Beijing to interfere in the domestic politics of the island countries.

By calling their programs, respectively, a "step up" and a "reset," Canberra and Wellington seem to be implying that before the arrival of China in the South Pacific they had neglected the region. Yet nothing could be further from the truth. Since the beginnings of the Bougainville Civil War in 1988, both Australia and New Zealand have been intensively involved in the South Pacific, most notably by leading a fourteen-year, AU$2 billion intervention in the Solomon Islands to restore law and order and to rebuild governance and economic institutions between 2003 and 2017.[19] One must suspect that the main audience for the step-up and reset titles is in Washington, D.C., rather than in the South Pacific.

Nevertheless, despite the policy focus of its allies, Washington seems to be in the process of developing its own renewed policy focus on the South Pacific. At the time of writing, this remains a work in progress, but the intent to do so from U.S. policymakers is clear. The United States has restructured the National Security Council to create an Office of Oceania and Indo-Pacific

---

[17] Primrose Riordan, "Concetta Fierravanti-Wells Warns PNG Not to Be China's Conduit," *Australian*, October 5, 2018.

[18] David Wroe, "Australia Will Compete with China to Save Pacific Sovereignty, Says Bishop," *Sydney Morning Herald*, June 18. 2018, https://www.smh.com.au/politics/federal/australia-will-compete-with-china-to-save-pacific-sovereignty-says-bishop-20180617-p4zm1h.html.

[19] Joanne Wallis and Michael Wesley, "Unipolar Anxieties: Australia's Melanesia Policy after the Age of Intervention," *Asia and the Pacific Policy Studies* 3, no. 1 (2016): 26–37.

Security, and senior members of the Trump administration, including Vice President Mike Pence, have visited the South Pacific. President Trump welcomed the leaders of the U.S. Compact of Free Association states to the White House in May 2019, issuing a joint statement with them on deepening cooperation on illegal fishing, the environment, and economic development.[20]

Intersection with Local Interests in Oceania

Australia and New Zealand

Responses to the United States. Australian and New Zealand elites have responded in complex ways to the increased Sino-U.S. rivalry in Oceania. The growing Chinese role in Southeast Asia and the South Pacific has seen both Canberra and Wellington cleave more closely to their relationships with Washington. The Australian government's 2017 foreign policy white paper, published in late 2017, characterized the importance of the United States in its region in these terms:

> The Australian Government judges that the United States' long-term interests will anchor its economic and security engagement in the Indo-Pacific. Its major Pacific alliances with Japan, the Republic of Korea and Australia will remain strong. Most regional countries, including Australia, clearly consider a significant U.S. role in the Indo-Pacific as a stabilising influence.[21]

Australia accepts that the period of uncontested U.S. primacy in the Pacific is over and that China's bid to dislodge the United States and establish its own form of primacy will be powerful and sustained. However, Canberra remains committed to its alliance relationship and is anxious to maintain U.S. commitment and attention to the Pacific. It has made several strategic commitments to underwrite the United States' presence, including hosting rotations of U.S. marines through Darwin and committing to doubling the size of its conventional submarine force with a range that will allow it to operate in the first island chain. Australia has also deepened its defense relationships with other U.S. allies and partners, such as Japan and Singapore, with the intention of partially "multilateralizing" the bilateral alliance architecture of the region.[22]

---

[20] Jesse Barker Gale, "Cooperation and Competition in the South Pacific," National Bureau of Asian Research, Brief, August 15, 2019, https://www.nbr.org/publication/competition-and-cooperation-in-the-south-pacific.

[21] Australian Government, *2017 Foreign Policy White Paper* (Canberra, 2017), 26.

[22] Peter J. Dean, "ANZUS: The 'Alliance' and Its Future in Asia," in *Australia's Defence: Towards a New Era?* ed. Peter J. Dean, Stephan Frühling, and Brendan Taylor (Melbourne: Melbourne University Press, 2014).

For over a decade now, New Zealand has been rebuilding its partnership with the United States, which had been damaged by its departure from the ANZUS alliance in 1985. Participation in coalition operations in Afghanistan saw it designated a major non-NATO ally of the United States in 2011. In 2010 the two countries signed the Wellington Declaration, a framework for strategic cooperation and political dialogue, and in 2012 they signed the Washington Agreement establishing official defense ties.[23] In 2015 the Edward Snowden leaks revealed close U.S.–New Zealand intelligence cooperation to penetrate the Chinese Foreign Ministry's computer systems.[24]

Both Australia and New Zealand have found that growing U.S. anxiety about China's activities in Oceania has given them greater access in Washington than they previously had. At the same time, the ascension of Donald Trump to the presidency of the United States has created some anxieties in both Canberra and Wellington. Trump has demonstrated on many occasions that he is not willing to treat allies any differently from rivals, as evidenced by his singling out of Japan, South Korea, and several NATO countries to criticize them for what he regards as their exploitation of U.S. generosity. The effect of these statements has been to cast doubt on the willingness of the United States under the Trump administration to come to the assistance of long-standing allies. A particularly bad-tempered phone conversation between Trump and then Australian prime minister Malcolm Turnbull in early 2017 has had an intimidating effect on elites in Canberra, who have since been particularly muted in their comments about U.S. policies that they find problematic, such as trade policies. At the very least, Trump's erratic foreign policy positioning has led Australia and New Zealand to think hard about "alliance plus" options—that is, strategies for managing China's growing presence and assertiveness that go beyond simply relying on U.S. power. These strategies include building strategic partnerships with other Indo-Pacific powers such as Japan, India, and Indonesia. More recently, in the context of the growing trade dispute and the possible "technology Cold War" between the United States and China, Canberra and Wellington have been working to clarify their interests in relation to the possibility of a bipolar confrontation in the Indo-Pacific. While Australia and New Zealand have welcomed the interest of European powers such as Britain, France, and Germany in the region, the main focus of their efforts has been on building partnerships with other Indo-Pacific states.

[23] The full text of the Wellington Declaration is available at http://www.stuff.co.nz/national/politics/4309206/Full-text-of-the-Wellington-Declaration.

[24] Tom Corben, "Louder Than Words: Actions Speak Volumes for New Zealand–U.S. Relations," *Diplomat*, October 12, 2016, https://thediplomat.com/2016/10/louder-than-words-actions-speak-volumes-for-new-zealand-us-relations.

Australia and New Zealand have reacted in complex ways to Washington's growing interest in the South Pacific. On the one hand, they have welcomed it as evidence of the United States' continued commitment to maintaining U.S. interests in the Pacific and have enjoyed greater access to policymakers in Washington as a consequence. On the other hand, policymakers in Canberra and Wellington are quietly irritated at the implication that the United States has become involved in the South Pacific because they have somehow created space for Chinese influence by neglecting their relationships in the region. The past quarter century has seen intensified Australian and New Zealand interest and activities in the South Pacific, and their access and influence across the region are arguably greater than at any time since the independence of the Pacific Island countries. As noted earlier, designating their policies as a step-up and a reset may be a somewhat misdirected way of reiterating their focus on the South Pacific to the United States.

Australia and New Zealand are also apprehensive that intensified U.S. activities may complicate their own efforts to maintain access to and influence in the South Pacific. The region is now awash with new initiatives, many of which are pursued by different agencies in Canberra and Wellington that often have little coordination with each other. Australian and New Zealand officials worry that additional U.S. activities will only add to this crowding-out effect, particularly if these activities are not accompanied by signs of genuine and long-term U.S. engagement, such as the establishment of fully fledged diplomatic missions in the region.

Responses to China. Australian and New Zealand responses to China have evolved markedly over the past half decade. For much of the post–Cold War period, both countries' attitudes toward China have largely been defined by their growing economic complementarity with the Chinese economy. They were two of the first countries in the region to register China as their largest trading partner, and this economic interdependence has become more marked over time. For Australia, and to a lesser extent for New Zealand, China has been the source of a remarkable terms-of-trade boom, enabling both countries' economies to ride out the downturns experienced by the rest of the world during the bursting of the technology bubble in 2000 and the global financial crisis in 2008. This economic complementarity has also meant that there have been few domestic losers from their interdependence with China, which generates positive elite and popular perceptions of bilateral relations. New Zealand became the first Western country to sign a free trade agreement with China in 2007, and Australia followed in 2014. For much of this period, Canberra's and Wellington's challenge was one of maintaining positive relations with both China and the United States, even as Sino-U.S. rivalry deepened.

However, these positive perceptions of China have shifted in both countries in recent years. The scale of China's economic growth, the rise in the power of the party-state under Xi Jinping, and the assertive nature of China's statecraft in the South China Sea have all contributed to a souring of attitudes in Australia and New Zealand. Official and public anxiety about the scale and nature of Chinese investment in both economies has increased. Canberra and Wellington have gradually broadened their definitions of what constitutes strategically sensitive elements of their economies, partly in response to public uproar over issues such as (in the case of Australia) the leasing of the port of Darwin to a Chinese company in 2016.

In particular, Australia has pushed backed more forcefully against China in recent years. In 2017, following a hack of the parliament's email network that allegedly originated in China, Australia legislated against activities that promoted foreign interference in its domestic affairs. Although not mentioning China, the legislation clearly implied that China was one of the main culprits behind the move. Australia was also the first country to explicitly ban Huawei from having any role in building the core components of its 4G mobile telephone network or any part of its 5G network. New Zealand, the United States, and several other Western countries have since followed suit. Australia has been particularly vocal in its opposition to China's claims and activities in the South China Sea, repeatedly calling on Beijing to respect international law and freedom of navigation in the waterway. In multiple public contexts, Australian government ministers and officials have rehearsed a mantra that calls for the respect of the rules-based order in the Indo-Pacific, with the clear implication that China's activities in the South China Sea and elsewhere pose the greatest challenge to it. Australia has also refused to sign on to China's Belt and Road Initiative, unlike New Zealand and many other countries in the Indo-Pacific. As a consequence, China has put bilateral relations with Australia into the cooler, suspending the annual strategic dialogues between the two countries and all but stopping bilateral ministerial visits.

New Zealand has been less confrontational with China than Australia or the United States. Although it too has banned Huawei from building its 5G network and has publicly voiced its concerns over China's activities in the South China Sea, Wellington has been careful to keep its relationship with Beijing in good repair. In April 2019, Prime Minister Jacinda Ardern made a state visit to China, and the two countries have commenced negotiations on updating their 2008 free trade agreement.[25]

---

[25] Jason Young, "Is New Zealand's Relationship with China on the Rocks?" East Asia Forum, May 2, 2019, https://www.eastasiaforum.org/2019/05/02/is-new-zealands-relationship-with-china-on-the-rocks.

Pacific Island Countries

In marked contrast to Australia and New Zealand, the Pacific Island countries refuse to align with the United States in its growing rivalry with China. Many are apprehensive that the island states of the Pacific will again be given no voice in the strategic alignments forming around them. In the words of the Samoan prime minister Tuilaepa Sailele Malielegaoi, "The renewed vigour with which a 'free and open Indo-Pacific' is being advocated and pursued leaves us with much uncertainty. For the Pacific there is a real risk of privileging the 'Indo' over the 'Pacific.'"[26] The period of strategic competition has coincided with a new assertiveness and solidarity from within the Pacific. According to Christelle Pratt, the deputy secretary-general of the Pacific Islands Forum, "For our region these similar yet different frames [i.e., Asia-Pacific vs Indo-Pacific] appear both complementary and competing, but what matters to this region is our own collective ambition to define our place. The Blue Pacific cannot and will not become an aside in this new Indo-Pacific frame."[27]

Many Pacific Island countries also worry about the polarizing effects of Sino-U.S. competition on intraregional relations and fear that it will become a pretext for overbearing neocolonial manipulation of the small island states. In the dramatic words of the Samoan prime minister,

> There is a polarisation of the geopolitical environment. The concept of power and domination has engulfed the world, its tendrils extending to the most isolated atoll communities. The Pacific is swimming in a sea of so-called "fit for purpose" strategies stretched from the tip of Africa, encompassing the Indian Ocean and morphing into the vast Blue Pacific Ocean continent—that is our home and place....The reality is stark—we are again seeing invasion and interest in the form of strategic manipulation.[28]

In a form of preemptive opposition, the Pacific Island countries rejected the framing of any such manipulation from the outset:

> Pacific Island countries and the U.S. have different approaches to this new phase of great power competition. The U.S. National Security Strategy portrays Pacific Island Countries as "fragile states"....[I]t states that the U.S. will work with Australia and New Zealand to "shore up" these fragile Pacific Island Countries. This narrative continues to paint the picture of a region that is willing to stand

---

[26] Tuilaepa Sailele Malielegaoi (remarks at the Lowy Institute, Sydney, August 30, 2018).

[27] Christelle Pratt, "Strengthening the U.S.–Pacific Islands Partnership" (opening remarks to the CSIS U.S.-Pacific Dialogue, Nadi, March 4, 2019), https://www.forumsec.org/opening-remarks-to-the-center-for-strategic-international-studies-us-pacific-dialogue-strengthening-the-us-pacific-islands-partnership-by-deputy-secretary-general-cristelle-pratt.

[28] Tuilaepa (remarks at the Lowy Institute).

by and allow its future to be shaped and directed by others. I would like to encourage you to move away from this narrative.[29]

Moreover, Pacific leaders emphatically refuse to be stampeded into making binary choices between China and their traditional partners, Australia and New Zealand. Many of the outspoken leaders in the region reject the "China threat" language that has accompanied the step-up and reset policies, as dramatically set out by secretary-general of the Pacific Islands Forum Dame Meg Taylor:

> I reject the terms of the dilemma which presents the Pacific with a choice between a China alternative and our traditional partners....In general, Forum members view China's increased actions in the region as a positive development, one that offers greater options for financing and development opportunities—both directly in partnership with China, and indirectly through increased competition in our region.[30]

There is a strong economic component to this perception. Between 2007 and 2017, China's trade with the Pacific Islands grew by a factor of four. China is now the Pacific Island countries' largest trade partner. Bilateral trade totals $8.2 billion, whereas Australia's annual trade with the region is only $5 billion.[31] Moreover, Pacific leaders have been quick to point out the hypocrisy of the Australian, New Zealand, and U.S. statements about the dangers of doing business with China when the countries making such statements have benefited greatly from their economic interdependence with China. Taylor's language on this is stark: "If there is one word that might resonate among all Forum members when it comes to China, that word is access. Access to markets, technology, financing, infrastructure. Access to a viable future."[32] Moreover, Australia and New Zealand had not offered or provided the Pacific Island countries with such access until they became concerned about China doing so, as Taylor highlights:

> To a large extent, Forum countries have been excluded from the sorts of technology and infrastructure that can enable us to fully engage in a globalised world. Many countries see the rise of China and its increasing interest in the region as providing an opportunity to rectify this. Indeed, we have seen large increases in both financing for development and trade with China over the past decade or so.[33]

---

[29] Pratt, "Strengthening the U.S.–Pacific Islands Partnership."

[30] Dame Meg Taylor, "The China Alternative: Changing Regional Order in the Pacific Islands" (speech at the University of South Pacific, Port Vila, February 8, 2019).

[31] Matthew Dornan and Sachini Muller, "The China Shift in Pacific Trade," DevPolicy Blog, November 15, 2018, https://devpolicy.org/china-in-the-pacific-australias-trade-challenge-20181115.

[32] Taylor, "The China Alternative."

[33] Ibid.

Yet even though there is a large amount of positivity about China across the Pacific Island region, it is not unanimous. Tonga, for example, has expressed uncertainty regarding its ability to repay concessional loans to Beijing. When Prime Minister Akilisi Pohiva voiced such concerns in August 2018, several other Pacific leaders, such as long-standing Samoan prime minister Tuilaepa, were quick to silence these concerns.[34] The Pacific Island states that are the most eager to defend Beijing are those that have signed on to the Belt and Road Initiative, including Papua New Guinea, Fiji, Samoa, and Vanuatu. There remain six states that have no diplomatic relations with China, some of which are the subject of active lobbying and counter-lobbying efforts by Beijing, Canberra, and Wellington. The Federated States of Micronesia is formally associated with the United States under the Compact of Free Association agreement. However, most of the Micronesian states have felt the gravitational pull of the Chinese economy, at times with uncomfortable effects. In 2017, for example, Palau found itself the subject of a sudden Chinese regulation against group tours to the island. The move had significant impact on the country, whose economy is dependent on tourism for almost half of its revenue and which had become dependent on China for half of its tourists by 2017.[35]

While the governments of Fiji, Vanuatu, and Samoa are strong advocates for China in diplomatic forums, there is also a divide opening up between them and their own populations over the benefits of growing Chinese influence. Public resentment of Chinese economic activity is rising among many Pacific Island populations, who perceive Chinese immigrants and small businesses as excluding local people from retail sectors. In some states, there is growing public anger that Chinese commercial success is being parlayed into corrupt political influence. In the Solomon Islands and Tonga, public unrest in 2006 erupted into direct attacks on Chinese-owned shops and enterprises, which continue to be the target of attacks in the Solomon Islands to this day. These sentiments have not gone unheeded by the political classes. Relations with China have become a significant domestic political issue in Cook Islands, Niue, Palau, Papua New Guinea, and Vanuatu. There is also growing anger in Fiji at the government's close relationship with Beijing, with a focus on incidents such as the decision to allow Chinese police to effect the

---

[34] Stephen Dziedzic, "Tonga Urges Pacific Nations to Press China to Forgive Debts as Beijing Defends Its Approach," ABC (Australia), November 19, 2018, https://www.abc.net.au/news/2018-08-16/tonga-leads-pacific-call-for-china-to-forgive-debts/10124792; and "China Must Not Write Off Pacific Island Debts, Says Samoan Leader," Agence France-Presse, August 20, 2018, available at https://www.scmp.com/news/china/diplomacy-defence/article/2160429/china-must-not-write-pacific-island-debts-says-samoa.

[35] Edward White and Nicolle Liu, "Palau Holds Out as China Squeezes Taiwan's Allies," *Financial Times*, December 30, 2017.

deportation of 77 Chinese sex workers from Fiji in 2017.[36] In addition, there is anecdotal evidence that awareness of Beijing's repressive measures against evangelical Christian churches in China is spreading in the deeply Christian societies of the South Pacific, leading to growing anti-China sentiment among populations and political elites.[37]

An even greater gap, however, has opened up between the Pacific Island countries and the United States, Australia, and New Zealand over the very framing of security priorities. While the metropolitan powers frame their security agendas in traditional terms focused on rising geopolitical rivalry with China, the Pacific Island states have adopted a nontraditional framing of security through the Pacific Island Forum's Boe Declaration and the Blue Pacific narrative. The latter seeks to upturn the traditional image of the Pacific Island states as small, marginal, and fragile. As Prime Minister Tuilaepa stated, "the Blue Pacific identity…represents our recognition that as a region, we are large, connected and strategically important. The Blue Pacific speaks to the collective potential of our shared stewardship of the Pacific Ocean."[38] While evoking the importance of the region and the countries it contains, this narrative is also motivated by anxieties about illegal and unsustainable fishing in the island states' vast exclusive economic zones:

> UNCLOS has been a game-changer of Pacific Island countries. It has literally transformed small island nations into large oceanic states with vast exclusive economic zones, increasing their territory along with sovereign rights to resources in the ocean and the untapped potential on and below the seabed… Forum leaders continue to emphasise the critical importance of a strong governance regime in the high seas. Such a regime is necessary to ensure the security and integrity of our Blue Pacific continent.[39]

But if there is one issue that galvanizes security concern across the island states, it is climate change. For atoll states such as Kiribati, Tuvalu, and Niue, climate change is not a future scenario; it is already a compelling reality. The issue of climate change has fostered arguably a greater degree of solidarity among the island states than has existed at any time in their post-independence history. It has also given them a more prominent voice on the global stage than ever before, as several regional leaders have become the most vocal advocates for drastic action. And more than any other issue, climate change has opened up a major division between the Pacific Island countries and Australia, New Zealand, and the United States. Pacific Island

---

[36] "Mass Deportation of Chinese from Fiji in Latest Offshore Crackdown by Beijing," Agence France-Presse, August 8, 2017.

[37] Author's correspondence with Graeme Smith on his fieldwork in Solomon Islands, August 15, 2019.

[38] Tuilaepa (remarks at the Lowy Institute).

[39] Pratt, "Strengthening the U.S.–Pacific Islands Partnership."

leaders question the sincerity of their traditional partners' concerns for their well-being, given that those partners seem to refuse to take the Pacific Island countries' top security concern seriously. Particularly galling have been the United States' withdrawal from the Paris Agreement and Australia's status as one of the largest producers and exporters of coal. In the words that prime minister of Fiji Josaia Voreqe Bainimarama chose for the benefit of Australian prime minister Scott Morrison during his visit to the Pacific Islands, "From where we are sitting, we cannot imagine how the interests of any single industry can be placed above the welfare of Pacific people and vulnerable people in the world over."[40]

The larger Pacific Island countries such as Papua New Guinea and Fiji have also placed transnational security challenges at the top of the list of regional security priorities enshrined in the Boe Declaration. Oceania's increasing integration into global trade, investment, and information networks has opened up social vulnerabilities that the island governments feel they will struggle to counteract. Into this space have stepped Australia and New Zealand through their capacity-building activities in Pacific states' security sectors. Over the past decade, several fusion centers have been established in regional capitals, each enabling a greater degree of coordination against prominent transnational threats. But progress on transnational threats only seems to further emphasize the gulf between the island states and their traditional metropolitan partners. The United States, Australia, and New Zealand have not succeeded in convincingly integrating climate change into the ways in which they frame their own traditional security challenges. Instead, climate change has become an awkward topic, one used by Pacific Island leaders to goad and castigate their traditional partners when they are minded to do so but otherwise left embarrassingly off the agenda.

Policy Responses

Oceania today resembles a roiling, incoherent geopolitical auction, with player after player offering the bemused locals slightly different versions of the same thing, which may or may not be what the locals actually want. Canberra's step-up and Wellington's reset policies were conceived separately, but seem to be aimed at the same targets. There are some indications that Washington is consulting with Canberra and Wellington on its own version of this approach, but there is also a sense in which U.S. policy in the Pacific

---

[40] Quoted in Stephen Dziedzic and Erin Handley, "Climate Change Is 'No Laughing Matter,' Fiji's PM Frank Bainimarama Tells Australia during Scott Morrison's Pacific Trip," ABC (Australia), January 18, 2019, https://www.abc.net.au/news/2019-01-18/climate-change-is-no-laughing-matter-fiji-pm-says/10724582.

will be determined by what the United States believes is at stake in the region. Britain has announced that it will be opening diplomatic posts in Samoa, Tonga, and Vanuatu, while France has signaled its recommitment to its Pacific presence, and Japan has signed on to a partnership with Australia and the United States to bring electricity to 70% of Papua New Guinea.[41] In contrast to these actions by the United States and its allies, China has not outlined a strategic blueprint of intent in the Pacific. Instead, it has used the language of shared interests and prosperity, the importance of multilateral commitments (in pointed contrast with the United States), and its leadership in taking practical action against climate change. China has also denounced actions that seek to interfere or compete with its growing role in the South Pacific as "protectionist" and "overbearing."[42] The Pacific Island states are under no illusion that the renewed interest from all sides stems from fears over China's growing role, and many are encouraging interest from all the rival powers.

Once again, Australia and New Zealand face the old dilemma of reconciling alliance responsibilities with diverging alliance commitments. In an era when their security imperatives diverge from those of their island neighbors, Canberra and Wellington face a real challenge of maintaining access and influence. Their success in building access to and influence in the South Pacific during the 1990s and 2000s relied on socializing Pacific Island states to their own overarching policy imperatives. During the 1990s, this imperative was trade and investment liberalization, and in the 2000s it was the transnational security agenda. But beginning with the run-up to the 2015 UN Climate Change Conference, Canberra and Wellington began to lose their ability to shape the Pacific Island states' diplomatic and security imperatives. While Australia in particular used its membership in the Pacific Islands Forum to tone down Oceania's collective voice on climate change, the island states became increasingly frustrated with being silenced in global forums and willing to caucus outside established regional organizations. As a result of the island states' climate change activism and solidarity on nontraditional security concerns, Australia and New Zealand now find themselves somewhat sidelined within formal regional settings.[43]

---

[41] Latika Bourke, "UK to Open Three New Posts in the Pacific, Citing Security Concerns," *Sydney Morning Herald*, April 20, 2018; Florence Parly, "Asia's Evolving Security Order and Its Challenges" (speech at the Shangri-La Dialogue, Singapore, June 1, 2019), https://www.defense.gouv.fr/english/salle-de-presse/discours/discours-de-florence-parly/discours-de-florence-parly-ministre-des-armees_allocution-au-shangri-la-dialogue; and "The Papua New Guinea Electrification Partnership," Prime Minister of Australia, Media Release, November 18, 2018, https://www.pm.gov.au/media/papua-new-guinea-electrification-partnership.

[42] See, for example, "China Cries Foul over Move to Block Huawei," *Australian*, September 17, 2018.

[43] See Greg Fry and Sandra Tarte, eds., *The New Pacific Diplomacy* (Canberra: ANU Press, 2015).

Meanwhile, in trying to drum up regional fears of China's growing role in honoring their alliance commitments, both countries are further damaging the sense of solidarity that exists between them and their island neighbors. Some Pacific Island leaders find the metropolitan powers' rhetoric about the China threat polarizing and patronizing, while others, such as Solomon Islands prime minister Sogavare, have actively sought relations with China as leverage enabling them to "stand up to Australia."[44]

The Pacific Island states have engaged pragmatically with the U.S., Australian, and New Zealand agenda while not buying into its geopolitical logic. They have forcefully foregrounded their own, nontraditional security agenda through the Blue Pacific narrative and the Boe Declaration as a direct pushback against the geopolitical agenda of the metropolitan powers. The Boe Declaration asserts that climate change is the region's primary concern, before acknowledging "an increasingly complex regional security environment driven by multifaceted security challenges, and a dynamic geopolitical environment leading to an increasingly crowded and complex region." It then forcefully restates the region's commitment to the Blue Pacific concept and to the sustainability of peoples and resources.[45] The document is replete with language declaring that the Pacific Island nations will not tolerate, once again, outside powers imposing their interests and agendas on the region to advance their own, rather than the regional countries', interests. Australia and New Zealand pragmatically signed and have since rhetorically supported the Boe Declaration, even though its identification of climate change as the major security concern is substantially at odds with their own priorities.

Meanwhile, China has also not had its way on everything in the South Pacific in recent years. While Beijing's rhetoric has emphasized its solidarity and the mutuality of its interests with the Pacific Island states, there are growing concerns among these countries that China's activities are deeply threatening to the Pacific's own security priorities. Despite having pledged to take action on climate change, China is still the world's largest emitter of greenhouse gases. It has the world's largest distant-water fishing fleet, which is enabled by generous government subsidies and tax exemptions and poses a major challenge to the sustainability of the Pacific's major resource—its fisheries. China's tuna-fishing fleet in the western-central Pacific has grown from 244 vessels in 2010 to 418 in 2016.[46] As noted earlier, there is also rising

---

[44] Andrew Fanasia, "Taiwan Reacts to Comments," *Solomon Star*, September 13, 2019.

[45] Pacific Islands Forum Secretariat, "Boe Declaration on Regional Security," September 5, 2018, https://www.forumsec.org/boe-declaration-on-regional-security.

[46] Ethan Meick, Michelle Ker, and Han May Chan, "China's Engagement in the Pacific Islands: Implications for the United States," U.S.-China Economic and Security Review Commission, Staff Research Report, June 14, 2018, https://www.uscc.gov/sites/default/files/Research/China-Pacific%20 Islands%20Staff%20Report.pdf.

awareness in the Pacific Islands of the Chinese government's repressive actions against Christians in China and growing resentment of the dominance of Chinese businesses. China's overbearing and aggressive diplomacy in the region has also caused major concerns. On two occasions in 2018, at the Pacific Islands Forum in September and during the APEC Leaders' Summit in Port Moresby in November, Chinese diplomats caused offence by aggressively demanding that their views be heard.[47] Whether these incidents were the result of an increasingly assertive diplomatic culture or an overestimation of China's prestige in the South Pacific, Beijing does not seem to realize that such actions can rapidly undermine years of effort and billions of dollars of investment in trying to build soft power.

There are some very early signs that China may become the cause of discord in the years ahead in what is now a very united region. Some Pacific Island states have expressed concerns about China's actions and activities. In February 2019 the leaders of five Micronesian states called on the Pacific Islands Forum to treat Taiwan and China as equals in its meetings.[48] Nauru publicly called on China to apologize for its behavior at the summit in September 2018, while Tonga called for the region to urge China to forgive Pacific Island states' debts.[49] Conversely, other Pacific Island nations have emerged as Beijing's defenders in the Pacific. Fiji protested against Nauru's treatment of the Chinese delegation at the 2018 Pacific Islands Forum summit, and the Samoan prime minister immediately rejected his Tongan counterpart's call for debt forgiveness from China.[50] The Tongan prime minister withdrew his comments and praised China's generosity shortly afterward.[51] In a region that is producing strong and outspoken leaders, many of whom are being skillfully courted by Beijing, such divisions over China's behavior could become increasingly polarizing.

[47] See "Nauru Demands China Apologize for 'Disrespect' at Pacific Forum," Reuters, September 6, 2018, https://www.reuters.com/article/us-pacific-forum-china/nauru-demands-china-apologize-for-disrespect-at-pacific-forum-idUSKCN1LM0HM; and Josh Rogin, "Inside China's 'Tantrum Diplomacy' at APEC," Washington Post, November 20, 2018, https://www.washingtonpost.com/news/josh-rogin/wp/2018/11/20/inside-chinas-tantrum-diplomacy-at-apec.

[48] "Micronesia Calls for Equal Recognition of Taiwan and China at Pacific Islands Forum," Radio New Zealand, February 26, 2019, https://www.rnz.co.nz/international/pacific-news/383371/micronesia-calls-for-equal-recognition-of-taiwan-and-china-at-pacific-islands-forum.

[49] Dziedzic, "Tonga Urges Pacific Nations."

[50] "China Must Not Write Off Pacific Island Debts, Says Samoan Leader."

[51] Charlotte Greenfield and Jonathan Barrett, "Tonga Backs Down on Pacific Plan to Pressure China on Debt," Reuters, August 17, 2018, https://www.reuters.com/article/pacific-debt-tonga/tonga-backs-down-on-pacific-plan-to-pressure-china-on-debt-idUSL4N1V82FW.

Policy Implications

Oceania's new security dynamics have the potential to do great harm to the region, a fact that the South Pacific's traditional partners need to recognize. Several Pacific Island states have histories of fractious internal politics, which are often intensified by allegations of corruption and nepotism. There are real dangers that competing offers of money, capacity building, and infrastructure could exacerbate these internal rivalries to the detriment of both the societies of the South Pacific and the stability of the region. The new geopolitical competition could also ignite dangerous intraregional rivalries, particularly if countries begin to become polarized by supporting one side or another. Several policy implications need to be acknowledged by the South Pacific's traditional partners.

First, the United States, Australia, and New Zealand should regard the key commitments of the Boe Declaration—solidarity, political resilience, and assertion of Pacific interests—as essential elements in Oceania's ability to endure ongoing geopolitical competition in its neighborhood. They must find ways to engage proactively with the Pacific's own security agenda, providing space for the island states to define a collective set of security commitments. In the current environment, the appearance of imposing alien security priorities on the region will be supremely counterproductive. This will be a new experience for the three traditional partners, which are more accustomed to leading rather than following in the region.

Second, the United States, Australia, and New Zealand need to drop their polarizing approaches to the island states' relationships with China. They need to realize that China is in the region to stay, with all the benefits and drawbacks that entails. Resurrecting a *cordon sanitaire* in the Pacific is not feasible or even desirable. Rather, the traditional partners should be working to build the island states' capacity to engage pragmatically with China and other new partners. Concerns about debt must be taken seriously, but not as an anti-China rallying cry. Rather, helping build the capacity of island states to negotiate and manage debt is likely to be a much more effective strategy.

Third, the traditional partners should abandon efforts to compete directly with Chinese initiatives. Doing this cedes the initiative to China and is in effect an admission that its activities are so appropriate to the region that they are worthy of copying. Instead, the United States, Australia, and New Zealand should build on decades of experience in and deep contact with the societies of the Pacific Island region. Despite the alarmism, all three countries have enormous soft power in the region and are its first points of contact when it needs help. Allowing this soft power to erode while competing with Beijing would be a colossal mistake. At this time, the traditional partners must double down on building soft-power assets across Oceania. New Zealand's and Australia's temporary worker schemes are a huge success in this regard. Australia should reconsider its visa restrictions on Pacific Islanders, which are causing major damage to its image. All three traditional partners should also invest heavily in education and training in the Pacific and encourage sustainable projects. Fiji's and Vanuatu's tourism industries should be a model for other regional economies.

Conclusion

Deepening strategic competition between the United States and China is having increasingly profound impacts across the Pacific. Australia and New Zealand have each seen their relationships with both the United States and China changed. In the current geopolitical environment, neither country can return to the simpler times when it could concentrate on building a security partnership with the United States and an economic relationship with China. Particularly in Australia, there is a growing anxiety about the security implications of economic interdependence with China, and a growing awareness that a potential decoupling of China's and the United States' technology sectors could have serious repercussions. At the same time, Trump's United States poses serious challenges to Australia and New Zealand. It is hard for both governments to discern what Trump's approach to Asia is. Though there is undoubtedly confrontation with China, the place of allies and security partners in the president's thinking is unclear. While both Canberra and Wellington are continuing to build their relationships with the United States, they are seeking new partnerships in Asia as a way of hedging against the turbulence in their relations with Beijing and Washington.

Sino-U.S. rivalry has brought geopolitics to Oceania in a way not seen since 1942. For Australia and New Zealand, this has made their relationships and responsibilities in Oceania vastly more complicated. China's investments and diplomacy in the region have focused attention in the Pacific Island countries on the adequacy of Canberra's and Wellington's past engagement in Oceania. This has coincided with a growing assertiveness among Pacific Island countries in advancing an alternative security agenda prioritizing climate change and transnational security. Australia and New Zealand face the challenge of reassuring Washington that they are up to the task of managing China's presence in Oceania, while at the same time maintaining their access and influence among Pacific Island states. Meanwhile, the United States has become sufficiently alarmed about China's activities in Oceania to have stepped up its own engagement in the region.

Oceania is no longer a strategic backwater that can be "managed" with a light touch by Australia and New Zealand as part of their alliance obligations to the United States. China has compelling diplomatic, strategic, and economic interests to build its presence in Oceania, where the scale of the region will not tax its resources. Moreover, its presence is largely welcomed by Pacific Island governments. As Australia, New Zealand, and the United States respond with their own diplomatic and aid initiatives, Oceania has become awash with offers of infrastructure and capacity-building. Pacific Island governments have engaged with these initiatives without taking sides in the geopolitical competition motivating them. At the same time, they have advanced an alternative security agenda, which they have used to criticize Australia and the United States as not sufficiently committed to action on climate change.

Amid this rising rivalry and proliferation of security agendas, Australia and New Zealand risk losing the access and influence with Pacific Island governments on which their security depends. If they allow their activities to be shaped by direct and polarizing competition with China, they will find themselves increasingly at odds with Pacific Island governments' own concerns. It is imperative that Canberra and Wellington find a way to engage genuinely with these governments' security agendas. They need to moderate their competition with China and move away from rhetoric that seeks to scare Pacific Island governments about engaging with Beijing. Most crucially, they should rethink how they capitalize on their insider status within Pacific regional organizations, building on long-term society-to-society relationships to help Oceania manage an enduring phase of geopolitical competition.

EXECUTIVE SUMMARY

This chapter examines the impact of Sino-U.S. competition on Southeast Asia and assesses the individual and collective response of regional countries.

MAIN ARGUMENT

While Southeast Asia has a long history of coping with great-power rivalry, the current state of affairs is different on a number of counts. The first factor is the unpredictability and uncertainty in U.S. foreign policy associated with the Trump administration. Second, the role of China has evolved over the last two decades; the country is no longer merely a great power but one whose regional influence is more substantial than any other such power in recent history, with the exception of the U.S. Third, the stakes of great-power rivalry for Southeast Asia today are arguably higher than during the Cold War due to the risks that a major downturn in Sino-U.S. relations would pose for the prosperity that the region has enjoyed in the post–Cold War years.

POLICY IMPLICATIONS

- The U.S. needs to realize that interdependence and integration between China and Southeast Asia have grown so deep that any effort to compel a "decoupling" is not only impractical but would be detrimental for regional security and U.S. interests in the region.

- Washington's current emphasis on strategic imperatives tends to obscure the extensive U.S. economic interests that over the years have contributed considerably to the prosperity of Southeast Asia. While the U.S. security presence is imperative for stability, a wider strategic edifice is needed to frame and guide U.S. policies as part of a holistic engagement strategy.

- Although the "free and open Indo-Pacific" strategy could promote regional stability, the prevailing ambiguity surrounding it and the perception that this strategy suffers from incoherence in terms of the integration of security and economic requirements and objectives remain causes of regional consternation.

Southeast Asia and Sino-U.S. Competition: Between a Rock and a Hard Place

Joseph Chinyong Liow

The end of the Cold War ushered in an era of strategic equilibrium in East Asia that had at its core a stable Sino-U.S. relationship. This equilibrium allowed the region to flourish economically (notwithstanding the Asian financial crisis of the late 1990s). Growing prosperity and deepening interdependence worked to keep the centrifugal pressures of strategic and political competition at bay. But there are concerns that this equilibrium is in danger of unravelling as tensions in Sino-U.S. relations escalate across a range of issues from trade and technology to Taiwan and territorial claims.

As a collection of small and medium-sized countries, Southeast Asia is inevitably caught up in the turbulence of these geostrategic crosswinds. Not unexpectedly, this current state of affairs has hastened discussion on how the region should position itself amid growing rivalry between Washington and Beijing. For years, regional leaders have stressed the point that Southeast Asian states should not be placed in a position of having to choose sides between the two great powers. Yet this very backdrop of uncertainty has prompted growing concern that the rivalry portends a precarious future for Southeast Asian states.

What follows is an analysis of the geostrategic considerations affecting Southeast Asia, including how these considerations are manifest in and shape domestic politics, and an exploration of how Southeast Asia has, and should, position itself in the wake of escalating Sino-U.S. rivalry. The chapter begins by assessing U.S. and Chinese strategic aims and objectives

Joseph Chinyong Liow is the Tan Kah Kee Chair in Comparative and International Politics and the Dean of the College of Humanities, Arts, and Social Sciences at Nanyang Technological University in Singapore. He can be reached at <iscyliow@ntu.edu.sg>.

in Southeast Asia. Focusing on several specific regional countries, the following section examines how the rhetoric and realities of Southeast Asian approaches to both the United States and China are shaped by domestic political and economic imperatives. A penultimate section then discusses the region's responses to U.S. and Chinese policies. The chapter concludes by considering how and where the region has needed to adjust to the tensions that have emerged from Sino-U.S. rivalry. By way of this framework, the chapter argues that the shifts in policy thinking and implementation in both Beijing and Washington in recent years, and the bilateral competition this has generated, portend a real and new challenge for Southeast Asia. At the same time, the strategic complexity has been further heightened by domestic political and economic priorities and exigencies confronting several regional states. These two phenomena have combined to cast greater uncertainty on the region's strategic landscape.

U.S. and Chinese Strategic Aims in Southeast Asia

Southeast Asia is fast becoming an arena for acute Sino-U.S. strategic competition. Here, more so than anywhere else, tensions and strategic differences are playing out over Chinese and American views as to what the Asia-Pacific (or the Indo-Pacific, as it is reconceived in the most recent U.S. National Security Strategy) should look like, as well as the norms that should govern affairs in the region.[1] At issue is a fundamental divergence between core U.S. and Chinese strategic interests that threatens to undermine the regional security architecture. This structural disconnect between the United States and China has been catalyzed by the role of personalities and domestic politics in both countries. On the one hand, the populist Trump and some in his administration have expressed intent to walk away from the international order that their postwar predecessors labored so hard to build and to ratchet up punitive pressure on China, the United States' only global strategic competitor, to effect a change of behavior. On the other hand, under Xi Jinping the Chinese state has jettisoned its previous low-key approach to international affairs, engaged in nationalist posturing, and articulated grand ambitions to transform China into a technological superpower in the process of the country's "grand national rejuvenation."

---

[1] White House, *National Security Strategy of the United States of America* (Washington, D.C., December 2017).

U.S. Aims in Southeast Asia

U.S. efforts to articulate a strategic edifice to guide policy toward Southeast Asia found expression in the "free and open Indo-Pacific" concept, which was introduced by President Donald Trump at the APEC CEO Summit in Hanoi in 2017.[2] This concept was subsequently developed in the National Security Strategy and National Defense Strategy.[3] Encapsulated in the U.S. Indo-Pacific strategy is the U.S. objective that Southeast Asia should be a region where states are free to assert their sovereignty and pursue their national interests without being subject to strategic or economic pressures from external powers. Concomitantly, in the eyes of the Trump administration, U.S. engagement policy should be directed at assisting Southeast Asian states with achieving these ends.

The Trump administration has been emphatic in its efforts to press this agenda. This is evident from the number of State Department and especially Defense Department delegations that have been dispatched to East and Southeast Asia, with the objective of explaining the free and open Indo-Pacific concept to regional friends and allies. How does this strategy fare in terms of the United States' security, economic, and ideational aims?

Security. There is a strong element of continuity in U.S. defense engagement with Southeast Asia, which is largely attributable to the fact that the United States already has a long established security presence in the region. Despite President Donald Trump's desire to distinguish his administration's policies from those of his predecessors, the fact is that the long-standing tradition of defense cooperation with key Southeast Asian partners and allies has for the most part remained unchanged. Simply put, the military support that the United States is currently committing to the region under the auspices of the free and open Indo-Pacific strategy bears considerable similarity to what was undertaken during the "rebalance" years of the Obama administration.

That said, there has been an uptick in commitment and activity in certain strategic areas. For instance, the United States has ramped up its freedom of navigation operations in the South China Sea: more operations were conducted in the first two years of the Trump administration than in the entire two terms of the Obama administration.[4] The United States has invited

---

[2] "Remarks by President Trump on His Trip to Asia," White House, Office of the Press Secretary, November 15, 2017, https://www.whitehouse.gov/briefings-statements/remarks-president-trump-trip-asia.

[3] White House, *National Security Strategy of the United States of America*; and U.S. Department of Defense, "Summary of the 2018 National Defense Strategy of the United States of America: Sharpening the American Military's Competitive Edge," January 2018.

[4] This view was expressed to the author on several occasions by different U.S. Defense Department officials who made visits to the region.

its security partners to conduct joint freedom of navigation operations with the U.S. Navy. Moreover, in May 2019 the United States initiated joint drills with security partners in the South China Sea, and in September it conducted drills with the navies of all member states of the Association of Southeast Asian Nations (ASEAN).

Arguably the most significant development in U.S. security engagement in Southeast Asia, however, is the assurance that the United States provided to the Philippines that the South China Sea would be covered by the mutual defense treaty between the two countries. Washington had hitherto been unwilling to stake a clear position on the issue, but Secretary of State Mike Pompeo clarified during his visit to the Philippines in February 2019 that because "the South China Sea is part of the Pacific, any armed attack on Philippine forces, aircraft or public vessels in the South China Sea would trigger mutual defense obligations under Article 4 of our Mutual Defense Treaty."[5] It remains to be seen, though, whether the United States is indeed prepared to see through this public commitment should China seek to test its resolve.

Economic. Although the U.S. Indo-Pacific strategy has been articulated by Trump administration officials to be an all-of-government strategy, its defense- and security-related dimensions have been most visible. This is evident from the dearth of nonmilitary aspects to the application of U.S. policy in Southeast Asia, as well as from the fact that the clearest articulations of this strategy take the form of documents on security posture, as mentioned previously. Whereas current defense and security policies may share much in common with preceding administrations, the departure is stark in the areas of trade and economic policy.

It is important to bear in mind that the United States is already heavily invested economically in Southeast Asia and has been so for a long time. Collectively, the U.S. private sector remains the largest foreign investor in the region, and this shows no sign of abating.[6] Indeed, with the ongoing trade war and tariffs that have been imposed on China, U.S. multinational firms have gradually been relocating manufacturing and assembly facilities to Southeast Asia as part of their reconfiguration of supply chains. But this investment has often gone unappreciated for a variety of reasons.

First, given that the majority of U.S. economic investments in Southeast Asia derive from the private sector, they tend to be disparate, depending on industries and the investment strategies of individual firms, and not

---

[5] Patricia Lourdes Viray, "U.S. Assures Philippines: Any Armed Attack in South China Sea Will Trigger MDT," *Philippine Star*, March 1, 2019.

[6] See Malcolm Cook, "Southeast Asia's Growing U.S. Market," ISEAS–Yusof Ishak Institute, ISEAS Commentary, September 4, 2019.

given to easy collation for the purposes of signifying strategic intent. This stands in stark contrast to recent Chinese investments, which have been primarily, though not exclusively, driven by state-owned enterprises (SOEs) and policy banks.

The second reason is the lack of visibility for U.S. commercial interests in the region. Simply put, since the end of the Cold War, the United States has stepped back from publicizing its efforts in the region, and this has diminished the visibility of the otherwise deep and extensive U.S. presence and commitment.

Third, U.S. government-led economic engagement under the Trump administration has suffered from poor messaging as a consequence of policy choices. The withdrawal from the Trans-Pacific Partnership (TPP) brought U.S. leadership of a major effort to redesign the regional trade and economics architecture to a grinding halt. Since then, the United States has offered no replacement architecture. Instead, the transactional approach of the Trump administration and the president's narrow obsession with trade deficits has dented regional confidence in the United States as a constructive economic partner committed to the growth and prosperity of the region. The administration's open accusations that regional partners like Malaysia, Vietnam, and Singapore are attempting to manipulate their currencies in order to gain a competitive edge have only further harmed the United States' reputation.

To rectify the perception that the United States is losing ground to China in regional economic engagement, the Trump administration introduced the Better Utilization of Investment Leading to Development (BUILD) Act in 2018. The BUILD Act aims to coordinate private-sector investment in developing countries in order to facilitate the transition from nonmarket to market economies while aligning these efforts with U.S. security and foreign policy objectives. While Washington has not stated so explicitly, the BUILD Act was likely designed in response to China's Belt and Road Initiative (BRI). It remains to be seen whether the administration can appropriate the required resources from Congress with minimum obstruction, how the BUILD Act will be implemented, and what its priorities will be. Nevertheless, the prospect of greater U.S. interest and investment in infrastructure development in Southeast Asia, which has been articulated as a priority in support of ASEAN's aspirations for greater connectivity between its members, or more targeted investments in specific areas such as the Lower Mekong region, would doubtless be welcomed.

Ideational. Though less pronounced compared to previous U.S. administrations, ideational factors are not altogether absent in current U.S. policy toward Southeast Asia. Under the Asia Reassurance Initiative

Act (ARIA), for instance, which has been articulated as a component of the Indo-Pacific strategy, the U.S. Congress has imposed restrictions on the nature and extent of military aid that can be provided to Myanmar, the Philippines, and Cambodia on the grounds of human rights concerns and violations.

Nevertheless, the most striking elements in the ideational content of current U.S. policy relate to the Indo-Pacific strategy itself. The stated objective of the Indo-Pacific concept, as noted earlier, is to emphasize the United States' interests in the region as a Pacific nation and to reinforce them through the distribution of resources to this "priority theater."[7] But there are several other aspects that speak to broader Trump administration foreign policy principles. By calling on regional states to play their part in a collective effort to build a "shared security order," the Trump administration is continuing to emphasize burden sharing.[8] Likewise, without drawing a direct connection, the emphasis on long-term threats to the rules-based international order suggests an implicit concern for the growing assertiveness of China. In fact, a senior official from the U.S. Department of Defense put simply and unequivocally that the Indo-Pacific strategy is "at the end of the day, driven by the logic of containment."[9] Therein lies the reality of U.S. objectives in Southeast Asia today: the region is seen as an arena, and regional states as partners, in a concerted effort not only to forestall China's rise but to actively curb it through strategic, economic, and diplomatic means. Much in the same vein, a former administration official's depiction of the challenge from China as coming from a country that is "not Caucasian" and has a "different civilization and different ideology" suggests that certain segments within the U.S. establishment understand the ongoing great-power competition in racial and cultural terms.[10] Needless to say, such an approach to policymaking is not one that is shared or that enjoys strong support in a region whose populations are "non-Caucasian."

Chinese Aims in Southeast Asia

Foreign and security policy thinking in China is presently at a crossroads. Despite continual protestations by many Chinese decision-makers that the country is still developing, there is a palpable sense that many Chinese believe

[7] See "Acting Secretary Shanahan's Remarks at the IISS Shangri-La Dialogue 2019," U.S. Department of Defense, Transcript, June 1, 2019, https://www.defense.gov/Newsroom/Transcripts/Transcript/Article/1871584/acting-secretary-shanahans-remarks-at-the-iiss-shangri-la-dialogue-2019.

[8] Ibid.

[9] Interview with a U.S. Department of Defense official in Singapore, April 8, 2019.

[10] See remarks by the director of policy planning at the U.S. Department of State, Kiron Skinner, at a public conference. Kiron Skinner (remarks at the Future Security Forum, Washington, D.C., April 29, 2019), 9 min., 35 sec., available at https://www.youtube.com/watch?v=JVl_eEmPoK4.

the time has come for China to assume its "rightful" place at the pinnacle of global affairs. This belief in manifest destiny is evident from statements by Chinese scholars and was further reinforced by Xi Jinping's speech at the 19th Party Congress of the Chinese Communist Party when he declared:

> National rejuvenation has been the greatest dream of the Chinese people since modern times began. At its founding, the Communist Party of China made realizing Communism its highest ideal and its ultimate goal, and shouldered the historic mission of national rejuvenation. In pursuing this goal, the Party has united the Chinese people and led them through arduous struggles to epic accomplishments.[11]

The consequence of this nationalist mood is quite simply a more assertive China in regional and global affairs, even as its interests expand internationally. At the same time, although the U.S.-led international order has clearly facilitated China's rise as an economic power, Beijing now views this same order as an impediment to its aspirations.

In contrast to the United States' attempts to craft a viable strategy to guide policy in Asia (including Southeast Asia), there is little evidence that China is constructing such an edifice to govern its regional engagement. This is not to say that China is devoid of grand narratives. BRI is certainly cast as one both by Chinese leaders and in media reports, although it is questionable how strategic the initiative is, given that it essentially comprises a range of mostly bilateral projects. Rather, the point is that China does not appear to be making any attempt to clearly articulate its military, economic, and ideational interests in the region and to knit together the efforts across the Chinese state to pursue these interests.

Nonetheless, there should be little doubt that China views Southeast Asia as its immediate backyard where it can and should rightfully be exercising influence. Even as Beijing seeks to create a more amenable regional environment by enhancing its engagement with Southeast Asian states both bilaterally and multilaterally (with ASEAN), its objective is to minimize the United States' role and influence in the region. China has demonstrated its readiness to pursue this goal through seemingly contradictory measures that involve economic inducements (which regional states welcome, though with some measure of discomfort about the inherent risks of dependence) and the flexing of military muscle (which holds little appeal). On occasion, Beijing

---

[11] Xi Jinping, "Secure a Decisive Victory in Building a Moderately Prosperous Society in All Respects and Strive for the Great Success of Socialism with Chinese Characteristics for a New Era" (speech delivered at the 19th National Congress of the Communist Party of China, Beijing, October 18, 2017).

has also sought to directly influence the policies of certain Southeast Asian states, with Cambodia frequently cited as the most obvious example.[12]

Two observations can be made about the fundamental premises on which China's policy toward the region is predicated. First, the country's outlook on regional security is shifting from one centered on diplomacy and outreach to one intent on shaping its strategic environment as a great power. While this orientation does not preclude diplomacy, China's focus is increasingly on asserting a presence based on its status as a great power and securing regional acceptance of this "reality." Second, as mentioned above, China has always considered Southeast Asia its strategic backyard. Indeed in geopolitical terms, it is the only bordering region where Chinese expansion does not immediately run up against a major power.

Security. China's military ventures into Southeast Asia have thus far been an exercise in contradiction. On the one hand, there has been an increase in military-to-military exchanges and cooperation of both a bilateral and multilateral nature, and China is increasingly also supplying arms to several regional militaries.[13] Chinese naval ships visited the Philippines in April 2017, the first such visit since 2010, while the Philippine Coast Guard has sent officers to train in China. Beijing also provided a $500 million soft loan to Manila for the purchase of military equipment.[14] Malaysia has purchased four littoral ships from China, the first naval purchase of its kind between the two countries.[15] The deal was signed during the administration of Najib Razak and was honored by the Mahathir administration. This is notable given the misperception immediately after Mahathir Mohamad unseated Najib that the former was prepared to take a tougher line against China. In addition, Thailand, after being shunned by the United States following its military coup, procured main battle tanks from China.

Defense cooperation between China and Southeast Asian countries has also increased. Significantly, the navies of China and ASEAN countries (which were either participants or observers) held their first maritime

---

[12] For example, when ASEAN failed to agree on a joint communiqué following its ministerial meeting in July 2012, numerous diplomats from member states privately explained that this was because of the Cambodian chair's reluctance to accept the inclusion of language that referred to the South China Sea disputes, claiming that those were bilateral issues. It is widely believed that Cambodia acted at the behest of China. In my interviews with former U.S. officials who were serving at that time, they shared that they were aware that Chinese officials were in fact present in the building during the ASEAN meeting and were consulted by Cambodian officials. Author's interviews, Washington, D.C., July 2014–June 2016.

[13] In response to the Marawi siege in the Philippines in 2017, China supplied weapons to the Philippines to bolster its counterterrorism capabilities.

[14] Manuel Mogato, "China Offers $14 Million Arms Package to the Philippines: Manila's Defense Minister," *Reuters*, December 20, 2016.

[15] Tom Allard and Joseph Sipalan, "Malaysia to Buy Navy Vessels from China in Blow to U.S.," *Reuters*, October 26, 2016.

exercise in October 2018.[16] This cooperation continued in 2019 when China conducted further military exercises with six ASEAN states in April.[17] Further underscoring China's growing security interest in the region, the 2019 iteration of the Shangri-La Dialogue marked only the second time that China sent its defense minister.

Controversy was stirred in January 2019, however, when three Chinese warships appeared in the port of Sihanoukville in western Cambodia, prompting suspicions that China was leaning on Cambodia for the provision of naval facilities.[18] These suspicions have been predicated on both the close relationship between the two countries and the extensive presence of Chinese investment in Cambodia. Given that the location of the purported naval base was proximate to two U.S.-funded military facilities, China's actions have attracted the attention of the U.S. defense establishment.[19]

China also has deployed military assets on the features that it has built and reinforced in the South China Sea. In so doing, it has asserted a military presence in the geographic heart of Southeast Asia. Despite the ambiguities surrounding China's claims to maritime rights as well as the scope and extent of its nine-dash line (which forms the basis of these claims), it is clear that the South China Sea is an area of priority for China. Although the South China Sea lies in the heart of Southeast Asia, the interests of regional states are incidental to China's aims in this body of water. Rather, Chinese leaders and policymakers see the South China Sea as an important strategic domain in its own backyard that must be defended against the activities of the U.S. Navy. On the occasion of an inspection of the Southern Theater Command whose operations cover the South China Sea, Xi called on the command to "bear the heavy military responsibility…and concentrate preparations for fighting a war."[20] This is at the center of the prevailing difference of opinion between Beijing and Washington over the interpretation of the United Nations Convention on the Law of the Sea (UNCLOS) as it relates to military

---

[16] Lim Min Zhang, "China, ASEAN Kick Off Inaugural Maritime Field Training Exercise in Zhanjiang, Guangdong," *Straits Times*, October 22, 2018.

[17] Minnie Chan, "China Begins Joint Naval Drills with Six Southeast Asian Nations," *South China Morning Post*, April 26, 2019.

[18] Jeremy Page, Gordon Lubold, and Rob Taylor, "Deal for Naval Outpost in Cambodia Furthers China's Quest for Military Network," *Wall Street Journal*, July 22, 2019. These allegations, however, have been denied by Cambodia. See "'Nothing to Hide': Cambodia Gives Glimpse of Base at Centre of China Rumours," *Straits Times*, July 26, 2019.

[19] Philip Heijmans, "The U.S. Fears This Huge Southeast Asian Resort May Become a Chinese Naval Base," Bloomberg, July 19, 2019, https://www.bloomberg.com/news/features/2019-07-18/u-s-fears-cambodia-resort-may-become-china-naval-base.

[20] Kristin Huang, "'Prepare for War,' Xi Jinping Tells Military Region That Monitors South China Sea, Taiwan," *South China Morning Post*, October 26, 2018.

activity within China's exclusive economic zone (EEZ).[21] In addition, the South China Sea is also a strategic priority for China because of the access to natural resources that control of the waters and features would afford. These resources are critical to the growth of the Chinese economy.

In pursuit of these interests, China has moved to occupy features in the South China Sea. This began with the occupation of features in the Paracel Islands in the early 1970s following clashes with South Vietnamese naval forces and escalated in the late 1980s when China occupied vacant features in the Spratly Islands (also after military encounters with the Vietnamese navy). China's occupation of Mischief Reef in 1995, however, is what precipitated reactions from regional countries and the search for diplomatic solutions to the competing claims. Since then, and notwithstanding the signing of the 2012 Declaration of Conduct on the Conduct of Parties in the South China Sea and its attendant "guidelines" document, China has continued to expand and fortify the features it occupies (as have Vietnam and the Philippines, but not to the same scale) on grounds that it is only doing what other claimant states had already done. These actions have taken place even as China and ASEAN are engaged in dialogue on this issue, leading some critics to argue that China is only buying time through dialogue and ASEAN is structurally unable to impose a moratorium on activity in the South China Sea.[22] Needless to say, the situation has been rendered more tense by the heightened presence of naval, coast guard, and merchant vessels of claimant and non-claimant states. Viewed in tandem with the increased frequency of U.S. freedom of navigation operations, the increasingly aggressive behavior of Chinese vessels has unnerved regional states and hastened efforts to complete a code of conduct.

Economic. Whereas defense initiatives are the most visible expression of the United States' presence in Southeast Asia, in the case of China trade and economic initiatives are undoubtedly the most visible sign. While much has been made—especially in Chinese sources—about the altruistic intentions behind BRI, at the heart of the grand vision for this initiative lies the matter of Chinese global ambitions and leadership. Chinese officials are quick to note that China is still a "developing country," citing the fact that its per capita income remains below $7,000. BRI is part of China's "grand national rejuvenation" and ambition to become a "medium developed country" by

---

[21] Simply put, China's interpretation of UNCLOS differs from the U.S. interpretation in that it does not accept the view that military activities should be recognized internationally as lawful uses of the sea and hence that the right to conduct such activities should be accorded to all states in the EEZs of other states.

[22] See, for example, David Martin Jones and M.L.R. Smith, "Can ASEAN Ever Solve the South China Seas Dispute through Multilateral Dialogue?" *Telegraph*, November 24, 2015.

2035 and "rich and strong socialist country" by 2050.[23] The salient point for present purposes is that many (though not all) of the projects that constitute this initiative are fundamentally strategic in nature, even if BRI as a whole appears piecemeal in implementation. BRI enhances China's already growing influence in regional trade and economics, and through these channels it will advance the country's broader strategic objectives in Southeast Asia. Indeed, if this is not already the case, China through BRI will become even more consequential to regional countries whose domestic political and economic agendas are, as this chapter will discuss in greater detail later, predicated on the provision of economic opportunity through infrastructure development.

Ideational. Ideational aims do not figure very prominently in China's relations with Southeast Asia. Shorn of the kind of pressure for normative change commonly associated with U.S. foreign policy, China has made much of its advocacy of noninterference in the internal affairs of other states. Nonetheless, as a later section will demonstrate, the reality on the ground in Southeast Asia is more complicated. Specifically, some have raised concerns that China's well-funded public diplomacy campaigns conducted through a range of vehicles, including cultural associations, Confucius Institutes, and various visitor and exchange programs, have sought to influence and shape regional thinking and discussions on China.[24]

Domestic Factors and Elite Interests in Southeast Asia

A common but somewhat mistaken description of the roles of the U.S. and China in Southeast Asia is captured in the trope "U.S. for security, China for prosperity." No doubt, the last two decades have seen regional states adopt a strategic outlook that embraces the United States as security guarantor (of various sorts and measures). Meanwhile, China has during this period emerged as a partner of growing importance in regional trade and economic development. However, as this chapter established earlier, the United States has been—and remains—an equally consequential economic partner by way of being the largest source of foreign investment in the region.[25]

These presumed roles, and the perceptions underpinning them, derive in large part from historical precedents. There is no question that since the

---

[23] This point has been made by numerous Chinese officials and experts in both public and private discussions.

[24] Russell Hsiao, "A Preliminary Survey of CCP Influence Operations in Singapore," Jamestown Foundation, China Brief, July 16, 2019. The Chinese embassy in Singapore immediately rebutted the report. See "Chinese Embassy Rebuts Report on Influence Operations in S'pore," *Straits Times*, July 20, 2019.

[25] Cook, "Southeast Asia's Growing U.S. Market."

Pacific campaign during World War II, the United States has assumed a paramount security position in Asia. In Southeast Asia, it was the role that the United States played during the Vietnam War that led non-Communist states to view—and rely on—Washington as a security bulwark. The United States' pivotal role in underwriting regional security was further amplified in the anxiety felt across the region on the occasion of the withdrawal of U.S. forces from bases in the Philippines at the end of the Cold War, and later in the U.S. support for counterterrorism efforts in the wake of the security challenge posed by regional terrorist groups such as Jemaah Islamiyah. In fact, paradoxically, this paramount security role is arguably the reason that the considerable investments that the United States has made in economic development and prosperity in Southeast Asia have tended to be downplayed, if not altogether ignored, by some commentators and analysts.

While regional countries looked to the United States as a security guarantor, China gradually assumed greater prominence in regional affairs on the back of its phenomenal economic growth beginning in the early 1990s. When the opportunity to advance its economic interests at the expense of regional economies presented itself after the Asian financial crisis in the late 1990s, China's restraint in not devaluing its currency was celebrated as not only a gesture of comity but an expression of regional leadership. This ushered in a halcyon decade in Sino-ASEAN relations during which regional economies grew on the back of China's manufacturing boom while the United States was distracted with its war on terrorism. Indeed, despite the fact that the United States remains the largest source of foreign investment in Southeast Asia, and Japan is the largest investor in realized infrastructure projects (as distinct from the promised funding of BRI), China's economic growth and the opportunities its huge market afforded Southeast Asia have ensured that China is a major, and in the case of some Southeast Asian states the preferred, economic partner.

The current turn in Sino-U.S. relations, however, is compelling the region to rethink and reconfigure its relations with both great powers. Amid the increasingly acrimonious Sino-U.S. competition and persistent talk of "decoupling," maintaining a balance is proving challenging.[26] The political climate in most Southeast Asian states today, where domestic priorities render long-term strategic thinking more difficult, further complicates matters. Even in Singapore, long celebrated as possessing some of the sharpest strategic minds in its foreign policy establishment, and where foreign policy has

---

[26] Decoupling here refers to the creation of entirely separate supply chains, one centered on U.S. industry and markets, and the other on Chinese industry and markets. Needless to say, if it materializes, such decoupling would be a fundamental shift away from the interdependence that has underpinned the global economy in the age of globalization.

hitherto been for the most part insulated from domestic political posturing, three senior foreign policy office holders ended up relinquishing their seats after a general election where opposition forces made significant headway.[27] Hence, against the backdrop of shifting geostrategic currents briefly sketched above, the recalibration of foreign policy across Southeast Asia is intertwined with domestic political trends. Specifically, regime interests, national interests, and economic opportunities and costs have influenced the shape and manner in which regional states have positioned themselves amid the growing strategic rivalry between the United States and China.

The following discussion analyzes the domestic factors and elite interests influencing relations with the United States and China in five key Southeast Asian countries: Indonesia, Vietnam, Thailand, the Philippines, and Malaysia.

Indonesia

Crucial to any discussion of regional autonomy for Southeast Asia is the role of Indonesia—the largest state in the region and one which continues to harbor aspirations to be recognized as a regional power. These aspirations have found expression in an Indo-Pacific strategic outlook that has informed the thinking of the foreign policy elite in the governments of the two most recent presidents, Susilo Bambang Yudhoyono and Joko Widodo (known as Jokowi).

A new assertiveness defines Indonesia's maritime behavior and ambitions in the 21st century. Jakarta's tough stance against foreign fishing boats in Indonesian waters and opposition to China's nine-dash line and claims to historical fishing rights are the result of Indonesia's strategy of establishing control over its maritime space. Similar assertiveness is seen in Indonesia's South China Sea strategy as the country embarks on strengthening its military presence in and around the Natuna archipelago. Former defense minister Purnomo Yusgiantoro highlighted the urgency to secure the territories that border the South China Sea, given regional tensions. President Jokowi's maritime focus has given a fresh push toward securing maritime outposts and areas of strategic interest. The Sino-Indonesian altercations off the Natuna archipelago in the South China Sea in March and May 2016 not only incited nationalistic sentiments in Indonesia but also compelled the Jokowi government to strengthen naval deployment in the Natuna Sea, increase the defense budget, and enhance the budgetary allocation for the Indonesian Navy.

---

[27] The three were Singaporean foreign minister George Yeo, the second minister for foreign affairs Raymond Lim, and the senior minister of state for foreign affairs Zainul Abidin Rasheed. Yeo and Zainul Abidin lost their seats. While Raymond Lim did not, he stepped down soon after the election.

In 2014, Jokowi articulated a major strategic concept designed to enhance Indonesia's position as a maritime power. The "global maritime fulcrum" vision was promulgated to ensure maritime security and enhance connectivity across the Indonesian archipelago.[28] The announcement coincided with China's launch of its plans for the maritime Silk Road, and Indonesia soon found itself a recipient of Chinese loans and investments for projects that include a $6 billion high-speed-rail link connecting Jakarta and Bandung, a $1.5 billion hydroelectric dam, and hydropower plants worth almost $18 billion in Kalimantan to be built by a Chinese SOE.

While integral to the building of necessary infrastructure, Chinese loans and investments have posed a dilemma for the Indonesian government. Under Jokowi, Indonesia's trade deficit with China surged to $18.4 billion in 2018, up from about $13 billion in 2014, Jokowi's first full year in office.[29] The magnitude of Chinese investment exposed Jokowi to criticism from political opponents. The apparent increase in the number of Chinese workers in steel plants, smelters, mills, construction sites, and even the tourism industry sparked protests.[30] In fact, protests have caused delays in several projects and compelled the Indonesian government to renegotiate others. In his 2019 re-election campaign, Jokowi was careful to downplay his administration's dealings with China. Meanwhile, Jokowi's opponent Prabowo Subianto and his running mate Sandiaga Uno vowed to review the high-speed-rail project as well as to negotiate a fairer trade deal with Beijing.[31]

Notwithstanding popular consternation about Chinese economic presence in Indonesia and attempts by Jokowi's opponents to politicize the issue, the China factor was surprisingly marginal in the politics surrounding the election. A survey by Saiful Mujani Research and Consulting showed that the percentage of Indonesian respondents who felt negatively about China's influence in Indonesia remained stagnant at 10%–15% over the campaign period.[32] Furthermore, the survey found that those respondents

---

[28] Vibhanshu Shekhar and Joseph Chinyong Liow, "Indonesia as a Maritime Power: Jokowi's Vision, Strategies, and Obstacles Ahead," Brookings Institution, November 7, 2014.

[29] Karlis Salna and Arys Aditya, "Indonesia May Be Next Asian Country to Spurn China in Election," Bloomberg, March 20, 2019, https://www.bloomberg.com/news/articles/2019-03-31/indonesia-may-be-next-asian-country-to-spurn-china-in-election; and "China: Export of Goods to Indonesia from 2007 to 2017 (in Billion U.S. Dollars)," Statista, https://www.statista.com/statistics/525325/china-export-of-goods-to-indonesia.

[30] In May, angry local tour guides on the popular resort island of Bali stormed the immigration office in protest of Chinese tour guides taking their jobs. Jeffrey Hutton, "A Catch-22 from China That Could Derail Indonesia's Widodo," South China Morning Post, May 12, 2018.

[31] Aloysius Unditu, "Indonesia Election: Prabowo's Adviser Says Jokowi Is Too Good to China, Country Needs New Friends," South China Morning Post, April 16, 2019.

[32] This national survey by Saiful Mujani Research and Consulting was conducted in December 2017 and has not been published.

tended to be anti-Jokowi voters already and by definition were predisposed to dislike his policies. In another popular survey conducted by the same agency in December 2017, more Indonesians believed that the benefits from Chinese investment outweighed the threat to sovereignty (32% compared with 27%). In the run-up to the election, the head of the election commission was quoted as saying that hackers from China had tried to "manipulate and modify" the electoral roll, which contains data on more than 187 million eligible voters. But these allegations were found to be unsubstantiated.[33] At the same time, however, rumors have periodically circulated regarding the purported influx of Chinese migrant labor, which has caused consternation in the general public.[34]

Vietnam

Of all Southeast Asian states, Vietnam arguably has the most complicated relationship with both the United States and China. It fought a long, bloody war against the United States from which it prevailed at the cost of an estimated 1.5 million Vietnamese lives. While not of the same magnitude, intermittent conflict with China has defined Vietnamese history for centuries. This includes several armed confrontations in the modern era in the South China Sea and Cambodia. Vietnam is acutely wary of Chinese ambitions, all the more so because it stands alone against China in their dispute over the Paracel Islands in the South China Sea.[35] In fact, some recent episodes were so acrimonious that several representatives in the National Assembly publicly castigated China for being "an invader and an enemy" when it dispatched an oil rig into Vietnam's EEZ in 2014.[36] More to the point, antipathy toward China in Vietnamese society has always been a significant factor in bilateral relations, particularly given that Chinese assertiveness in the South China Sea has often been directed at Vietnam.

At the same time, Vietnam and China have a comprehensive strategic cooperative partnership, and the Vietnamese Communist Party continues to enjoy strong ties with its Chinese counterpart. This has come to be expressed not only in party-to-party links but perhaps more importantly in the exercise of restraint during crises. For example, during the oil rig standoff in 2014, Hanoi refused to use its naval forces and also dampened public protests that threatened to boil over against Chinese actions. Moreover, Vietnam has also

---

[33] Kate Lamb, "Indonesia Election Mired in Claims of Foreign Hacking and 'Ghost' Voters," *Guardian*, March 19, 2019.

[34] Leo Suryadinata, "Anti-China Campaign in Jokowi's Indonesia," *Straits Times*, January 10, 2017.

[35] By contrast, the dispute over the Spratly Islands also involves the Philippines, Malaysia, and Brunei.

[36] Alexander Vuving, "A Tipping Point in the U.S.-China-Vietnam Triangle," *Diplomat*, July 6, 2015.

benefited greatly from an upsurge of Chinese investment in the country, as China, by virtue of being one of Vietnam's largest foreign investors, seeks to leverage the Comprehensive and Progressive Agreement for Trans-Pacific Partnership (CPTPP) by taking advantage of Vietnam's status as a signatory to the agreement.[37] Vietnam has also embraced BRI, although project delays and cost overruns have soured the mood of economic cooperation with China in the Vietnamese government, SOEs, and private sector.

In some respects, Vietnamese policy toward the United States and China has been colored in recent years by domestic political competition between reformers and conservatives. An upturn in relations with the United States during the Obama administration was a consequence of the rise of a reformist faction within the Communist Party of Vietnam, led by Nguyen Tan Dung, then prime minister and outspoken critic of China. This faction was wary of China and advocated a strategic adjustment to new developments in the regional security architecture—namely, China's deployment of an oil rig in Vietnam's EEZ and the Obama administration's rebalance policy. The sidelining of Dung, whose allies were caught up in corruption scandals involving several SOEs, and the centralizing of power in Nguyen Phu Trong, the president of Vietnam and secretary-general of the Communist Party, have been seen not only as a resurgence of conservatives in the establishment but also as heralding a turn in bilateral relations with China, given Nguyen's close relationship with its political leadership. The domestic attitude in Vietnam toward China is likely to remain a complex dynamic for years to come, where strong party-to-party relations are juxtaposed against wider popular concerns about Chinese encroachment on Vietnamese sovereignty in the South China Sea.

Thailand

In Thailand, a military coup in 2014 deposed the popularly elected government of Yingluck Shinawatra, the sister of controversial former prime minister Thaksin Shinawatra (himself removed through a coup in 2006), prompting an immediate shift in relations with both the United States and China. Relations between Thailand and the United States grew frosty, despite a string of visits by Thai diplomats and politicians to Washington in 2014 and 2015 to explain the coup and reinforce the importance of the relationship. These efforts proved futile, and the United States imposed restrictions on arms sales and military education and training, thus straining its oldest diplomatic relationship in Asia.

---

[37] Lam Thanh Ha, "Chinese FDI in Vietnam: Trends, Status, and Challenges," ISEAS–Yusof Ishak Institute, ISEAS Perspective, no. 34, April 24, 2019, 2.

However, with a new administration in power in Washington—one that has paid little attention to human rights issues—bilateral relations were set back on track as the United States restored strategic dialogue with Thailand and resumed arms sales. In addition, U.S. officials curbed their criticism of the military junta and found ways to keep the relationship on course. Given the polarized nature of Thai society, these overtures to the military junta alienated opposition groups to some extent without necessarily boosting the domestic credibility or popularity of the junta.[38]

Having been kept at a remove by the Obama administration in the immediate aftermath of the coup, the Thai military junta turned its attention to China, which made clear it would not allow the domestic political crisis to affect its relations with Thailand. Since 2014, China has become the second-largest foreign investor in Thailand behind only Japan. To illustrate the magnitude of this development, in 2012 China was not even among the top-ten foreign investors in the country. Bilateral defense cooperation was enhanced when Thailand purchased 34 armored personnel carriers and 28 VT-4 battle tanks from China and signed a deal to buy 3 Chinese-made S26T submarines.[39] The value of FDI applications from China approved by the military junta for the Eastern Economic Corridor and beyond jumped almost 1,500% in January through March 2018 from the previous year.[40]

Opposition leaders who participated in the election in March 2019 have raised concerns about growing Chinese investment in Thailand. These concerns were captured in the following statement by Thanathorn Juangroongruangkit, the popular billionaire leader of the opposition Future Forward Party: "When can China best increase its influence? It's here and now in Thailand. They're [the junta] turning to China, saying we don't have to be a democracy, we don't have to respect human rights, we don't have to uphold the rights of freedom of speech in order to be prosperous—we can be like China."[41] Expressing similar views, the leader of the Bhumjaithai Party, Anutin Charnvirakul, opined in August 2018 that one of his biggest priorities was to push for the delay of the high-speed-rail projects under BRI that would link the airport in Bangkok to an airport near Pattaya and another in China in order to deny China a foothold in Thailand.

[38] Benjamin Zawacki, *Thailand: Shifting Ground between the U.S. and a Rising China* (London: Zed Books, 2017).

[39] Olli Suorsa and Koh Swee Lean Collin, "Thailand Takes Advantage of China's Arms Market," *National Interest*, October 4, 2018.

[40] Suttinee Yuvejwattana and Anchalee Worrachate, "Thai Junta Eyes Chinese Investment for $51 Billion Spending Plan," Bloomberg, July 12, 2018.

[41] Natnicha Chuwiruch, "Thai Politicians Criticize China as Election Comes into Focus," Bloomberg, August 31, 2018.

The Philippines

At first glance, the recalibration of Philippine foreign policy is arguably the most striking shift in Southeast Asia in terms of relations with the United States and China. A U.S. treaty ally, the Philippines adopted an antagonistic stance against China during the Benigno Aquino III administration. Most notably, it brought the territorial dispute over the Spratly Islands before the Permanent Court of Arbitration, which eventually ruled in its favor in July 2016. The election of the populist Rodrigo Duterte, however, has resulted in a discernible shift in Philippine policy toward both the United States and China.

Soon after his election, President Duterte moved to distance Philippine foreign policy from the United States, launching frequently into tirades against Washington for its presumably overbearing approach and threatening to withdraw the Philippines from the security alliance (threats he has yet to carry out). Meanwhile, the Philippines under Duterte pivoted toward China. He made a visit to China early in his term and reportedly obtained a commitment for $24 billion in investments from Chinese interests, although it is unclear how much has actually materialized since then. Major Chinese projects that have been announced include a railway from Manila to Legazpi, a port-expansion project in Manila, a landfill project in Cebu, the Kaliwa and Cagayan dams, and an expansion of the port in Davao Harbor.[42] In 2017, China became the top trading partner of the Philippines (with trade volume exceeding $50 billion) and one of its largest investors.[43] Chinese support for developing infrastructure in the Philippines dovetailed strategically with the Duterte administration's domestic priorities, captured in its "build, build, build" initiative.

Once the most vocal Southeast Asian critic of Chinese adventurism in the South China Sea, the Philippines is now presided over by a president who refuses to draw attention to the countries' maritime dispute, to the extent of even welcoming Chinese fishing activities in the Philippine EEZ and downplaying the sinking of a fishing boat by a Chinese merchant vessel in June 2019. Rather than adopt a confrontational posture, Duterte has preferred to stress cooperation with China through the establishment of a de-escalation mechanism: the Bilateral Consultation Mechanism (BCM) on the South China Sea.[44] Another intriguing prospect is the idea of joint exploration of the disputed areas for oil and gas, without prejudice to their

---

[42] Raymund F. Antonio, "Chinese Investors Interested in Partnership with R-11 Builders," *Manila Bulletin*, February 28, 2017.

[43] "Philippine-China Ties as Warm as Manila Weather—Li," *Philippine Star*, November 15, 2017.

[44] Consultations between the two countries under the rubric of the BCM have not been reported publicly, although at least two meetings have been held. While the BCM is a positive step, whether the mechanism can outlive the Duterte administration is an open question.

respective claims. This echoes a 2004 attempt by the Philippine National Oil Company to conduct joint operations with the China National Offshore Oil Corporation, which was eventually scuttled in the wake of popular opposition. Nevertheless, a major obstacle still exists in the form of the Philippine Supreme Court, which has legislated that any joint exploration within the Philippine EEZ is unconstitutional. It is worth nothing that Gloria Arroyo was accused of "treason" for proposing cooperative ventures that were much more restrained than those proposed by Duterte.

The overlap between China policy, elite interests, and domestic politics was thrown into sharp relief at the midterm elections held in May 2019. Opposition parties attempted to discredit the Duterte presidency by drawing attention to his downplaying of Chinese actions against Philippine interests in the South China Sea. In doing so, these parties were hoping to capitalize on widespread popular apprehension toward China's assertiveness in the South China Sea and growing hold over the Philippine economy.[45] Attacks on Duterte for his China policy were especially acute in the contest for senate seats, half of which were up for election in the midterms. However, the patriotism card failed to pay dividends as Duterte allies managed to secure nine of the twelve contested senate seats.

Despite Duterte's provocative public statements, Philippine policy toward the United States and China exhibited considerable continuity, suggesting that complex calculations were being made in Manila to deal with complicated strategic circumstances. In point of fact, the public expressions of disdain for the United States on the part of Duterte, especially in the early months of his presidency, had but a marginal effect on defense cooperation, much of which continued uninterrupted. Threats by the president to scrap bilateral defense exercises have not been carried out. On the contrary, the security relationship with the United States has in some ways even been enhanced. For instance, not only did the Philippines proceed with the Balikatan exercises, the quality of the exercises has increased during the Duterte presidency with the introduction of the F-35B Lightning II aircraft and the USS *Wasp*. In April 2018, the United States and the Philippines signed the Enhanced Defense Cooperation Agreement, which provided for an increase in the number and scope of annual military exercises and also initiated discussions on the expansion of U.S. access to military locations in the Philippines, including at Bautista Airbase in Palawan, which is close to the disputed Spratly Islands.

Arguably the most striking example of this close security relationship was the assurance provided by Secretary of State Pompeo, mentioned earlier,

---

[45] A 2018 Pew survey found that 43% of Filipinos held unfavorable views of China. Pew Research Center, "Trump's International Ratings Remain Low, Especially among Key Allies," October 2018, https://www.pewresearch.org/global/2018/10/01/international-publics-divided-on-china.

that the United States would come to the aid of the Philippines should its forces come under attack in the South China Sea.[46] The significance of this assurance lies in the fact that hitherto the United States had been ambivalent about the application of the mutual defense treaty to the South China Sea.

Malaysia

Perhaps the most controversial and direct example of the intersection of Chinese interests with domestic politics in Southeast Asia in recent years is Malaysia. Chinese intervention in local affairs has been a sensitive issue since the early days of the postcolonial era, when the Chinese Communist Party sought to exercise varying degrees of influence over the brewing Communist insurgency in British Malaya. Even as the Communist threat petered out, states with sizable ethnic Chinese populations like Malaysia and Singapore remained wary of Chinese influence through cultural associations. Recent provocative actions on the part of Chinese diplomats in Malaysia have served only to reinforce some of these concerns.[47]

The election of a new government in Malaysia in May 2018 and the return of Mahathir Mohamad as prime minister suggested that, on the face of it, Malaysia would be resetting its China policy—moving away from the initial embrace of China by the Najib administration—and in the process would galvanize ASEAN to hold the diplomatic line against China in the South China Sea. The reasons for this view are that during the Najib administration there were concerns that Malaysia was prepared to remain silent on Chinese assertiveness in the South China Sea, presumably in return for BRI-related loans that could offset some of the losses in the 1Malaysia Development Berhad, which is the subject of a highly publicized ongoing corruption trial that has implicated Najib himself. Despite being a strong advocate of China during his previous tenure as prime minister, Mahathir emerged as a vocal critic of Chinese infrastructure projects, which he argued imposed an unnecessary debt burden. The fact that soon after assuming office Mahathir canceled two BRI projects in the East Malaysian state of Sabah and hinted that his government would also cancel the East Coast Railway Link, which had become a symbol of Chinese economic presence, served only to increase such speculation.

---

[46] Karen Lema and Neil Jerome Morales, "Pompeo Assures Philippines of U.S. Protection in Event of Sea Conflict," *Reuters*, March 1, 2019.

[47] On several occasions in 2015 and 2016, the Chinese ambassador to Malaysia was reported to have involved himself in local politics through either comments made on interethnic relations in Malaysia or appearances on the campaign trail of local politicians. These instances were widely reported in the local media.

Not unlike the case of the Philippines, however, public statements by the Malaysian leadership belie more complex undercurrents. To be sure, an acute sense of concern about Chinese activities in the South China Sea persists in the country's security establishment. At the same time, under the new government, Malaysia has successfully renegotiated the East Coast Railway Link project by reducing the loan required from China as well as increasing the business opportunities for local industries and the local population. In other words, Malaysia's move to stall and renegotiate the railway link was not driven by a strategic imperative, as many analysts and commentators had suggested, but rather by the economic reality. More to the point, it had to do with the internal dynamics of regime change in Malaysia, which saw BRI-related projects come under scrutiny not so much because they were Chinese but because they were negotiated by Najib. Nonetheless, any scenario in which Mahathir plays a galvanizing role as leader and elder statesman of ASEAN to push it to become more independent and assertive toward external powers is likely to be diminished by the unstable state of his ruling coalition and the increasing weight of domestic political priorities, namely, succession.

Regional Responses

Southeast Asia's Response to the United States

When the Indo-Pacific concept was introduced by the Trump administration in 2017, the response of Southeast Asian states was for the most part lukewarm, not least because of the ambiguity surrounding the concept as well as anxiety about ASEAN's place in the Indo-Pacific. The most skeptical states were the Philippines and Cambodia, with both being wary of the risk that the concept posed to the principle of ASEAN centrality. Other states such as Laos, Brunei, and Myanmar mostly stayed silent on the issue. The rest of the ASEAN members—Indonesia, Vietnam, Malaysia, Singapore, and Thailand—were broadly prepared to accept it without betraying exuberance or despite harboring varying degrees of apprehension.

Because the free and open Indo-Pacific concept has been articulated as U.S. strategy and represented an attempt by the Trump administration to signal its interest in remaining engaged in the region, it had to be taken seriously by ASEAN.[48] To that end, the challenge for Southeast Asia was to sustain its relevance in the regional security architecture in the wake of the emergence of this new conception of regional security. The significance of

---

[48] This is especially important given the region's congenital anxiety toward any prospect of U.S. disengagement. See Joseph Chinyong Liow, *Ambivalent Engagement: The United States and Regional Security in Southeast Asia after the Cold War* (Washington, D.C.: Brookings Institution Press, 2017).

this challenge cannot be overemphasized. It was the first time in some years that a security concept with direct implications for ASEAN had emerged from outside the grouping.[49] To that effect, regional states harbored doubt toward the free and open Indo-Pacific concept on several scores.

First, beyond the matter of geography, the ideological impetus to the Indo-Pacific strategy—in particular, the U.S. emphasis on "free and open"—occasioned some degree of consternation. Indeed, despite the fact that Japan's conception of the Indo-Pacific also includes the notion of free and open, the United States' formulation has been a cause for concern because of how it reflects the U.S. propensity to project and impose norms and values on other states. Over the years, this has been evident in the agenda of human rights advocacy and democratization, which at various times and under various administrations have been together presented as the linchpin of U.S. foreign policy and impeded cooperation with some allies and friends.

A second concern against the backdrop of intensifying Sino-U.S. rivalry is that, despite the claims of U.S. officials otherwise, the U.S. Indo-Pacific strategy appears designed as a means to contain China. As a result, regional countries were concerned that they would be implicated in this policy if they were to categorically embrace the free and open Indo-Pacific concept.

Third, the unpredictability of the White House, which has been manifest in sharp policy U-turns taken without consultation with allies, has exacerbated regional anxieties. These concerns have rendered more acute the fear of abandonment. While advocates of continued U.S. engagement in Washington think-tank circles are quick to point out the need to look beyond the idiosyncrasies of the president so as to appreciate the continuities in the U.S. commitment, the reality is that this is a very different administration with a very different approach to policy formulation. Suffice to say, President Trump's unorthodox means of communicating policies—via tweets and casual off-the-cuff remarks—have rendered the implementation and translation of policy difficult for American officials and the interpretation of these policies challenging for U.S. partners and allies in the region.[50]

Fourth, the Indo-Pacific strategy exposes a fundamental contradiction in U.S. foreign policy under the Trump administration, whereby the emphasis on collective effort in the security sphere appears to be undermined by a transactional approach in the economic sphere. In doing so, the administration appears intent on decoupling its security and economic

---

[49] Previous efforts by the former Australian prime minister Kevin Rudd and the former Japanese prime minister Yukio Hatoyama fell by the wayside precisely because they failed to get ASEAN support.

[50] One need only consider the laments of former Trump administration officials and cabinet members to appreciate the severity of the situation. See Jeffrey Goldberg, "The Man Who Couldn't Take It Anymore," *Atlantic*, October 2019.

approaches in ways that discomfit regional states. Despite his intriguing call for an open Indo-Pacific, there is a widely held view that by withdrawing the United States from the TPP, Trump has done considerable damage not only to the standing that the United States commands in the region as a leader but also to the commitment and reliability of the United States to regional stability and growth.

Southeast Asia's Response to China

When BRI was introduced by Xi Jinping in 2013, it was immediately evident that Southeast Asia would play a pivotal role in the initiative. At the 2014 ASEAN-China Summit, Xi announced a $10 billion loan from the China Development Bank for development projects in the ASEAN region and pledged to increase the China-ASEAN Investment Cooperation Fund to $4 billion. An Indonesian project was the recipient of the first tranche of loans disbursed by the China-led Asian Infrastructure Investment Bank (AIIB), and it was followed soon after by further projects in Indonesia as well as Myanmar and the Philippines.

Even as some Southeast Asian states have wholeheartedly embraced BRI, others have tried to keep it at a safe remove. Following the initial euphoria, Indonesia, Malaysia, and Thailand have witnessed a reduction in the scope of projects, such as the construction of high-speed-rail lines. Cambodia, Myanmar, and Laos are even more vulnerable to and dependent on China. Unlike the maritime Southeast Asian states, they have fewer options because of their historical links and geographic proximity to China. For these states, the reality is that their economies need massive infrastructure investment, and China is likely to be the best source for this funding through BRI.

For maritime Southeast Asia, the territorial disputes that some countries have with China in the South China Sea further complicate their relations with Beijing. China's efforts to fulfill its objectives in the South China Sea have been frustrated by the reactions of some Southeast Asian states toward its actions to enforce those claims. In 2013 the Philippines brought the dispute over the Spratlys to the Permanent Court of Arbitration. Meanwhile, relations with Singapore experienced a downturn when China took issue with the island-state in 2016 for its vocal advocacy of the rule of law, which Beijing viewed as unwelcome in the aftermath of the arbitral tribunal ruling in favor of the Philippines.

Although only four Southeast Asian states are claimants in the South China Sea disputes (Malaysia, Brunei, the Philippines, and Vietnam), the region has sought to assume a collective stance on the issue given the risks that any open conflict would pose for stability. To that end, ASEAN has engaged

China in discussions about a code of conduct that aspires to defuse tension. The regional organization has managed to secure Chinese commitments to conflict-prevention initiatives such as the Code for Unplanned Encounters at Sea (CUES), designed to improve the operational safety of and communication between naval vessels and aircraft of the respective countries.[51]

Ultimately, China's peaceful rise to prosperity and great-power status is significant for Southeast Asia on at least three counts. First, Chinese prosperity will have a positive spillover effect for the region. Second, from a strategic perspective, a weakened China would pose a major security threat. As Singapore's former prime minister Goh Chok Tong once described vividly, "a prosperous and globally integrated China is in all our interests. The alternative of a poor and isolated China will be like having sixty North Koreas at our doorstep. It will pose challenges without the opportunities." Finally, regional decision-makers are fully cognizant of the fact that growing Chinese influence in Southeast Asia is an inescapable reality. Hence, a key objective of regional countries is to do whatever they can to nudge China to wield this influence in ways that would advance regional stability and economic growth.

Challenges and Opportunities in Southeast Asia's Relations with the United States and China

Against the backdrop of escalating Sino-U.S. competition, the abiding questions for Southeast Asia are how and whether the region can remain nimble enough to weather the storms of great-power rivalry without compromising on national and regional interests. The immediate impact of the ongoing trade war is instructive. While some regional countries might benefit from the reconfiguration and relocation of supply chains—Vietnam, for instance, has seen an upsurge in demand for its workforce for the assembly of smartphones previously done in China—the larger picture of disruption spells significant challenges for a region whose countries have collectively contributed considerable value to Chinese manufactured products through their place in regional and global supply chains.

The challenge posed for Southeast Asia by the intensification of the Sino-U.S. rivalry will also be manifest with respect to strategic issues, most prominently in the South China Sea. The United States will continue conducting its freedom of navigation operations, and indeed the renamed Indo-Pacific Command has already indicated its intention to ramp up these operations, much to the chagrin of Beijing. Most of the states in the region

---

[51] Tan See Seng, "ADMM-Plus: Can It Do 'CUES' in the South China Sea?" S. Rajaratnam School of International Studies (RSIS), RSIS Commentary, October 26, 2017.

do not want to provoke China by publicly voicing their support. Because China cannot be removed from the features it currently occupies, and the United States cannot be stopped from conducting freedom of navigation operations, activities in the South China Sea will soon settle into a pattern. The concern, however, is that these militarized activities increase the risk of unplanned encounters.

Another area where Southeast Asia will find itself vulnerable is in the technology sphere. With the ambitious plan for the Smart Cities Network, ASEAN states will be looking to build and synchronize their respective information and communications technology (ICT) platforms. China is already deeply involved with various ASEAN states in this regard, having assisted them in the building of national ICT platforms. The United States, however, is dialing up the pressure on its friends and allies, cautioning against the use of Chinese technology due to the risk of cyberespionage. While Washington has yet to turn its attention to Southeast Asia, should the United States eventually call on its ASEAN partners to reconsider collaboration with Chinese technology companies, this would pose problems for the region, which is an increasingly important recipient of Chinese investments along the Digital Silk Road. Instead, ASEAN's preferred approach has been to encourage the United States to support its Smart Cities initiative, and in the process serve as a platform for Sino-U.S. cooperation rather than competition.

Notwithstanding these vulnerabilities, Southeast Asia is potentially positioned to maximize benefits from this superpower contest. This is because Sino-U.S. competition may not necessarily result in the imposition of a choice or a *fait accompli* on regional states; it could also afford opportunities if superpower rivalry means enhanced efforts to coax and persuade regional states with inducements. How has Southeast Asia attempted to cope with prevailing strategic uncertainties and seize on opportunities?

First, Southeast Asian states have hastened regional integration. Clearly, the impetus for a stronger, more united and cohesive ASEAN is growing. While ASEAN has always staked a claim to centrality in the regional security architecture (most recently, to centrality in the Indo-Pacific) it is increasingly urgent that substance be given to this concept. Recent developments have been encouraging in this regard. Under pressure from the growing interest in the Indo-Pacific as a strategic concept, which could render Southeast Asia—and the concept of ASEAN centrality—less relevant in the regional architecture, ASEAN managed to sufficiently align the strategic outlooks of member states in order to formulate the "ASEAN Outlook on the Indo-Pacific." Following several discussions and iterations at the working level marked by differing perspectives and opinions, leaders eventually converged on an agreement at their June 2019 summit. Unlike Washington's approach to the Indo-Pacific, however, the outlook stressed economic cooperation and regional connectivity as its priorities. Issues related to defense and security were deliberately downplayed. Additionally, the outlook is predicated on ASEAN centrality, something that the non-ASEAN advocates have paid lip service to.

While no member state was under any illusion that the articulation of the "ASEAN Outlook on the Indo-Pacific" would substantially influence the thinking of external powers on this issue, they believed it was nevertheless imperative that ASEAN itself demonstrate some modicum of unity in response to a strategic concept being imposed from beyond.[52] Another recent example of regional unity is ASEAN's successful finalization of a common position toward ongoing negotiations for the Regional Comprehensive Economic Partnership (RCEP), which is crucial in terms of positioning the grouping to weather the storm of the Sino-U.S. trade war.[53]

Second, Southeast Asia has been deepening and widening its relations with other extraregional powers, whether as an institutional collective (ASEAN) or as individual states on a bilateral basis. While regional scholars, analysts, and decision-makers are consumed with the deterioration in Sino-U.S. relations, strategic competition in the region need not be dyadic in nature, and the U.S.-China relationship is certainly not the only one that matters. In order to diversify strategic actors and enmesh the interests of other major powers in the region, especially since the inception of the Trump administration, Southeast Asia has enhanced its cooperation with countries like Japan, India, and Australia, both bilaterally and through the ASEAN process with dialogue partners. For its part, Japan has already demonstrated an inclination and ability to play a proactive leadership role in a manner that is aligned broadly with Southeast Asian interests. In the wake of the U.S. withdrawal from the TPP, Japan took the lead in negotiations of the CPTPP (which includes four Southeast Asian states, with several more indicating interest in joining), established strategic partnerships with several Southeast Asian states (through which Japan has provided maritime assets not just for the respective coast guards but the navies as well), significantly increased naval visits, enhanced the provision of quality infrastructure, and accommodated the concerns articulated by ASEAN in its own "free and open Indo-Pacific" vision.[54] India has also increased its engagement

---

[52] The fact of the matter is that whether it is presented as an idea, concept, vision, or strategy, the term "Indo-Pacific" did not arise from ASEAN's own strategic lexicon.

[53] See Phuwit Limviphuwat, "ASEAN Finalises Common Position on RCEP," *Nation* (Thailand), June 23, 2019.

[54] In the latter instance, Japan was prepared to stress ASEAN centrality and to change the nomenclature of the free and open Indo-Pacific from "strategy" to "vision" at the behest of ASEAN. See Kuni Miyake, "What Does the 'Indo-Pacific Strategy' Mean?" *Japan Times*, March 11, 2019.

and activism in Southeast Asia, most notably on security cooperation with various Southeast Asian states, especially Singapore and Thailand, focused on the maritime domain.[55] Some Indian initiatives include the Indian Ocean Rim Association, the Indian Ocean Naval Symposium, and the increased presence of the Indian Navy in Southeast Asian waters.

Notwithstanding the efforts of Southeast Asian states to recalibrate their postures and policies in response to the uncertainties occasioned by the downturn in Sino-U.S. relations, there remains one challenge that is likely to exercise foreign policy decision-making among most regional states in the foreseeable future. As this chapter has demonstrated, superpower competition is increasingly overlapping with domestic politics and elite interests. Hence, ASEAN leaders must be able to raise their sights above the parapets of momentary domestic electoral interest in order to foster a shared strategic outlook on regional developments that affect all the member states. Otherwise, they risk being overwhelmed—and ASEAN itself risks being rendered irrelevant—by the shifting tides of geostrategic rivalry.

Conclusion

In a major speech delivered at the 2019 Shangri-La Dialogue, Singapore prime minister Lee Hsien Loong emphasized that Southeast Asia has often found itself a subject of and arena for rivalry and competition between external powers and, concomitantly, that the region has a long history of resisting such interference. Hence, coping with the centrifugal pulls exerted by external powers is nothing new for the region.

However, there is good reason to believe that things might be different this time around. First, the level of unpredictability and uncertainty in U.S. foreign policy has never been as disconcerting for regional countries as it is currently under the Trump administration, even though the administration is at the same time single-minded in its objective of curbing the expansion of Chinese power and influence. The fact that the Trump administration has demonstrated on numerous occasions its penchant for sudden policy U-turns and shifts cannot but give pause. In fact, this perverse combination of resolve to counter China and unpredictability in the conduct of foreign policy is precisely what triggers anxiety within ASEAN. Second, the influence of China today is far more extensive than that of any other superpower (with the exception of the United States itself) in recent decades. In fact, China not only is thoroughly integrated into the international order but is in some

---

[55] Sinderpal Singh, "The Dilemmas of Regional States: How Southeast Asian States View and Respond to India-China Maritime Competition," *Asian Security* 15, no. 1 (2019): 44–59.

respects also reshaping it (for instance, through the AIIB and BRI). The challenge for Southeast Asian states is to seize the opportunities afforded by Chinese engagement but avoid overdependence, while also managing Chinese assertiveness and overreach.

What does this all mean? Southeast Asia desires and requires the United States' presence to ensure that the region does not become overly beholden to China. Yet the unpredictability of U.S. foreign policy during the Trump administration has invariably prompted Southeast Asian states to reassess strategic options and recalibrate their postures accordingly. As the downturn in Sino-U.S. relations continues and the rivalry between the superpowers accelerates, the region will find itself increasingly confronted with a strategic dilemma as pressure mounts to align with one side or the other. This will impose pressing policy challenges on individual states as well as on ASEAN. Navigating the rough waters ahead will require the development of a unity of purpose among the states of the region.

EXECUTIVE SUMMARY

This chapter investigates Europe's role in and responses to U.S.-China competition and assesses whether great-power competition for influence is fostering greater European unity and policies that put European interests first.

MAIN ARGUMENT

U.S. and Chinese pressure on Europe to choose sides and become a great-power dependent have encouraged it to move toward greater unity across a wide spectrum of issues, ranging from trade and industrial policy to Indo-Pacific security and defense. High levels of popular support for the EU have strengthened efforts to carve out an independent position that allows the EU to cooperate with both Washington and Beijing. European policies are increasingly based on interests rather than values, enabling Europe to accommodate the rise of authoritarianism. Putting European interests first also facilitates the diversification of the region's partners. A more self-reliant, interest-based Europe could contribute to international stability by motivating the U.S. and China to be more willing to compromise.

POLICY IMPLICATIONS

- Europe continues to prefer transatlantic cooperation over other partnerships due to common interests in preserving a liberal world order. Provided both sides acknowledge that their policies are often complementary rather than competitive, transatlantic relations will remain cooperative.

- Europe will continue to cooperate with China on reforming and preserving multilateral institutions such as the World Trade Organization and pursuing diplomacy-based conflict resolution. At the same time, it will establish defensive mechanisms against unfair Chinese trade and industrial practices.

- The EU is adopting a more united position in policy areas such as trade, defense, industry, technology standards, export controls, external and internal security, and multilateral institutions, making its footprint across a wide range of economic and security issues larger than ever.

Europe's Place in Sino-U.S. Competition

Liselotte Odgaard

The trade war between the United States and China demonstrates that Europe is caught in the crossfire between an ally that demands more help to counter an economic and military rival and a rising power that is rolling out a major global economic vision that could transform the regional order at the expense of European political cohesion and economic autonomy. U.S. aims in Europe focus on pushing what is seen as an unruly, free-riding, and ineffective group of allies into place while trying to revitalize cooperation on central U.S. priorities. Old themes that have been thorns in the side of transatlantic relations, such as burden sharing in NATO, the trade imbalance in Europe's favor, and a greater U.S. willingness to use force against security threats, have turned into festering crises. At the same time, the United States still looks to Europe for cooperation in pursuing global interests. Defense cooperation in the Indo-Pacific is seen as important for preventing China from acquiring military and strategic dominance. Economic cooperation to push back at Chinese disregard for intellectual property rights and reciprocal market access is likewise considered crucial to preserving U.S. and European economic prosperity.

Europe has responded ambiguously to U.S. aims. On some issues, it has caved when faced with U.S. demands. Many European countries, for example, are taking steps to increase defense expenditure to 2% of GDP.[1] On other issues, such as reform of the World Trade Organization (WTO),

Liselotte Odgaard is a Senior Fellow at the Hudson Institute in Washington, D.C. She can be reached at <lodgaard@hudson.org>.

[1] Lucie Béraud-Sudreau, "On the Up: Western Defence Spending in 2018," International Institute for Strategic Studies, Military Balance Blog, February 15, 2019, https://www.iiss.org/blogs/military-balance/2019/02/european-nato-defence-spending-up.

Europe has attempted to work with China to demonstrate that the country is both a systemic rival and a partner.[2] On still other issues, such as Indo-Pacific defense cooperation, Europe has yet to define and develop its contribution.

Chinese aims in Europe focus on developing economic relations. To this end, Beijing has prioritized implementing a Chinese version of world order—the Belt and Road Initiative (BRI)—and establishing a regional strategic foothold. It aims to ensure access to profitable markets, technological know-how, and infrastructure and to establish a strategic presence in Europe that will enhance its regional economic clout and political influence.[3] Europe's position as a leading global economic force with reservations about U.S. cooperation on key European priorities such as security guarantees, the centrality of multilateral institutions such as the WTO and the United Nations for global economic and security management, and the maintenance of strategic arms control mechanisms makes it a potential jewel in the crown of Chinese strategic partners.

China's implementation of BRI is only beginning in Europe, with a current focus on building infrastructure such as ports in Southern Europe. Of greater concern to European countries, China has invested in the region's high-technology sectors.[4] This emerging economic and political influence sometimes undermines European unity—for example, by establishing the 17+1 initiative made up of eastern and southern EU member states to allow China a greater voice in Brussels. Chinese economic statecraft has adversely affected European coherence on security issues where Europe and the United States largely have common objectives. For example, the EU's South China Sea policy refrains from criticizing China because countries such as Hungary and Greece prioritize attracting Chinese investment.[5] On the other hand, Europe and China cooperate on issues such as WTO reform and the Iran nuclear agreement. China has sufficient common interests with Europe that it will continue to look at Brussels as a partner on economic and security issues even as a growing mismatch between European and Chinese strategic priorities increases competition and confrontation between the two sides.

---

[2] Delegation of the European Union to China, "Joint Statement of the 21st EU-China Summit," April 10, 2019, https://eeas.europa.eu/delegations/china_en/60836/Joint%20statement%20of%20 the%2021st%20EU-China%20summit.

[3] Joel Wuthnow, "China's Belt and Road: One Initiative, Three Strategies," in *Strategic Asia 2019: China's Expanding Strategic Ambitions*, ed. Ashley Tellis, Alison Szalwinski, and Michael Wills (Seattle: National Bureau of Asian Research 2019), 210–35.

[4] Thilo Hanemann, Mikko Huotari, and Agatha Kratz, "Chinese FDI in Europe: 2018 Trends and Impact of New Screening Policies," *MERICS Papers on China*, March 2019, https://www.merics. org/sites/default/files/2019-03/190311_MERICS-Rhodium%20Group_COFDI-Update_2019.pdf.

[5] Mikko Huotari et al., "China's Emergence as a Global Security Actor: Strategies for Europe," *MERICS Papers on China*, July 2017, 109.

This chapter concludes that the challenges that Sino-U.S. competition presents for European unity encourage a division of labor between EU institutions that formulate general policies and establish supportive mechanisms, on the one hand, and groups of member states that implement policies, on the other. Innovative institutional cooperation allows Europe to position itself as a strategic influence beyond its traditional stronghold of trade in areas such as industrial policy and security. This strategic positioning is based on putting European interests first. Common interests in pushing back against Chinese industrial, security, and human rights policies that undermine fundamental liberal principles will facilitate continued transatlantic cooperation. At the same time, Europe is diversifying its portfolio of partners to hedge against growing differences of interest with the United States and thus continues to engage in cooperation with China on multilateral institutions and diplomatic conflict resolution.

The rest of this chapter is organized as follows. The first main section defines Europe as an actor and examines the security, economic, and normative challenges engendered by Sino-U.S. competition. The second section examines Europe's geopolitical, security and defense, economic, and normative responses to these challenges. The third section then discusses the consequences of Europe increasingly putting its own interests first with a view to establishing an independent strategic role in the world order.

How to Understand Europe's Role in Sino-U.S. Competition

The Interplay between Regional Institutions and States

As an actor, Europe is politically rather than geographically defined and consists of the member states of the European Union and the EU institutions. The EU comprises 28 member states, which is expected to drop to 27 if the United Kingdom follows through on plans to leave the EU. The most important EU institutions are the European Council, which convenes the EU heads of state and government to set general objectives and priorities; the European Commission, which has the executive power to submit legislation, implement policies, administer the budget, and set policies on trade beyond the EU's borders; the European Parliament, which exerts democratic control and approves European Commission members; and the European External Action Service, which prepares foreign and defense policy proposals.[6]

---

[6] Simon Usherwood and John Pinder, *The European Union: A Very Short Introduction*, 4th ed. (Oxford: Oxford University Press, 2018).

The relative power of the EU institutions depends on the issue area. On trade issues, the institutions are at their strongest. The EU rather than the individual member states legislates on trade and concludes international agreements. Capital market regulation is a case of medium institutional strength. In this area, legislation has been passed that deepens and further integrates the capital markets of the member states. In addition, the EU provides support for initiatives taken by industrial actors within member states to facilitate objectives such as increasing FDI and providing sources of business funding. The EU institutions are at their weakest on security and defense issues. In this area, the EU creates measures and tools such as the European Defence Fund to encourage groups of member states to develop and strengthen cooperation on and coordination of security and defense capabilities and policies.[7]

The EU's ambition is to advance European interests independently from great-power aims across a wide range of economic, security, and normative issue areas. According to the secretary-general of the European Council, Jeppe Tranholm-Mikkelsen, after ten years of economic crises, migration problems, and Brexit, the EU is beginning to have the capacity to look beyond Europe's borders. In a world defined by Sino-U.S. competition, individual member states can no longer exercise sovereignty as they once did. They recognize that they must exercise joint sovereignty to influence the global order.[8] To realize this objective, the EU must demonstrate that it is sufficiently powerful that the United States and China cannot ignore its objectives and policies. The EU institutions are central actors in facilitating coordination between member states by providing frameworks for both dialogue and the adoption of general policy guidelines. From this common basis, groups of member states form to fly the flag for Europe on issues on which the institutions do not have the power to act.

The four biggest EU member states (Britain, Italy, Germany, and France) each have different positions that influence the EU's place in the global order. Britain and Italy tend to embrace both U.S. and Chinese aims in Europe, challenging EU aspirations toward greater unity. Each country maintains close defense and security ties with the United States by hosting U.S. troops, participating in U.S.-led wars, and governing some of the most pro-U.S. populations in Europe. In Italy, 52% of the population holds a favorable opinion of the United States, and in the UK, 50% expresses a favorable view. By comparison, only 38% of the French population and 30% of Germans

---

[7] European Council, "Policies," October 10, 2018, https://www.consilium.europa.eu/en/policies.

[8] "Caught in the Crossfire: Balancing EU Relations with the U.S. and China" (transcript from panel debate at Hudson Institute, Washington, D.C., April 16, 2017).

hold a favorable opinion of the United States.[9] At the same time, the UK and Italy embrace Chinese policies that leave them vulnerable to Chinese leverage. The UK, for example, is lobbying for British companies to provide either financing or engineering expertise for BRI and advocating that London's financial district connect with China's capital market.[10] Irrespective of the outcome of Brexit, Britain will have to choose to side more closely with the EU, the United States, or China. The country's deepening economic downturn and prolonged domestic political quarrel on future relations with Europe indicate that Britain is too weak to exercise independent international influence. Italy's economic recession at the end of 2018 and retreat from a standoff with Brussels over the country's budget deficit of 2.4% of its GDP indicate that, despite the occasional protest over the EU's economic policies, Italy will opt for cooperation within the EU to exercise sovereignty. It has no appetite for joining Britain's journey toward great-power dependency without influence.[11]

Germany and France continue to be the motors that drive Europe toward more unitary action. Germany is the economic heavyweight that has been historically more oriented toward Eastern and Northern Europe. France provides greater military muscle and traditionally has maintained close ties to Southern and Western Europe. They are thus complementary powers with the shared aspiration of being the caretakers of the EU in its role as a strong guarantor of peace, security, and prosperity. This was confirmed with their 2019 agreement on bilateral cooperation at Aachen.[12] Germany and France cooperate with the United States and China from very independent positions, manifesting support for core liberal economic and political values and refusing to succumb to geostrategic U.S. or Chinese policies that in their view enhance great-power competition.

Despite suspicions in the other EU member states that Germany and France are exercising hegemonic decision-making power in Brussels, at times deepening conflicts, German-French cooperation on uniting Europe at a time of Sino-U.S. competition is a precondition of the success of such an ambition. The rest of this section investigates economic, security, and

---

[9] Pew Research Center, "Trump's International Ratings Remain Low, Especially among Key Allies," October 2018, 19.

[10] Lucy Hornby and George Parker, "Hammond Courts China Economic Ties on Beijing Trip," *Financial Times*, April 27, 2019, https://www.ft.com/content/a791f700-6812-11e9-9adc-98bf1d35a056.

[11] Peter Schechter, "Italy Will Keep Blinking in 2019," EUobserver, February 4, 2019, https://euobserver.com/opinion/144054.

[12] *Traité entre la République Française et la République Fédérale d'Allemagne sur la coopération et l'intégration Franco-Allemandes* [Treaty between the French Republic and the German Federal Republic on French-German Cooperation and Integration], January 22, 2019, https://www.diplomatie.gouv.fr/fr/dossiers-pays/allemagne/relations-bilaterales/traite-de-cooperation-franco-allemand-d-aix-la-chapelle.

normative challenges to European cohesion and transatlantic cooperation engendered by U.S.-China rivalry.

Challenges from U.S.-China Security Competition

For decades, the United States has complained about a free-riding Europe with small defense budgets and tight political constraints on its use of hard power (see **Figure 1**). Since NATO's inception, Washington has shouldered most of the burden of defending the United States and its allies against military threats.[13] The United States continues to constitute the backbone of NATO deployments to deter threats against European security such as

FIGURE 1   European defense spending as a percentage of GDP, 2014–17

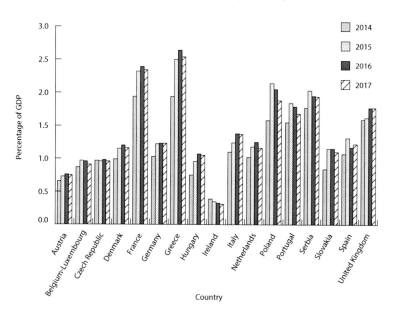

SOURCE: Trading Economics, 2018, https://tradingeconomics.com.

---

[13] Charles Cooper and Benjamin Zucker, "Perceptions of NATO Burden-Sharing," RAND Corporation, Report, 1989, https://www.rand.org/pubs/reports/R3750.html.

those from Russia in Eastern Europe and the Baltic states.[14] However, China's emergence as a competitor that seeks to displace the United States as the principal security provider in Asia has encouraged Washington to gradually shift military resources toward Asia and away from Europe.[15] Moreover, Russia's and China's limited nuclear war capabilities and strategies have prompted the United States to change its nuclear force strategy to allow for precisely tailored nuclear attacks that fall far below the threshold of mutually assured destruction.[16]

The United States explained its withdrawal from the 1987 Intermediate-Range Nuclear Forces (INF) Treaty in 2019 with reference to Russian treaty violations. However, the predominant reason for the U.S. withdrawal was widely thought to be that China does not form part of the Cold War arms-control regime. This omission prevents the United States from installing intermediate-range missiles in Asia directed against China.[17] The EU argued that Washington's decision left Europe especially vulnerable because it is within reach of both U.S. and Russian missiles that the INF Treaty prohibits.[18] The United States' decision to withdraw from the treaty is part of a pattern of actions to prioritize threats to U.S. security interests and assets. Similarly, the 2018 U.S. Nuclear Posture Review was received with dismay in Europe.[19] Washington's greater willingness to consider using nuclear weapons to counter threats destabilizes the world in Europe's view by increasing the risk that nuclear weapons could be used at lower levels of conflict. Nevertheless, save for France and Britain, Europeans are not yet ready to travel the route of strategic nuclear autonomy. For example, Europe remains unwilling to place French nuclear capacities under EU command.[20]

China's strategic partnership with Russia is also a growing concern. BRI might help Russia realize its geopolitical agenda of pushing back against NATO's presence from the Arctic down to the Mediterranean. Xi Jinping's

---

[14] Grzegorz Kuczyński and Krzysztof Kamiński, "U.S. Permanent Military Base in Poland: Favorable Solution for the NATO Alliance," Warsaw Institute, Special Report, November 2019, https://warsawinstitute.org/u-s-permanent-military-base-poland-favorable-solution-nato-alliance.

[15] Ashley J. Tellis, "Pursuing Global Reach: China's Not So Long March toward Preeminence," in Tellis, Szalwinski, and Wills, *Strategic Asia 2019*, 40–43.

[16] U.S. Department of Defense, *Nuclear Posture Review* (Washington, D.C., February 2018), https://dod.defense.gov/News/SpecialReports/2018NuclearPostureReview.aspx.

[17] Mercy A. Kuo, "U.S. Withdrawal from IMF Treaty: Impact on Asia," *Diplomat*, March 1, 2019, https://thediplomat.com/2019/03/us-withdrawal-from-inf-treaty-impact-on-asia.

[18] Sico van der Meer, "The Demise of the INF Treaty: Can the EU Save Arms Control?" EUobserver, May 18, 2019, https://euobserver.com/opinion/143980.

[19] U.S. Department of Defense, *Nuclear Posture Review*.

[20] Manuel Lafont Rapnouil, Tara Varma, and Nick Witney, "Eyes Tight Shut: European Attitudes towards Nuclear Deterrence," European Council on Foreign Relations, December 2018, https://www.ecfr.eu/specials/scorecard/eyes_tight_shut_european_attitudes_towards_nuclear_deterrence.

launch of the Polar Silk Road in Russia in July 2017 envisages expanded cooperation in the energy sector, a joint venture to build ice-class cargo vessels, and the development of a northeast Arctic underwater fiber-optic telecommunications cable. China has also offered to build railway links from Norway through Finland and the Baltic states, making the Northern Sea Route that runs through Russia's territorial waters in the Arctic more economically profitable.[21] Chinese economic investments provide Russia with resources and infrastructure that will enable it to expand its influence in Europe's eastern border regions. Growing military cooperation between Russia and China adds to the long-term concerns about the emergence of an additional Chinese military threat.[22]

The U.S. withdrawal from the Joint Comprehensive Plan of Action agreement for preventing Iran from acquiring nuclear weapons, which resulted in the United States reinstating sanctions against Iran, highlights the importance of using the potential complementarity of different U.S.-European instrumental preferences for conflict resolution. Europe has continued to collaborate with China, Japan, and Russia on preserving the agreement. The Iran nuclear issue is a reminder that internal European decisions on the instruments used to protect regional security, rather than looking to the United States as a security provider, are necessary in an international order of fluctuating alliances and faltering multilateral frameworks. Indeed, European insistence on institutional instruments for diplomacy complements the continued U.S. sanctions pressure on the Iranian economy, and the combination could sufficiently weaken Iran to prevent it from further destabilizing the Middle East.

European policies toward the South China Sea also highlight the possibilities and limitations of transatlantic cooperation. The Sino-U.S. strategic rivalry has produced a confrontational and uncompromising atmosphere with regular incidents involving U.S. and Chinese navies, coast guards, and paramilitary forces that risk escalation. The United States seeks greater European cooperation on confronting Chinese challenges in the

---

[21] Elizabeth Wishnick, "Russia and the Arctic in China's Quest for Great-Power Status," in Tellis, Szalwinski, and Wills, *Strategic Asia 2019*, 48–78; and M. Taylor Fravel, Kathryn C. Lavelle, and Liselotte Odgaard, "China in the Arctic: Melting and Freezing of Alliances as the Climate Changes in the Polar Zone" (paper presented at the International Studies Association annual conference, Toronto, March 27–30, 2019).

[22] Dick Zandee, "The Future of NATO: Fog over the Atlantic?" Clingendael Institute, Strategic Monitor 2018–2019, 2018, https://www.clingendael.org/pub/2018/strategic-monitor-2018-2019/the-future-of-nato.

South China Sea, but Europe does not see China as a direct military threat.[23] However, China's militarization of the South China Sea and its encroachments on the freedom of navigation of civilian and military vessels in areas that are defined as international waters are seen by both Europe and the United States as threats to globally recognized interpretations of international law. If China succeeds in limiting freedom of navigation in its neighborhood, persuading weaker powers to accept such restrictions in return for peaceful and profitable relations, it may set a global precedent.

Europe's South China Sea policy consists of general policy declarations that do not directly criticize China. The EU's statement on the Permanent Court of Arbitration's award in the dispute between the Philippines and China stated that the EU was committed to upholding international law in the maritime domain.[24] The watered-down statement reflects that China's growing economic presence in Europe has political consequences. Countries such as Hungary and Greece that want to attract Chinese investments are hesitant to oppose Chinese actions. Because of these internal divisions, a growing number of member states coordinate operations in support of freedom of navigation in the South China Sea to circumvent internal disagreements on how much to contest China far from European shores.

Challenges from U.S.-China Economic Competition

Europe has welcomed the U.S. attack on the structural problems of Chinese market economic practices, which violate international regulatory regimes of the WTO. The EU also agrees with the United States that China is no longer a developing country and should not be entitled to special treatment in the WTO.[25] However, the EU disapproves of the economic costs of using punitive tariffs to force China to comply. The European commissioner for trade, Cecilia Malmström, has stated that although the EU and the United States share many concerns about China's economic policies, the EU does not approve of the Trump administration's approach

[23] Fidel Sendagorta, "The Triangle in the Long Game: Rethinking Relations between China, Europe, and the United States in the New Era of Strategic Competition," Belfer Center for Science and International Affairs, Project on Europe and the Transatlantic Relationship, June 2019, 97, https://www.belfercenter.org/publication/triangle-long-game.

[24] European Union External Action Service, "Declaration on the Award Rendered in the Arbitration between the Philippines and China," July 15, 2016, https://eeas.europa.eu/headquarters/headquarters-Homepage/6873/declaration-award-rendered-arbitration-between-philippines-and-china_en.

[25] European Commission, "EU-China—A Strategic Outlook," March 12, 2019, https://ec.europa.eu/commission/news/eu-china-strategic-outlook-2019-mar-12_en.

of using tariffs to achieve political goals. Europe sees China as an economic rival but not a political enemy.[26]

In the economic sphere, the United States has long-standing complaints about the trade imbalance in Europe's favor (see **Figures 2** and **3**). Its imposition in May 2018 of tariffs on EU steel and aluminum exports and refusal to allow the appointment of new WTO appellate body members—a refusal that impairs the WTO's ability to work—have led the EU to impose retaliatory tariffs on select U.S. exports and cooperate with China on upholding the WTO as a central institution for managing global trade issues through reform measures. U.S. actions thus have aligned Europe

FIGURE 2   European exports, 2017 (selected countries, $ billion)

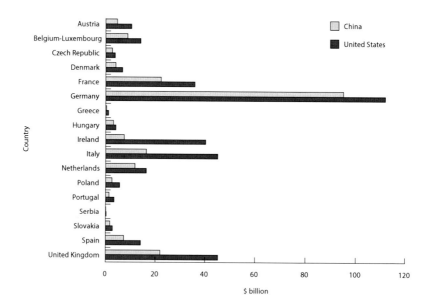

SOURCE: Alexander Simoes, Observatory of Economic Complexity database, https://atlas.media.mit.edu/en.

---

[26] Peter Müller and Christian Reiermann, "EU Commissioner on the U.S.-China Trade War: 'Our List of Countermeasures Is Ready,'" *Der Spiegel*, June 26, 2019, https://www.spiegel.de/international/europe/eu-commissioner-cecilia-malmstraem-on-the-u-s-china-trade-war-a-1274479.html.

FIGURE 3   European imports, 2017 (selected countries, $ billion)

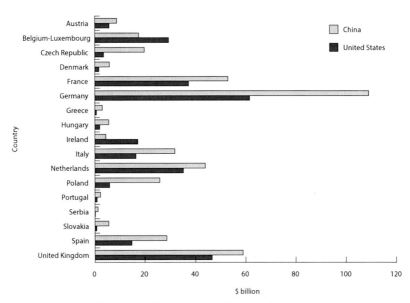

SOURCE: Simoes, Observatory of Economic Complexity database.

more closely with China. Given that many European countries consider U.S. trade policies to be an imminent threat to the viability of multilateral trade regulation, the issue of tariffs and the WTO is seen as a litmus test for future transatlantic cooperation.[27]

Another area of U.S.-China competition with economic implications for Europe is technology standards. Such standards establish boundaries for technology usage, specifying the technology to be used and restricting access to technology outside these limits. The controversy both over Huawei's use of network devices to provide data access to the Chinese government and over Facebook's collection of data from users without compliance have made this issue an urgent European concern. In 2018 the EU General Data Protection Regulation (GDPR) went into force, requiring private and public organizations to gain consent before using data and to protect the data in their possession. As artificial intelligence becomes a key driver of economic development, Europe is grappling with ensuring competitiveness while shaping the conditions for the development and use of technology through

[27] "Caught in the Crossfire."

instruments that build on the GDPR.[28] The United States and Asia host 79% of the world's most valuable tech companies.[29] Europe's weak position in the global technology market leaves it at a disadvantage in terms of both standard setting and competitiveness. The U.S. technology industry is basing its long-term strategic plans on Balkanization, relying on regionalized supply chains that decrease economic and technological interdependence between the United States and China.[30] Rumors that China is considering establishing an Asian standardization organization, which would be available to Asian partners of BRI, is another indication that global standards organizations may not have a future.[31] This development would leave Europe with little influence in an area of major importance for economic growth and security.

The U.S.-China dispute over Huawei illustrates Europe's vulnerability in this regard. In May 2019, the United States took retaliatory action against Huawei, warning that Chinese state-owned companies are legally obliged to share information of importance to state security with the Chinese government. Huawei equipment has already been incorporated into the 4G networks of numerous European countries. In 2018, Huawei controlled more than 40% of the European base-station market, surpassing the market shares of the European companies Nokia and Ericsson.[32] For the time being, France, Germany, and several European countries have moved away from a ban against Huawei and are opting instead for a regulatory approach aimed at securing sensitive data.[33] This has underscored the need for an EU approach that carries sufficient weight to enable Europe to compete with the United States and China.

Export controls are central to Europe's role in the U.S.-Chinese economic competition, being closely connected to the technological standards on which export licenses are based. Technological standards regulate data production and access and hence also determine which entities can get a license to be involved in sensitive sectors with dual-use technology and patented

[28] European Commission, "Digital Single Market: Policy: Artificial Intelligence," July 4, 2019, https://ec.europa.eu/digital-single-market/en/artificial-intelligence.

[29] Casper Klynge, "Tech Diplomacy," Ministry of Foreign Affairs (Denmark), September 3, 2019.

[30] Off-the-record briefing with a chief technology officer at a U.S. telecommunications company, Hudson Institute, Washington, D.C., April 29, 2019.

[31] Björn Fagersten and Tim Rühlig, "China's Standard Power and Its Geopolitical Implications for Europe," Swedish Institute of International Affairs, Brief, no. 2, 2019, 16, https://www.ui.se/globalassets/ui.se-eng/publications/2019/ui-brief-no.-2-2019.pdf.

[32] Minoru Satake, "Europe Adopts Huawei Gear into 5G Networks over U.S. Objections," *Nikkei Asian Review*, May 16, 2009, https://asia.nikkei.com/Spotlight/5G-networks/Europe-adopts-Huawei-gear-into-5G-networks-over-US-objections.

[33] Achour Messas et al., "5G in Europe: Time to Change Gear!" Institut Montaigne, May 2019, https://www.institutmontaigne.org/ressources/pdfs/publications/5g-europe-time-change-gear-part-1-note.pdf.

intellectual property. Export controls highlight the weakness of existing EU regulatory mechanisms at a time when Europe shares U.S. concerns about Chinese forced technology transfers and intellectual property theft. Export controls limit the spread and use of specific goods and services for purposes of national security. Regional and national export control regimes are challenged by technological developments. Intangible technology transfers occur in the form of FDI, mergers and acquisitions, research and education cooperation, and the transfer of data in nonphysical forms. These transfers have helped China's arms industry, for example, compete with more established arms exporters on global markets. The key question for Europe is to what extent the EU should build more restrictive export controls for European industry and R&D at a time when Europe is already facing serious issues of competitiveness in the technology industry as a result of the growing Sino-U.S. rivalry.

In sum, U.S.-China economic competition poses a challenge to Europe insofar as it relies on global standards and markets. The escalating rivalry between the two countries thus encourages the EU to put regional interests first, diversify its portfolio of partners, and facilitate regional collaboration on an industrial policy that would make Europe more self-reliant and competitive.

Challenges from U.S.-China Normative Competition

The United States and Europe share an emphasis on the liberal values of democracy, human rights, and market economic principles as the route to global prosperity and order. These values have formed the basis of the globalized post–World War II liberal institutions.[34] In contrast with Europe, however, the American public is more inclined to support the use of force to uphold world order, less inclined to seek UN approval, and less inclined to assist other nations.[35] Thus, during a time of waning U.S. power, there is considerable popular support for the United States' withdrawal from multilateral institutional and diplomatic commitments in order to facilitate the unilateral protection of U.S. national interests.

The United States, Britain, and France hold three of the five permanent seats with veto-wielding power in the UN Security Council. The remaining two permanent seats are held by China and Russia. This position allows the Western member states to set the agenda. However, with the surge of U.S.-China competition, the Security Council has become a forum in which conflict resolution is stymied and political divisions prompt the permanent

---

[34] G. John Ikenberry, "Power and Liberal Order: America's Postwar World Order in Transition," *International Relations of the Asia-Pacific* 5, no. 2 (2005): 133–52.

[35] Pew Research Center, "The American-Western European Values Gap: American Exceptionalism Subsides," Global Attitudes Project, February 29, 2012, https://www.pewglobal.org/2011/11/17/the-american-western-european-values-gap.

members to frequently use their veto powers.[36] This institutional paralysis, combined with the UN system's bias against legitimizing the unilateral use of force for purposes of international conflict resolution, makes UN institutions increasingly unattractive instruments for the United States to pursue its interests.[37]

European support persists for the UN's emphasis on the legal equality of states, irrespective of size and ideological basis. In an era of U.S.-China competition, this norm allows weaker states to wield considerable influence. Internal challenges to Europe's commitment to UN multilateralism have arisen, as illustrated by the refusal of nine EU member states to sign on to the UN's Global Compact for Safe, Orderly and Regular Migration. Nevertheless, such incidents remain exceptions to the general pattern that the EU countries act together on most UN resolutions.[38] China's growing role in the United Nations is seen as both an opportunity for and a challenge to promoting this and other European values. China aspires to be recognized as a responsible power that is concerned with protecting not merely Chinese interests but also the common interests of peace and security for all states.[39] To this end, it has become a major contributor to UN responsibilities such as peacekeeping.[40] As wars in Iraq, Afghanistan, and Libya worsened the human rights situation for civilians, Europe recognized that, in contrast to the United States, China's UN policy offered support for Europe's preferences for avoiding the use of force and addressing problems of poverty and education to protect against human atrocities.[41]

European recognition of China's contributions to the UN humanitarian agenda exists alongside a growing concern that the country is a systemic rival that promotes an alternative model of governance that undermines the core European tenets of rule of law, human rights, democracy, and good governance. China's failure to observe basic human rights in Xinjiang and

---

[36] Ian Martin, "In Hindsight: What's Wrong with the Security Council?" Security Council Report, March 29, 2018, https://www.securitycouncilreport.org/monthly-forecast/2018-04/in_hindsight_whats_wrong_with_the_security_council.php.

[37] Ted Piccone, "U.S. Withdrawal from UN Human Rights Council Is 'America Alone,'" Brookings Institution, June 20, 2018, https://www.brookings.edu/blog/order-from-chaos/2018/06/20/u-s-withdrawal-from-u-n-human-rights-council-is-america-alone.

[38] Richard Gowan, "How Not to Save the World: EU Divisions at the UN," European Council on Foreign Relations, January 22, 2019, https://www.ecfr.eu/article/commentary_how_not_to_save_the_world_eu_divisions_at_the_un.

[39] Rosemary Foot, "'Doing Some Things' in the Xi Jinping Era: The United Nations as China's Venue of Choice," International Affairs 90, no. 5 (2014): 1085–1100.

[40] Sunghee Cho, "China's Participation in UN Peacekeeping Operations since the 2000s," Journal of Contemporary China 28, no. 117 (2019): 482–98.

[41] Liselotte Odgaard, "Responsibility to Protect (R2P) Goes to China: An Interpretivist Analysis of How China's Coexistence Policy Made It an R2P Insider" (paper presented at the International Studies Association convention, San Francisco, April 4–7, 2018).

its disregard for civil and political rights, as witnessed by the crackdown on human rights lawyers and defenders, are key sources of European skepticism toward China's ability to play a constructive normative role.[42] In 2018, China worked with states such as Sudan, Syria, and Venezuela to push a resolution through the UN Human Rights Council that promotes human rights by way of "mutually beneficial" or "constructive" cooperation. The resolution does not negate individual rights but emphasizes interstate cooperation. Whereas the United States opposed the proposal, the EU abstained due to the vagueness of the text.[43] The incident indicates that Europe still considers the jury to be out as to whether China's domestic human rights policies shed light on the positions that Beijing will take on future international human rights issues. As China's presence in the region grows, Europe is also closely watching to assess whether it will be subject to Chinese soft-power influence such as the large-scale financing of academic cooperation and strategic media communications.[44] However, on global normative issues, Europe is hesitant to choose sides between the United States and China as long as China is partially cooperative regarding Europe's liberal internationalist agenda.

Thus, at this early stage of U.S.-China competition, Europe is still trying to cooperate with both countries. The EU continues to prefer liberal transatlantic cooperation across a wide range of security, economic, and normative issues. At the same time, it works with China on preserving the central role of multilateral institutions and diplomacy at a time when the United States is putting unilateral measures and national interests first. China's tendency to revise multilateral institutions from within, while demonstrating domestic indifference to liberal political values such as the rule of law, democracy, and good governance, calls into question whether Europe and China have compatible interests and preferences. As in the economic sphere, Sino-U.S. competition is pushing Europe to develop instruments that allow it to pursue regional interests independently from Washington and Beijing. In the following section, this chapter investigates Europe's efforts to advance these interests.

---

[42] European Commission, "EU-China—A Strategic Outlook."

[43] François Godement, "China's Promotion of New Global Values," in Tellis, Szalwinski, and Wills, *Strategic Asia 2019*, 358–59.

[44] Fidel Sendagorta, "Triangle in the Long Game," Belfer Center for Science and International Affairs, Project on Europe and the Transatlantic Relationship, June 2019, 66, https://www.belfercenter.org/publication/triangle-long-game.

European Responses to U.S.-China Competition

Geopolitical Responses

Europe can no longer rely on transatlantic cooperation for meeting challenges. The president of the European Council Donald Tusk stated in May 2018 that the EU must be prepared to act alone without the United States.[45] China is not an alternative to the United States because of fundamental differences of interests and worldviews. However, on some issues, Europe and China have sufficient common interests to cooperate. The EU Commission's Strategic Outlook seeks reciprocal conditions governing relations with China to protect European economies against the distortive effects of Chinese economic practices.[46] But the EU's intention to cooperate with Beijing on climate change, interconnectivity, and the Iran nuclear deal has also encouraged it to define a platform for cooperation that is distinct from U.S. policies.

Europe is attempting to become more self-reliant by diversifying its international partnerships and multilateral institutional connections. U.S. pro-Israeli policies stop Washington from seeking cooperation with the League of Arab States. By contrast, the EU has established cooperation with this regional institution consisting of 22 member states in North Africa, the Horn of Africa, and Arabia. The two sides seek cooperation on the common security concerns of terrorism, radicalization, and organized crime. In addition, Europe's rapprochement with the league is a means of countering growing Russian and Chinese influence. The EU can cooperate with the Arab League because on some political issues, such as the 1967 Israeli settlements in Palestinian territories, the EU agrees with the Arab countries rather than with the United States.[47]

South Korea was the first Asian country to establish a trade deal with the EU in July 2011.[48] Since 2017, the EU also has enhanced its cooperation with Japan, the Association of Southeast Asian Nations (ASEAN), India, and Australia to facilitate an independent European influence in Asia. With these countries, the EU shares a commitment to free trade, multilateralism, and a rules-based order that protects the legal equality of states against great-power dominance. The EU and Japan acceded to an economic partnership agreement

---

[45] Mehreen Khan, "EU's Tusk: 'With Friends Like Trump, Who Needs Enemies?'" *Financial Times*, May 16, 2018, https://www.ft.com/content/c3002464-5907-11e8-b8b2-d6ceb45fa9d0.

[46] European Commission, "EU-China—A Strategic Outlook."

[47] European Council, "Sharm El-Sheikh Summit Declaration," February 25, 2019, https://www.consilium.europa.eu/en/press/press-releases/2019/02/25/sharm-el-sheikh-summit-declaration.

[48] European Commission, "Countries and Regions: South Korea," May 7, 2019, http://ec.europa.eu/trade/policy/countries-and-regions/countries/south-korea.

in December 2017, sending a powerful signal against protectionism to the United States and against undermining market economic principles to China.[49] In October 2018 the EU and Singapore signed a landmark free trade agreement (FTA), which Europe sees as a pathfinder to a wider FTA with ASEAN.[50] The EU contributes considerable capacity building to ASEAN to provide alternatives to China's BRI. The budget for 2014 to 2020 provides approximately 200 million euros for economic integration and 2 billion euros for poverty reduction and connectivity.[51] Since 2018, maritime security has become a focus area for EU-India cooperation. This focus includes the stationing of Indian escorts for humanitarian aid deliveries from the EU, cooperation on antipiracy efforts, and the strengthening of the links between European and Indian naval forces.[52] Substantial EU-Australian cooperation began to take shape in August 2017 when the two sides established a security dialogue. In June 2018, the EU and Australia began negotiating an FTA.[53]

The EU's heightened cooperation with Japan, South Korea, Australia, India, and ASEAN complements U.S. efforts to expand relations with liberal Indo-Pacific states. However, EU priorities deviate from U.S. priorities in that they put a higher premium on multilateral institutional cooperation and comprehensive FTAs than on unilateralism and protectionism. Europe's diversified strategic partnerships leave the door open for enhanced transatlantic cooperation in Asia. U.S. and European policies in Asia aim to push back at unsolicited Chinese economic and security policies. Their preferences for using different instruments to achieve this goal can be seen as complementary, provided that both sides accept that they have conflicting policies on some particular geopolitical and geoeconomic issues such as the Arab-Israeli conflict, the Iranian nuclear issue, and comprehensive FTAs.

[49] European Commission, "Key Elements of the EU-Japan Economic Partnership Agreement—Memo," December 12, 2018, http://trade.ec.europa.eu/doclib/press/index.cfm?id=1955.

[50] Zakir Hussain, "Singapore, European Union Sign Landmark Free Trade, Partnership Agreements," *Straits Times*, October 20, 2018, https://www.straitstimes.com/world/europe/singapore-eu-sign-landmark-free-trade-partnership-agreements.

[51] Mission of the European Union to ASEAN, "40 Years of EU-ASEAN Partnership and Prosperity: Trading and Investing Together," 2016/17, 28, https://eeas.europa.eu/sites/eeas/files/eu_asean_trade_investment_2017.pdf.

[52] Delegation of the European Union to India and Bhutan, "European Union Naval Forces—Port Visit to Mumbai," January 25, 2019, https://eeas.europa.eu/delegations/india/57118/european-union-naval-forces-port-visit-mumbai_en.

[53] "Australia–European Union Free Trade Agreement," Department of Foreign Affairs and Trade (Australia), June 18, 2019, https://dfat.gov.au/trade/agreements/negotiations/aeufta/Pages/default.aspx; and "Framework Agreement between the European Union and Its Member States, of the One Part, and Australia, of the Other Part," Department of Foreign Affairs and Trade (Australia), https://dfat.gov.au/geo/europe/european-union/Documents/european-union-australia-framework-agreement.pdf.

Security and Defense Responses

Doubts about the United States' commitment to European security and defense encourage Europe to redirect its security and defense policies. Germany and France, in particular, have pursued initiatives to kick-start European ambitions to develop an independent defense profile. The EU's next budget for 2021 to 2027 will be the first to directly allocate EU funding to defense.

In December 2017 the European Council decided to establish the Permanent Structured Cooperation (PESCO), in which 25 EU member states participate. This framework for defense cooperation was the result of a German-French compromise and allows member states to develop joint defense capabilities and invest in shared projects. By November 2018, the projects covered areas such as training, capability development, cyberdefense, and operational readiness on land, at sea, and in the air.[54] Although the European Council regards PESCO as complementary to NATO,[55] the United States views it as a competitor and as an example of Europe's unwillingness to engage in mutually beneficial defense cooperation.[56] In September 2017, France launched the European Intervention Initiative to equip Europe with a common intervention force, defense budget, and doctrine for action to enable European militaries to act convincingly together within a decade. France, Germany, Denmark, Belgium, the Netherlands, Spain, Estonia, Portugal, the United Kingdom, and Finland are members. Germany has criticized the initiative for not being sufficiently integrated into EU institutions to be open to all member states. However, the initiative ensures that European states that are not part of the EU's common security and defense policy, such as Britain and Denmark, are included in European defense projects. In addition, it sets out to create a common threat perception and shared instruments to address these threats.[57] At a time of mounting threats from Russia, North Africa, the Middle East, and Asia, this effort to develop a common strategy is essential to establishing a credible European defense. German-French quarrels over

---

[54] "Defence Cooperation: Council Assesses Progress Made in the Framework of PESCO after First Year of Implementation," European Council, Press Release, May 14, 2019, https://www.consilium.europa.eu/en/press/press-releases/2019/05/14/defence-cooperation-council-assesses-progress-made-in-the-framework-of-pesco-after-first-year-of-implementation.

[55] Dick Zandee, "PESCO Implementation: The Next Challenge," Clingendael Institute, Policy Report, September 28, 2018, https://www.clingendael.org/publication/pesco-implementation-next-challenge.

[56] Sebastian Sprenger, "European Union Rejects U.S. Claims to Internal Defense Coffers," *Defense News*, May 16, 2019, https://www.defensenews.com/global/europe/2019/05/16/european-union-rejects-us-claims-to-internal-defense-coffers.

[57] Frédéric Mauro, "The European Intervention Initiative: Why We Should Listen to German Chancellor Merkel," Institut de Relations Internationales et Stratégiques, July 16, 2018, https://www.iris-france.org/115776-the-european-intervention-initiative-why-we-should-listen-to-german-chancellor-merkel.

whether inclusion or ambition should be prioritized are minor rifts in their fundamental agreement about the need to ensure that the region can defend itself at a time of waning U.S. defense commitments to Europe.

These European defense initiatives are in the early planning stages, and it is too early to assess whether their implementation has been successful. However, the inclusion of countries that are skeptical of the EU, such as Britain and Denmark, in the construction of a European defense profile indicates that the structural forces for moving Europe toward greater unity on defense issues trump tendencies to regional fragmentation.

In the Indo-Pacific, Europe has begun to establish the preconditions for an independent security and defense presence, having realized that economic instruments of influence may be insufficient to address China's geopolitical agenda. Security concerns such as ensuring open shipping lanes in key trade corridors and guarding against the threat posed by China's cyberwarfare capabilities are as important to Europe as they are to the United States.[58] However, the EU is distancing itself from U.S. pressures to adopt a confrontational stance against China and thus needs to develop an independent Asian security and defense presence. EU institutions can facilitate a greater presence, but they do not have the powers to lead these efforts.

France has emerged as Washington's main European partner in adding military strength in Asia. Since 2016, France has mobilized support for an annual European deployment in the Indo-Pacific with a rotating cast from other European countries.[59] Initially, the UK was France's main partner, deploying vessels to conduct operations in support of freedom of navigation in the South China Sea. However, with Britain voting to withdraw from the EU, it is no longer positioned to play a key role in revitalizing transatlantic security cooperation.[60] At the same time, France is careful to maintain a balancing act of strengthening defense cooperation with the United States without alienating China. For example, in May 2019 a French air-defense destroyer sailed through the South China Sea without emulating the United States in conducting exercises close to Chinese-claimed features. However, without directly challenging China's presence, France still signaled that it considers the South China Sea to be international waters. Likewise, in April 2019 a French frigate transited the Taiwan Strait. The Chinese navy shadowed

[58] Matthew Karnitschnig, "For NATO, China Is the New Russia," *Politico*, April 4, 2019, https://www.politico.eu/article/for-nato-china-is-the-new-russia.

[59] Jean-Yves Le Drian, "The Challenges of Conflict Resolution" (speech at Shangri-La Dialogue, Singapore, June 5, 2016).

[60] For further discussion, see Liselotte Odgaard, "European Engagement in the Indo-Pacific: The Interplay between Institutional and Naval Diplomacy," *Asia Policy* 14, no. 4 (2019): 129–59.

the frigate, and China later disinvited France to the navy's 70th anniversary celebration in Qingdao. Although France did not plan to attend the naval parade, the maneuver effectively singled out France as a culprit. China's 2019 defense white paper states that the People's Liberation Army will resolutely defeat any country attempting to separate Taiwan from China and take actions to safeguard national unity at all costs.[61]

With China's navy expanding at a rapid clip, France's naval diplomacy has been well received in Washington, which is looking for partners willing to adopt hard-power responses to China's growing presence. The French tradition of a strong and independent defense profile and the country's Indo-Pacific territories provide it with unique strengths. By joining forces with like-minded Asian partners and including its overseas territories in base-sharing arrangements, France could help prove the point that European contributions to Indo-Pacific security are not to be dismissed. It remains to be seen in coming years whether other European states also contribute capabilities to the French effort on a scale that gives Europe, and not just France, a substantial regional defense footprint.

Europe is still in the early stages of developing an independent security and defense profile. Minor skirmishes between Germany and France over the relative importance of inclusiveness versus ambition are not enough to override the structural pressures for European countries to work together on independent defense capabilities.

Economic Responses

The EU is an important trading partner with both the United States and China. Approximately 30% of the EU's exports and more than 12% of its imports are from the United States, while more than 10% of its exports and almost 22% of its imports are from China. This makes the United States the EU's largest trade partner and China its second-largest trade partner.

The EU's 2019 summit statement with China demonstrated mutual interest in cooperation on issues where cooperation with the United States is impaired, such as free trade, WTO reform, and diplomacy toward Iran. It also committed China to addressing key European concerns regarding market access, discriminatory practices toward European companies, and forced technology transfers.[62] The agreement reflects enhanced European unity toward China and the two sides' mutual interest in signaling to Washington that they have alternative partners if the United States does not compromise.

---

[61] See Odgaard, "European Engagement in the Indo-Pacific."

[62] Author's interview with an EU government official, Washington, D.C., April 2019; and European Commission, "EU-China—A Strategic Outlook."

Stalled U.S.-European trade negotiations, postponed due to the U.S.-China trade war, are seen as a litmus test for the future of transatlantic relations.[63] Trade agreements with Asian states give Europe attractive alternatives to the United States. The EU's willingness to prioritize other trade partners and the United States' ongoing demands to include agriculture in negotiations, despite the EU's clear unwillingness to do so, indicate that both sides need to make significant compromises to restart negotiations.

On industrial policy, the EU performs an advisory role with some powers of enforcement toward the member states, making it harder for Europe to act as a unified bloc. China has rolled out BRI with negligible European participation in the process. Its state-focused economic policies have challenged market economic principles rejecting intellectual property theft, forced joint ventures, and unfair competition due to state subsidies. These differences demonstrate that China is an economic competitor to the EU in the pursuit of technological leadership.[64] China's practices have encouraged cooperation between the EU institutions and its member states on establishing defensive mechanisms to ensure a more balanced and reciprocal economic relationship with China. The EU Commission's ten action points on industrial policies to protect member states against the downsides of Chinese economic practices provide a platform of knowledge and networking that is intended to facilitate cooperation on defining best practices when entering into investment arrangements with Chinese actors.[65] China endorsed the action points by signing a joint statement at the 2019 EU-China summit, which provides Europe with a green light for closely surveilling Chinese compliance with European market economic regulations.[66]

The unfair advantages of Chinese industrial giants such as Huawei have sparked a debate in the United States and Europe about how to ensure competitiveness, either by strengthening antitrust regulations to protect start-up companies and consumer rights or by allowing for mergers with the economies of scale that let them compete with Chinese companies. In 2019 the European Commission blocked a merger of the largest regional suppliers in the rail market, Alstom and Siemens, despite prior French and German governmental approval, because it believed that the merger would harm competitiveness. The merger was meant to create a European match for China's state-owned China Railway Rolling Stock Corporation, which is forecast to become dominant in global rail markets. The case has sparked a

---

[63] Author's interview with an EU government official, Washington, D.C., April 2019.

[64] European Commission, "EU-China—A Strategic Outlook."

[65] Ibid.

[66] "EU-China Summit Joint Statement," European Council, April 9, 2019, https://www.consilium.europa.eu/fr/press/press-releases/2019/04/09/joint-statement-of-the-21st-eu-china-summit.

debate on how to reconcile European industrial and competition policies in a way that ensures that European companies are sufficiently sizeable to enjoy economies of scale that allow them to compete with gigantic U.S. and Chinese companies with major financial resources. This must be balanced by the concern not to violate European consumer interests in maintaining multiple European companies in any given manufacturing and service sector to ensure reasonable price levels and long-term industrial interests that allow innovative start-up companies to enter European markets.[67]

Europe recognizes that the issue of standards will be key in the development of new technologies. The lack of unified EU rules brings additional costs to companies and constitutes a security problem. In 2019 the president of the European Commission, Ursula von der Leyen, pledged that upgrading safety and liability rules for the development of digital platforms, services, and products and for the completion of the EU's proposed digital single market—which would eliminate internet barriers within the bloc—is a priority. In attempting to standardize the patchwork of national regulations, the EU intends to put particular emphasis on regulating artificial intelligence by harmonizing rules across the bloc and creating a dedicated regulator to ensure oversight and enforcement.[68]

Negotiations for a comprehensive EU-China agreement on investments have been ongoing since 2013. This would be "a key tool in rebalancing investment relations and in securing fair and equal treatment for EU companies operating in China."[69] While the outcome of these negotiations remains unknown, in 2019 an EU investment screening system entered into force. Chinese acquisitions in strategic sectors, such as semiconductors, robotics, and aerospace, have helped promote European unity.[70] The screening system will affect intangible technology transfers as well as China's targeting of Europe to acquire control or influence over European undertakings that may have repercussions for critical technologies, infrastructure, or sensitive information.[71] Although this leaves out export controls in areas such as

---

[67] Konstantinos Efstathiou, "The Alstom-Siemens Merger and the Need for European Champions," Bruegel, March 11, 2019, https://bruegel.org/2019/03/the-alstom-siemens-merger-and-the-need-for-european-champions.

[68] Valentina Pop, "No Relief for Big Tech under New EU Leadership," *Wall Street Journal*, September 2, 2019, https://www.wsj.com/articles/no-relief-for-big-tech-under-new-eu-leadership-11567428651.

[69] European Commission, "EU-China—A Strategic Outlook."

[70] Mathieu Duchâtel, "EU-China Relations Face a Bumpy Road in the Year Ahead," *South China Morning Post*, January 5, 2019, https://www.scmp.com/news/china/diplomacy/article/2180817/eu-china-relations-face-bumpy-road-year-ahead.

[71] "Regulation (EU) 2019/452 of the European Parliament and of the Council of 19 March 2019 Establishing a Framework for the Screening of Foreign Direct Investments into the Union," *Official Journal of the European Union*, March 19, 2019, https://eur-lex.europa.eu/eli/reg/2019/452/oj.

education and research, it is a promising beginning to the restructuring of EU-China relations in a way that takes the competitive elements seriously.

The EU's industrial policy initiatives address long-standing complaints in European business communities that Brussels has not offered guidelines for proper conduct regarding investment agreements with China. Companies focus on making a profit, and the Chinese market is attractive. For fear of being left out, most companies accept short-term gains in exchange for the transfer of know-how, even if Europe suffers long-term economic losses as a result.[72] It remains to be seen whether Chinese and European businesses comply with the EU's industrial policy guidelines. This will partially depend on the member states' adoption of legislation that reflects EU recommendations and partially on the EU's ability to develop coherent and enforceable regulations. Recent developments indicate that, although Europe may have a long way to go before its industrial policies offer sufficient protection against illicit Chinese business practices, progress has been made.

The Italian memorandum of understanding (MOU) on BRI in April 2019 did not receive much applause in Brussels. The EU refrained from signing on to BRI in 2017 because the initiative does not ensure adherence to basic EU and WTO market economic rules. However, the Italian MOU is in line with EU industrial and economic policies and arguably even makes progress on persuading China to sign on to European and global economic standards. The MOU commits China to transparency, reciprocity, openness, and environmental and financial sustainability, and the multilateral Asian Infrastructure Investment Bank (AIIB) is mentioned as the bilateral financial cooperation channel rather than murky Chinese banks.[73] Moreover, at the second BRI Forum held in April 2019, the leaders' joint communiqué stressed the importance of debt sustainability, environmental sustainability, transparency, and the rule of law. [74] At the inaugural forum two years ago, Beijing was not willing to adopt such language, despite the fact that doing so might have persuaded the EU to endorse BRI.[75] China is known to be long on words and short on actions when it comes to committing to demands that are not aligned with its interests and practices. Nevertheless, widespread

---

[72] Author's interview with a Danish executive officer from the Danish Industry Association, Copenhagen, November 2018.

[73] Giulio Pugliese, "As Rome Embraces the New Silk Road, Beijing May Be Turning the Corner," *South China Morning Post*, April 6, 2019, https://www.scmp.com/news/china/diplomacy/article/3004386/rome-embraces-new-silk-road-beijing-may-be-turning-corner.

[74] "Joint Communiqué of the Leaders' Roundtable of the 2nd Belt and Road Forum for International Cooperation," Ministry of Foreign Affairs of the People's Republic of China, April 27, 2019, https://www.fmprc.gov.cn/mfa_eng/zxxx_662805/t1658766.shtml.

[75] Mathieu Duchâtel, "China's Flexibility on Display at the Belt and Road Forum," Institut Montaigne, April 25, 2019, https://www.institutmontaigne.org/en/blog/chinas-flexibility-display-belt-and-road-forum.

criticism of Chinese BRI practices and cancellations of projects could ensure greater future Chinese compliance with such agreements.

Europe is also adopting offensive mechanisms to address the challenges posed by BRI. The 2018 Europe-Asia connectivity plan offers alternatives to the initiative across a wide range of security, trade, and cultural issues.[76] Although it is too early to assess its effects, the plan complements similar initiatives from the United States, which launched the Indo-Pacific infrastructure initiative in 2018, and from Japan, which established the Partnership for Quality Infrastructure Initiative in 2015. Multiple liberal alternatives are emerging to BRI, further increasing the likelihood of greater Chinese compliance with standards that Europe considers preconditions for economic cooperation.

In sum, Europe and the United States largely agree on the substance of their responses to illicit Chinese trade and investment practices. However, growing U.S. willingness to question the benefits of free trade and multilateral economic regulatory standards has prompted the emergence of independent European responses to China's economic challenges. These responses are founded on conditional cooperation with China rather than the U.S. model of competing with China across the board.

Normative Responses

The EU is committed by treaty to the values of human dignity, freedom, democracy, equality, the rule of law, and human rights.[77] The EU was awarded the Nobel Peace Prize in 2012 for its work on these issues. According to the Nobel committee, the stabilizing role that the EU has played has helped transform most of Europe from a continent of war to a continent of peace.[78] The rise of authoritarian populist governments in Europe, however, has challenged these normative foundations of the EU and provoked considerable debate. EU skeptics in Washington argue that the greatest threats to European unity do not come from the United States but from Europe itself.[79]

---

[76] European Commission, "Connecting Europe and Asia: Building Blocks for an EU Strategy," September 19, 2018, https://eeas.europa.eu/headquarters/headquarters-homepage/50724/connecting-europe-and-asia-building-blocks-eu-strategy_en.

[77] "Consolidated Versions of the Treaty on European Union and the Treaty on the Functioning of the European Union," *Official Journal of the European Union*, December 13, 2007, https://eur-lex.europa.eu/legal-content/EN/TXT/HTML/?uri=CELEX:12016ME/TXT&from=EN; and "Charter of Fundamental Rights of the European Union," *Official Journal of the European Union*, December 13, 2007, https://eur-lex.europa.eu/legal-content/EN/TXT/HTML/?uri=CELEX:12016P/TXT&from=EN.

[78] "The Nobel Peace Prize for 2012," Norwegian Nobel Committee, Press Release, October 12, 2012, https://www.nobelprize.org/prizes/peace/2012/press-release.

[79] Walter Russell Mead, "Europe's Challenge Is Decline, Not Trump," *Wall Street Journal*, February 18, 2019, https://www.wsj.com/articles/europes-challenge-is-decline-not-trump-11550519599.

The 2019 elections for the European Parliament did not see the broader gains for nationalist populist parties that many polls had projected. Although these parties did win a majority of the national vote in France, Italy, and the UK, there was a surge in support for liberal and green parties in France and the UK, as well as in Germany.[80] Perhaps more importantly, the differences within nationalist parties over issues such as migration and Russia cloud prospects for a united political right. The big voter turnout for the elections may be the most important trend. More than 50% of European voters participated, which was the highest turnout in two decades and a sharp increase from the last election in 2014.[81] The high turnout testifies to the widespread recognition in Europe that Brussels has a major influence on people's lives. That realization bodes well for Europe's ability to move toward greater unity.

Much attention has been given to the rise of parties in Europe with hard-line views on immigration and national sovereignty. Hungary and Poland have been singled out as EU countries that do not subscribe to basic European values of human rights. They view states such as Singapore, China, and Russia as political models, while abolishing independent judiciaries, changing the electoral system to favor the incumbent, exercising political control over the media, and nationalizing large parts of the private sector.[82] Such reforms constitute a broad assault on European political, economic, and social values. The U.S. administration's 2019 charm offensive in Eastern Europe to push back at growing Chinese influence as a result of the 17+1 initiative has been received with suspicion in Europe. Many in the region see this effort as fuel for the nationalist populist wave that has spread across the Western world because of the focus on economic deals that favor the United States rather than on the erosion of democracy.[83]

Despite all the fuss about the rise of nationalist populist forces in Europe, even in the most hard-nosed nationalist Eastern European countries there is little appetite for leaving the EU. A survey of the 28 EU member states found that 61% of respondents believe that their country's EU membership is beneficial, and 68% believe that their country has gained from being part of the EU. Support has returned to the peak level last recorded between the fall of the Berlin Wall in 1989 and the adoption of the Maastricht Treaty in 1992.

---

[80] "European Parliament 2019: Election Results," Bloomberg, June 7, 2019, https://www.bloomberg.com/graphics/2019-european-parliament-elections.

[81] Meg Anderson, "4 Takeaways from the European Parliament Election Results," NPR, May 27, 2019, https://www.npr.org/2019/05/27/727293356/4-takeaways-from-the-european-parliament-election-results.

[82] Dalibor Rohac, "Authoritarianism in the Heart of Europe," American Enterprise Institute, August 2018.

[83] Marc Santora, "In Eastern Europe, U.S. Officials Talk Deals, Not Erosion of Democracy," New York Times, February 15, 2019, https://www.nytimes.com/2019/02/15/world/europe/pence-pompeo-eastern-europe.html.

If a referendum on membership were held in each country, an absolute majority of respondents in 25 member states would vote to remain in the EU, while a plurality of respondents still share this view in the remaining 3: Italy, the Czech Republic, and the UK.[84] The main bearer of anti-liberal values among the EU heads of state, Hungarian prime minister Viktor Orbán, is reportedly among the most cooperative participants in the EU's work on most internal issues.[85]

These trends indicate that there is strong support for European unity because of a widespread recognition that only if Europe acts collectively will it carry enough weight to exercise influence in an era of U.S.-China competition. The political chaos of Brexit has driven the point home in EU-skeptical countries that they must work within the union to exercise influence. The low level of support for the nationalist populists in Denmark's 2019 election for the European Parliament exemplifies this tendency.[86] The rise of authoritarian populism reflects greater popular engagement in Europe, and with that comes a wider spectrum of voices, including those critical of EU institutions. This development does not mean that Europe is abandoning its value base, but it does mean that values promoted by specific policies must be directly tied to European interests. For example, extensive freedom of navigation and overflight rights serve European economic interests. This type of argument will increasingly define Europe's future international engagement.

Consequences and Political Implications

Paradoxically, the challenges that U.S.-China competition pose to European unity have increased the unity of the region. A United States that is increasingly skeptical of Europe and focuses more on its Asian partners, and a China that is rolling out its economic vision across Europe, with little concern for liberal market economic standards, help raise regional awareness that sovereignty is best exercised by working within Europe's institutional frameworks. This realization that uniting is necessary to exercise influence in a world of volatile alignment patterns and faltering global institutions facilitates a tendency to define European interests and to prioritize them over normative concerns. Interest-based policies allow EU institutions to accommodate the rise of authoritarianism and nationalism. The main drivers of greater unity are Germany and France. These countries have taken the lead

---

[84] "Spring 2019 Eurobarometer: Closer to the Citizens, Closer to the Ballots," European Parliament, Special Eurobarometer 91.1, 2019.

[85] Author's interview with an EU government official, Washington, D.C., April 2019.

[86] "European Parliament 2019: Election Results."

in developing innovative institutions that allow Europe to position itself as a strategic influence beyond its traditional stronghold of trade. Industrial policy and security and defense policy are areas in which a division of labor is emerging between the general recommendations of the EU institutions and the groups of countries that manage implementation.

Europe has looked to China as an alternative partner on some issues. For example, it does not share the U.S. view of China as a strategic opponent across the board and is likely to continue to work with Beijing on issues such as trade, Iran, and UN peacekeeping. However, China's implementation of economic policies in Europe without concern for European liberal values has caused the region to exuviate its trust in China's commitment to the rules-based international order. Likewise, the use of international institutions and agreements to advance Chinese interests, often at the expense of European interests, has compelled Europe to establish defensive and offensive mechanisms against Chinese policies that are considered detrimental to European stability and prosperity. Future cooperation between Europe and China is thus likely to be based on a more cautious approach and include continuous reassessments of the benefits derived from cooperation.

In an era of escalating U.S.-China competition, transatlantic cooperation continues to be the cornerstone of European efforts to strengthen regional unity and global influence. The challenges that China poses to U.S. security, economic prosperity, and global leadership encourage the United States to look for partners with both vested interests in pushing back at Chinese behavior and the capabilities to deliver meaningful contributions. Europe remains the most reliable and capable partner in this venture. It is the only other actor with a major global economic presence and worldwide security interests whose social, political, and economic structures are built on liberal values such as private-sector competition, liberal democracy, and individual freedom. This shared transatlantic identity aligns the United States and Europe regarding fundamental objectives such as basing economic prosperity on competition rather than on monopolistic behavior and state support, promoting sociopolitical stability through information sharing and freedom of expression rather than surveillance and oppression, and building security through freedom of movement and mutual defense obligations rather than spheres of influence and coercion. The challenges that China presents, such as the economic advancement of large state-owned enterprises, intellectual property theft and unsolicited information sharing, and encroachments on freedom of navigation, are of equal concern to the United States and Europe.

Transatlantic differences of interest are mainly instrumental. These differences emerge in quarrels over the usefulness of multilateral institutions in a world that is showing signs of the Balkanization of international standards. Another issue of contention is determining the proper balance between the use of force, diplomacy, and the rule of law at a time when coercive measures, authoritarian political mechanisms, and disregard for the sanctity of international treaties are gaining traction. However, the United States and Europe agree that China is at least partially promoting these tendencies.

Answering the question of how to manage these challenges could be facilitated by recognizing that there is a lot of low-hanging fruit to be picked in focusing on the complementarity of U.S. and European instrumental preferences. For example, EU–Arab League summits help address rising Chinese influence in the Arab world in ways that are not feasible for the United States. European economic, security, and defense partnerships with U.S. allies in Asia help build a formidable counterbalancing coalition against China and open avenues for coordinating infrastructure projects to push back against BRI. The right mix of U.S. punitive measures and European diplomacy may help keep Iran's destabilizing influence on the Middle East at bay. The establishment of independent European defense forces that are capable of addressing regional and global security challenges to partners in the Indo-Pacific and Eurasia and to principles such as freedom of navigation is necessary to defend the liberal world order. Focusing on the benefits of complementarity in transatlantic relations is key to effective cooperation on the common objective of demonstrating the superiority of liberal policies for promoting peace and prosperity.

EXECUTIVE SUMMARY

This chapter analyzes how bilateral tensions between the U.S. and China have played out in the Western Hemisphere.

MAIN ARGUMENT

Since 1978, China has been exporting manufactured goods to Latin America, and the latter sends back a rich array of raw materials to China. This cross-Pacific trade exploded upon China's 2001 entry into the World Trade Organization. Nevertheless, the core of China's relationship with Latin America is developmental in nature, something that Washington needs to grasp. The U.S. has adopted a hard-power narrative toward China's rising presence in the Americas, while Chinese soft power is the glue that binds the China–Latin America relationship. The U.S. towers over China in terms of trade and investment inflows to the Americas, while U.S.-China military competition in the region is negligible. In terms of the impact on specific countries, Canada and Mexico have been most adversely affected by U.S.-China competition.

POLICY IMPLICATIONS

- The U.S. needs to rely less on a hard-power narrative and harsh language about the evolving relationship between China and the countries of Central and South America. This discourse fails to capture the nature of China's ties with Latin America and drives possible allies further from the U.S.

- The U.S. insistence on renegotiating NAFTA in a mercantilist mold was misplaced. The new U.S.-Mexico-Canada Agreement puts the automobile sector most at risk, as content requirements that favor the U.S. market will disrupt regional value chains and disadvantage this sector at large.

- Rather than seeking to compete with China's Belt and Road Initiative, the U.S. needs to work with the Latin American countries to strengthen business practices (especially contract negotiations, transparency, and the rule of law) such that the initiative becomes a positive developmental force in the Americas rather than an economically destabilizing one.

U.S.-China Competition in the Western Hemisphere

Carol Wise

Until the late 1990s, China's interaction with the Western Hemisphere was primarily a G-7 affair focused on the United States and Canada. In the period between the launching of China's "reform and opening" project in 1978 and the advent of the Trump administration in 2017, relations between China and the Western Hemisphere were more or less manageable. Canada, for example, maintained a relationship with China throughout the Cold War and established formal diplomatic ties with the People's Republic of China (PRC) in 1970. On balance, Canada has been more flexible than the United States in its interactions with the non-Western authoritarian regime, but also more critical of China's dismal human rights record.[1] Given its status as the hegemonic leader of the liberal political-economic global order, the United States has had a more conflictual relationship with China, and formal diplomatic recognition did not occur until 1979. Since then, the stance of both Canada and the United States toward China has been one of constructive engagement, relying on some combination of incentives and disincentives.

With China's accession to the World Trade Organization (WTO) in 2001, economic and strategic tensions have increasingly come to define

Carol Wise is Professor of International Relations at the University of Southern California. She can be reached at <cwise@usc.edu>.

The author thanks an external reviewer for astute comments, the editors for their patience and guidance, and Claire He, Erin Piñeda, Lucy Santora, Yuhao Wang, and Chenyan Zhou for their consistently excellent research assistance. The Center for International Studies at the University of Southern California provided partial funding for this research. Parts of this chapter draw on Carol Wise, *Dragonomics: How Latin America Is Maximizing (or Missing Out on) China's International Development Strategy* (forthcoming from Yale University Press, 2020).

[1] Paul Evans, *Engaging China: Myth, Aspiration, and Strategy in Canadian Policy from Trudeau to Harper* (Toronto: University of Toronto Press, 2014), 23.

each country's respective relationship with China. Both the United States and Canada have long-running trade deficits with the PRC, both carefully vet FDI inflows from China as an economic security measure, and both have taken a vigilant stand against China's industrial espionage and violation of intellectual property rights. Both countries have also signed strategic partnership agreements initiated by China—the United States back in 1993 and Canada in 2005. From China's viewpoint, a strategic partnership refers to a mutually beneficial relationship, one that is win-win, reciprocal, and established on equal footing.[2]

With respect to Latin America and the Caribbean (LAC), in the late 1990s the possibility that China would come to play a significant role was remote, and it was even less probable that any such role would become a major point of contention between Beijing and Washington. In 2005, some in the U.S. Congress began to question "whether China will play by the rules of fair trade" in the region.[3] When Brazil-China trade surpassed the level of Brazil-U.S. trade in 2009, concerns arose around the Beltway. More recently, President Donald Trump's foreign policy team has shifted the China-U.S. bilateral relationship onto more conflictual terrain and defined the explosion of Chinese investment, loans, and trade with LAC since 2003 as a "threat."

There is no doubt that the Western Hemisphere is vital to the political, economic, and security interests of the United States. However, in this chapter I offer an alternative explanation for the burgeoning China-LAC relationship. Despite projecting the image of a behemoth Asian developmental state, China faces serious natural resource constraints. Most pressing is its urgent need to feed the world's largest population and to access resources to fuel the world's soon-to-be largest economy. Of necessity, the PRC has had to internationalize its development strategy through the incorporation of select resource-rich emerging economies in Africa, Southeast Asia, and increasingly Latin America. At a time when the focus of the Western multilateral banks is on reducing poverty and achieving the United Nations' sustainable development goals, China has funded projects that fill crucial infrastructure gaps in other emerging economies as part of its own internationalized development strategy.[4] These projects are closely linked to the production of goods and the extraction of resources that are then shipped back to China to spur domestic development.

---

[2] Feng Zhongping and Huang Jing, "China's Strategic Partnership Diplomacy: Engaging with a Changing World," European Strategic Partnerships Observatory, Working Paper, no. 8, June 2014.

[3] Dan Burton, "China's Influence in the Western Hemisphere," statement before the House Subcommittee on the Western Hemisphere, Washington, D.C., April 6, 2005, 5–7, https://www.govinfo.gov/content/pkg/CHRG-109hhrg20404/pdf/CHRG-109hhrg20404.pdf.

[4] Kevin Gallagher, The China Triangle: Latin America's China Boom and the Fate of the Washington Consensus (New York: Oxford University Press, 2016), 72.

This chapter proceeds as follows. The first section sets the historical backdrop for Chinese and U.S. relations with the Americas and identifies North America as the region most adversely affected by U.S.-China tensions. The second section then explores regional responses to U.S.-China competition in the Western Hemisphere from the standpoint of public diplomacy, elite interests, the winners and losers outside North America, and U.S.-China acrimony over China's Belt and Road Initiative (BRI). The concluding section briefly summarizes the chapter's main arguments and identifies possible policy implications.

How U.S. and Chinese Interests and Ambitions Intersect in the Americas

History Matters

China-LAC relations. Upon the founding of the PRC in 1949, there began a rich commercial, political, and cultural exchange between the leaders of the Chinese Communist Party (CCP) and civil-society groups within a number of countries in Latin America. Long before the normalization of diplomatic ties between China and its LAC partners, and even amid the U.S. embargo against trade with China, the PRC built people-to-people relations with civil-society factions in various LAC countries.[5] On the commercial front, Argentina and Mexico sold wheat to the PRC in the early 1960s, as did Canada, when a severe drought and the mismanagement of grain stocks during Chairman Mao Zedong's Great Leap Forward led to widespread death and famine. By the 1970s, Brazil was trading iron ore in exchange for Chinese oil, China had become the third-largest buyer of Chilean copper, and Chile was importing light industrial goods, chemical products, tools, and machinery from China.[6] Furthermore, Mexican producers had met with measured success in selling value-added manufactured goods to their Chinese counterparts.

Despite these growing economic ties, cross-Pacific relations were mostly political and cultural from roughly 1949 to 1989. The PRC's political outreach to LAC was twofold. First, Beijing was determined to gain diplomatic recognition from afar and to isolate the "renegade province" of Taiwan. On this count, the CCP made considerable gains within the LAC region (see **Table 1**). It was Mexican president Luis Echeverría's impassioned speech

---

[5] People-to-people contact refers to exchanges occurring between private, nongovernmental parties and was the cornerstone of the PRC's outreach to LAC states until the normalization of relations with regional countries.

[6] William A. Joseph, "China's Relations with Chile under Allende: A Case Study of Chinese Foreign Policy in Transition," *Studies in Comparative Communism* 18, no. 2 (1985): 140.

TABLE 1 Diplomatic relations between Western Hemisphere states and China

Country	Date established
Cuba	September 28, 1960
Canada	October 13, 1970
Chile	December 15, 1970
Peru	November 2, 1971
Mexico	February 14, 1972
Argentina*	February 19, 1972
Guyana	June 27, 1972
Jamaica	November 21, 1972
Trinidad and Tobago	June 20, 1974
Venezuela*	June 28, 1974
Brazil*	August 15, 1974
Suriname	May 28, 1976
Barbados	May 30, 1977
United States	January 1, 1979
Ecuador*	January 2, 1980
Colombia*	February 7, 1980
Antigua and Barbuda	January 1, 1983
Bolivia*	July 9, 1985
Uruguay*	February 3, 1988
Bahamas	May 22, 1997
Dominica	March 23, 2004
Grenada	January 27, 2005
Costa Rica	June 1, 2007
Panama	June 13, 2017
Dominican Republic	May 1, 2018
El Salvador	August 25, 2018

SOURCE: *The Republic of China Yearbook* (Taipei: ROC Government Information Office, 1996), 792–96; Dennis Van Vranken Hickey, *Taiwan's Security in the Changing International System* (Boulder: Lynne Rienner, 1997), 116, 118; Francisco Haro Navejas, "China's Relations with Central America and the Caribbean States: Reshaping the Region," in *China Engages Latin America: Tracing the Trajectory*, ed. Adrian H. Hearn and José Luis León-Manríquez (Boulder: Lynne Rienner, 2011), 203–20; Neil Connor, "Panama Cuts Ties with Taiwan in Major Diplomatic Coup," *Telegraph*, June 13, 2017; Austin Ramzy "Taiwan's Diplomatic Isolation Increases as Dominican Republic Recognizes China," *New York Times*, May 1, 2018; and Tracy Wilkinson, "U.S. Decries Salvadoran China Policy," *Los Angeles Times*, August 25, 2018.

NOTE: Asterisk indicates that the Republic of China (Taiwan) maintains an unofficial representative office. Taiwan maintains diplomatic relations with Belize, Guatemala, Haiti, Honduras, Nicaragua, Paraguay, St. Kitts and Nevis, and St. Vincent and the Grenadines.

before the United Nations in 1971 that rallied LAC votes for Taiwan's expulsion and China's entry later that same year.[7] UN entry for China dovetailed with Canadian prime minister Pierre Trudeau's strategy of "having Canada play a middle power role in bringing China in from the cold."[8] By 1974, Argentina, Brazil, Chile, Mexico, and Peru had all formally recognized the PRC and normalized diplomatic relations.

The CCP's second political strategy toward LAC was the recruitment of fellow radicals of a socialist-communist bent. Beijing interpreted Cuba's revolutionary victory of 1959 as a signal that "the Latin American peoples are standing in the forefront of...[the] struggle against U.S. Imperialism."[9] Prospective Latin American radicals were invited to China to meet personally with Mao and to participate in a six-month course on indoctrination. However, Fidel Castro's eventual siding with the Soviet Union against the PRC prompted the majority of LAC leftist political parties and would-be revolutionaries to follow suit. Of the 59 Communist parties that existed across the region in 1970, only 8 still looked to Beijing for guidance. By the time of Mao's death in 1976, China had stopped funding Communist parties and training insurgents from various LAC countries.

Cultural outreach toward the LAC region was embedded in China's "propaganda and invitations" strategy. William Ratliff writes that, beginning in 1953 "small groups of Chinese visited Latin America in cultural, trade, journalist, and youth delegations; larger numbers went in performing troupes on tour. Leading members of the Chinese delegations...talked with university presidents and newspaper editors, visited overseas Chinese communities, and went to meetings of local friendship associations."[10] The Chinese government returned these invitations to Latin Americans in kind. In 1956, a rare exhibit of Mexican art in Beijing displayed the mural painting *Gloriosa Victoria* by Diego Rivera, which in turn inspired a generation of Chinese mural artists painting in this tradition.[11] Another example is the outreach of Mexico's first ambassador to China, Eugenio Anguiano Roch, who sponsored an exhibit of Aztec artifacts at museums in Beijing and Shanghai in 1974. He also aired at the embassy in Beijing a Mexican movie about the 1938 nationalization of

---

[7] Frank Mora, "The People's Republic of China and Latin America: From Indifference to Engagement," *Asian Affairs* 24, no. 1 (1997): 35–58.

[8] Evans, *Engaging China*, 27.

[9] Quoted in William Ratliff, "Chinese Communist Cultural Diplomacy toward Latin America," *Hispanic American Historical Review* 49, no. 1 (1969): 55.

[10] Ibid., 66.

[11] *The Winds from Fusang: Mexico and China in the Twentieth Century* (Los Angeles: USC Asia-Pacific Museum, 2018), available at https://pacificasiamuseum.usc.edu/exhibitions/past/winds-from-fusang.

Mexico's oil industry under President Lázaro Cárdenas.[12] Both exhibits were a huge hit with the Chinese people.

In the wake of China's Cultural Revolution, the CCP began to quietly shed its aim of promoting a worldwide proletarian revolution and moved from its "third-worldist" stance toward the advocacy of multilateralism and nonintervention. Chinese leaders stressed their support for Argentina's claim over the Falkland/Malvina Islands, for the efforts of the Contadora Group to mediate the violent U.S.-sponsored Central American conflict underway at that time, and for the Cartagena Group's efforts to broker a more reasonable sharing of the debt burden with commercial lenders.[13] The Tiananmen Square massacre in 1989 appears to be what stunted the references to real-world politics and heartfelt cultural exchanges between China and the LAC region. Although Western governments shunned China, newly democratizing regimes in Latin America hardly missed a beat in welcoming the country back into their fold. The difference this time was China's insistence on framing the relationship in mainly business and economic terms.

Just a year after Tiananmen, President Yang Shangkun made China's first executive-level visits to Argentina, Brazil, Chile, Mexico, and Uruguay. During this trip, he announced his country's priorities for engaging with LAC (trade, joint FDI ventures, collaboration in the extraction of natural resources, and exchanges in science and technology) and touted the distinctly apolitical "five principles of peaceful coexistence."[14] The PRC went so far as to designate Brazil as its first strategic partner in 1993, an added enticement to sweep Tiananmen under the carpet while bestowing on Brazil the status of a great power. If anything, both China and its LAC partners have since been overly cautious by ignoring or enshrouding possible political frictions in diplomatic euphemisms. This includes silence on China's systematic abuse of human rights and mutual attempts to bury the social protests over environmental damage that both Chinese investors and LAC host governments have faced in launching mining and hydroelectric projects.[15]

---

[12] Adrian H. Hearn, "Mexico, China and the Politics of Trust," *Latin America Perspectives* 42, no. 6 (2015): 120–21.

[13] Wolfgang Deckers, "Latin America: How the Chinese See the Region," *Pacific Review* 2, no. 3 (1989): 246–51.

[14] Mapped out by the Chinese leadership before 1949, the five principles of peaceful coexistence are (1) mutual respect for each other's territorial integrity and sovereignty, (2) mutual nonaggression, (3) mutual noninterference in each other's internal affairs, (4) equality and mutual benefit, and (5) peaceful coexistence.

[15] Rebecca Ray, Kevin P. Gallagher, Andrés López, and Cynthia A. Sanborn, eds., *China en América Latina: Lecciones para la cooperación Sur-Sur y el desarrollo sostenible* [China in Latin America: Lessons for South-South Cooperation and Sustainable Development] (Lima: Universidad del Pacífico Press, 2016).

U.S.-LAC relations. For decades, the literature on U.S. foreign policy toward Latin America has lamented the benign neglect and sporadic nature of bilateral relations in the post–World War II era, including intermittent military interventions. During the war, political and economic cooperation was at one of its high points. The United States signed commodity agreements with various LAC countries and negotiated bilateral defense agreements with Brazil and Mexico, while Congress granted funds for the modernization of regional infrastructure, including the construction of the Pan-American Highway.[16] Early in the post–World War II era, political leaders in Latin America welcomed this developmental thrust of U.S. policy and interpreted it as a fresh start in relations. However, they were taken aback when Washington made clear that the postwar focus of U.S. foreign policy would be the reconstruction of Europe and Northeast Asia. Not only would there be no equivalent of the Marshall Plan for Latin America, but U.S. attention toward the region would turn narrowly on the imperative to block the spread of Communism to the Western Hemisphere.

From this period all the way up to the fall of the Berlin Wall in 1989, Latin America was a pawn of sorts in the game of Cold War politics. We have seen that during the 1950s and 1960s the CCP did indeed set its sights on the recruitment of Latin American radical parties to its cause, but these efforts failed in the end. The Communist regime in the Soviet Union stoked the biggest U.S. fears of Communist encroachment in the Western Hemisphere. As in times past, the United States stood ready to intervene in the event of a perceived threat from the Soviet bloc. Washington successfully unseated reformist presidents in Guatemala and the Dominican Republic, as well as Marxist-Communist heads of state in Chile and Nicaragua. The Castro brothers in Cuba were the only radicals to survive repeated U.S. attempts at intervention.

Following his 1961 Bay of Pigs fiasco, President John F. Kennedy sought to intermingle some carrots with this big stick approach. He launched the Alliance for Progress in 1961, which saw some $10.2 billion in aid allocated to the region until the program's termination in 1969. Following Kennedy's death, his successors quietly began to reduce the program's budget, which dwindled to around $335 million by 1969.[17] Hindsight shows that this would be the last big burst of U.S. development aid allotted to the LAC region, as subsequent administrations began advocating private enterprise and self-help. Despite repeated proclamations by consecutive U.S. administrations

---

[16] Victor Bulmer-Thomas, *The Economic History of Latin America since Independence*, 2nd ed. (Cambridge: Cambridge University Press, 2003), 250–51; and Michael J. Kryzanek, *U.S.-Latin American Relations*, 4th ed. (Westport: Praeger, 2008), 55–56.

[17] Jerome Levinson and Juan de Onís, *The Alliance That Lost Its Way* (Chicago: Quadrangle Books, 1970).

concerning the need to prioritize ties with Latin America, Washington's lost opportunities for a more constructive working relationship with the region are palpable.

The nadir was perhaps 2005, when President George W. Bush's arrival at the Summit of the Americas ministerial meeting in Argentina elicited angry street mobs and the burning of both effigies in his likeness and U.S. flags to protest the U.S. invasion of Iraq. Although the advent of the Obama administration in 2008 saw a renewed commitment to mending relations with the region, and President Barack Obama did indeed make three diplomatic trips to Latin America during his first term, by 2011 a number of loose ends continued to dangle. According to a news report in 2011, "diplomatic tensions have left the United States without ambassadors in Bolivia, Venezuela, Ecuador and Mexico. Free trade agreements (FTAs) long sought by Panama and Colombia…remain stalled by domestic political fights, while China has moved ahead of the United States to become Brazil's most important trading partner."[18] These leadership lapses suggest the extent to which U.S. policymakers have come to take the United States' primacy in the Americas for granted and failed to exercise regional leadership on a par with its status.

Toward the end of the Obama years, Secretary of State John Kerry offered an olive branch in a speech made before the Organization of American States: "The era of the Monroe Doctrine is over.…The relationship we seek…is not about a United States declaration about how and when it will intervene in the affairs of other American states. It's about…the decisions that we make as partners to advance the values and the interests that we share."[19] But since Donald Trump entered office in 2017, Washington has dropped any semblance of this soft-power, liberal internationalist discourse and replaced it with the reassertion of U.S. dominance in the region. Nor are there any of the proclamations characteristic of the Clinton and Obama administrations about the need to prioritize and revitalize ties with Latin America. During a February 2018 tour of the region, then secretary of state Rex Tillerson trumpeted a revival of the Monroe Doctrine and warned regional leaders about China's predatory trade and investment practices. Tillerson's criticism of China prompted a handful of South American policy officials to boast publicly of their more constructive partnership with China.[20]

---

[18] Ginger Thompson and Simon Romero, "Clinton Aims to Improve Ties with Latin America," *New York Times*, May 18, 2011, http://www.nytimes.com/2011/05/19/world/americas.

[19] Zachary Keck, "The U.S. Renounces the Monroe Doctrine?" *Diplomat*, November 21, 2013, http://thediplomat.com/2013/11/the-us-renounces-the-monroe-doctrine.

[20] "Perú defiende a China tras críticas de EE.UU. sobre su influencia en la región" [Peru Defends China after U.S. Criticism of China's Influence in the Region], *Gestión*, February 7, 2018, https://gestion.pe/economia/peru-defiende-china-criticas-ee-uu-influencia-region-226664.

The North American Quagmire: Bearing the Brunt of U.S.-China Hostilities

As a candidate, Trump vilified the North American Free Trade Agreement (NAFTA) and made its renegotiation one of the main economic pillars of his campaign. Mexico was the villain in this narrative, due to its long-running trade surplus with the United States and its failure to halt the entry of undocumented workers into the U.S. market. Once elected, Trump fulfilled a campaign promise by renegotiating NAFTA, now the U.S.-Mexico-Canada Agreement (USMCA).[21] The USMCA actually raises trade and investment barriers in North America and is problematic for Mexico, in particular. Another of Trump's pledges on the campaign trail was to reduce the U.S. trade deficit with China. The White House launched a trade war against China in March 2018. As a result, Canada has found itself on the outs with China due to its entanglement in the U.S.-China fight over the trade practices of the Chinese telecom giant Huawei. The following discussion will consider the effects of U.S.-China competition on both Mexico and Canada.

Mexico. After gaining independence from Spain in 1821, Mexico was most at odds with the United States over what it perceived as the latter's imperialistic stance and chronic interference. As the Mexican historian Enrique Krauze wrote, "The first and most serious offense was of course the American invasion of Mexico in 1846 and the subsequent Mexican-American War, which resulted in Mexico losing more than half of its territory."[22] Nearly 175 years later, the U.S.-Mexico relationship had matured, culminating with Mexico's entry into NAFTA in 1994. By the turn of the new millennium, China had become more problematic for Mexico. Although the two countries had enjoyed a cordial bilateral relationship until the early 1990s, this evaporated under the thrust of chronic trade disputes.[23] With the election of Trump in 2016, Mexico could no longer seek political-economic solace from its position within NAFTA. As Krauze explains, "The victory of Mr. Trump has changed all the rules…a new period of confrontation has arisen, not military but surely commercial, diplomatic, strategic, social and ethnic."[24]

[21] Alan Beattie and James Politi, "How Is Donald Trump's USMCA Trade Deal Different from NAFTA?" *Financial Times*, October 1, 2019, https://www.ft.com/content/92e9ce0a-c55f-11e8-bc21-54264d1c4647.

[22] Enrique Krauze, "Trump Threatens a Good Neighbor," *New York Times*, January 17, 2017, https://www.nytimes.com/2017/01/17/opinion/trump-threatens-a-good-neighbor.html. See also Michael Reid, *Forgotten Continent: The Battle for Latin America's Soul* (New Haven: Yale University Press, 2007), 74–75.

[23] Romer Cornejo, Francisco Javier Haro Navejas, and José Luis León-Manríquez, "Trade Issues and Beyond: Mexican Perceptions on Contemporary China," *Latin American Policy* 4, no. 1 (2013): 57–75.

[24] Krauze, "Trump Threatens a Good Neighbor."

Thus, in the run-up to its own presidential election in 2018, Mexico found itself wedged quite uncomfortably between the two largest and most powerful players in the global economy. Tensions with China first began when the bilateral trade balance swung in China's favor in the early 1990s (and have not abated since). The second blow came with China's accession to the WTO in 2001, which Mexico had tried unsuccessfully to veto. In 2003, China bumped Mexico down to third place in the ranking of U.S. trade partners, and by 2012 more than half of Mexico's manufactured exports to the U.S. market were under direct threat from Chinese competition.[25] To their credit, Mexican policymakers had seized on NAFTA as a means to diversify away from commodity exports and build a manufacturing-based export-led development model. The rise of China, however, has been the Achilles heel in this strategy, as consecutive Mexican administrations fought Chinese competition through protectionism and the filing of antidumping complaints against the PRC at the WTO. Hindsight suggests that Mexico would have benefited more by designing its own set of Asian-style public policies to promote manufactured exports that could compete with China.

One important feat is that Mexican producers still outperform China in the quality of cars, trucks, and related parts and accessories. Despite the sophisticated automobile production and export value chain that spans North America under NAFTA, the Trump administration has repeatedly threatened and intermittently imposed tariffs on Mexico as a punishment for its failure to halt the northward flow of undocumented workers into the United States. Within the renegotiated USMCA, the automobile sector will be subject to higher North American content requirements and biased toward boosting production in the United States. This is protectionism, and it is most detrimental to Mexico, which was given an ultimatum by Washington. China, for its part, has tried and thus far failed to invest significantly in Mexico's automobile and transportation sectors. The 2018 election of President Andrés Manuel López Obrador on an unprecedented third-party ticket also augured a new wave of Mexican nationalism, which has led the government to reconsider China's $2 billion investment in Mexican oil exploration contracts.

Like the United States and Canada, Mexico has a strategic partnership with China. Negotiated in 2003, from China's perspective "strategic" means that cooperation is long-term, stable, and transcends ideology and individual events; "partner" suggests that the bond is mutually beneficial and established on equal footing.[26] China's Ministry of Commerce and Mexico's

---

[25] Enrique Dussel Peters and Kevin P. Gallagher, "NAFTA's Uninvited Guest: China and the Disintegration of North American Trade," *CEPAL Review*, no. 110 (2013): 83–108.

[26] Yanran Xu, *China's Strategic Partnerships in Latin America: Case Studies of China's Oil Diplomacy in Argentina, Brazil, Mexico and Venezuela, 1990 to 2015* (Lanham: Lexington Books, 2017).

Secretariat of Economy bolstered this strategic partnership with the creation of a permanent bilateral commission and three high-level groups to focus generally on the strengthening of trade and investment ties between the two countries. Together, China and Mexico have contributed to a $2.4 billion fund, and the two countries established a joint action program to enhance a comprehensive strategic association.[27] These various ventures, however, have thus far resulted in naught, with each side blaming the other. Until the advent of the Trump administration, Mexico's political and economic orientation toward NAFTA superseded its relationship with China. To date, Sino-Mexican institutional venues have been treated as a fallback strategy. Yet it seems that the time has come for the Obrador administration to embrace these mechanisms and pursue better relations with China through them as a hedge against U.S. hostility.

Canada. Since entering into its strategic partnership with China in 2005, Canada has further pursued the bilateral relationship through the G-20 and, as of 2018, through the new Canada-China Economic and Financial Strategic Dialogue. Both countries managed to set aside earlier differences over human rights and resource exploitation that prevailed during the premiership of Stephen Harper from 2006 to 2015 and were on track to declare 2018 as the "China-Canada tourism year," complete a feasibility study for the negotiation of an FTA, and open up a chain of Canada's iconic Tim Horton coffee shops in mainland China.[28] But all these initiatives froze in December 2018 with the Canadian government's arrest of Huawei CFO Meng Wanzhou in British Columbia under an extradition treaty with the United States. Because of the treaty, Canada had no choice but to arrest Meng, and it has since held her under house arrest in Vancouver. Canada's relations with China have all but collapsed as a result.

Since the arrest of Meng, Chinese trade officials have cited phytosanitary reasons for banning imports of all Canadian meats, the bulk of canola oil, and most grains. Beijing also has arrested two Canadians on charges of spying and pronounced a death sentence on a Canadian citizen for selling illicit drugs in China. These are just the highlights of Chinese retaliation against Canada as a direct result of U.S.-China tensions over Huawei. In January 2019, Canada recalled its ambassador from China.

---

[27] "China, Mexico Vow to Enhance Political Dialogue," Xinhua, May 6, 2013, http://news.xinhuanet.com/english/china/2013–06/05/c_132432564.htm.

[28] "2018 Will Be the China-Canada Tourism Year," Xinhua, December 4, 2017, http://www.xinhuanet.com/travel/2017-12/04/c_1122054927.htm; "Chinese Ministry of Commerce: The Feasibility Study of the China-Canada Free Trade Agreement Is Basically Completed," Xinhua, December 12, 2017, http://m.xinhuanet.com/2017-12/07/c_1122075998.htm; and "Canadian Famous Brand Tim Hortons Gets into China," Xinhua, July 12, 2018, http://m.xinhuanet.com/2018-07/12/c_1123116405.htm.

According to one Canadian policymaker, "China is important, but not big enough to impact the Canadian economy."[29] Only 4%–5% of Canadian exports go to China, and total Chinese FDI inflows to Canada from 2005 to 2019 were around $54.7 billion.[30] Like the United States, Canada is a service-based economy, and the bulk of its trade and FDI are oriented toward the U.S. market in a range of high value–added sectors.[31]

A U.S.-China Arms Race in the Americas?

On a global scale, in 2015 the United States accounted for 41% of arms transfer agreements with developing nations and China accounted for just 9%.[32] China's arms transfers to LAC have more than tripled since 2008 and averaged $2.7 billion annually from 2012 to 2015; average U.S. arms transfers to the region held steady at $2.6 billion annually during the same period. To put these numbers in perspective, from 2012 to 2015 China's arms sales to LAC averaged 16% of the country's total arms sales, whereas around 46% went to Africa and 10% went to Asia over the same period. Given that the United States and China are now close competitors in arms sales to LAC, does China pose a challenge to U.S. dominance in this area?

A report from the U.S.-China Economic and Security Review Commission states that China poses no obvious security threat to the region at this time.[33] The report identifies two phases of Chinese arms sales to LAC: "First, low-level military sales and exchanges of items like transport aircraft and anti-tank missiles (1990–2000), and second, sales worth approximately US$100 million a year of more sophisticated equipment such as aircraft, radar, and air-to-air missiles, mainly to Venezuela but also to Ecuador, Peru, Bolivia, and Argentina (2000–2015)."[34] More recently, China has ventured into high-tech military agreements with LAC countries. For instance, former Argentine president Cristina Fernández de Kirchner negotiated a number of clandestine agreements with China, including the purchase of expensive fighter jets and the construction of a satellite and space control station

[29] Author's off-the-record interview with a senior Canadian policymaker.

[30] "China Global Investment Tracker," American Enterprise Institute, https://www.aei.org/china-global-investment-tracker.

[31] Carol Wise, "The U.S. Competitive Liberalization Strategy: Canada's Policy Options," in *Canada among Nations 2007*, ed. Jean Daudelin and Daniel Schwanen (Montreal: McGill-Queens University Press, 2008).

[32] The data cited in this paragraph can be found in Catherine A. Theohary, "Conventional Arms Transfers to Developing Nations, 2008–2015," Congressional Research Service, CRS Report for Congress, R44716, December 19, 2016, https://fas.org/sgp/crs/weapons/R44716.pdf.

[33] Quoted in Ted Piccone, "The Geopolitics of China's Rise in Latin America," Brookings Institution, Geoeconomics and Global Issues Paper, no. 2, November 2016, 24.

[34] Ibid., 8–9.

in Patagonia. The subsequent administration of President Mauricio Macri canceled this order and negotiated an agreement with Beijing that the use of the Patagonian station would be solely for "peaceful purposes."[35]

However, others are more equivocal about these trends. Allan Nixon points to China's lower prices and lack of conditionality in selling arms to LAC countries.[36] This is an important consideration, especially given that in 2017 China built its first overseas military base in Djibouti. If China were to attempt to do the same in Buenos Aires or Rio de Janeiro, this would be a geopolitical catastrophe from the standpoint of the entire Western alliance. Michael Beckley argues why this scenario is improbable:

> Inefficiencies and barriers drag down China's military might. On average, Chinese weapons systems are roughly half as capable as those of the United States in terms of range, firepower, and accuracy....Moreover, border defense and internal security consume at least 35 percent of China's military budget and bog down half of its active-duty force.[37]

The breakdown of democracy in Venezuela in August 2017 offered a concrete opportunity for China to step into the fray and thus intrude on U.S. regional dominance. The United States and a number of Latin American states refused to recognize the fraudulent Venezuelan vote, and the United States promptly announced sanctions against both President Nicolás Maduro and Venezuela. At least one Chinese scholar has argued that Beijing is waiting in the wings "to create a 'sphere of influence' in the traditional 'backyard' of the United States…in retaliation for the U.S. containment and encirclement of China" in Asia.[38] Evan Ellis lent credence to this view in congressional testimony, arguing that Chinese credit lines and arms sales to Venezuela have bolstered its ability to defy the United States.[39] Venezuela's estimated $20 billion in debt-payment arrears to China is omitted from Evans's testimony, as is any reference to the creditor trap in which Venezuela has now ensnared China.

China has reached out to Venezuela's democratic opposition in hopes that it would honor the country's contractual obligations post-Maduro and has

---

[35] Ernesto Londoño, "From a Space Station in Argentina, China Expands Its Reach in Latin America," *New York Times*, July 28, 2018, https://www.nytimes.com/2018/07/28/world/americas/china-latin-america.html.

[36] Allan Nixon, "China's Growing Arms Sales to Latin America," *Diplomat*, August 24, 2016, https://thediplomat.com/2016/08/chinas-growing-arms-sales-to-latin-america.

[37] Michael Beckley, "Stop Obsessing about China," *Foreign Affairs*, September 21, 2018, https://www.foreignaffairs.com/articles/china/2018-09-21/stop-obsessing-about-china.

[38] Lei Yu, "China's Strategic Partnership with Latin America: A Fulcrum in China's Rise," *International Affairs* 91, no. 5 (2015): 1048.

[39] R. Evan Ellis, "The Influence of Extra-Hemispheric Actors on the Crisis in Venezuela," testimony to the House Subcommittee on Western Hemisphere Affairs, Washington, D.C., September 13, 2017.

sought to renegotiate $67.2 billion in outstanding loans to Venezuela.[40] For hawks, this is a strategic ploy to lure Venezuela further into China's orbit.[41] For others, this is one of any number of efforts on China's part to rectify earlier errors related to its nonconditional lending practices.[42] To be clear, both Russia and China have sold arms to Venezuela, and the phenomenon of large arms sales to authoritarian leaders like Maduro is nothing new in Latin America. What is new is the passivity of the United States when faced with the dissolution of a democratic regime in its own backyard. As for China's military incursions into the Western Hemisphere, Beijing is emphatic that its only motive is to explore the opportunities and challenges for military and security cooperation between China and Latin America.[43]

The Economic Scenario: Complementarities and Asymmetries

Arms transfers and military expenditures are one way of assessing the projection of hegemonic power in a given region. Other traditional measures of hegemonic might are in the economic realm, including trade and FDI flows. On trade, in 2018 total exports and imports between China and Latin America amounted to nearly $306 billion, whereas total U.S.-LAC trade was around $896 billion in the same year. U.S. direct investment in LAC reached an unprecedented $1 trillion in 2017,[44] whereas China's FDI in LAC amounted to only $109 billion the same year.[45] A sizeable share of FDI inflows to Latin America from the United States and China are channeled through the Cayman and British Virgin Islands, mainly for tax purposes, which makes it difficult to gauge the precise amount that has actually been invested in each country. Although China has become the most important partner in terms of

---

[40] Lucy Hornby and Andres Schipani, "China Seeks to Renegotiate Venezuela Loans," *Financial Times*, June 19, 2016, https://www.ft.com/content/18169fbe-33da-11e6-bda0-04585c31b153.

[41] This, for example, is the position of Ellis, "The Influence of Extra-Hemispheric Actors on the Crisis in Venezuela."

[42] Tom Hancock, "China Renegotiated $50 Billion in Loans to Developing Countries," *Financial Times*, April 29, 2019, https://www.ft.com/content/0b207552-6977-11e9-80c7-60ee53e6681d.

[43] "China Has No Military Base in Latin America, No Imperialist Goals," Xinhua, February 5, 2018, http://www.xinhuanet.com/mil/2018-02/05/c_129805866.htm; and Baiyun Yi, "Head of the Latin American Division of the Ministry of Foreign Affairs Refutes Pompeo's Comments," *Global Times*, April 17, 2019, https://world.huanqiu.com/article/9CaKrnKjRfj.

[44] "U.S. Direct Investment Abroad: Selected Items by Country of Foreign Affiliate, 2014–2017," U.S. Department of Commerce, Bureau of Economic Analysis, https://www.bea.gov/international/di1usdbal.

[45] Enrique Dussel Peters, "Monitor de la OFDI de China en América Latina y el Caribe" [OFDI from China to Latin American and the Caribbean Monitor], Latin America and the Caribbean Network on China, National Autonomous University, March 21, 2019, http://www.redalc-china.org/monitor/images/pdfs/menuprincipal/DusselPeters_MonitorOFDI_2019_Esp.pdf.

total trade for Argentina, Brazil, Chile, Peru, and Uruguay, the United States is still indisputably the dominant economic actor in the region.

Further examination of the participation of both the United States and China in Latin America suggests an emerging division of labor. Whereas raw materials captured just 10% of U.S. FDI in LAC in 2017, less than 10% of the total Chinese FDI to the region from 2000 to 2017 flowed into the manufacturing sector. Raw materials captured close to 50% of Chinese FDI inflows to LAC during this period, while services related to raw material extraction and transport counted for about 30% over the same period. In sum, the data depicts a mirror image with regard to U.S.-China economic participation. U.S. investors will no doubt continue to promote property rights, the rule of law, and investment in services and manufacturing in the region, while China will do the heavy lifting with trade expansion, resource extraction, infrastructure investment, and a range of other developmental endeavors.

The China-LAC trade and investment relationship is similarly complementary, although not entirely satisfactory from the standpoint of regional countries. With the exception of Costa Rica and Mexico, both of which carry large trade deficits with China and export a small share of value-added manufactured goods to the mainland, the pattern of trade between China and its other strategic partners has conformed to the old-fashioned comparative advantage model that existed in the region at the beginning of the twentieth century. LAC countries mainly export raw materials to China and import value-added manufactured goods back from China. FDI patterns reflect this same asymmetry. Total LAC FDI outflows to China from 2003 to 2018 are estimated at around $5.3 billion, whereas Chinese outflows of FDI to LAC during the same period are estimated to be around $129.8 billion.[46]

Put simply, LAC countries have not kept pace with China in the manufacturing sector over the past twenty years. China's gains in this area since the early 1980s are the result of highly focused expenditures and policies that have promoted science, technological adaptation, advanced education in hard science fields, and R&D.[47] Although Latin America is not unique in facing these competitiveness challenges, Secretary of State Mike Pompeo has attributed this trend to China's resource imperialism. As will be discussed in

---

[46] "Meet the Latin Americans Making It Big in China," *Americas Quarterly*, April 23, 2019, https://www.americasquarterly.org/content/meet-latin-americans-making-it-big-china-2; and Dussel Peters, "Monitor de la OFDI de China en América Latina y el Caribe."

[47] Kevin P. Gallagher and Roberto Porzecanski, *The Dragon in the Room: China and the Future of Latin American Industrialization* (Stanford: Stanford University Press, 2011).

the next section, China has sought to take some of the sting out of these trade and FDI asymmetries by establishing several funds to help close the gaps.

Regional Responses to U.S.-China Competition in the Americas

Traditional Diplomacy

The analysis thus far has delineated the ways in which China's global reach has crystallized in Latin America. As evidence of its growing commitment to the region, China obtained permanent observer status at the Organization of American States in 2004 and paid the $300 million entry fee to become a full-fledged member of the Inter-American Development Bank (IDB) in 2008. Under an arrangement between the Export-Import Bank of China and the IDB, China also established a $1.8 billion Latin American fund to spur equity investments in the region's infrastructure, medium-sized enterprises, and natural resources. Moreover, China has set up three separate regional finance platforms that together total $35 billion in credit for industrial cooperation, infrastructure, and other productive projects.[48] In January 2016, China led the establishment of the Asian Infrastructure Investment Bank (AIIB) for the explicit purpose of financing transportation infrastructure and connectivity. Canada is a founding member of the AIIB, Brazil is a prospective founding member, and Argentina, Bolivia, Chile, Ecuador, Peru, Uruguay, and Venezuela are all prospective members.

Despite strident U.S. criticism, all these ventures fall under the umbrella of standard economic diplomacy. Although the Obama administration did all it could to thwart the launch of the AIIB, four of its G-7 partners broke ranks and joined on. Interestingly, the World Bank and the Asian Development Bank have partnered with the AIIB on a number of projects that surpass the resources of any one of these institutions.[49] Even if it will remain symbolic for some time to come, the inclusion of eight LAC countries as prospective members is an example of Beijing's effective use of soft power in the economic realm. This, in turn, has enabled China to achieve some of its own goals with regard to the "one China" policy; the negotiation of FTAs in the LAC region with Chile, Costa Rica, and Peru; and the expansion of BRI into the Western Hemisphere.

[48] Rebecca Ray and Kevin Gallagher, "China–Latin America Economic Bulletin 2015 Edition," Boston University, Global Economic Governance Initiative, Discussion Paper, September 2015.

[49] Hong Yu, "Motivation behind China's 'One Belt, One Road' Initiative and Establishment of the Asian Infrastructure and Investment Bank," *Journal of Contemporary China* 26, no. 105 (2017): 353–68.

With respect to the one-China policy, between 2004 and 2018 six LAC countries (Dominica, Grenada, Costa Rica, Panama, the Dominican Republic, and El Salvador) switched diplomatic recognition from Taiwan to China.[50] In particular, Panama's 2017 break from Taiwan was a major affront to U.S. hegemony in the region, at least from the perspective of Washington.[51] China brought considerably more material resources to the table in Panama and had established a sound record of working collegially with numerous countries in the region. El Salvador's 2018 decision to recognize China over Taiwan was interpreted as a direct salvo by the United States, even though the shift was based on Taipei's refusal to lend El Salvador funds to relaunch its defunct La Union port on the Pacific coast.[52]

As for the South American side, what stands out is the lack of a cohesive subregional response to China's assertive economic diplomacy. The first factor is the sizable intervals between China's strategic partner designations, such as between the designation of Brazil (1993) and Bolivia (2018). This has thwarted regional efforts to form a common identity and collective strategy related to this status. Second, the countries concerned belong to two distinct subregional integration schemes—with Argentina, Brazil, and Venezuela (which is currently suspended) in the Southern Cone Common Market (Mercosur) and Chile, Ecuador, and Peru in the Andean Community. This too has distracted China's strategic partners from articulating a concrete regional economic policy response to China's ongoing gestures. Third, in recent decades, these countries have been more divided than united on issues ranging from a collective response to the external debt shocks of the 1980s to the negotiation of a Free Trade Area of the Americas (FTAA) in the 2000s.

The failure of the FTAA is a case in point. First proposed by President George H.W. Bush in 1990, the FTAA would have linked all 34 democratic states in the Western Hemisphere into an encompassing free trade and investment agreement. With the launching of NAFTA in 1994, the North American bloc envisioned the FTAA as an expansion of NAFTA and a formidable competitor with the European Union. Small states in Central America and the Caribbean got on board, as increased access to the U.S. market was crucial to them. But in South America, Brazil flexed its muscles as the hegemon of that subregion and formed the Mercosur customs union

---

[50] A full explanation of these shifting commitments lies beyond the scope of this chapter.

[51] Neil Connor, "Panama Cuts Ties with Taiwan in Major Diplomatic Coup," *Telegraph*, June 13, 2017, http://www.telegraph.co.uk/news/2017/06/13/panama-cuts-ties-taiwan-major-diplomatic-coup-china; and An Baijie, "China, Panama Turn Page in Ties," *China Daily*, November 18, 2017, http://www.chinadaily.com.cn/china/2017-11/18/content_34675248.htm.

[52] Tracy Wilkinson, "U.S. Decries Salvadoran China Policy," *Los Angeles Times*, August 25, 2018; and Kinling Lo, "China's New Alliance Stirs U.S. Worries over Possible 'Military Base' in El Salvador," *South China Morning Post*, August 22, 2018.

with Argentina, Paraguay, and Uruguay. The Andean Community imploded, as Ecuador and Peru went to war in 1995 over border territory disputed since independence. In addition, the prospect of one seamless trade and investment bloc in the hemisphere reignited tensions between Bolivia and Chile over the former's loss to Chile of its access to the Pacific Ocean during the 1879 War of the Pacific. In 1999, Mercosur announced negotiations for a comprehensive trade agreement with the EU that took twenty years to complete.

China has astutely avoided engagement in these kinds of interstate theatrics in the Americas. Beijing did inadvertently open a can of worms when it ambitiously proposed building a railway to link the Atlantic and Pacific coasts, a project that would run from São Paulo, Brazil, to the southern coast of Peru.[53] Landlocked Bolivia lobbied hard to have a branch of the railway run through its territory all the way to the Pacific coast. This was a nonstarter for Chile, however, through which the route would pass. The project is on hold, as political strife, exploding costs, and concerns over environmental damage and indigenous rights have impeded progress. Nonetheless, China has benefited on balance from the inchoate nature of regional politics in the Americas. There has been little pushback on Chinese-backed projects and programs that are not necessarily in the best interests of some nations. The best outcomes have stemmed from China-related endeavors where rule of law, regulatory oversight, and a clear strategy exists on the Latin American side. Ecuador and Venezuela represent worst-case scenarios. In both countries, China lent populist governments millions for special projects as part of loans-for-oil deals, and a good share of these funds vanished into a vortex of corruption.

Managing Elite Interests across the Pacific

There is no question that China has been more effective than the United States over the past two decades in managing both sovereign and people-to-people relations with governments and civil societies across the Americas. This is so even if the rich political interactions characteristic of the pre-1989 period in China-LAC relations have been reduced to platitudes and the cultural exchanges largely boiled down to the Confucius Institutes and formalistic Chinatowns cropping up in LAC capitals.[54] The PRC's more collegial working relationship has highlighted the long-standing failures and tensions in U.S.–Latin America relations. China's comparative success recently

---

[53] "Update: Twin Ocean Railway," Inter-American Dialogue, June 2, 2016, https://www.thedialogue.org/blogs/2016/06/update-twin-ocean-railway.

[54] Monica DeHart, "Costa Rica's Chinatown: The Art of Being Global in the Age of China," *City and Society* 27, no. 2 (2015): 183–207.

was illustrated in a Pew Research Center poll that found "the U.S. image in Latin America…has taken a major hit since Trump took office."[55] Unthinkable even a decade ago, China is outpacing the United States as a preferred partner in the LAC region, except for Brazil, Colombia, and parts of Central America. U.S. weakness, however, does not automatically equate with Chinese success, as illustrated by the ease with which China's carefully crafted institutional venues in the Western Hemisphere can crumble under duress.

China has courted Latin American constituencies through the implementation of a three-pronged public diplomacy approach. The first prong is the designation of ten strategic partners within the LAC region: Brazil (1993), Venezuela (2001), Mexico (2003), Argentina (2004), Peru (2008), Chile (2012), Costa Rica (2015), Ecuador (2015), Uruguay (2016), and Bolivia (2018). As discussed earlier, according to Yanran Xu, "strategic" means that cooperation is long-term and stable, while "partner" suggests that the bond between China and a given country is mutually beneficial and fair.[56] For China, such partnerships tend to be an economic endeavor—albeit one cloaked in flowery terms of friendship, trust, and a long-term bilateral commitment. With the exception of Costa Rica, all these strategic partners have abundant supplies of oil, minerals, and other natural resources that are vital inputs for sustaining Chinese growth. The China–Costa Rica strategic partnership, as well as a 2013 FTA between the two countries, is rooted in Costa Rica's diplomatic recognition of China over Taiwan in 2007.

The second prong is the Chinese Ministry of Foreign Affairs' dissemination of two white papers on LAC, one in 2008 and the other in 2016.[57] The spirit of these white papers, rather than their actual content, is what has appealed to China's LAC partners. For the first time, China put Latin America explicitly and positively on its foreign policy agenda. The white papers emphasize its intentions to build a comprehensive and cooperative relationship with Latin America based on mutual benefit, mutual respect, and mutual trust. Both papers contain sections on political ties (e.g., high-level exchanges between legislatures and political parties as well as consultation mechanisms), economic relations (e.g., trade and investment, infrastructure construction, and financial, agricultural, and industrial cooperation), cultural and social exchange (e.g., in sports, science, technology, and education, as

---

[55] Cited in Andres Oppenheimer, "China Is Becoming More Popular Than the U.S. in Many Latin American Countries," *Miami Herald*, April 24, 2019, https://www.miamiherald.com/news/local/news-columns-blogs/andres-oppenheimer/article229621934.html.

[56] Xu, *China's Strategic Partnerships in Latin America*.

[57] For the white papers, see "Full Text: China's Policy Paper on Latin America and the Caribbean," *China Daily*, November 6, 2008, http://www.chinadaily.com.cn/china/2008-11/06/content_7179488_2.htm; and "Full Text of China's Policy Paper on Latin America and the Caribbean," Xinhua, November 24, 2016, http://english.www.gov.cn/archive/white_paper/2016/11/24/content_281475499069158.htm.

well as on environmental protection and combatting climate change), and cooperation on peace, security, and judicial affairs (e.g., military exchanges and policing). The 2016 white paper on Latin America added new topics like science and technology, space cooperation, and maritime cooperation.[58]

The third prong of Chinese public diplomacy in the Americas has been the hosting of two ministerial meetings with the 33 member countries of the Community of Latin American and Caribbean States (CELAC). The first occurred in 2015 in Beijing and the second in 2018 in Santiago. During the 2015 summit, the Chinese government committed to doubling trade with Latin America to $500 billion by 2025 and to investing $250 billion in Latin America over the next decade.[59] The 2018 summit resulted in a joint action plan for 2019–21 based on the areas of common interest identified in China's 2018 white paper on Latin America, such as renewable energy, science and technology, infrastructure, the environment, and greater connectivity between land and sea. The PRC delegates also issued a declaration on BRI, which was launched by President Xi Jinping in 2013. The initiative promotes stronger infrastructure links between Asia and Europe, with billions of dollars of infrastructure investment in roads, ports, and railways. Africa has since been included, and China invited the CELAC nations to join at the 2018 summit.

China's carefully orchestrated gestures toward LAC contrast sharply with the erratic and abrupt foreign policy stance of the United States, but these gestures are not without limits. The swift collapse in established diplomatic institutional structures between China and the United States, Mexico, and Canada in 2018 is a case in point. Rather than pursuing a comprehensive, affirmative approach to the region, the United States has focused narrowly on problem countries like Bolivia, Cuba, Venezuela, and more recently El Salvador and Mexico. With the worsening of this trend and the plummeting of U.S. popularity in LAC during the Trump era, China has moved quickly to fill the leadership void left by Washington. Through the efforts reviewed here, Beijing appears to have institutionalized its cross-Pacific relationships and thereby induced regional countries to respond in ways that promote the best economic interests of both sides.[60] Nevertheless, LAC countries that are strategic partners with China must resist the elite thrust of these

[58] Barbara Stallings, *Dependency in the 21st Century? The Political Economy of China–Latin American Relations* (New York: Cambridge University Press, forthcoming in 2020), 67–69.

[59] UN Economic Commission for Latin America and the Caribbean, "First Forum of China and the Community of Latin American and Caribbean States," January 2015; and Alicia Bárcena (remarks at the second ministerial meeting of the China-CELAC Forum, Santiago, January 22, 2018), https://www.cepal.org/es/discursos/segunda-ministerial-foro-celac-china.

[60] R. Evan Ellis, "Chinese Soft Power in Latin America: A Case Study," *Joint Force Quarterly*, no. 60 (2015): 85–91.

arrangements and work harder to root Chinese projects and initiatives within the sociopolitical settings in which they have been introduced.[61]

Winners and Losers

How do we assess the effects of China's rise in the Americas, including the tensions that Washington perceives regarding China's burgeoning presence within the United States' own sphere of influence? Despite the twelve strategic partnerships that China has signed with countries in the Americas (ten in LAC, plus the United States and Canada), only a handful of South American countries have benefited from Chinese largesse since the early 2000s. Even here, the benefits have been uneven and the effects difficult to discern. The winners in terms of Chinese inflows of FDI are Brazil, Peru, and Argentina (a distant third). Mexico has the strongest trade ties with China, although the bulk of this is on the import side. Brazil, Chile, and Peru follow Mexico in terms of total trade with China, the difference being that all three have consistently run a trade surplus with China.

The other major source of capital inflow to LAC from China is lending from China's two policy banks, the China Development Bank and the Export-Import Bank of China. As of 2017, the top loans have gone to Venezuela ($67.2 billion), Brazil ($28.9 billion), Ecuador ($18.4 billion), and Argentina ($16.9 billion).[62] Notably, the commodity price crash in 2013–14 sent all four of these LAC borrowers into an economic depression. The higher economic performers—Chile, Costa Rica, and Peru—readily outpace these borrowers on indexes of institutional modernization and policy reform. By negotiating separate bilateral FTAs with China, all three of these small, open economies have chosen to meet the China challenge in the realm of international norms and binding treaties. This strategy has afforded them a more predictable and stable relationship with Beijing.[63]

The most visible losers in the China-LAC game, at least according to the data, are Mexico and Central America. Costa Rica, for reasons just stated, is an outlier here. To the chagrin of the United States, Costa Rica was handsomely rewarded by Beijing for switching its diplomatic allegiance to the PRC. China built a new soccer stadium in the country's capital, offered $180 million in grants for projects of the government's choosing, and purchased $300 million

---

[61] Ruben González-Vicente, "The Limits to China's Non-interference Foreign Policy: Pro-state Interventionism and the Rescaling of Economic Governance," *Australian Journal of International Affairs* 9, no. 2 (2015): 205–23.

[62] Kevin Gallagher and Margaret Myers, "China–Latin America Finance Database."

[63] Carol Wise, "Playing Both Sides of the Pacific: Latin America's Free Trade Agreements with China," *Pacific Affairs* 89, no. 1 (2016): 75–101.

of Costa Rican government bonds on very favorable terms.[64] Although Chinese demand for South American commodities helped push average annual growth for LAC as a whole to 4.8% between 2003 and 2013, Mexico and Central America sat out the boom. Chinese-manufactured exports had inundated these subregional markets, but the countries involved possessed little that China wanted to buy in return. Mexico, with its overwhelming dependence on the U.S. market, registered the lowest returns on aggregate and per capita income growth compared to its South American counterparts during the boom between 2003 and 2013. Subsequently, the uncertainty created by the Trump administration's insistence on renegotiating NAFTA triggered currency volatility and capital flight from Mexico.

Argentina and Brazil, the two Western Hemisphere countries most closely integrated into China's internationalized development strategy, have struggled to stay on good terms with both China and the United States. Growth soared in these countries during the China-driven commodity price boom, but in both cases this fueled populist mismanagement and capital squandering. As the dust has settled since 2014, both countries have seen state and economic institutions erode and essential reforms stall. In Brazil, the boom set the backdrop for one of the world's biggest corruption scandals—the skimming of billions of dollars from the majority state-owned oil company Petrobras— while in Argentina it enabled executive interference and resource grabbing from a handful of private and public entities. Political backlash in Brazil led to the election of a China-bashing former military captain as president, while in Argentina voters re-elected the same populist coalition that gave rise to the need for a $57 billion bailout from the International Monetary Fund in 2018.[65] Although the aforementioned Pew public opinion poll found that a majority of Brazilians still prefer the United States as a diplomatic partner, while Argentines have expressed a stronger affinity for China, the irony is that in neither case do these alliance sentiments appear to be mutual.

A more obvious and immediate example of how mounting U.S.-China tensions can hurt the Americas has to do with the effects of the trade war. The prospect of a standoff is a losing endeavor around the world. In the Americas, it is important not to let short-term gains cloud the medium-term realities. Since the trade war began, Mexican officials report a first-ever bump in automobile part exports to China. Brazil and Argentina likewise have enjoyed a bonanza in soybean sales to China, as U.S. producers—once the top suppliers of soybeans

[64] Barbara Stallings, "Chinese Foreign Aid to Latin America: Trying to Win Friends and Influence People," in The Political Economy of China–Latin American Relations in the New Millennium, ed. Margaret Myers and Carol Wise (New York: Routledge, 2016), 84.

[65] Benedict Mander, "Cristina Fernández Is Back Centre Stage in Argentina," Financial Times, December 15, 2019.

to China—have been shut out of the Chinese market.[66] Yet analysts on both sides of the Pacific are sober about the long-term losses that a prolonged trade war implies.[67] With regard to LAC, in particular, the IDB has warned, "If we have a…combination of shocks in which China's growth falls, U.S. growth falls, and asset prices also fall, we could have a reduction in Latin American growth rates that could reach negative territory in 2020."[68]

China's Belt and Road Initiative

The "go out" prelude to BRI. When the CCP announced its "go out" mandate in 1999, LAC was a remote destination for this endeavor. Indeed, Chinese outward FDI to the region in massive resource-related projects would not take off for another decade. As China's entry into the WTO in 2001 further catapulted the country into the global trading system, increased demand for raw material inputs to propel industry and exports quickly exceeded domestic supply. A first round of outward Chinese FDI in LAC sought to access those materials needed to take China's manufactured export–led development model to the next level (such as copper, iron ore, and oil). This included Chinese investment in infrastructure related to the extraction of these resources and their transport back to the mainland. This goes to the heart of China's internationalized development strategy, which is possible due to the country's accumulation of the world's highest level of foreign exchange reserves, totaling nearly $3.1 trillion as of September 2019.[69]

Assessments of this first stage of China's go-out strategy in LAC vary. Perhaps the biggest "red elephant" is a Chinese-sponsored high-speed railway project in Venezuela that collapsed halfway through its construction. In reference to this debacle, Stephen Kaplan and Michael Penfold report that "railroad factories along the construction corridor were ransacked for their power generators, computers, metal siding and copper wiring."[70] Yet there

---

[66] Author's interviews with the Brazilian ambassador to China, Paulo Estivallet de Mesquita, Brazilian Embassy in Beijing, July 23, 2019; and the Argentine ambassador to China, Diego Guelar, Argentine Embassy in Beijing, July 18, 2019.

[67] Tao Liu and Wing Thye Woo, "Understanding the U.S.-China Trade War," *China Economic Journal* 11, no. 3 (2018): 319–40.

[68] Luc Cohen and Alexandra Valencia, "Latam's 2020 Growth May Turn Negative Due to U.S.-China Trade War," Reuters, July 17, 2019, https://www.reuters.com/article/us-latam-economy-iadb/latams-2020-growth-may-turn-negative-due-to-u-s-china-trade-war-iadb-idUSKCN1UC2NM.

[69] "China Foreign Exchange Reserves," Trading Economics, https://tradingeconomics.com/china/foreign-exchange-reserves.

[70] Stephen B. Kaplan and Michael Penfold, "China-Venezuelan Economic Relations: Hedging Venezuelan Bets with Chinese Characteristics," Wilson International Center for Scholars, Latin America Program, February 2019, 27.

are some positive counterfactuals, including China's modernization of major ports in Mexico and Peru, its bridge construction over the Panama Canal, and the State Grid Corporation of China's management of seven electricity transmission companies and thirteen transmission lines in Brazil. Again, the best outcomes have stemmed from China-related endeavors in which the rule of law, regulatory oversight, and a clear strategy exist on the Latin American side.[71] As a closer economic relationship moves into its third decade, the record suggests that political leaders, policymakers, and economic elites across the region need to step up in brokering deals around the numerous opportunities that China is offering, while also finding creative ways to minimize the risks.

The slowing of Chinese imports of LAC's natural resources in 2013–14 signaled a partial saturation of demand for raw materials and the need to export the overcapacity of engineering, construction, and shipping services that accrued as a result of China's 30-year high-growth trajectory. Mega companies like China State Construction Engineering Corporation, the State Grid Corporation of China, China COSCO Shipping Corporation, and China's "big three" oil companies—China Petroleum and Chemical Corporation (SINOPEC), China National Petroleum Corporation (CNPC), and the China National Offshore Oil Corporation (CNOOC)—were pressed to seek business abroad. Some of these ventures have received bleak reviews. China's construction of the $19 billion Coca Codo Sinclair dam in Ecuador is already infamous for corruption and shorting out the country's electrical grid.

Perhaps most controversial, however, were two other hydroelectric projects backed by the China Development Bank on the Santa Cruz River in the Patagonia region of Argentina. As in the case of Brazil's China-backed Belo Monte hydroelectric dam, environmentalists raised legitimate concerns that the two dams would inflict damage on the pristine ecosystem in Santa Cruz Province. Moreover, this scarcely populated province did not have the transmission capacity to handle the projected 1,740 megawatts of electricity that these hydroelectric projects would generate.[72] Having dealt previously with the idiosyncrasies of Argentine politics, the China Development Bank had inserted a cross-default clause in its loan stating that the cancellation of these two mega-projects would mean the immediate halt of Chinese funding for completion of the crucial Belgrano Cargas freight line in Argentina. Because these dams are the largest ever built overseas by a Chinese company (the Gezhouba Group), Xi Jinping had a personal stake in their completion.

[71] Carol Wise, *Dragonomics: How Latin America is Maximizing (or Missing Out on) China's International Development Strategy* (New Haven: Yale University Press, forthcoming 2020), 240.

[72] Luke Patey, "China Made Mauricio Macri a Deal He Couldn't Refuse," *Foreign Policy*, January 24, 2017, http://foreignpolicy.com/2017/01/24/china-made-mauricio-macri-a-deal-he-couldnt-refuse.

In the end, "China agreed to lower the capacity of [the] dams by including fewer turbines and adding another transmission line."[73]

There is no lack of information on the opaque, environmentally damaging, and exploitative nature of some of China's project-development contracts in other developing countries. The weaker a host government, the more likely that Chinese investors will violate best practices in this realm. Does this mean that U.S. officials are justified in their criticisms of China's infractions? Yes, but not because China is on the verge of superseding the United States in its own sphere of influence.[74] Rather, host governments must hold China's feet to the fire and be much more vigilant about upholding global investment norms around transparency, accountability, and environmental protection. In the best of worlds, the United States could play an essential role in the provision of technical assistance and training for LAC governments on everything from competitive bidding on procurement to contract negotiation and full disclosure. The strengthening of business practices and the rule of law vis-à-vis China or any other foreign investor entering the region is precisely the kind of regional public good that would reinforce the political vitality and competitiveness of the Western Hemisphere at large.

Infrastructure by any other name. Since the official incorporation of LAC into BRI at the 2018 China-CELAC summit, nineteen countries in the region have signed memoranda of understanding (MOUs) with China to join this initiative. The United States has been especially vehement in warning LAC countries not to accept Chinese loans for infrastructure.[75] During the 2018 Asia-Pacific Economic Cooperation summit, Vice President Mike Pence accused China of offering "a constricting belt or a one-way road."[76] Significantly, the top three emerging economies, Argentina, Brazil, and Mexico, have all declined to sign an MOU with China. This reticence is based on the combination of China's spotty track record thus far and a reluctance to cross diplomatic lines and affront Washington.[77]

Mexico, which can least afford to anger the United States, insists that China's MOU for joining BRI is under review at the Secretariat of Foreign

---

[73] Patey, "China Made Mauricio Macri a Deal He Couldn't Refuse."

[74] Weifeng Zhou and Mario Esteban, "Beyond Balancing: China's Approach toward the Belt and Road Initiative," *Journal of Contemporary China* 27, no. 112 (2018): 487–501.

[75] Owen Churchill, "Mike Pompeo Warns Panama and Other Nations about Accepting China's 'Belt and Road' Loans," *South China Morning Post*, October 18, 2018, https://www.scmp.com/news/china/diplomacy/article/2169449/mike-pompeo-warns-panama-and-other-nations-about-accepting.

[76] Andrew Chatzky and James McBride, "China's Massive Belt and Road Initiative," Council on Foreign Relations, May 21, 2019, https://www.cfr.org/backgrounder/chinas-massive-belt-and-road-initiative.

[77] Author's interviews with economic counselor Roberto Cabrera, Mexican Embassy in Beijing, July 19, 2019; Diego Guelar, Argentine Embassy in Beijing, July 18, 2019; and Paulo Estivallet de Mesquita, Brazilian Embassy in Beijing, July 23, 2019.

Affairs (apparently indefinitely). The Argentine ambassador to China, Diego Guelar, cites his country's special relationship with the United States, as well as a reluctance to step into the crosshairs of escalating U.S.-China competition over the Western Hemisphere. Guelar, along with Brazil's ambassador to China, Paulo Estivallet de Mesquita, points to weaknesses intrinsic to the MOUs for BRI. For Brazil, the lack of clarity and specificity in the MOU itself, rather than fear of Washington's wrath, is what has held the country back from joining the initiative. This has not stopped Beijing from claiming projects in both Argentina and Brazil under the banner of BRI. Such is the case with a $2.1 billion contract won in 2018 by China State Construction Engineering Corporation for highway construction in Argentina and with a 30-year concession for 90% of Brazil's Paranagua container terminal secured by the China Merchants Port Holdings Company in 2018.[78]

Panama was the first LAC country to sign an MOU with China (U.S. threats notwithstanding), and it is home to the first authentic BRI project in Latin America, the Panama-Chiriquí high-speed railway. With the feasibility study now completed, the project is expected to create 2,900 permanent jobs and reduce the time it takes to transport large containers within the domestic market by 400%.[79] After Panama, where China has a vital commercial stake as the second-largest user of the Panama Canal, the size and importance of other LAC participants in BRI shrinks considerably. Again, the highly asymmetrical relationship between China and these small states leaves them vulnerable to some of the worst excesses that have plagued BRI projects in other regions: lack of serious environmental impact assessments, the insistence that Chinese contractors control each point in the supply chain, and the reckless accrual of excessive debt.[80]

The United States itself has been out of the business of infrastructure investment in mega-projects in the developing Latin American countries since the "lost decade" of the 1980s debt crisis. This withdrawal of the United States and development institutions like the World Bank reflects, first, the increasingly risk-averse lending milieu in the West, characterized by strict fiduciary guidelines and ballooning transaction costs on infrastructure loans. Second, domestic politics have thwarted U.S. infrastructure investment in the developing countries, as politicians on both sides of the aisle have become

---

[78] "Brazil Hopeful of Rise in Trade after Inclusion in Belt and Road Initiative," *China Daily*, September 9, 2018, http://usa.chinadaily.com.cn/a/201809/09/WS5b947f5fa31033b4f4654ffd.html.

[79] "China Estimates Cost of Panama High-Speed Rail Line at $4.1 Bn," Agencia EFE, March 15, 2019, https://www.efe.com/efe/english/business/china-estimates-cost-of-panama-high-speed-rail-line-at-4-1-bn/50000265-3926478#.

[80] "China's Belt and Road Initiative Is Falling Short," *Financial Times*, July 29, 2018, https://www.ft.com/content/47d63fec-9185-11e8-b639-7680cedcc421.

more vigilant about corruption, corporate welfare, and environmental costs.[81] In a move meant to counter BRI, the Trump administration rescued rather than terminated the U.S. Overseas Private Investment Corporation in 2018, merged the agency with two other federal development agencies, and allocated it a $60 billion budget.

This U.S. budget, however, falls far short of the $1 trillion that China envisions spending on all BRI projects over the next several years. U.S. funds would be better spent on technical assistance and training for LAC governments to strengthen business practices, transparency, and the rule of law in their dealings with China. Both the FTAA and the WTO's Doha Development Round negotiations sought to include technical training, contract negotiation, and state capacity-building measures for developing countries. The failure of the FTAA and Doha Round has left a void with regard to the ability of developing countries like those in Latin America to negotiate effectively with the likes of China. While the PRC has trumpeted BRI as a linchpin of South-South solidarity, disastrous outcomes such as Ecuador's Coca Codo Sinclair dam and Venezuela's defunct bullet train reflect the deep asymmetries inherent in the China-LAC relationship. As plans to extend BRI into the Americas move forward, these earlier mistakes could well become business as usual. The United States has an essential role to play in shaping more productive development outcomes, not in direct competition with BRI, but rather through the strengthening of regional business skills and practices and the reinforcement of norms around transparency and the rule of law.

Conclusion

This chapter has traced how the rise of China in the Western Hemisphere went from a nagging concern in Washington during the early 2000s to today's strident exchange between the United States and China regarding the latter's motives. Mutual engagement has morphed into cross-Pacific barbs over China's increasing presence in the Americas and U.S. perceptions that this is somehow an encroachment on U.S. hegemony. Although Chinese arms transfers to Latin America have caught up to U.S. transfers, China's forging of realpolitik alliances or geopolitical maneuvering is a remote possibility. The region remains firmly in the sphere of the United States. On all three proxies—trade, FDI, and security—the United States is still the top political and economic broker in the Americas. Through a comparative historical

---

[81] Bushra Bataineh, Michael Bennon, and Francis Fukuyama, "Beijing's Building Boom," *Foreign Affairs*, May 21, 2018, https://www.foreignaffairs.com/articles/china/2018-05-21/beijings-building-boom.

analysis of China-LAC and U.S.-LAC relations, this chapter has argued that China's status as a relative newcomer to the Americas puts it at a distinct advantage. Conversely, a Pew Research Center poll conducted in 2018 suggests that hard-power discourse and other verbal lashings are driving once-solid Latin American allies further from Washington and closer to Beijing.[82]

This is certainly the case with Canada and Mexico, which have been the closest U.S. allies in the Western Hemisphere since the early 1990s. These countries have been the most adversely affected by U.S.-China tensions in the region. First, the renegotiation of NAFTA threatens to raise content barriers in the North American automobile sector and shift higher production levels toward the U.S. market. At least from Mexico's standpoint, the new USMCA—ratified by the U.S. House of Representatives on December 19, 2019—is essentially the North American correlate to the U.S. trade war on China. Second is the implosion of the China-Canada relationship over U.S. insistence that Canada arrest the Huawei CFO under an extradition treaty with the United States. While Canada is looking toward Europe to diversify away from its strong dependence on the United States, and Mexico is reaching out more to its regional neighbors, neither country can escape the fact of U.S. dominance in the Americas.

Similarly, the decision by several countries in Central America to diplomatically recognize the PRC shows the limits on U.S. demands for a level of loyalty from Latin American countries that is increasingly unwarranted. South America has pivoted toward Asia, with China as the focal point. The PRC has encouraged this pivot by placing the Americas explicitly on its foreign policy agenda with the release of two white papers, the hosting of two ministerial meetings with the 33-member CELAC group, and the incorporation of LAC into BRI. Generous development lending from China's two big policy banks has helped grease the wheels of the bilateral relationship. The United States, by contrast, has no cohesively stated policy toward Latin America. Nonetheless, despite the frictions in U.S.-LAC relations, leaders of the top three emerging economies in the region (Argentina, Brazil, and Mexico) have refrained from signing on to BRI, partly for fear of upsetting Washington.

Chinese political ties to countries in the Western Hemisphere run mainly through strategic partnerships. Yet such partnerships can quickly collapse, as happened in the case of Canada following its arrest of Huawei's CFO. On the cultural front, China's use of soft power to transmit its culture through the establishment of numerous Confucius Institutes and the construction of Chinatowns in some capitals has met with mixed reactions from populations

---

[82] Cited in Oppenheimer, "China Is Becoming More Popular."

across the region. But China has little historical baggage with LAC countries and thus nothing to ignite U.S. claims about its pernicious motives in the region. Whether measured by economic presence, political sway, or cultural penetration, evidence of China's efforts and ability to supersede the United States in the Western Hemisphere is thin.

Rather than squandering political capital in the Western Hemisphere, it is time for the United States to exercise regional leadership on a par with its status. Soft-power diplomacy and a few kind words from Washington could go a long way. First, Washington needs to rely less on hard power (such as military threats) and harsh language with regard to the evolving relationship between China and the countries of Central and South America. This discourse fails to capture the nature of China-LAC ties and further alienates regional countries. Second, in North America the Trump administration's insistence on a more mercantilist trade agreement is misplaced. The North American automobile sector is most at risk because content requirements that favor the U.S. market could disrupt regional value chains and disadvantage this sector at large. Finally, it is futile for the West to seek to compete with China's BRI. Instead, the United States needs to compensate for the failures of the FTAA and Doha Round and work with LAC countries to strengthen business practices (namely, contract negotiations, transparency, and the rule of law) such that BRI becomes a developmental force in the Americas rather than an economically destabilizing one.

About the Contributors

Frédéric Grare is a Nonresident Senior Fellow in the South Asia Program at the Carnegie Endowment for International Peace. His research focuses on South Asian security issues and the search for a security architecture. He has extensive professional experience working on India's Look East policy, Afghanistan's and Pakistan's regional policies, and the tension between stability and democratization in South Asia. Dr. Grare has served at the French embassy in Pakistan, as head of the Asia Bureau at the Directorate for Strategic Affairs in the French Ministry of Defense, and as the director of the Centre for Social Science and Humanities in New Delhi. He is the author of *India Turns East: International Engagement and U.S.-China Rivalry* (2017), in addition to writing extensively on security issues, Islamist movements, and sectarian conflict in Pakistan and Afghanistan. Dr. Grare received an advanced degree from the Paris Institut d'Études Politiques and a PhD from the Graduate Institute of International Studies in Geneva.

Ji-Young Lee is the inaugural holder of the Korea Policy Chair and a Senior Political Scientist at the RAND Corporation and an Associate Professor of International Relations at American University. Dr. Lee is the author of *China's Hegemony: Four Hundred Years of East Asian Domination* (2016). She is currently working on her second book, *The Great Power Next Door* (under contract), which concerns the past and present of Korea-China relations with a focus on security issues. Prior to teaching at American University, she was a Mellon postdoctoral fellow at Oberlin College, where she was also a visiting assistant professor. Dr. Lee served as a POSCO visiting fellow at the East-West Center, a nonresident James Kelly Korean Studies fellow at Pacific Forum CSIS, an East Asia Institute fellow, and a Korea Foundation–Mansfield Foundation scholar in the U.S.-Korea Scholar-Policymaker Nexus program. She holds an MA and a PhD from Georgetown University and an MA from Seoul National University.

Syaru Shirley Lin is Compton Visiting Professor in World Politics at the Miller Center of Public Affairs at the University of Virginia and a member of the founding faculty of the master's program in global political economy at the Chinese University of Hong Kong. Previously, she was a partner at

Goldman Sachs, responsible for private equity investments in Asia. Dr. Lin was appointed by the Hong Kong government as a member of the Hong Kong Committee for Pacific Economic Cooperation, and her board service includes Goldman Sachs Asia Bank, Langham Hospitality, Mercuries Life Insurance, Swire Pacific Group, and the Focused Ultrasound Foundation. Her current research project is focused on the challenges facing countries in East Asia in the high-income trap. Dr. Lin is the author of *Taiwan's China Dilemma: Contested Identities and Multiple Interests in Taiwan's Cross-Strait Economic Policy* (2016), which was also published in Chinese (2019). She earned an MA in international public affairs and a PhD in politics and public administration at the University of Hong Kong and graduated *cum laude* from Harvard College.

Joseph Chinyong Liow is the Tan Kah Kee Chair in Comparative and International Politics and the Dean of the College of Humanities, Arts, and Social Sciences at Nanyang Technological University (NTU) in Singapore. In addition to his academic work, he is Singapore's representative on the advisory board of the ASEAN Institute of Peace and Reconciliation formed under the auspices of the ASEAN Charter. Dr. Liow previously held the Lee Kuan Yew Chair in Southeast Asia Studies at the Brookings Institution, where he was also a senior fellow in the Foreign Policy Program. He is the author of *Ambivalent Engagement: The United States and Regional Security in Southeast Asia after the Cold War* (2017), *Religion and Nationalism in Southeast Asia* (2016), and *Dictionary of the Modern Politics of Southeast Asia* (2014), in addition to co-authoring and editing eleven books. His commentary on Southeast Asian affairs has been featured in many media outlets, including *Foreign Affairs*, *Foreign Policy*, and the *National Interest*. Dr. Liow holds an MSc in strategic studies from NTU and a PhD in international relations from the London School of Economics and Political Science.

Chris Miller is Assistant Professor of International History at the Fletcher School of Law and Diplomacy at Tufts University, where he co-directs the Russia and Eurasia Program. He is also the Eurasia Director at the Foreign Policy Research Institute. Dr. Miller previously served as the associate director of the Brady-Johnson Program in Grand Strategy at Yale University, a lecturer at the New Economic School in Moscow, a visiting researcher at the Carnegie Moscow Center, a research associate at the Brookings Institution, and a fellow at the German Marshall Fund's Transatlantic Academy. His research interests include Russian history, politics, economics, and foreign policy. In addition to many scholarly and media articles, Dr. Miller is the author of two books: *The Struggle to Save the Soviet Economy: Mikhail Gorbachev and the Collapse of the USSR* (2016) and *Putinomics: Power and Money in Resurgent Russia* (2018). He holds an MA and a PhD from Yale University.

Liselotte Odgaard is a Senior Fellow at the Hudson Institute in Washington, D.C. She has published numerous monographs, books, peer-reviewed articles, and research reports on Chinese and Asia-Pacific security, including *China and Coexistence: Beijing's National Security Strategy for the Twenty-First Century* (2012). Dr. Odgaard has been a visiting scholar at institutions such as Harvard University, the Woodrow Wilson International Center for Scholars, and the Norwegian Nobel Institute. She regularly participates in policy dialogues such as the Shangri-La Dialogue in Singapore and the Xiangshan Forum in Beijing. Dr. Odgaard holds a PhD from Aarhus University.

Sheila A. Smith is a Senior Fellow for Japan Studies at the Council on Foreign Relations. She is an expert on Japanese politics and the author of *Japan Rearmed: The Politics of Military Power* (2019), *Intimate Rivals: Japanese Domestic Politics and a Rising China* (2015), and *Japan's New Politics and the U.S.-Japan Alliance* (2014). She is also the author of the interactive guide "Constitutional Change in Japan." Dr. Smith is Vice Chair of the U.S. advisers to the U.S.-Japan Conference on Cultural and Educational Interchange, a binational advisory panel of government officials and private-sector members, and is an Adjunct Professor in the Asian Studies Program at Georgetown University. Dr. Smith earned an MA and a PhD from the Department of Political Science at Columbia University.

Alison Szalwinski is Vice President of Research at the National Bureau of Asian Research (NBR). She provides executive leadership to NBR's policy research agenda and oversees research teams in Seattle and Washington, D.C. She is the author of numerous articles and reports and a co-editor of the *Strategic Asia* series along with Ashley J. Tellis and Michael Wills, including the most recent volumes, *China's Expanding Strategic Ambitions* (2019), *Power, Ideas, and Military Strategy in the Asia-Pacific* (2017), *Understanding Strategic Cultures in the Asia-Pacific* (2016), and *Foundations of National Power in the Asia-Pacific* (2015). Prior to joining NBR, Ms. Szalwinski spent time at the U.S. Department of State and the Center for Strategic and International Studies. Her research interests include U.S. policy toward Asia, especially U.S.-China relations and the importance of great-power competition for U.S. alliances in the region. She holds a BA in foreign affairs and history from the University of Virginia and an MA in Asian studies from Georgetown University's Edmund A. Walsh School of Foreign Service.

Ashley J. Tellis is the Tata Chair for Strategic Affairs and a Senior Fellow at the Carnegie Endowment for International Peace. He has also served as Research Director of the Strategic Asia Program at the National Bureau of Asian Research (NBR) and co-editor of the program's annual volume since 2004. While on assignment to the U.S. Department of State as senior adviser to the undersecretary of state for political affairs, Dr. Tellis was intimately involved in negotiating the civil nuclear agreement with India. Previously, he was commissioned into the Foreign Service and served as senior adviser to the ambassador at the U.S. embassy in New Delhi. He also served on the U.S. National Security Council staff as special assistant to President George W. Bush and senior director for strategic planning and Southwest Asia. Prior to his government service, Dr. Tellis was a senior policy analyst at the RAND Corporation and professor of policy analysis at the RAND Graduate School. He is the author of *India's Emerging Nuclear Posture* (2001) and co-author of *Interpreting China's Grand Strategy: Past, Present, and Future* (2000). He holds a PhD in political science from the University of Chicago.

Michael Wesley is Deputy Vice-Chancellor International at the University of Melbourne in Australia. Previously he was dean of the College of Asia and the Pacific at the Australian National University, executive director of the Lowy Institute for International Policy (2009–12), director of the Griffith Asia Institute at Griffith University (2004–9), and assistant director-general for transnational issues at the Office of National Assessments (2003–4). Dr. Wesley is the author of *There Goes the Neighbourhood: Australia and the Rise of Asia* (2011) and *Restless Continent: Wealth, Rivalry and Asia's New Geopolitics* (2015). He is currently completing a history of the Regional Assistance Mission to Solomon Islands. He earned a PhD from the University of St. Andrews.

Michael Wills is Executive Vice President at the National Bureau of Asian Research (NBR). He manages all aspects of NBR's financial and business operations, serves as secretary to the Board of Directors, and is a member of the *Asia Policy* journal's editorial advisory committee. His research expertise includes geopolitics, international security, and the international relations of Asia, with a particular interest in China's relations with Southeast Asia. Mr. Wills is co-editor of eight *Strategic Asia* volumes (with

Ashley Tellis and, since 2015, Alison Szalwinski) as well as *New Security Challenges in Asia* (2013, with Robert M. Hathaway). Before joining NBR, he worked at the Cambodia Development Resource Institute in Phnom Penh, and prior to that with Control Risks Group, an international political and security risk management firm, in London. He holds a BA (Honors) in Chinese studies from the University of Oxford.

Carol Wise is Professor of International Relations at the University of Southern California (USC). She specializes in international political economy and development, with an emphasis on Latin America and specifically Argentina, Mexico, and Peru. Dr. Wise was the 2019 recipient of the Fulbright-Masaryk University Distinguished Chair Grant in the Czech Republic. She spent eight years at the Johns Hopkins University School of Advanced International Studies before joining USC. Dr. Wise is the author of *Dragonomics: How Latin America Is Maximizing (or Missing Out on) China's International Development Strategy* (2019) and has been widely published on trade integration, exchange rate crises, institutional reform, and the political economy of market restructuring in Latin America. Her other recent publications include *The Political Economy of China–Latin America Relations in the New Millennium* (co-edited with Margaret Myers, 2016) and "Playing Both Sides of the Pacific: Latin America's Free Trade Agreements with China" (2016). Dr. Wise holds an MPA and a PhD from Columbia University.

About Strategic Asia

The **Strategic Asia Program** at the National Bureau of Asian Research (NBR) is a major ongoing research initiative that draws together top Asia studies specialists and international relations experts to assess the changing strategic environment in the Asia-Pacific. The program combines the rigor of academic analysis with the practicality of contemporary policy analyses by incorporating economic, military, political, and demographic data and by focusing on the trends, strategies, and perceptions that drive geopolitical dynamics in the region. The program's integrated set of products and activities includes:

- an annual edited volume written by leading specialists
- an executive brief tailored for public- and private-sector decision-makers and strategic planners
- briefings and presentations for government, business, and academia that are designed to foster in-depth discussions revolving around major public policy issues

Special briefings are held for key committees of Congress and the executive branch, other government agencies, and the intelligence community. The principal audiences for the program's research findings are the U.S. policymaking and research communities, the media, the business community, and academia.

Previous Strategic Asia Volumes

Now in its nineteenth year, the *Strategic Asia* series has addressed how Asia functions as a zone of strategic interaction and contends with an uncertain balance of power.

Strategic Asia 2019: China's Expanding Strategic Ambitions assessed Chinese ambitions in a range of geographic and functional areas and presented policy options for the United States and its partners to address the challenges posed by a rising China.

Strategic Asia 2017–18: Power, Ideas, and Military Strategy in the Asia-Pacific identified how Asia's major powers have developed military strategies to address their most significant challenges.

Strategic Asia 2016–17: Understanding Strategic Cultures in the Asia-Pacific explored the strategic cultures of the region's major powers and explained how they inform decision-making about the pursuit of strategic objectives and national power.

Strategic Asia 2015–16: Foundations of National Power in the Asia-Pacific examined how the region's major powers are building their national power as geopolitical competition intensifies.

Strategic Asia 2014–15: U.S. Alliances and Partnerships at the Center of Global Power analyzed the trajectories of U.S. alliance and partner relationships in the Asia-Pacific in light of the region's shifting strategic landscape.

Strategic Asia 2013–14: Asia in the Second Nuclear Age examined the role of nuclear weapons in the grand strategies of key Asian states and assessed the impact of these capabilities—both established and latent—on regional and international stability.

Strategic Asia 2012–13: China's Military Challenge assessed China's growing military capabilities and explored their impact on the Asia-Pacific region.

Strategic Asia 2011–12: Asia Responds to Its Rising Powers—China and India explored how key Asian states have responded to the rise of China and India, drawing implications for U.S. interests and leadership in the Asia-Pacific.

Strategic Asia 2010–11: Asia's Rising Power and America's Continued Purpose provided a continent-wide net assessment of the core trends and issues affecting the region by examining Asia's performance in nine key functional areas.

Strategic Asia 2009–10: Economic Meltdown and Geopolitical Stability analyzed the impact of the global economic crisis on key Asian states and explored the strategic implications for the United States.

Strategic Asia 2008–09: Challenges and Choices examined the impact of geopolitical developments on Asia's transformation over the previous eight years and assessed the major strategic choices on Asia facing the incoming U.S. administration.

Strategic Asia 2007–08: Domestic Political Change and Grand Strategy examined internal and external drivers of grand strategy on Asian foreign policymaking.

Strategic Asia 2006–07: Trade, Interdependence, and Security addressed how changing trade relationships affect the balance of power and security in the region.

Strategic Asia 2005–06: Military Modernization in an Era of Uncertainty appraised the progress of Asian military modernization programs.

Strategic Asia 2004–05: Confronting Terrorism in the Pursuit of Power explored the effect of the U.S.-led war on terrorism on the strategic transformations underway in Asia.

Strategic Asia 2003–04: Fragility and Crisis examined the fragile balance of power in Asia, drawing out the key domestic political and economic trends in Asian states supporting or undermining this tenuous equilibrium.

Strategic Asia 2002–03: Asian Aftershocks drew on the baseline established in the 2001–02 volume to analyze changes in Asian states' grand strategies and relationships in the aftermath of the September 11 terrorist attacks.

Strategic Asia 2001–02: Power and Purpose established a baseline assessment for understanding the strategies and interactions of the major states within the region.

Research and Management Team

The Strategic Asia research team consists of leading international relations and security specialists from universities and research institutions across the United States and around the world. A new research team is selected each year. To date, more than 150 scholars have written for the program. The research team for 2019 is led by Ashley J. Tellis (Carnegie Endowment for International Peace), Alison Szalwinski (The National Bureau of Asian Research), and Michael Wills (NBR). Aaron Friedberg (Princeton University, and Strategic Asia's founding research director) and Richard Ellings (NBR, and Strategic Asia's founding program director) serve as senior advisors to the program.

Attribution

Readers of *Strategic Asia* and visitors to the Strategic Asia website may use data, charts, graphs, and quotes from these sources without requesting permission from NBR on the condition that they cite NBR and the appropriate primary source in any published work. No report, chapter, separate study, extensive text, or any other substantial part of the Strategic Asia Program's products may be reproduced without the written permission of NBR. To request permission, please write to publications@nbr.org.

Index